Self as Image
in Asian Theory and Practice

Self as Image
in Asian Theory and Practice

Edited by
Roger T. Ames
with
Thomas P. Kasulis *and* Wimal Dissanayake

STATE UNIVERSITY OF NEW YORK PRESS

Cover: Detail from *The 36 Poets on a Field of Flowers and Grasses,* Sakai Hoitsu, Japan, 1761–1828, Etsuko and Joe Price Collection, Los Angeles Museum of Art. Reproduced by permission.

Portions of chapter 5 will be published in Mark Elvin, *Changing Stories in the Chinese World,* forthcoming by Stanford University Press.

Quotes for *Kalidasa: The Loom of Time—Selections of His Plays and Poems* trans. Chandra Rajam, are reproduced by courtesy of the publishers (Penguin Books India Pvt. Ltd.) and the translator.

Selections from David McCraw's book, *Du Fu's Laments from the South* are reprinted by permission of the University of Hawaii Press.

Illustrations of the Japanese prints are from the James A. Michener Collection, the Honolulu Academy of Arts, Honolulu, reproduced with permission.

Published by
State University of New York Press

© 1998 State University of New York

For information, address the State University of New York Press,
State University Plaza, Albany, NY 12246

Marketing by Nancy Farrell
Production by Bernadine Dawes

Library of Congress Cataloging-in-Publication Data

Self as image in Asian theory and practice / edited by Roger T. Ames with
    Thomas P. Kasulis and Wimal Dissanayake.
        p. cm.
    Papers originally presented at seminars held at the East-West Center in
    Honolulu.
    Includes index.
        ISBN 0-7914-2725-0 (alk. paper). — ISBN 0-7914-2726-9 (pbk. :
alk. paper)
        1. Self (Philosophy)—Asia—History—Congresses. 2. Self-perception—
    Asia—History—Congresses. I. Ames, Roger T., 1947-   . II. Kasulis,
    Thomas P., 1948-   . III. Dissanayake, Wimal.
B5015.S34S43   1998
126—DC20   95-34253
                                                              CIP

1 2 3 4 5 6 7 8 9 10

Contents

Editors' Preface

This is the third book in a series published by SUNY Press devoted to the exploration of the concept of self as it finds articulation in Asian theory and practice. The first of them titled, *Self as Body in Asian Theory and Practice* was edited by Thomas P. Kasulis with Roger T. Ames and Wimal Dissanayake. The second book was edited by Roger T. Ames with Wimal Dissanayake and Thomas P. Kasulis and was titled, *Self as Person in Asian Theory and Practice*. The present volume continues our cross-cultural and cross-disciplinary explorations of various notions of self that ground alternative cultural traditions.

The process of editorship of the three volumes was as follows. Each volume had a primary editor responsible for the overall book project, yet all major editorial decisions were shared by the three editors. For all three volumes, Dissanayake had special responsibility for the Indian section, Ames for the Chinese section, and Kasulis for the Japanese section. One of the editors for each volume wrote the general introduction, setting the context for the investigations that were to follow, but in all cases the introduction to each geographical section was the responsibility of the appropriate area specialist. The purpose of this format was to prevent any crude overgeneralizations that would have attenuated the diversity of voices represented by the three cultural areas and the methodological differences among the editors. We believe that this division of labor guaranteed not only a plurality of cultural perspectives on broad themes but also a plurality of individual perspectives on the more specific issues and themes articulated in edited volumes of this nature.

This SUNY Press series of anthologies on self emerged out of a project initiated and organized at the East-West Center in Honolulu by Wimal Dissanayake, a senior fellow at the center. Over the past few years, relatively small seminars—approximately twenty scholars on each occasion—were convened at the center to bring experts representing different cultures and disciplinary perspectives into conversation. Most of the essays included here were selected from papers presented and discussed in this forum. A major criterion in the selection process was the achievement of a nice balance between reflection on those specific practices that define cultural differences and the application of emergent theories, once shaped and abstracted, as instruments of explanation for cultural practices.

All three volumes are committed to the task of exploring the concept of self from cross-cultural and cross-disciplinary vantage points. Clearly, there are thematic affinities and shared conceptual orientations among the three volumes, and each volume purposefully complements the other two. However, it needs to be stated that each volume stands on its own, and can be usefully read independently of the other two, if the reader so desires.

The concept of self has once again assumed a position of importance in contemporary cultural description. Broadly speaking, one can identify two main approaches to the concept of self. On the one hand, there are those who seek to valorize the self as the center of power, of consciousness, of action, and of epistemic privilege. On the other hand, there are those who vigorously challenge such an approach, maintaining that selfhood is socially constituted, is a product of language, and that it lacks unity and coherence. They wish to emphasize the determining influence of discourse at the expense of the autonomy of selfhood. Whatever the approach—and there are many more in between those mentioned—it is patent that the concept of self has become a compellingly useful point of departure and an enabling proposition for cultural description. This conviction informs all three volumes.

We believe that these three books taken together would add up to a significant exploration of the concept of self as it finds expression in Chinese, Indian, and Japanese cultures. If in the earlier two volumes the emphasis was on religion, philosophy, and intellectual history, the present volume focuses much more heavily on art, literature, cinema, and other representational practices and symbolic media.

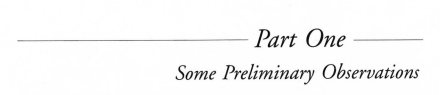

Part One

Some Preliminary Observations

INTRODUCTION

Wimal Dissanayake

The fifteen essays included in this book primarily focus on two sets of important questions related to the understanding of the interplay among self, image, and culture. The first set of questions deals with the nature and significance of the interconnections of self and image. What is the nature of an image? How is it related to the concept of self? How do images—visual, auditory, tactile, and so on—serve to define the contours of the self and the dynamics of self-formation? The second set of questions addresses issues related to the ways in which cultural variabilities affect the relationship between self and image, the importance of culture in the construction of self and image, the role of cultural epistemology in self-constitution and image-construction. Both these sets of questions, it need hardly be added, are vital to an understanding of the interlinkages among self, image, and culture. Interestingly, the second set of questions serves to define more clearly the import of the first set of questions. In order to locate these questions in a larger discursive framework and horizon of understanding, it is important to pay attention to the conceptual cartography of self and image.

To think of self in terms of image is to open up an important avenue of understanding of self. Here I use the word "image" in its broadest sense to include the graphic, optical, perceptual, mental, verbal, and conceptual dimensions. Self and image are inextricably linked, and an inquiry into the complex functioning of images in human communication at various levels would underline their inseparably close linkages. Etymologically, the word "image" is derived from the Greek word *eikon,* connecting such meanings as imitation, similarity, and likeness. Anyone familiar with Plato's dialogues will realize that this word constitutes an important dimension in his metaphysical speculations. The word image has been closely associated with metaphysical, aesthetic, and epistemological thinking in both the East and the West from ancient times, and hence a just estimate of its true nature and importance demands a study of the fascinating ways in which it is embedded in cultural, social, and political discourses of various types.

The relationship among self, image, and cultural communication is as complex as it is fascinating, as is borne out by the essays that follow. For purposes of analysis, we can examine this relationship at three levels: the way self is conceived through images, the way images are textualized, and the way readers and spectators respond to images and attribute meaning and significance to them. Let us first consider the ways in which self is conceived and produced in terms of image. Here I would like to focus on the work of three scholars representing the disciplines of philosophy, cultural anthropology and psychoanalysis. They are George Herbert Mead, Irving Hallowell, and Jacques Lacan. One can, of course, add to this list with profit. Mead addressed himself to the question of a unified and coherent self. He placed great emphasis on the concept of role in social life, but realized that a role or a number of roles by themselves will not generate a unified self. Mead conceptualized self as a phenomenon of cognition and hence questions of a unified and coherent self and self-consciousness are inextricably linked. A number of American social scientists have shown a great interest in the concept of self and its relationship to society. The theoretical writings of George Horton Colley, James Baldwin, and George Herbert Mead are particularly important in this regard. All of them have pointed out the crucial role played by society in the formation of self. The work of Mead deserves very close attention. His book, *Mind, Self and Society* has exercised a profound influence on many who have been concerned with the problematic of self. Mead, in his theory of symbolic interactionism, maintained that the self is essentially social and that it arises as a consequence of the interaction with other members of society. Its stability and changeability depends upon social interaction. This is indeed a phenomenon that one can observe in the earliest stages of human growth right up to adulthood and beyond. In childhood the self emerges as a result of symbolic interactions with a significant other that in later times paves the way for the interaction with a generalized other.

According to Mead and the symbolic interactionists, the self is what an individual is able to see for himself or herself as an object, an image. The individual, through the exercise of the imagination, is able to become disengaged from his or her personhood and is capable of looking at the self as others do. What this really means is that the individual is able to assume the role of significant others and reference groups and see himself or herself from their perspectives. The self, then, according to the symbolic interactionists, is a social object that we can identify and categorize in a world of social objects. The idea of image is central, in the view of symbolic interactionists, to the constitution of self. The self is in point of fact the image that a person constructs of himself or herself in relation to the interactions with others.

Anthropologists who have written persuasively about the construction of self, too, have focused on the idea of image, although they may not necessarily have used that word. A. Irving Hallowell has pointed out the significance of what he has termed the "behavioral environment" on the formation of self, and this behavioral environment, as he saw it, was essentially culturally constituted. While agreeing with the notion that self-awareness is a generic human trait, Hallowell goes on to make the observation that the nature of the self, taken in its conceptual context, is a culturally identifiable variable. The human individual acts and behaves in accordance with a normative image that he or she creates on the basis of this behavioral environment. Clifford Geertz, who does not totally endorse Hallowell's views of the self, nevertheless makes the point that becoming human is becoming individual, and we become individual under the guidance of cultural patterns, historically created systems of meaning, in terms of which human beings impart form, order, point, and direction to their lives. Hence the role of culture and inherited history is crucial to Geertz's understanding of self. Some of the concerns of Hallowell and Geertz have been fruitfully extended by modern ethnopsychologists who are interested in the cultural understandings and cultural formations of the self and the processes and dynamics of interplay by means of which these formulations find expression in quotidian life. The idea of culturally validated and normative images is at the heart of their thinking on the constitution of the self. As Hallowell remarked, an individual's self-image and interpretation of his or her experiences cannot be divorced from the concept of self that is characteristic of that society. Indeed, such concepts are the primary means through which different cultures promote self-orientation in ways that make self-awareness of crucial importance in the maintenance of social order. As he observed, "in so far as the needs and goals of the individual are at the level of self-awareness, they are structured with reference to the kind of self-image that is consonant with other basic orientations that prepare the self for action in a culturally constituted world."[1]

The work of Jacques Lacan, in its own distinct way, also serves to highlight the importance of the concept of image in the constitution of the self. Lacan, while reinterpreting Freud in the light of cultural anthropology and linguistics, focused attention on the social and linguistic construction of self, and the idea of image is central to his project. According to Lacan, it is in what he refers to as the mirror stage that the articulation of self takes place. He believes that the recognition of the self by the child in the mirror proceeds in three stages. First, the child who is in the presence of an adult confuses his own image with that of the adult who is with him or her. Second, the child begins to realize that it is an image that he sees and not his or her real self. Third, he comes to the realization that what he sees is not only an image but that it is dissimilar to the images of others. Lacan develops these ideas in terms of the constitutive power of language in the making of the self. Once again we see an important dialectic between self and image.

I have so far discussed very briefly the role of image in the constitution of self. Next, it is important to reflect on the complex ways in which the image is textualized in various representational practices. Images do not produce meanings naturally and immanently. Indeed, as commentators like Roland Barthes have cogently pointed out, meanings are generated through various codes that are operative in representational practices, and they are consciously produced. What this means is that the generation of meaning through images takes place in diverse social, cultural, political, philosophical, and ideological domains. The relationship between text and image can be examined fruitfully at different levels of analysis. In terms of the themes explored in many of the essays gathered in this volume, the cultural encodings of images as they appear in various texts and representational practices can prove to be a productive line of inquiry. Let us, for example, consider a genre-like portraiture where one would think that cultural codes and conventions play a very inconsequential role. In point of fact, however, the opposite is the case. As Richard Vinograd points out, one of the central paradoxes of portraiture in any culture is that it purports to be about individuals, but to communicate effectively it must of necessity rely on the shared codes and conventions. Commenting specifically on Chinese portraiture, he says that it is important to bear in mind the fact that while Western cultures place greater emphasis on the value of individualism and personal autonomy, Chinese culture stresses family affiliations as the source of identity and the acting out of designated social roles as the realization of the self. These characteristics and valorizations find eloquent expression in Chinese portrait paintings in interesting and complex ways. As Vinograd remarks, "One culturally wide-spread system of signification that was relevant to the experience of portraits at large was that of physiognomy. The lore of physiognomic and phrenologic fortune-telling was part of everyday culture of traditional China. Human appearances were thought to be revelatory not only of personal characterolog-ical traits but also of fated destiny in terms of familial prosperity, professional success, and other crucial life events. Physiognomy and portraiture were thus both linked to the performance of familial and social roles."[2] What these remarks point to is the centrality of codes, conventions, and discourses of a given culture in shaping images of self.

Next we need to discuss the relationship between image and audience as a way of probing into the constitution of self through images. Images, whether they be in poetry or in cinema, tend to act as signifying systems positioning and addressing the audiences in diverse ways. This does not, of course, mean that the audiences have to passively accept the self-positioning decreed by the images. Indeed, very often they resist such positionings. What is interesting to observe here is the interaction that texts set in motion be-tween images and audiences in different cultural practices. How readers, lis-teners, and spectators make sense out of the images presented to them in symbolic contexts has much to do with the cultures that they have been born into. Similarly the social and historical conjunctures from which images arise and in which audiences are located are crucial to the constitution and com-munication of self through images. Let us for example consider Jawaharlal Nehru's autobiography.[3] The "prison" is clearly the dominant trope in it, operating at a number of levels of signification. One can identify at least five dimensions. First, there is the physical presence of the prison in the narrative with all the connotations of restrictiveness, loneliness, and oppression. The prison constitutes a massive presence in Nehru's autobiography, and some of the most memorable accounts deal with the life of the prison. Second, the prison becomes a metonym for the British administration that Nehru and his colleagues in the Congress were so vigorously fighting against. In prison, Nehru saw the inhuman side of the British administrative apparatus of re-pression at its worst. Third, the prison becomes for Jawaharlal Nehru a met-aphor for the constricting ways of thought that India has inherited from feudal times and within which he has to operate in his struggles to emancipate India both politically and spiritually. His attempts to break out of the prison house of tradition constitutes a significant dimension of the book. Fourth, the way in which the autobiographical narrative unfolds, the prison becomes emblematic of the troubled relationship that he had with Mahatma Gandhi. Fifth, the trope of the prison becomes an enabling device to give definition to, and provide us with, a hermeneutic for understanding Nehru's agonizing consciousness that he was a member of the bourgeoisie who was seeking to lead the Indian masses. In his autobiography, Nehru seeks to convey a complex image of himself. However, this image derives its force and emotive power from the social and historical conjunctures from which it arises and in which the readers are located. Without a deep awareness of the intertextualities, the roots of his cultural life, the complex image that he constructs will not yield its full significance. As John Berger rightly points out, although every image embodies a way of seeing, our perception and recognition of an image also depends upon our own ways of seeing and understanding.

The importance of image in the understanding of self cannot be overemphasized. As many scholars have convincingly argued, self can best be understood in terms of narration, and the end product of narrative is a powerful image or a complex of images related to the character or characters in the narrative. This is most evident in autobiography, lyric poetry, and first person narratives in fiction. The French philosopher Paul Ricoeur observed that, "Our own existence cannot be separated from the accounts we give ourselves. It is in telling our own stories that we give ourselves an identity. We recognize ourselves in the stories that we tell about ourselves. It makes very little difference whether these stories are true or false; fiction as well as verifiable history provides us with an identity."[4] What this remark underlines is the fact that self is produced through the instrumentality of narrative, and what all narratives end up with is an image or complex of images of the self. What these narrativized images serve to accomplish is to give concretion to what we valorize and hold in high esteem and to articulate in terms of cultural representation what a person is and what he or she desires. It provides the orientation for living. Scholars like Alasdair MacIntyre and Charles Taylor in their different ways have explicated the centrality of narrativized images in the construction and understanding of images.[5]

Most intellectual traditions, in both the East and West, posit an idealized image of the self, and the aim of virtuous men and women should be to approximate that image as closely as possible in day-to-day life. Let us, for example, consider Confucianism. The concept of self found in Confucianism is most interesting and can help us better understand the relationship between self and image. Confucianism abhors the all too familiar polarities of body and mind, sacred and profane, self and society, inner world and outer world, which in many ways have contributed to the current understanding of self. As Tu Wei-ming remarks, it seeks to emphasize the relationship between part and whole, inner and outer worlds, surface and depth, root and branches, substance and function.[6] The emphasis shifts from the static, mechanistic, and analytical distinctions of earlier Chinese thought to subtle relationships, internal resonance, dialogical interplay, and reciprocity of influence. Consequently, Confucianism seems to promote an idealized image of human beings that valorizes connectedness, interdependence, and the infinite potential for development.

According to the teachings of Confucius, the self needs to be perceived as the center of relationships in an open system. The idea of self-actualization entails the promotion of human interrelatedness in ever-widening circles that would include the self, the family, the nation, the world, the cosmos. Indeed, the search for self-actualization needs to be seen as search for interrelatedness. As Tu Wei-ming has observed, since the self as a center of relationships is an open system, self-actualization entails the establishment of an ever-widening circle of human relatedness.[7] Such a circle must also rise above selfishness, nepotism, anthropocentrism, and ethnocentrism in order to preserve its authenticity and dynamism. Clearly, there is a dominant moral strain in Confucian thinking. When poets seek to create idealized images against which their lives can be measured, they invoke this Confucian image. The essay on Du Fu's poetry contained in this volume aims to bring this out. Similarly, most other religious and intellectual traditions of Asia, as indeed in the West, embody an idealized image of an exemplary person that needs to emulated and against which the successes and failures are measured.

Similarly we can examine the Hindu and Buddhist traditions. The *Bhagavad Gītā* is a religious and philosophical poem that continues to exert a profound influence on the thought and sensibility of the Hindus, inflecting their attitudes to self and social order.[8] Just as in the *Analects* by Confucius, in the *Bhagavad Gītā* is enfigured an image of an ideal person that invites admiration. The idealized image that emerges from the *Bhagavad Gītā* is of a person committed to the maintenance of the *Dharma* or the sacred law and order and duty as decreed in Hinduism. He follows meticulously the norms of conduct prescribed in accordance with his social background, age, kinship structures; the term *Dharma* carries with it associations of religious and social duties that one has to perform in keeping with one's position in the social ladder. It is also linked to one's own mental and spiritual development. The idealized image given figurality in the *Bhagavad Gītā* is of a person who pursues diligently his duties and is deeply aware of his moral obligations. He is committed to the proposition of performing actions without attachments to the fruits of action. The ideas of discipline, duty, spiritual knowledge, love of and devotion to the divine are central to the constitution of this idealized image as represented in the *Bhagavad Gītā*. He constantly seeks to transcend his egotistical desires through the devotion and pursuit of spiritual knowledge; he is engaged in a profound quest for self-actualization that is to be achieved through the total identification with the power of Being. This ideal person aims to emancipate himself from the fetters of worldly existence through detachment and union with the Absolute. It is a composite image of this nature that emerges from the *Bhagavad Gītā* and that becomes the norm against which later writers have sought to measure their own projected valorized selves in their writings.

If we take a poem like the *Dhammapada* from the Buddhist tradition we can find the emergence of an image that is somewhat different.[9] Behind all texts such as the *Dhammapada* that seek to influence our moral conduct, we can discern an image of a highly valorized ideal person who inspires emulation. In the case of the *Dhammapada,* this ideal person is one who is thoughtful, mentally serene, disciplined, free of excessive sensual desire. He is engaged in a quest for real freedom through the instrumentalities of nonattachment, self-control, and the cultivation of wisdom and insight. He is one who does not depend upon any supernatural powers and seeks by dint of his own effort to overcome the suffering that inheres in the world. Indeed, it is this complex image that gives coherence to the poem and invests it with emotional power.

In the essays that follow, the way images of self are represented in literature, painting, cinema, and so on, are discussed in relation to Chinese, Indian, and Japanese cultures. Hence the idea of representation deserves closer study. Traditionally, representation was seen as a transparent act. A poet, for example, writes about an incident and the language that he or she uses is merely an instrument of communication; it is transparent. However, as a consequence of newer theorizations on this subject it has become evident that language is not transparent; the poet is not totally in command of the language. Language always exceeds the writer's intentions and creates ambiguities of meaning. Moreover, questions of cultural discourse, power, ideology, and so forth, are never absent from representation. Hence when we examine the ways in which images function to construct meaning in works of literature, cinema, and art, we need to pay closer attention to the problems associated with representation. In this volume, one such problem that is repeatedly stressed is the role of culture—how cultural codes, conventions, discourses, and valorizations shape these images and give them life.

The papers included in this volume, needless to say, do not explore all the varied and knotty interconnections between self and image that I have hinted at. However, they do focus attention on the cultural work of images and the role that culture plays in shaping the idea of self as image. They underline the need to examine the relationship of self and image in the context of a larger thought world. Many of the essays contained in this book deal with representational practices like art, literature, and cinema. The point that often emerges from these essays is that works of art are not transhistorical and transdiscursive and that they serve both to reflect and inflect social discourse. Any discussion of the construction of self through images has to bear this in mind. With this line of thinking as a backdrop, many of the chapters in this volume explore the role of images in the life of individuals as well as cultures, especially as manifested in China, India, and Japan. Hence, this book as a whole, I believe, opens an interesting window onto the complex ways in which culturally grounded, culturally produced, and culturally legitimized images connect with the concept of self in China, India, and Japan.

Arthur Danto's essay serves the purpose of widening the discursive boundaries of self and image and introducing a newer angle of approach. Although it does not specifically deal with Asian cultures, the distinction it draws between sign and manifestation, symbol and expression, is extremely helpful in understanding the elusive nature of self and how it gets constructed discursively in representational practices.

Notes

1. A. Irving Hallowell, *Culture and Experience* (Philadelphia: University of Pennsylvania Press, 1955).

2. Richard Vinograd, *Boundaries of the Self: Chinese Portraits 1600–1900* (Cambridge: Cambridge University Press, 1992), p. 5.

3. Jawaharlal Nehru, *An Autobiography* (New Delhi: Oxford University Press, 1980).

4. Paul Ricoeur, "History as Narrative and Practice," *Philosophy Today,* Vol. 29, N. 4 1985, p. 214.

5. See Alasdair MacIntyre, *After Virtue* (Notre Dame, Ind.: University of Notre

Dame Press, 1984), and Charles Taylor, *Sources of the Self* (Cambridge: Harvard University Press, 1989).

6. Tu Wei-ming, *Confucian Thought* (New York: State University of New York Press, 1988).

7. Ibid.

8. Wimal Dissanayake, "*Bhagavad Gītā* and the Discourse of Social Order." Typescript.

9. Wimal Dissanayake, *The Path of Virtue*—An English translation of the *Dhammapada,* with a critical introduction. Forthcoming.

1

Symbolic Expressions and the Self

Arthur C. Danto

In seeking to define the contours of the Other, each of us — with psychiatrists no less immune to error than sweethearts or even parents — must somehow learn to discriminate between what any of us would call *expressions* and what, for want of a better term, I shall merely call manifestations. The task is complicated by the fact that a good many things the Other does could be either, but it is simplified by the fact that nothing can be both. Manifestations will in general have different kinds of explanations than expressions, which in any given case tend to rule one another out. And because of that, of course, they license very different sorts of response.

The expressions to concern me will be cultural rather than physiognomic, and though expressions of both sorts refer to feelings, the feelings themselves will be complicated by the internalization of a culture, which for the most part is not the case with those dispositions of limb and feature that Darwin, in a great book, was at some pains to establish as continuous between animals and humans. That would make them very largely invariant to culture, since animals have none to speak of. That, of course, does not mean that physiognomic expressions themselves are invariant from culture to culture, though the manifestations, as against the expressions of basic feelings, may in fact be. Consider, for example, the look of terror on someone's face that we would count as the expression of fear. Clammy palms or facial pallor might be merely among the physical manifestations of fear, the distinction resting on the fact that what we call expressions can with some degree of success be feigned or inhibited, whereas keeping our palms dry and face ruddy normally exceeds the limits of the will. It is rarely a matter of cultural indifference what feelings its members have, hence physiognomic expressions fairly readily fall within the class of cultural feelings and their expressions accordingly are among those that I shall want to discuss. It is as important to American culture that people look happy as it is to the society of the French that its members look serious, and it will come as a form of anthropological relief to the tourist in Auvergne that the dour looks are not expressions of disapproval occasioned by some gaucherie of his but mere manifestations of an internal-ized enjoined *Auvergnat* sobriety. This means that the members of that culture will have to find ways of expressing what a dour look in our culture expresses as disapproval. But I have begun with a digression, mainly to indicate that the feelings and expressions that I am concerned with can assimilate without quite being reduced to the concept that Darwin expressed in his book title, *The Expression of Emotions in Animals and Humans,* which was meant, after all, only to remove a difficulty from his theory of our common origins.

Let me then begin with an example of quite another kind, that of a disordered room, where the disorder is of a kind that is ordinarily to be explained with reference to negligence rather than violence, where strewn contents of spilled drawers, the ripped mattress, and the dashed and broken pictures really imply, as in a later example, an alien intervention. Here, in-stead, I have in mind a room where clothes are flung about, where empty—or worse, half-empty—soda cans occupy windowsills with dead plants, where soiled linen lies rumpled on the unmade bed, and dust is everywhere. If, in response to "Your place or mine?" the fastidious swinger has opted for "Yours" he (let him be *he*), will want to know if this is a manifestation or an expression before he goes any further with the affair, if indeed he wants to go further at all. It will be a (mere) manifestation when the room belongs to someone who just never learned to straighten things up, or never so much as learned that this was something to do, having grown up in a household where all this was a matter of indifference. This domestic indifference is made manifest in the room, but the room is not then an expression of what it manifests. As a manifestation, it does not tell him what kind of a person she (let her be *she*) is, but only things for which she has no responsibility as a person, any more than for her accent: it tells only something about her world. And I suppose it begins to tell what the distance is between that world and the world of the one who finds it a problem. It gets instead to be an expression when the conditions under which it is a manifestation fail, when the occupant, as we say, knows better but has decided to live in the room that way for certain reasons. In some way explanations through reasons (as against explanation through causes) connect with our distinction and tend to defeat one another.

It is not difficult to think of the kinds of reasons someone might have for allowing a room to stand in disorder. The occupant may be a woman repudiating the tidiness associated in her mind with a form of oppression to which women, as unpaid household workers—as *slaves*—have for too long been subjected. The room is a political statement (and in my scenario it could mean, to whomever she brought home: Sex, yes, but don't expect me to be the kind of girl your mother wants you to bring home). Or it can, by another woman, be a skirmish in the marital wars, a way of getting back at a man who has not done what she has a right to have expected of him: and the room is a punitive act. Or it can, this time when its occupant is an adolescent, be a declaration of independence from the detested and contemptible values of his awful parents in the medium of flaunted mess. These are all reasonably familiar scenarios, and they operate only under a code, well understood by the occupants of rooms, under which tidiness means something and untidiness also means something or is a repudiation of the first meaning. In these cases, there certainly are feelings that the disordered room expresses, but the feelings themselves are structured by the internalized culture in which the orderly room has a meaning that gives the individual an avenue for expression. But so has, or can have, almost everything else. And any member of any culture can cite or invent example after example of cases where the distinction between manifestations and expressions is underdetermined by what meets the eye, as is the further question of what is expressed if it is an expression.

I am now going to graft onto this distinction another one, that between symbols and signs. An expression, as distinguished from a manifestation (and which could, under different auspices just be a manifestation), is a symbol, whereas manifestations are merely signs. And what we have to do in defining the contours of the Other can be rephrased as distinguishing symbols from signs, which means we have to decide when to give a certain sort of interpretation, and then what specific interpretation to give.

It will give us a fair sense of the distinction by thinking for a moment of the moral philosophy of Kant. Kant's test in making a moral judgment (making, I suppose, a moral decision), is this: could I, as a rational being, will that the principle that justifies the action be a universal law of nature: would that principle fit coherently with the remaining laws of the universe to yield a rational world in which no one has the choice, as I have, but would be constrained, as a matter of natural law, to behave the way I now choose to act? I will put this somewhat differently: can I will as actual a possible world in which what I have decided is the right thing to do in this world happens instead as a matter of course in that possible world because of the way that world is made. Kant's famous negative example is a world in which everyone breaks promises, which is a world that would fall apart: hence I have no moral right to break a promise in the actual world. There is a great deal more to Kant's formulation than this, but the structure of judgment, relativized to possible worlds, is all I need from him here. An expression implies a world in which it would instead be a manifestation. The expression symbolizes the reality in which it would be a manifestation or in which it would be a mere sign, if that world instead of this one were real. The symbol, that is, represents this world as different by embodying that world as if it were in this world instead. It brings into this world another world through something that I am saying *embodies* it.

Now, a sign is part of reality; it is the way something makes itself manifest to whoever knows how to read the sign, which is perhaps an effect of the signified reality. In the real world in which the disordered room is an expression rather than a sign, an ordered room might be a sign that a certain set of imperatives have been internalized and enacted. In the real world in which a disordered room is a sign, there are either no imperatives of the sort that regulate the *Lebenswelt of the real world in which the disordered room is an expression of repudiation,* or there are contrary imperatives of the kind expressed in the long-suppressed pages of *Poor Richard's Almanack:* "Only the whore, sweepeth the floor." Or "A dull heade maketh a bed." The protesting feminist is in effect already endeavoring to live in that world in which the disordered room is a manifestation rather than an expression. It is as if, in the medium of this room, that world is already real. The disordered room in her case is a symbol because it contains a fragment of reality from another world. And it is a symbol because it is only a fragment. It is surrounded by a world to which it does not belong and which she rejects. The same is true of the adolescent who endeavors to live in his parent's world as if he already belonged to another one, one in which their values did not exist, and where he would be free. The formula is: find the world in which the expression of this world would be but a sign. Then the expression is a symbol of that world.

The individuals I have been discussing exist in a world alternative to the world they reject, and live in the rejected world like prisoners. Their true world is embodied in a world to which it does not otherwise belong—the way a god is a being from another world but enfleshed in this world. In *Les Chemins de la liberté,* Sartre depicts a Communist in a prison camp who makes a great point of shaving daily. He is rejecting his identity as a prisoner; he is affirming his identity as a free man by living in the prison as he would live outside it. Outside, in ordinary life, shaving is just a manifestation and so a sign, but in the prison camp it has become a symbol of the reality in which it is a mere sign. Hence it is a rejection of the circumstances of the captivity by someone who, under the circumstances, has perhaps only the recourse of symbolic enactment. His life as a free man, if to a degree reduced to the dimensions of a razor blade, is an expression that means different things to his fellow prisoners and to his custodians. But of course someone in the world shaving symbolizes in this world could, by growing a beard, affirm his citizenship in a world in which the conformity of shaving is condemned.

Let me round things off at this preliminary stage by considering cases where the advent of psychoanalytical theories of the mind make it difficult and urgent to decide whether something is a manifestation or an expression, when either way it is still a symptom. The cases I have sketched are not symptoms, it seems to me, but rather cases of persons acting symbolically under circumstances in which non-symbolic action is for the moment ruled out—or where, for reasons not worth going into, direct rather than deflected communication is excluded. Let the symptom once again be a disordered room, and the question is whether this is a symbol or a sign. Suppose the room belongs to someone extremely depressed, so depressed as to have pretty much lost the will to do anything—depressed to the point of abulia. Then no special explanation of a disordered *room* is called for, any more than, within the room, no special explanation is called for as to why the clothes are thrown here and there. All these things would be part of the disturbance: the sufferer has let his work slip and social relationships lapse, has stopped taking care of himself, just can't bring himself to do anything. Or: there is some point to the fact that it is a disordered room, as if the room were a kind of text through which the owner of it expresses a feeling through modifying, to be sure only symbolically, a certain reality. Then the therapist has to understand the disorder *through the disorder,* which must be interpreted. What alternative reality is embodied here, what statement is being made about the reality in which the sufferer lives? These questions arise with many other things—with sexual disfunction, with anorexia, and with phobic behavior of various sorts. They all give rise to the question of what the patient is endeavoring to say, or better, in what world it is that the patient is endeavoring to live. Obviously, the anorexic is not saying that the world in which he wants to live is one in which he does not eat—he does that in *this* world—but in some sense he is, by not eating, living in that world "symbolically" and by way of criticism of this one. Obviously, a certain amount of transformation is undergone by the alternative world as the symbolizer finds a way of bringing it into this one. Even a god undergoes some pretty humiliating transformations when he takes on a fleshly identity: he has to acquire the appurtenances of gender, become subject to pain, and show the mark of lashes across his perfect back.

So we might, as a sort of exercise, consider two views of transubstantiation. On the one view, the wine really turns to blood in the mouth, complicating the laws of chemistry, insisting upon miraculous occurrences, so that Christ's body and blood are really manifest in wine and wafer. The other view leaves the laws of nature intact and insists only that wine and wafer in this world are body and blood in another, so that Christ is symbolically present in the act, a transfigured way of being in this world while belonging to another. On the one view, a transformation actually occurs of an order so momentous that there is no way of understanding it through science. On the other view, we coparticipate in a symbolic reality at right angles to the plane of science, leaving the world as it was. On this view, the wine and wafer embody a reality that is of an altogether different order than that to which wine and wafer belong.

Perhaps the example puts too heavy a stress on a fragile theory, so let us turn to a case that returns me to my structures but is a bit more compelling than the simple gestures with which I began. Consider the way in which George VI of England, but really any king, is held to be the symbolic embodiment of his people. (In this sense Louis XIV was not so much boasting as acknowledging some mystical bond between himself and his kingdom when he said *l'état, c'est moi*.) In the London Blitz of the 1940s George's behavior just *was* the behavior of the British people in the mode of exemplification. So even if it was a natural manifestation of his natural inclination as a person, the fact that as a king he did by choice what others had to do as a matter of course, that as a king he did publicly what commoners did privately, meant that the people saw him as themselves, inverting Louis's thought to read: *le roi, c'est nous*. This meant that literally everything he did in this period was symbolic; it was the life of the ordinary person inscribed in the life of the king. Thus in not leaving London, he did as a matter of choice what most of his subjects did as a matter of necessity; in visiting bomb sites he in effect was declaring that it was he that had been bombed; in celebrating, or rather, in just taking as given the virtues of family life, he in effect gave symbolic weight to the spontaneous system of values that defined his people domestically. It was as though he were an ordinary person, but also king, so that king and people were one. His brother Edward's abdication obviously put personal happiness above duty, and it is unclear what his behavior would have been had he instead become king, given his character. He would have represented but not embodied his people: he might have done what was expected of him as king, but he would not have done as king what people have expected of themselves. So George did what he would have done otherwise as manifestation, but, as he was king, it became expressive and became symbolic. So seriously did he take his role that the public and the private were one, providing perhaps an impossible model for the British royal family. Demanding some privacy is in effect fighting a paradigm of symbolic existence created by George VI, whose example cannot any longer be erased from British consciousness. With George's conduct in the war, we have a beautiful example of the kind of relationship I am striving to characterize: his conduct expressed symbolically what would have been manifested had he been an ordinary person instead. It was commonplace behavior transfigured, enabling everyone to be a kind of king. Something of the same sort evidently held with Barbara Bush, whose conmonplace American ways became symbolic when transferred to a different plane of reality.

The concept of symbol that I am advancing is almost entirely Hegelian, in that it consists in giving sensuous or material embodiment to what Hegel would have called Idea: it is, as it were, Idea made flesh. Hence it involves rather a complex kind of understanding, if we think of symbols as representations, in distinction, say, from signs or manifestations, where the representational function is straightforward and in a way evidential. I shall think of a sign as an effect that is *taken* as standing for its cause—something is a sign *for* somebody—as a footprint is the effect of a footfall and, forensically, a sign of its cause. There are causal theories of proper names, according to which something is a name if a causal history connects it to an act of naming, so it stands for what it names only if caused to. Symbols, by contrast, *contain* the reality they represent, or embody it, and to respond to the symbol is to respond to that content. That, I think, would explain the special power of symbols, in that they distill the very reality signs merely stand for. In a way, if one encounters signs of something fearful, one may be afraid, but the thing in question is still at a distance, whereas with the *symbol* of something fearful, what is feared is already present, embodied in the vehicle of its representation. The paradigm of the symbol, perhaps, would be the tragic hero as depicted in *The Birth of Tragedy*. That member of the chorus, perhaps the leader of the chorus, is, at a special moment, possessed by the god. The god then becomes enfleshed in an individual who, to all outward appearances, is of a piece with his neighbors, but notwithstanding that ordinariness, has become the vehicle of divinity that has chosen him as the way of becoming present among men. I imagine much the same account can be given of the Virgin Mary; the mysterious notion of possession or embodiment is given an affectingly ordinary exemplification through pregnancy and impregnation by the Holy Spirit. But there is a very ancient concept of representation according to which the thing represented is present, literally, in its images. This is why certain images are taken to be holy or miraculous, or powerful in ways that images would not ordinarily be. The art historian David Freedberg speaks of this as "the power of images" where the power, in effect, is of the entity that is *captured* (a phrase we still use) in the icon or effigy—or, for those who find these notions offensive, in the idol. Freedberg's theory is that we are still responsive to the power of images, as evidenced by the forms iconoclasm still takes, as well as by the way certain images move us. With photographs of loved ones, for example, the impulse may seem uncontrollable to feel, however irrationally, that in kissing the photograph we are kissing the loved one, even (or especially) if dead—she or he "lives on" in her or his images. My overall sense is that if one believes in gods, there are only symbols and never signs: the gods express themselves in symbols, like the stirring of leaves or the flights of birds, as a kind of divine natural language that simply collapses into natural events when the belief in divine expression through them fades. But this takes me off in a direction I do not especially feel it important to pursue here, largely because it seems to me that the mode of symbolic representation divine discourse was supposed to exemplify in whatever medium it chose, remains in the far less extravagant notion of symbolic embodiment that connects us to the concept of expression.

   Let us consider photographs, which provide some marvelous examples of the same thing being manifestation or sign, on the one hand, and expression or symbol, on the other. They do this especially through the fact that in recent times, artists have begun to use photographs to make works of art; they draw on certain connotations of the concept of photography, but themselves are only technically to be classed as photographs. I am thinking of the works of Cindy Sherman or Louise Lawlor, or of the remarkable French artist, Christian Boltansky, or, in the case I want to consider, the Canadian artist, Jeff Wall. All these artists *use* photography, but they need not themselves be photographers, and in fact most of the ones I have mentioned may not make their own photographs, anymore than a film director, say, would ordinarily stand in as cameraman for his own films. It could be done, but like conducting from the piano in a concerto, it comprises two distinct functions, so that though the product is a photograph, the art in question is not the art of photographing.

Let me bring to the mind's eye then, a 1978 work by Jeff Wall: a fairly large (63 x 92) cibachrome print whose title is "The Destroyed Room." It has a more violent degree of disorder than I considered in my first example, and what I want to bring out with *this* example is that it could in the ordinary course of things be simply a photograph of a destroyed room—a forensic record of an act of vandalism, where the photograph was caused by the interior it represents, in the straightforward manner of snapshots. The violently disordered room is perhaps itself an expression, but it could also be a manifestation. It could be the latter if it were caused by a particularly zealous search on the part of police who looked for something and did not care what the room looked like so long as they could find it. It is manifestation through the fact that it is explained as the way the police act when they search. It is, though it sounds funny to say it, a "sign" of the police having been there—or of somebody. The room is the way it is as the consequence of the search. But it could also be an expression. Someone may have wanted to intimidate the occupant and communicate through a medium of ransacked drawers and ripped mattresses that the owner had better watch out. Since the owner is a woman, evidently, from the shoes, the clothing, and the ornaments, the attack on her room is a vicarious rape. It is a terribly violent gesture. The photograph as sign will not discriminate between these two statuses; it will not tell us if it is manifestation or expression. (It seems it could be both, but I think not: the police may have made their search and expressed their warning—but in that case we have to distinguish between the search and letting the evidence of the search stand, viz., not concealing it, not because it is too much trouble to clean things up but because the police *also* want to intimidate.)

Now, in fact this photograph is neither of these. It is an expression, not the documentation of what might be an expression. This room was arranged this way. I don't even know if there was a room there before—the entire thing may be a piece of stage setting, arranged by Jeff Wall, who discussed with his associates how to make it convincing. It was like arranging fruit on a table for the purposes of painting a still life. In a sense, the meaning of the photograph is interior to the photograph, not an external relationship between the photograph and the room. As a work of art, as an expression, it has the structure of a symbol. Note, as a symbol, that its being a photograph in part enters into the structure of its meaning, largely in consequence of the documentary connotations of photography and the nearly universal knowledge that a photograph records what is set before it.

Still, as is methodologically central to such inquiries, the same image could be sign or symbol, and it is instructive to reflect that theories of pictorial representation such as Nelson Goodman's will not help discriminate, just because both are (what Goodman would call) "destroyed-room-pictures" and each "stands for" destroyed rooms. Nor will it especially reduce the somewhat mysterious dimensions of the symbol to say that, in the case of Wall's work, it contains a representation, as it does, since the presumption is that he assembled the garments, the slashed mattress, and the like, so that the assembled jumble is itself a model, with representational properties in its own right, like a movie set. I don't think this takes us very far in working out the distinction, mainly because the identical photograph could be both sign and symbol, depending upon how it is used: Warhol used ordinary newspaper photographs of disasters like plane crashes or automobile accidents as expressions, and one of the things one has to work out in interpreting Warhol's art is the difference. My sense, once more, is that the representation the symbol "contains" is an idea, and it contains it in the sense of embodiment; and the question, as always in criticism, is to identify the idea and then explain the way it is embodied. I don't think you can dissolve the matter quite so mechanically as the internal representation idea might suggest, viz., that a symbol is a representation of a representation. A rephotographed photograph by Sherrie Levine fits that formula to perfection, and though it is true that Levine's (re)photographs of the works of Walker Evans really are expressions in their own right, as mere photographic reproductions of the images of Walker Evans are not, they are so in virtue of embodying rather complex ideas of ownership, originality, appropriation, and the like. And these are not the kinds of things that especially meet the eye.

My sense is that it was probably important to Wall's intention that there be a settled uncertainty between sign and symbol in this work, though it is worth stressing that the circumstances of display go some distance toward resolving it. Wall uses light boxes to frame his images, which are then internally illuminated, and in this case he adapted the window of his gallery as an improvised light box, so that the window in effect became an artwork rather than the space in which an artwork was displayed. According to one critic, Wall thereby meant to set up a comparison with the shopwindows along that street which displayed the kinds of material objects—feminine finery, bedroom furniture, bibelots—that he shows as destroyed in his photograph. So perhaps he was making a statement about material possessions; perhaps, as a Marxist, he was making a statement about consumption and bourgeois society. These are things that have to be worked out in order to find the interpretation of the work, which is no great concern of mine to establish here. Secondly, and I attach a certain importance to this, one must take the image in this instance *as part of a corpus,* as one work among many, in each of which the same order of question could be raised, but where, slowly, the sense emerges that these works were staged and that Wall is making some kind of statement about the place of violence in ordinary life. The ordinariness of life seems underwritten by the ordinariness of the photographs themselves, which are not in the least arty and seem the kind of color prints Everyman and Everywoman get back from the Photorush of their neighborhoods. Here, I think, this ordinariness is thematized by the fact that it distances the artiness of artistic photography, and even by the fact that it is colored, as the artistic photograph makes something of being in black-and-white. In one image, an Oriental youth is walking toward us, sharing a sidewalk with a couple, a boy and girl, holding hands. The picture is called "Mimic," and it is quite large again, billboard size. The title refers to a gesture by the Occidental man, who uses his finger to slant one of his eyes, in mimesis of the characteristic facial feature of the Oriental. It is a racist gesture, an insult, a provocation. The Oriental youth sees it, and the scene becomes filled with impending violence. In another, "Outburst," an Oriental man clenches his fists and shouts at a surprised worker, seated at one of the sewing machines in what one supposes is a garment factory or even a sweatshop. The other workers look on apprehensively. And the message may have to do with the violence provoked by the manufacturing process. In any case, as we situate the work in a context of other works, it acquires a certain clarity of intention and even of philosophical identity it might not have on its own, vivid as the destroyed room is as an image. Each work seems to embody the same overall idea or kind of idea, and, in particular, I think, it gets clearer and clearer that these works are staged, as much so, as I see it, as Poussin. I know nothing of Wall's training as an artist, so I don't know even if he knows how to paint. But these works could all have been painted, though it seems to me, at a considerable loss in artistic power as against their being photographs.

It seems to me that symbolic expressions, as I have been constructing the concept they exemplify, are *communications,* and presuppose a code that is supposed accessible to those to whom the communication is addressed. When a woman in a backward corner of Asia burns the millet, or lets the millet burn, she is (or can be) expressing resentment, or discontent, or contempt for those who have every reason to expect, who count on, the millet being cooked just right. It is a mode of symbolic expression her culture and her station within that culture makes available to her, and it can be read for those conversant in the code of cooked millet. Symbolic expressions function as ways of saying what cannot be said, or saying more effectively what can be said, and they demonstrate the degree to which every item of social existence is penetrated by meaning. The artist Christian Boltanski at one period exhibited works that consisted of objects from his childhood displayed in biscuit tins. Those tins are, as he puts it, "Minimal objects, cubes, very close to objects by Donald Judd" and it would be instructive to imagine a work made of biscuit tins by Boltanski and a work made of fabricated metal cubes by Judd, which, as usual with the sorts of examples I use, look altogether alike. Judd's would be a very complex expression of a set of ideas about originality, creativity, the social nature of art—all those things that are condensed in the formulas of Minimalism. And we might be struck, aesthetically, by regularity, repetition, unadornedness, and the like. Formally, Boltanski's work would look quite like Judd's, but his would condense the sort of emotional feeling that it is, one is certain, an axiom of minimalism to hold at bay. "Biscuit tins in France are also childhood objects with many associations," Boltanski says. "The task is to create a formal work that is at the same time recognized by the spectator as a sentimentally charged object. Everyone brings their own history to it." Indeed, for someone who grew up in France at a certain moment, the biscuit tin carries a charge of feelings that bear out almost to perfection what Proust describes in the prologue to *Contra Saint-Beuve:*

> What intellect restores to us under the name of the past, is not the past. In reality, as soon as each hour of one's life has died, it embodies itself in some material object, as do the souls of the dead in certain folk-stories, and hides there. There it remains captive, captive forever, unless we should happen on the object, recognize what lies within, call it by its name, and set it free.

Boltanski's project as an artist is to present objects to consciousness in such a way that the viewer's past will be awakened to consciousness, and it is to this end that he uses the objects he does use—children's clothing, snapshots, and of course biscuit tins. And his work is successful when the viewer is overpowered with emotion, encountering his or her forgotten self embedded in familiar objects, and afflicted, abruptly, with the consciousness of their recoverability of the past, the death of childhood, and the ephemerality of life. And in a way Proust does this as well in his stunning meditation on the tea-steeped madeleine (or, in *Contra Saint-Beuve,* tea-steeped rusk). What is remarkable is that the objects that meant so much to Boltanski as a child mean just as much, and in the same way, to all those who shared his childhood, who were children at a certain moment in history in France. The rest of us do not know what is going on. Boltanski's works define an entire culture and communicate in much the same way and with much the same intensity with all who share the culture. (Boltanski's works when exhibited in the United States, or in Canada, elicit very different responses). Symbolic expressions, as communications, in general define communities of implicit understanders, individuals whose feelings and thoughts will be modified (or at least it is the intention of the expressor that they be modified) upon understanding the expressions.

My sense, if this is true, is that the self, as the author of symbolic expression, is defined reciprocally by the community that may be expected to grasp the symbolic expressions: the self *is* that community, internalized, as it were, and it alone makes expression a possibility. There is a work by Boltanski called *Purim* that consists in great quantities of children's clothing hung up, as if displayed, and illuminated. Because of the title, it suggests a Jewish content, and it is impossible to repress the idea that the owners of this clothing are all dead, and this is a pathetic and touching memorial to the children who perished in the camps. The clothing is colorful and in a way anonymous: it is cheap, mass produced—the kinds of things Anychild would wear. But the associations are available only to a community in which the components of these associations have the intended meanings and where the encounter with the reality embodied in the mass of clothing evokes the kinds of feeling intended by the work. For those outside that community, the work requires interpretation, and perhaps can never be responded to at all.

Chomsky famously stresses the truth that any child can learn any language, and that each of us—American, Chinese, Japanese Indian—might have been thrust, as infants, in a language community other than our own and grown to fluency there. The same must be said about the field of symbolic expression. Any of us might have grown up through a different symbolic field, as I shall designate that domain of meanings symbolic expressions activate. There are these differences. Chomsky supposes, or supposed, that we have a common grammatical core, the same from individual to individual, which is what makes it possible to learn the language. Does the language in any way penetrate the speaker of it, so that we would be different persons were we to have spoken another language than the one we in fact speak? No one knows the answer to this. But I think it reasonably clear that if the self is defined by the symbolic field within which it expresses itself, we would have been very different selves as a function of the accidents of cultural locus. How striking it is to reflect, if this is true, that in addition to its art, literature, and architecture, all the different cultures have different selves as their products. The vexing, unanswerable question is what would *I* be had, as Santayana says, I been born under a different sky? There is, in the philosophy of Kant, a distinction between the pure self, the self *an sich,* and the empirical self that is as it appears to itself. It is the empirical self that I have been speaking of, defined by the way in which it appears to itself through the refractions of the symbolic fields in which it conducts its expressional experiments. I suppose we need the self *an sich* only in order to be tormented by the question of what would I have been had I been a different self in a different field of symbolic operations.

─────── *Part Two* ───────
Self as Image in Chinese Theory and Practice

INTRODUCTION

Roger T. Ames

The five essays dedicated to geographical China in this anthology cover the broad sweep of Chinese history, reporting on both high and popular culture. The central concern that provides continuity throughout this section is the porous relationship between aesthetic presentation and established values. It is certainly the case that art is instrumental, reinforcing traditional social and political values and serving as a discourse to express cultural importances. But it is also true that poetry and painting have a performative, ontological dimension, figuring, shaping, and "realizing" (in the sense of "making real") the world called China.

The first essay is Stephen J. Goldberg's exploration of the way in which gendered subjects are constructed in the visual arts of traditional China. Goldberg begins by contextualizing the Chinese experience, drawing comparisons with those conventions of objective space and mimetic representation familiar in Western art. There is an immediately discernible distance between the dualistic "subject/object" presuppositions that can be excavated from a consideration of Western artistic representations and the mutual resonance among correlated elements *(ganlei)* that undergirds a traditional Chinese worldview, making Chinese artistic expression self-consciously presentational, productive, and normative—the Chinese artist knowingly images and recommends a world.

Goldberg uses gender construction to survey the tradition and to illustrate the sometimes hegemonic social and political implications of embedding female subjects in conventionalized topoi: the palace, the garden, the hermitage, and the rock and tree by a riverbank. Throughout this essay, Goldberg relies upon the artist's brush and figured subject to make the Chinese tradition an early precursor to the Foucaultean claim that art is performative, producing what it might pretend to merely represent. For Goldberg, the awareness and sensibilities encouraged by his analysis are a basis for formulating strategies necessary to challenge the negative social and political inequities that have been reinforced by their materialization in China's tradition of artistic representation.

John Hay in his essay, "Construction and Insertion of the Self in Song and Yuan Painting," examines the visual image as a resource for recovering notions of self that prevailed in medieval China. In assessing traditional notions of creativity, Hay takes careful account of seemingly conservative influences such as "categories" (motifs, conventions, subject matter) and "grades" (the vocabulary of evaluation) that ensured continuity within the structure of the tradition and guaranteed a cultural as well as social and political stability. As Hay observes, the Chinese obsession with these formal aspects is itself revealing. For the schematics of categorization is the semiotic ground of a kind of correlative thinking pervasive in Chinese cosmology. So considered, these same categories are at different periods and in differing degrees reflexive and have a dynamic, performative function, locating the "person" of the artist effectively within the artifact itself. Good persons paint good paintings.

The increasing importance of calligraphy, "at once one of the most controlled of all cultural practices and one of the most spontaneous," seems to be natural outcome of this reflexivity within the life of the Chinese literati. It is in calligraphy that the person of the artist is revealed in the most unambiguous form—the organism of the body itself. Hay then moves from the physiology of the body as it "dwells" in the calligraphic product to the ecology of place as it is disclosed both in geomancy and landscape painting: "the phenomena of landscape and culture in China are closely related to the ecological issues of place, space and self." To illustrate this insight about the interplay among fundamentally aesthetic discourses, Hay closes with a compelling interpretation of a fourteenth-century handscroll painted by Huang Gongwang in which the artist himself is inscribed into the work as an imposing, solitary mountain, erupting from the surface of the scroll.

In Martin Huang's contribution, "Stylization and Invention: The Burden of Self-Expression in *The Scholars*," he appeals to an eighteenth-century novel as a mirror of the life of the literatus *(wenren)* in a period when rigid conventionization constricted personal expression. During the seventeenth and eighteenth centuries, the hydraulics of an identity crisis among the literati emerged in which marginalization and exclusion from political life was countered by an increasingly visible degree of cultivated and often stereotypical eccentricity. The inhospitable times and circumstances of the early Qing forced the man of letters into a kind of self-parody as he undertook an often futile attempt at self-invention. This cult of eccentricity reached its peak in the eighteenth century, when scholars so keenly felt the need to be noticed that self-expression became synonymous with the compulsion to startle one's contemporaries.

In Huang's study of *The Scholars,* which dramatizes the complexity of this period, he reports on the ironies that subvert the authentic self-expression of the literati class. Eremitism—the literatus's refusal to perform within the institutions of government—is co-opted by imperially sanctioned and celebrated hermitic lifestyles, where public impact becomes the dominant concern of the recluse. In *The Scholars,* a sociology of "public" self overrides all other concerns, becoming the guiding thematic of the work. Accumulated culture and the demands of conformity that distinguish the Qing from the late Ming dynasty have a devastating affect on genuine self-expression, transforming the existential project of self-cultivation into a veritable predicament.

"Unseen Lives" by Mark Elvin is subtitled: "The emotions of everyday existence mirrored in the Chinese popular poetry of the mid-seventeenth to the mid-nineteenth century." It is an unconventional piece in many ways. It is unconventional in being twice as long as any of the other essays in this volume, in using an idiosyncratic romanization system, in appealing to poetry of sometimes marginal aesthetic merit, and in following conventions in the English translation that are often quite at variance with the Chinese text. At the same time, it is of extraordinary cautionary value—it gives voice to what is too often left silent. China has a vast agrarian tradition which is almost always characterized on the basis of the surface and visible "citified" civilization. Our elitist approach to Chinese history and culture generally leaves the lives and values of the ordinary people unnoticed, and to the extent that we ignore the balk of the Chinese people, we remain ignorant of China. Elvin's corrective lays bare the seasonal concerns and expectations of Everyman, using popular poetry to explore earthy themes such as poverty, family relations, sexual license, the harvest cycle, female infanticide, the unhappy arranged marriage, prison conditions, and so on, providing us with a composite and complex profile of daily life in Qing China.

John Kwok-kan Tam and Terry Siu-han Yip begin from a characterization of Confucian self as being socially embedded and relationally defined. It is against this model that "Mr. Science" and "Mr. Democracy," introduced into China in the early twentieth century, represent much more than a call to modernization. Under the banner of a newly discovered individualism, May Fourth cultural leaders such as Lu Xun and Hu Shi appealed to an anti-traditional notion of self to undermine the stagnation blamed on traditional Confucian values. This iconoclasm in different guises became the life blood of the new playwrights, dramatizing the existential dilemma of being an individual in a majority-dominated traditional society. Tam and Yip use the revolutionary drama of Guo Moruo, Tian Han, and Cao Yu to illustrate alternative models of the new Chinese self and the actual complexity of the post–May Fourth mentality. At issue here is nothing less than the viability of "Chineseness" as we know it. For if China were successful in embracing the values of Western individualism, such a turn would herald a psychological and sociological revolution that would challenge the very core of traditional Chinese ways of thinking and living.

2

Figures of Identity
Topoi and the Gendered Subject in Chinese Art

Stephen J. Goldberg

In this essay, I shall be concerned with an investigation into the ways in which the identities of masculine and feminine-gendered subjects are represented in traditional Chinese art. This will necessitate the formulation of an interpretive strategy that is based on a different set of assumptions than those embraced by Western mimetic representational practices. Generally speaking, Western art, at least since the Renaissance, is premised on a belief in the universality of artistic concern for visual appearance, a concern that is informed by an objective conception of *space* which is fundamentally Western, but alien to Chinese culture.

The modern Western conception of self finds its earliest paradigmatic expression in Leonardo da Vinci's *Study of Human Proportions According to Vitruvious,* Venice Accademia, and the Cartesian cogito. The self is conceived as a perceiving, conceiving, enunciating ego that occupies a position of mastery at the geometrical center of an objective space, constructed in the transparent, universal discourse of geometry and light. For Descartes, "It is the order of the *cogito—ergo—sum:* mind—signs—world."[1] This exemplary formal statement is a spatial metaphor predicated on a fundamental dualism between rationality, conceived as the procedural property of the mind to construct orders of representation, and the self and phenomenal world of which it seeks certainty. It is a model of rational mastery—"mastery at a distance"—in which the space that separates the object world and the rational

33

subject is the space of instrumentality. Galileo's telescope is the operative metaphor for this stance of disengagement. As Charles Taylor puts it: "Descartes calls on the enquiring mind to disengage from the cosmos. . . . The proper stance to self and nature is one of disengagement."[2]

In Chinese art, I shall try to show that the identity of the human subject is represented as an idealization that is determined precisely in terms of its correlation to the topos or *place* in which it dwells. Wimal Dissanayake has observed that "the relation between topoi and a given culture is an intimate one, in that topoi both reflect and intervene in the deeper structures of culture."[3] Following a brief preliminary reassessment of the Western conception of mimesis, I shall offer a rhetorical description of the culturally specific roles of topoi in the figuration of the human subject in Chinese art.

Mimesis and the Dissimulation of Place

An essential tendency of Western art has been the mimetic representation of the visual appearance of the phenomenal world. It is the result of what Timothy Reiss, in his book entitled *The Discourse of Modernism,* has characterized as "an 'analytico-referential' class of discourse [that] becomes the single *dominant* structure and the necessary form taken by thought, by knowledge, by cultural and social practices of all kinds."[4] Ascending to dominance in the art of the Renaissance, it is a discourse of "resemblance" primarily preoccupied and guided by the discrete separateness of appearance. "Appearance," in the Heideggerian perspective of Joseph Fell, "is first and foremost displacement, which dissimulates the placement whereby the appearance originally becomes what it is."[5] The epochs of later Western art history mark the successive stages of a working out of the consequences of the "dis-placement" or nonsituatedness of appearance that occurred at or near its beginnings in the Renaissance.

For example, in a Quattrocento drawing such as Leonardo da Vinci's study for the *Adoration of the Magi,* in the Uffizi in Florence, we are presented a geometrical experience of pictorial space as a perspectival construction through what Michael Baxandall has characterized as "the imposition of a network of calculable angles and notional straight lines."[6] Whether Baxandall is correct or not in suggesting that this may have been interpreted—or better still, rationalized—from a theological point of view as connoting "moral certainty" and "spiritual beatitude," it is, in any case, the result of a rational or analytic factoring of the world into objective and subjective relata.

The iconic power or seeming naturalness of this metaphor is still discernible in the constructionist space of recent abstraction. In much of twentieth-century art, as the end or last consequence of this dissimulation of place, there is the appearance of beings as independent of place, as standing in and by themselves, either in a physical space or virtual space that is ultimately empty and groundless.

The Western conception of mimesis is essentially predicated on the dualistic notion of metaphor as "identity in difference." This binary logic has led to two fundamentally opposing positions concerning the image, be it poetic or pictorial. Classical views of mimesis treat the image as an imitation *(imitatio)* of a preexisting phenomenal world. Advocates of this position tend to embrace a "perceptualist" theory of art. The romanticist, however, construes the image as the pure artifice *(inventio)* of the artist, representing — yet distinctly different from — the sensible world.

The deconstructive turn in recent poststructuralist criticism posits an ontological doubt with respect to the predication of a fundamental disjunction between a mimetic representation and the essential otherness of a transcendent concrete reality that is its referent. Following Michel Foucault, we have come to recognize that art, in fact, produces that which it purports merely to represent. From this perspective, "identity" is understood as an effect of the discursive practice of artistic representation and not an preexisting attribute of the represented subject. This can be demonstrated in terms of: (a) the juridical power of the regulatory norms of artistic practice to extend visibility and thus legitimacy to certain individuals, while being exclusionary of others,[7] and (b) the productive power of the conventions of rhetorical figuration that govern the culturally intelligible representation of a subject's identity in its coherence and continuity.

Topoi and the Principle of Categorical Correlation

I now propose to show that the self-identity of the gendered subjects represented in Chinese art are constituted in terms of the topoi or commonplaces in which they appear. Topoi are represented as the "natural dwelling places" in which human subjects and the object world come to be as they are, in their essential relatedness and situatedness.

This practice can be understood as grounded in the ancient Chinese concept of *ganlei,* "responding according to categorical correlations." *Lei,* or "categorical correlation," is central to the ancient Chinese cosmological principle that "similar natures or kinds *[lei]* mutually influence or respond to each other" *(wei lei xiang dong)*. Joseph Needham considers this the basis of traditional Chinese causation theory. In pre-Han and Han texts, the principle of *ganlei* became the normative basis for the ethical system in which human actions, particularly those of the ruler, are deemed to be linked in a chain of causality to the larger human order as well as the cosmic order. This is predicated on the existence of fundamental correlations between natural patterns *(wen)* and objects and human situations. This can be seen, for example, in the following passage from a chapter in the *Huainanzi,* entitled "Tian wen xun" (Discourse on the cosmic happenings): "The spirit of the ruler of the people is associated with the heaven above. Therefore, when he collects taxes relentlessly and beyond reason, tornados result."[8] *Ganlei,* which Needham has termed "a symbolic correlation system," provides us with an implicit, non-mimetic, normative principle of representation, regulating the correct correlation between specific individuals and the topoi in which they appear to be situated. Accordingly, a pictorial or poetic image *(xiang)* or representation may thus be construed as "stimulating" *(xing)* the drawing forth *(yin)* of a "comparison" *(bi)* between the topos and the identity of the individual based on their categorical correlation *(lei)*. This can be illustrated in the following passage from Zong Bing's *Hua shanshui xu* (A preface to the painting of mountains and rivers):

> Now the sage, with his spirit realizes the Way; thus the worthy can pass through it. Mountains and rivers (likewise), with their forms, relish the Way; thus the virtuous can enjoy it. How similar they are to each other![9]

The concepts of *lei* and *ganlei* figure prominently in Zong Bing's *Hua shanshui xu,* which, as Kiyohiko Munakata has noted, "is not only the earliest extant theory of landscape painting, but the earliest systematic treatise on visual art in the history of China."[10]

The concept of *lei* may be posited as a foundational correlative principle for the elicitation of coherent readings in which the relational identity between topoi and human subjects is established. If, however, as I shall try to demonstrate, this can be shown to conceal or repress the fact that it proceeds with certain sociopolitically motivated legitimating and exclusionary aims, it can be argued that the concept of categorical correlation is invoked as a *naturalized* foundational premise that subsequently legitimates that law's own regulatory hegemony.

The key to this deconstruction lies precisely in the concepts of *bi* ("comparison") and *lei* ("categorical correlation"), which bring into a relation of identity two terms, place and subject, which usually stand in varience to each other. This opens the possibility for a tropological description of topoi as enframing the identity of the human subject within a rhetoric of persuasion. That is to say, topoi may be shown to swerve away from their literal meaning as iconic signs, denoting a setting, toward their figurative meanings, as rhetorical tropes, which connote the specific identities of the represented individuals.

The Rhetoric of Place and the Identity of Gendered Subjects

This study will focus on the pictorial representation of that privileged social group, the scholar-officials, and their female counterparts, particularly the ladies of the court, in terms of four fundamental topoi: the palace, the garden, the hermitage, and a rock and tree by a riverbank. In each instance, the specific topos will be shown to figure the identity of the represented subjects in asymmetrical—or more precisely, dissymmetrical—relations of social status and power, depending upon their gender. The term "dissymmetry" is employed in Mieke Bal's compelling study, *Death and Dissymmetry: The Politics of Coherence in the Book of Judges:* "I call it dissymmetry because, more than an absence of symmetry—asymmetry—the issue is a fundamental struggle to enforce and strengthen dissymmetrical (unequal) power relations."[11] For this reason, I shall term the elicitation of such coherent readings the "politics of coherence" as it is invested with the values of a particular social group and gender.

The corresponding identities of topos and subject, although seemingly stable and permanent, can instead be understood as an event-structure, as, in other words, what is constantly being reinterpreted, reproduced and refigured in the pictorial representations of different historical periods. This occurs in accordance with specific coherence-generating, figurative operations responsible for the formal articulation and ordering of the human subjects and object world into intelligible representations. These strategies of figural coherence come to take on a paradigmatic status as codes of representation during specific periods in history. The decision to adopt a particular figurative mode, though it may be motivated by external conditions, is ultimately made on the basis of the persuasive power and hence the rhetorical efficacy of a given paradigm.[12]

Identity, we must conclude, is a shifting and contextual phenomenon denoting a relative point of convergence among culturally and historically specific sets of determinant relations. The recognition of the event-structure of the topos-subject relation, as something that occurs in the unique circumstances of each interpretive representation and its reading, requires a microhistorial approach to Chinese art, in which the identities of the represented topoi and subjects are accounted for as *provisional unities* that emerge in the contexts of concrete practices.

The Palace

The earliest topos represented in Chinese art is the "palace." Since it was the place where ritual ceremonies, official banquets, and the affairs of state were conducted, the palace figures prominently in Han and pre-Han pictorial art. Among the earliest examples of this topological theme are the late Eastern Zhou engravings on the inside of an oval bronze bowl, in the Shanghai Museum of Art, and the inlaid representations on the bronze *hu* of the Werner Hannings collection, kept in the Palace Museum, Beijing. In each instance, the foundation, columns, and roof of a palace enframe what Mary H. Fong has identified as depictions of a wine-drinking ritual and musical performance in celebration of the ritual of archery:

> the archery contest as a means through which the Zhou king selected his feudal lords and ministers to assist him in governing, was an important state observance. The chapter, "The Ritual of Archery," in the *Liji* (*Book of Rites;* early 1st century B.C.) points out that an archery contest, being an affair of state, should be embellished with *li yue* (ceremonial music).[13]

The male figures in elaborate headgear and long flowing robes are portrayed engaged in the preparation and serving of wine as well as in the playing of such musical instruments as the bronze bell and stone or jade chimes. Fong has noted the close similarity between these early schematic figural representations and the pictographic characters in Shang dynasty bronze inscriptions.

The persistence of the Eastern Zhou themes can be seen in a rubbing from an Eastern Han stone relief, from the funerary stone shrine of Wu Liang, Jiaxiang, Shandong province, c. A.D. 147–51. This representation of a homage scene depicts a ritualistic observance taking place inside a palace. In the main hall, the identities of the individuals are mapped within a hierarchy of social relations, signified by their relative size, deportment, and spatial disposition. It is a didactic narrative that exemplifies the Confucian principle of reciprocal respect between the ruler and his ministers.

The topos of the "inner palace" is actually embedded within two other topoi or "overlapping universes,"[14] each of which elaborates the implications and consequences of maintaining or destabilizing the harmonious hierarchy of relations that characterize the Confucian notion of sociopolitical order represented in the first world. The spiritual realm of the mythical Queen Mother of the West (Xiwangmu) and her ministers, represented *above,* on the second storey, symbolizes the just rewards in the afterlife for those officials who are paragons of Confucian virtue. *Before* the gate of the palace, the legendary Archer Yi is poised atop a carriage with bow and arrow in hand, about to shoot down nine of the ten suns that one day appeared in the sky, here symbolized by black birds in a Wusong tree. This can be interpreted as the attempt to reestablish order after corrupt rulership brought about an instability in the natural world and the loss of the Mandate of Heaven *(tianming).*

In each of the instances discussed above, the palace is represented as the place where male subjects are portrayed engaged in rituals of power. This can be seen, for example, in *Confucian Scholar and Disciples,* a rubbing of a Han dynasty pottery tomb relief, from the vicinity of Chengdu, in the Chongqing Museum, Shandong Province, which represents the education of gentlemen in the Confucian *Classics,* preparatory for official service. According to the teachings of Confucius, there were six arts *(liu yi)* of learning: rites *(li),* music *(yue),* archery *(she),* charioteering *(yu),* writing *(shu),* and mathematics *(shu).* These activities were traditionally denied to the ladies of the court.

Where the topos of the palace, as seat of power, figures the identity of the male subjects engaged in the external *(wai)* matters concerning the affairs of state, it figures that of female subjects in domestic roles with responsibility for such *internal (nei)* household tasks as preparing food, weaving, rearing children, and participating in sacrifices for the husband's ancestors. This can be seen in two Han dynasty rubbings: one of a stone relief entitled *Weavers at their Looms,* from a vaulted brick tomb of the Later Han at Zhengjiabao near Chengdu, and the other, *Kitchen Preparations,* from Tomb Number One at Mixian, Henan Province.

By the eighth century, the theme of women within the palace was taken up by court painters who specialized in *meiren* or beautiful women. Representative of this genre are *Ladies Preparing Newly Woven Silk*, attributed to Song emperor Hui Zong (reigned 1101–26), after a lost painting by the Tang painter Zhang Xuan (active 713–41), in the Museum of Fine Arts, Boston and *Ladies of the Court*, an anonymous Southern Song handscroll after a painting by Zhou Wenju of the tenth century, in the Cleveland Museum of Art.

As these works clearly demonstrate, when women are represented in the palace, they are invariably depicted fulfilling the behavioral prescriptions set down in the *Liji* or *Book of Rites*, one of the *Five Classics (wujing)* of the Confucian canon:

> A girl the age of ten ceased to go out (from the women's apartments). Her governess taught her (the arts of) pleasing speech and manners, to be docile and obedient, to handle the hempen fibers, to deal with the cocoons, to weave silks and form fillets, to learn (all) women's work; how to furnish garments, to watch the sacrifices, to supply the liquors and sauces, to fill the various stands and dishes with pickles and brine and to assist in setting forth the appurtenances for the ceremonies.[15]

From this we may conclude that one of the principal purposes of pictorial representations of ladies in a palace setting is didactic: to illustrate exemplary feminine behavior for emulation by the ladies of the court.

The Garden

Literary Gathering in the Apricot Garden, in the Wango H. C. Weng Collection, Lyme, New Hampshire, was painted in 1437 by the early Ming court painter Xie Huan (active ca. 1368–1436). It commemorates a gathering of eight high officials in the Apricot Garden *(Xing Yuan)* of Yang Rong (1371–1440), in Beijing. In this section, "the 'Tree Yangs' all of whom were members of the Grand Secretariat, are depicted in the weighty poses associated with formal and imperial portraiture."[16] However, their identity as cultivated scholars is connoted by the garden setting. They are surrounded by a carefully selected variety of flora and "fantastic" rockery, the finest specimens of which come from Lake Tai, in the Jiangnan region of Jiangsu Province. Most telling are the "accoutrements of the scholar's studio—brush, ink, ink stone and paper,"[17] which serve by their very contiguity as metonyms for the cultivation and erudition of the represented officials. In rendering their group portrait, the artist thus invokes the traditional theme of "enjoying cultural pursuits in a garden setting."[18]

As Alice Hyland has observed:

> This practice of scholarly gatherings was a time honored one in China and became an important theme in painting and poetry. The "elegent gathering in the western garden," reputed to have brought together sixteen literati in a scenic garden in the Song capital Bianliang in 1087, became the model gathering of literati for centuries afterwards, even though it probably never actually took place.[19]

One of the earliest representations of this theme is the *Literary Gathering*, presently in the Palace Museum, Beijing. An inscription, dated 1107, in the "slender gold" calligraphy of Song Huizong (reigned 1101–26) informs us that it was painted by the Tang master Han Huang (723–87). Zhan Jingfeng, a sixteenth-century scholar, has identified the work as depicting a gathering of prominent literary figures of the mid-eighth century at the Liuli Hall.[20] In this work, a metaphorical relation is drawn between the self-cultivation of the male subjects, represented as actively engaged in scholarly pursuits, and the cultivated nature of the garden setting.

A comparison of Han Huang's *Literary Gathering* with contemporaneous representations of ladies in a garden setting reveals how radically different the topos of the garden figures the identities of male and female subjects. In *Ladies in a Garden*, a recently excavated mural, from the Tomb of Zhanghui (711), near Xian (the ancient Tang capital of Chang'an), *Court Ladies Adorning Their Hair*, a handscroll by the Tang court painter Zhou Fang (active ca. 780–810), in the Liaoning Provincial Museum, and *Ladies Under Trees*, a set of screen paintings from the eighth century, in the Shoso-in, Nara, executed in the figural style of Zhou Fang, the women are portrayed engaged in polite distractions, such as catching cicadas, or simply gazing longingly for the return of their loved ones. The garden serves as a metonym for the sheltered self of the female subjects protected within its walls. Through the principle of juxtaposition, a metaphorical relation is also drawn between the cultivated beauty of the garden setting (e.g., the magnolia blossoms in *Court Ladies Adorning Their Hair*) and the sheltered beauty of the female subjects cloistered within its walls.

All of these pictorial representations dated to the Tang dynasty are rendered in a mode of figural coherence that permitted the artist to apprehend the human subject and the phenomenal world as a succession of discrete entities, each with its own particular attributes and structure. When an event is enframed within the terms of this strategy of coherence, the entities inhabiting the pictorial space are provisionally integrated with one another on the basis of mere proximity, as occupants of a shared contextual field. Visual image is set alongside visual image in a formal coincidence that is additive and serial in fashion. Spatial organization is defined in terms of binary, trinary, and annular or "framing" patterns, constructed in terms of figural motifs that are essentially self-contained and unitary.

The Ming artist Tang Yin (1470–1523) was particularly known for his metaleptic translations of the Tang treatment of this theme. Metalepsis is a strategy of refiguration, prevalent in the sixteenth century, in which the identity of an earlier mode of figural coherence is retained, marking the explicit inscription of an historical or archaistic dimension in pictorial representations that the Chinese identify by the term *gu-yi,* the "sense of antiquity." This can be seen in his *Lady Ban Holding a Fan,* in the National Palace Museum, Taipei. The painting represents Ban Jieyu (active 48–6 B.C.), a concubine to the Han emperor Chengdi (r. 32 B.C. to 7 A.D.). Upon falling out of favor, Lady Ban composed a poem for the emperor that she inscribed on a fan. In this poem, she compared herself to a fan that is stored away in autumn and forgotten along with the summer heat.

Lady Ban was made the subject of the following poem by Xie Tiao of the Tang dynasty:

> At dusk in the hall she lowers the pearl screen.
> Fireflies drift by in flight, then cease.
> In the long night she stitches a gauze shirt.
> Thoughts of her lord: when will this end?
>
> Wisteria grazes the blossoming trees;
> Yellow orioles cross their verdant limbs.
> Thoughts of her lord: a single sigh.
> Bitter tears answering words course down.[21]

Tang Yin has represented Lady Ban holding a fan within the palace garden. The delicate beauty of her white face, as she gazes wistfully at the autumn moon, is compared to the fragile beauty of the white chrysanthemums that grace the foreground of the garden setting and also appear on the painted fan. The chrysanthemum is associated with the autumn season and is thus a poignant reminder that all things must wane. The formal coincidence draws a metaphorical relation of identity with Lady Ban to bring out the sentiment of the theme.

Where the scholar-officials in a garden setting, represented as *active* agents of self-cultivation, are models for emulation by male viewers, the court ladies are displayed as graceful and delicate *meiren* or "beauties"—*passive* "objects of desire" for the male viewer's gaze. The correlation between the binaries of male self-cultivation/female natural beauty and the active *yang*/passive *yin* principles in nature have their origins in the belief in the cosmological correlations underlying the *Classic of Changes (Yijing)*. This can be found in "the *Wenyan*" commentary to the second hexagram *kun*, where one finds the principle of *kun* described as that of *yin* in the complementary pair of forces, *yin* and *yang:*

> Though it has its beauty, it conceals it in order to follow along in service to the king and does not dare fulfill it [alone. *Kun/yin*] is the way of the earth, the way of the wife, the way of the minister.[22]

The Hermitage

The third of our topological themes is the hermitage. One of the earliest representations of this theme is *A Noble Scholar,* in the Palace Museum, Beijing. Attributed to the Five Dynasties artist Wei Xian (active 937–75), the painting represents the Han dynasty retired scholar *(yingshi)* Liang Hong and his wife, Meng Guang. It exemplifies the rhetorical function of the hermitage as a metonym for the reclusive self of the scholar who has sought refuge from the political affairs of state. A repoussé of trees, a river, fantastic rocks, and a fence stand between and distance the viewer from the hermitage and its occupants, effectively creating the sense of a retreat. From this vantage point we observe the "noble scholar," seated before an open scroll, and his wife, kneeling with a raised lacquer tray and serving bowls, in a distinct position of subservience.

Thus, for the female subject, the topos of the hermitage does not function figuratively. When she appears in this setting, she is merely portrayed in a domestic role as a caretaker and attendant. These women are not technically subjects in their own right: they do not figure within the rhetoric of identity in Chinese art. They occupy a position of relative subordinance in order to sustain the identity of the dominant male subject within the Confucian hierarchy of social relations. The "noble scholar" may have retreated from the politics of the state, but he is still engaged in the politics of gender.

It is here that we begin to see these ancient paintings, "not as sources for knowledge that lie outside them, but as the materialization of a social reality that they do not simply and passively reflect, but of which they are a part and to which they respond."[23] The lack of subject-position that characterizes the women with respect to the topos of the hermitage, is an example of the politics of exclusion practiced in the discursive economy of Chinese pictorial art.

An examination of the figural operations responsible for the formal articulation and ordering of *A Noble Scholar* as an intelligible whole will reveal its persuasive power to elicit coherent readings that situate the dissymmetrical relations of its human subjects within the natural order of things.

A Noble Scholar represents the transition from earlier figure painting to true landscape painting. This development occurs following the fall of the Tang dynasty and is marked by the emergence of a new paradigm of figural coherence in which the phenomenal world is represented as a field of integrated entities governed by a clearly specifiable structure or syntax of relationships. Beginning in the tenth and extending through the early twelfth century, the phenomenal world is increasingly conceived through what may be considered a Neo-Confucian *analytical reduction* to processes that govern the integration of the individual entities in metonymical terms of part-part relationships of contiguity.

Each motif is conceived as a discrete unit, precisely articulated so as to correlate with other units within an integrated hierarchy of stable relations. Meaning no longer resides, as it did earlier, in the individual motif but rather in its correlation with other motifs in the realization of a coherent order to which they are all subordinated. The order of the images mirrors the order of things, that is to say, the cosmos. The beholder of the work discovers himself or herself in a position of viewing subject offered by the precisely articulated, explicitly structured closure in the pictorial field. From this position, the signifying operations become intelligible and seemingly natural as we move from the general to the particular.

Wei Xian has envisioned a most stable landscape in which each of the constituent parts, including the human subjects, occupies its proper place within the *just* order of things. This can be attributed to the figurative effect associated with the metonymical relations of contiguity whose persuasive force lies precisely in establishing a seamless linear coherence among the individual motifs.

A Noble Scholar is perfectly in keeping with a contemporary foundational statement about landscape painting, the "Six Essentials of Painting," which appears in an essay by Jing Hao (active ca. 900–950) entitled "Notes on Brushwork" *(Bifaji)*.[24] Jing Hao was a Confucian scholar who, during the social and political turmoil of the Five Dynasties Period, retired to the Taihang mountains of southern Shensi.

In this essay, Jing Hao put forth that which would become *the* prevailing aesthetic norm for the next three centuries: transparency as an explicit ideal for pictorial representation. It prescribes artistic conventions and brush and ink techniques that are self-effacing, concealing all traces of the material process of representation, and by implication, all traces of personal expression, in order to give transparent access to that which is represented.

The "Six Essentials of Painting" exhibits the influence of emerging Neo-Confucian values when it defines the ultimate goal of painting—the achievement of a rational order among the compositional elements, in their mutual relationships—as an expression of the essential reality of nature. As we have seen in Wei Xian's *Noble Scholar,* so we now find in the writings of Jing Hao, the work of art, in the transparency of its discourse, is thus conceived "as a manifestation of cosmos, the harmonious and orderly structure based on Confucian moral virtues. . . ."[25]

A Rock and Tree by a Riverbank

The last of the topological themes is the rock and tree by a riverbank. As a microcosom of the natural world, it functions rhetorically as a synecdoche for the harmonizing self of the scholar who is usually portrayed either standing or seated in contemplation of nature.

Liang Kai's (active early thirteenth century) *Scholar of the Eastern Fence,* in the National Palace Museum, Taipei, is an imaginary portrait of the fourth-century poet-recluse Tao Yuanming. He is represented standing, with a chrysanthemum in his hand, on the bank of a river beside a rock and two types of trees. As Cahill has observed, the combination of pine and red-leaf trees framing the figure juxtaposed the ideals of constancy and integrity, symbolized by the evergreen pine, with the autumnal theme of age and decline. The dual theme is suited to the poignant personage of T'ao Yuan-ming who renounces the corruptions of worldly ambitions.[26]

Holding the chrysanthemum refers us back to a passage in the "Li sao" or "Encountering Sorrow," attributed to Qu Yuan (ca. 343–278 B.C.), the longest poem in the *Songs of Chu:*

> In the mornings I drank the dew that fell from the magnolia;
> At evening ate the petals that dropped from chrysanthemums.

It has been interpreted ever since as a symbol of virtuous conduct for the official who has had to leave the court in times of political corruption.[27]

Ma Yuan (active ca. 1190–1225), like his contemporary Liang Kai, was a painter at the court of the Southern Song. In his *On a Mountain Path in Spring,* in the National Palace Museum, Taipei, a scholar stands beside a rock and willow tree on the bank of what is most certainly West Lake, in the Southern Song capital of Hangzhou. He is accompanied by an attendant who carries the scholars *qin* or lute. The scholar, intent on harmonizing his spirit with nature by playing the *qin,* has stopped momentarily to enjoy the sweet song of two birds. However, his very presence has caused the birds to take flight, thus disturbing the very harmony that he sought.

The image of the willow in painting as well as in poetry is associated with parting and separation. As Hans Frankel noted, its earliest literary association appears in a poem in *The Classic of Songs:* "When we left/The willows were lush;/As we come back/Snow is falling."[28] The willow appears in another painting by Ma Yuan entitled *Bare Willows and Distant Mountains,* in the Museum of Fine Arts, Boston. Here it marks the place and the season where the man in the lower right, now returning in the Fall, originally departed in the Spring. Presenting a willow branch to a departing friend was believed to have the power of delaying his departure—the word *liu* "willow" is homonymous with *liu* "to keep, detain."[29]

As we see especially in *On a Mountain Path in Spring,* the human subjects and the phenomenal world are represented as experienced from a single point of view, in a single moment or extended series of moments of feeling and perception. The viewer is, for the first time, offered a position at the spatio-temporal center around which the painting is held in place. This is accomplished by the introduction of formal devices that function as deictic markers to establish the spatiotemporal perception of the viewing subject. It is by these means that we experience the articulation of the pictorial equivalence of such linguistic oppositional relationships as the first person *I* to a reciprocal object *it;* the demonstratives *this/that;* and the relative adverbs *here/there.* All of these "signs of person" help to represent the "presence" of a viewer, situated "here" in a temporal present, within the foreground of the painting, to dramatize the individual gaze of the viewing subject.

Ma Yuan's painting relies on the principles of parallelism and proximity in the formal contours of the imagery in order to establish a metaphorical relation of equivalence in the symbolic value or meaning of the corresponding iconographical motifs. This can be seen, for example, in the implied equivalence between the overarching branches of the autumnal willow with its song birds in momentary flight—symbolic of separation and the impermanence of the natural and human order—and the distant mountains whose upper peaks, rendered in curving washes of ink, give the impression of appearing to float ever so insubstantially and ephemerally above the softly diffused veils of mist. It is as if, in an intense lyrical moment, all of the forms and substance of the world appear dissolved into a series of vivid perceptual qualities—a totalizing vision of a world in flux, grasped in an instant of time from a single point of view.

In spite of the brevity of form and simplicity of motifs, the painting sets forth a synecdochic vision of the vast world of nature from the limited or partial perspective of the implied viewer in the foreground of the scene. It is a small, self-contained pictorial structure that depends on internal correspondences and formal and semantic parallelisms to an expression of the poignancy of transience, impermanence, and separation as the condition of the phenomenal world.

The "poignancy of things" is a central feature of Southern Song painting and the synecdochic mode of figural coherence was the most efficacious means of expressing this. This sensibility among members of the court in Hangzhou was no doubt in part a response to the historical circumstances in which half the country was no longer under Chinese sovereignty.

The topos of the rock and tree by a stream is conspicuous for the absence of the female subject, whose proper place traditionally is within the walls of her residence or the palace. When a female does appear in nature, she is in the form of a fairy *(nuxian)*. This can be represented by *Nymph of the Lo River,* attributed to the most famous painter of the Six Dynasties, Gu Kaizhi (ca. 344–ca. 406) and *Illustrations to the Nine Songs of Qu Yuan,* a section of a handscroll, attributed to the Song painter Zhang Dunli, in the Museum of Fine Arts, Boston.

A section from the *Illustrations of the Nine Songs of Qu Yuan* depicts the Princess of the Xiang *(Xiang Jun)* and the Lady of the Xiang *(Xiang Furen)* seated beneath trees on the bank of Dungting Lake. Originally these two were the wives of the legendary emperor Shun. Upon his death, they were overcome with sorrow and drowned themselves in the Xiang River, a foreshadowing of Qu Yuan's fate. They ultimately became the spirits of the Xiang river. As Osvald Siren aptly described it:

> In the picture they are shown wandering mournfully along a riverbank. An autumn wind is rustling in the old trees which are bending protectingly over the women. The curving lines of the trees as well as of the long robes of the ladies seem to express the emotional rhythm of longing and mourning which forms the *Leitmotif* of the poem.[30]

Qu Yuan's encounter and pursuit of both the Princess and Lady of the Xiang, on the banks of Dongting Lake, ultimately end in a similar lament: "For time once gone cannot be recovered / And I wish we could sport but a little longer."[31]

Chinese commentators have traditionally interpreted the use of women in Qu Yuan's elegy as metaphorical images for the ruler he so desperately longs to serve. The modern commentator You Guoen argues that they are used as images of Qu himself.[32] In either case, as will also become apparent in Gu Kaizhi's *Nymph of the Lo River,* the fairies are not true female subjects in their own right but ultimately metaphorical projections of the political power that male subjects desire but sorely lack.

The *Nymph of the Lo River* is a narrative handscroll that illustrates the "Loshen Fu," a prose poem written in 222 by Cao Zhi (192–232). Once again, it tells of the author/narrator's encounter and enchantment with the bewitching beauty of the river goddess. He is moved to a declaration of his love which ultimately must go unfulfilled, since, "between men and gods no converse can endure."

As Thomas Lawton has suggested, the prose poem can be read as an allegory of Cao Zhi's tragic love for the daughter of Zhen Yi, a magistrate in Honan province. Lady Zhen eventually became the wife of Cao Zhi's rival, his older brother Cao Bei, and was made empress when he became Wendi

of the Wei dynasty, in 220. On a visit to the capital, Loyang, in 222, Cao
Zhi was made the recipient of her jewelry and informed of her execution one
year earlier, after having fallen out of favor with the emperor. In his preface
to the "Loshen Fu" (originally titled "Ganhen Fu"), Cao Zhi informs us that
he composed the prose poem as he crossed the Lo River on his return from
the capital Loyang in 222.[33]

The enframing of the females as river goddesses within a natural setting
serves to establish their identity as that of the enchanting beauty of nature
itself. Once again we have the binary "male-culture/female-nature," in which
the male by a rock and tree is represented as actively seeking to harmonize
his nature with that of the natural world, and the female, in contrast, is always
represented as already possessing nature's beauty.

As we have seen in the representations of "ladies in a garden," women's
identity (and power) can simply be derived from their sexuality and the males
upon whom they depend. In the *Nymph of the Lo River,* the identity of the
male depends entirely upon his control over the female as sexual being. Here,
we become aware of a reality that is also represented in the work: the repressed
reality of male sibling rivalry in which the desire for control, lacking in the
author-narrator, is projected onto the unobtainable object of his desire: the
river goddess.

The last example that we shall consider is *A Tall Pine and Daoist Immortal,*
in the National Palace Museum, Taipei. It was painted by the late Ming master
Chen Hongxiu (1598–1652) in 1635, just nine years before the fall of the
dynasty to the Manchus. According to the artist's inscription, it is actually a
portrait of himself, referred to as Master Lotus, and his nephew, Bohan.

A Tall Pine and Daoist Immortal constitutes a moment of moral agency in
which the artist attempts to fashion for himself a romantic image of self-identity against the very norms and conventions of traditional representational
practice. He stages this resistance through a rhetorical strategy of ironic skepticism. As we have already noted, the representation of a scholar by a rock and
tree was a synecdochical expression of the harmonizing self in communion
with nature. Chen Hongxiu effectively undermines this traditional theme by
introducing a series of fundamental displacements that ultimately serve to
establish himself as the alienated locus of subjectivity of his pictorial world.

The radical subjectivization of self-identity is achieved, first of all, through
an emphatic discontinuity in the manner in which the scholar and his surroundings are visually represented. Chen Hongxiu refigures the traditional
theme through a highly mannered exaggeration of the Six Dynasties landscape

style associated with Gu Kaizhi's *Nymph of the Lo River*. This entails rhetorical operations that can be best modeled in terms of catachresis.

Catachesis, like metalepsis, is a strategy of refiguration that may be thought of as a metaphor at the secondary level of figuration. They both generate figural effects via the operations of troping upon previous modes of rhetorical figuration. However, whereas metalepsis, as we have seen in Tang Yin's *Lady Ban Holding a Fan,* is founded on sameness, catachresis is a trope of difference.[34]

Catachresis involves the transference of a previous mode of figural coherence "beyond its proper-use context." Its employment in the new domain tends to be excessive, "producing significations outside its usual connotative horizon."[35] Catachresis thus generates figural effects that dis-figure the primary figural base, that which is troped upon, essentially problematizing or undermining its original representational function in the process of refiguration.

In *A Tall Pine and Daoist Immortal,* great liberty is taken with the rather awkward spatial conception and naïve treatment of the landscape motifs characteristic of the earlier work. By fracturing the horizon line and placing the landscape elements to the right of center higher than those to the left, Chen Hongxiu constructs a most unstable pictorial world. Even his nephew is moved to gaze up incredulously at the bizarre central tree. The one seemingly stable, still point in this unsettling landscape is the artist, who gazes out at the viewer from within his solidly defined form. This brings us to the second displacement.

In contrast to earlier paintings in which the figural subjects are represented as objectifications of a detached spectator, Chen Hongxiu portrays himself as a center of subjectivity. As the represented human subject now gazes out in the direction of the viewer, this makes of the self of the viewer a specular object in relationship to this otherness. In Sartrean terms, the irruption of this subjective specular alterity or otherness on the viewer's horizon threatens to decenter the viewer from the traditionally established position of detached spectator.[36] The objectification of the viewer by the other's gaze serves actually to heighten his or her sense of being a subject, in other words, of being subjected to a pictorial practice that now implicates the viewer in the representation. This brings us to the third and final displacement: that of the artist with respect to the traditional modes of pictorial representation.

Chen Hongxiu's appropriation of the landscape style associated with Gu Kaizhi is markedly different from the references to the past in earlier paintings. Consciously aware of the historicity of the ancient styles and themes, previous artists unquestioningly invoked their authority as a means of legitimating their own stylistic interpretations with the "sense of antiquity." Chen Hongxiu's extreme, though coherent, deformation of the landscape style of the Six Dynasties Period effectively undermines its validity as a means of rendering a plausible image of the world, especially in view of the fact that it stands in sharp contrast to his descriptively realistic self-portrait. However, by bringing these two radically opposing modes of representation into juxtaposition, with neither one holding sway over the entire work, Chen has, in effect, disclosed the shaping power and limitations of each to articulate an intelligible representation of self-identity in its relationship to the phenomenal world. From the late Ming on, Chinese scholars increasingly express in their painting and literature an uncertainty concerning their identity that often results in a conscious self-stylization.[37] The conventions of pictorial and literary practice are no longer simply taken as natural and transparent means of self representation. How may we account for this crisis of representation?

The intellectual milieu of the late sixteenth century was colored by the radical individualistic philosophy of Li Zhi (1527–1602) and the antirevivalist Yuan brothers of the Gungan School of poetry. In general, there was a transformation in literati thinking, a questioning of the manners of life and scholarly orientation of the early Ming. This led to a movement away from introspection and preoccupation with self-cultivation in literature, scholarship, and art. In the Qing dynasty (1644–1912), there was the linguistic skepticism of the Evidential Movement, in which exegetical studies increasingly focused on textual criticism, revealing the spurious portions of long-venerated texts.[38] All of these extra-artistic circumstances suggest a historical context conducive to the Chen Hongxiu's ironic skepticism concerning the traditional styles at this time.

The traditional treatment of the theme of the scholar beside a rock and tree portrayed him gazing in contemplation of and harmonizing his spirit with the mist-filled landscape, his natural dwelling place. In Chen Hongxiu's interpretation there is a fundamental displacement of the human subject from his natural setting, as he gazes out, this time, apprehensively in the direction of the beholder of the work. James Cahill has interpreted this as an expression of:

> Ch'en's ambivalent feelings about his status as a professional artist, his bitter sense
> of the degeneration of an artistic mode that had once been used for fresh images

of a comprehensible world, his awareness that the past could no longer function as a repository of truth on which he and his contemporaries could draw in the old way.[39]

It may, as well, have been caused by an experience of radical otherness in the form of an alien means of pictorial representation, the introduction of European art.

Here I wish only to cite *Portrait of a Scholar,* in the University Art Museum, Berkeley, painted in 1639, just four years after Chen Hongxiu's *Tall Pine and Daoist Immortal,* by the most prominent portraitist of the late Ming, Zeng Qing (1568-1650). In the subtle layers of colored wash, used to define the planes of the scholar's face, we witness a style and pictorial concern distinctively influenced by the European art available in Nanking, where Matteo Ricci had an important mission.

Expressions of alienated self-identity often occur during periods of foreign domination. This can be seen, for example, in the landscape paintings of Ni Zan (1301-74) and Wang Meng (1308-85) of the Mongol Yuan dynasty (1260-1368), and the Nanking master Gong Xian (ca. 1617-89) of the Manchu Qing dynasty. In each instance, the scholar-painter confronted a situation of political disempowerment that precipitated a crisis of social and cultural identity. Mobilizing conditions for change already present within the signifying system, he was able to effect a "discursive displacement" through a catachretic transgression of an earlier style.[40] The artist was thus able to introduce certain coherent deformations that tranformed what was originally a representation of the landscape as a natural dwelling place into an expression of displaced alienated self-identity. For Ni Zan, it was the Dong-Zhu tradition of the Five Dynasties Period; for Wang Meng and Gong Xian, it was the monumental landscapes of the Northern Song.

Gong Xian's *Thousand Peaks and Myriad Ravines,* in the C. A. Drenowatz Collection, in the Rietburg Museum, Zurich, is surely one of the most "surreal" landscapes in the history of Chinese art. As James Cahill convincingly demonstrated, it represents a refiguration of the idiom of Northern Song landscape paintings, transposed in terms of Western conventions derived from Anton Wierix's *View of Thessaly and the Vale of Tempe,* an engraving from Abraham Ortelius, *Teatrum Orbis Terrarum* (1579). In Gong Xian's view,

> Paintings by other artists are all of places where people have gone. They cannot
> paint places where no one has ever gone. This painting of mine greatly resem-

bles a place where no one has ever gone—or at least, where people do not ordinarily go.[41]

Conclusion

In conclusion, the representation of human subjects in dissymmetrical relations of power and status, based on topoi and gender differences, must be understood as serving social and ideological purposes as well as being traditionally justifiable on the basis of fundamental principles of cosmological correlations. "Ideology in action," Gayatri Chakravorty Spivak has observed, "is what a group takes to be natural and self-evident, that of which the group, as a group, must deny any historical sedimentation. . . . In turn, the subject(s) of ideology"—here I have in mind both the artist-as-authorial-subject and the represented subject in pictorial art—"are the conditions and effects of the self-identity of the group."[42]

My own efforts have been directed toward an analysis of the strategies of rhetorical persuasion and figural coherence in the discursive construction of self-identity in Chinese art. They also represent a modest step toward the formulation of strategies of "countercoherence," in order to counter the politics of coherence in the pictorial figuration of gender-bound dissymmetry. We can now understand this representational practice as the materialization of a social reality governed by the coherence of dissymmetry in the politics of male/female relations as defined within the canon of Confucian *Classics* and the *Lieh-nu* tradition of literature on virtuous and virtueless women.[43] It is an effort to resist identification with those very positions articulated by the ideological correspondences of the work of art, positions that subject the beholder to its perspectives on gender inequality and repression.

As Richard Guisso has observed:

> The classics have little to say of women as persons, but deal almost entirely in idealized life-cycle roles of daughter, wife and mother. They have in common an insistence . . . that there is a natural and immutable difference between male and female . . . since this difference is part of the cosmic order, it must be maintained to preserve and continue that order. In other words, women's place in the classical canon was not determined by the fiat of any supernatural force or deity, but rather by the Confucian certainty that order and harmony were supreme values and that only in hierarchy were they preserved.[44]

It is the politics of this coherence of dissymmetry that has to be countered (e.g., the tendency to argue in terms of "a natural and immutable difference," in terms that reduce the multiplicity of female subjects to the binary of male/female and essentializes and universalizes women's identity in terms of male-dependent "life-cycle roles": the obedient daughter, the faithful wife, and the sacrificing mother). The topological figuration of women's identities solely in terms of familial roles ultimately served the didactic purpose of affirming and maintaining their subordinate "place" in the sexual hierarchy of Confucian society, so as to preserve the order and harmony that privileged the male gender. To the extant that pictorial representation replicates this politics of coherence, it can be discussed as both "a meaningful act of cultural expression as well as an instrument of political and social oppression."[45]

Lastly, as our brief discussion of those painters associated with the tradition of political resistance has shown, there are moments in the history of art when certain individuals have succeeded in opening up a discursive space within which to exert moral agency in the face of political domination and social oppression. That is to say, they were able to "act otherwise," within and against the traditional constraints of artistic practice, in order "to intervene in the world . . . with the effect of influencing a specific process or state of affairs."[46] Here we need not account for this by positing a notion of the artist as authorial subject, that is, as sovereign cause of this agency of resistance. In place of this positivist essentialism, we may speak of a subject-effect:

> that which seems to operate as a subject may be part of an immense discontinuous network ("text" in the general sense) of strands that may be termed politics, ideology, economics, history, sexuality, language, and so on. (Each of these strands, if they are isolated, can also be seen as woven of many strands.) Different knottings and configurations of these strands, determined by heterogeneous determinations which are themselves dependent upon myriad circumstances, produce the effect of an operating subject.[47]

Accordingly, each instance of moral agency would be understood as a resistance-effect of the subject-effect, itself produced by the "particular conjunctions called forth" by the given crisis. The implications of this approach for the ways we continue to practice art historiography are truly enormous.

Notes

1. Timothy J. Reiss, *The Discourse of Modernism* (Ithaca: Cornell University Press, 1982), 33.

2. Charles Taylor, "The Moral Topography of the Self," in Messer, Sass, and Woodfolk, eds., *Hermeneutics and Psychology Theory* (New Brunswick, N.J.: Rutgers University Press, 1988), 307.

3. Wimal Dissanayake and Steven Bradbury, eds., *Literary History, Narrative, and Culture*. Selected Conference Papers, vol. 2 (Honolulu: College of Languages, Linguistics and Literature, University of Hawaii and the East-West Center, 1989), 49.

4. Reiss, *Discourse of Modernism*, 23.

5. Joseph P. Fell, *Heidegger and Sartre: An Essay on Being and Place* (New York: Columbia University Press, 1979), 204.

6. Michael Baxandall, *Painting and Experience in Fifteenth Century Italy: A Primer in the Social History of Pictorial Style* (Oxford: Oxford University Press, 1972), 107-8.

7. Judith Butler, *Gender Trouble: Feminism and the Subversion of Identity* (New York: Routledge, 1990).

8. Kiyohiko Munakata, "Concepts of *Lei* and *Kan-lei* in Early Chinese Art Theory," in Bush and Murck, eds., *Theories of the Arts in China* (Princeton: Princeton University Press, 1983), 108.

9. Ibid., 118.

10. Ibid., 116.

11. Mieke Bal, *Death and Dissymmetry: The Politics of Coherence in the Book of Judges* (Chicago: The University of Chicago Press, 1988), 18.

12. Gianni Vattimo, *The End of Modernity: Nihilism and Hermeneutics in Postmodern Culture,* trans. Jon R. Snyder (Cambridge: Polity Press, 1988), 92.

13. Mary H. Fong, "The Origin of Chinese Pictorial Representation of the Human Figure," *Artibus Asiae* 48 (1989): 11.

14. Shirley Ardener, "Ground Rules and Social Maps for Women: An Introduction," in Ardener, ed., *Women and Space: Ground Rules and Social Maps* (New York: St. Martin's Press, 1981), 13.

15. Richard W. Guisso, "Thunder Over the Lake: The Five Classics and the Perception of Women in Early China," in Guisso and Johannesen, eds., *Women in China: Current Directions in Historical Scholarship* (Youngstown, N.Y.: Philo Press, 1981), 58.

16. James Cahill, *The Compelling Image: Nature and Style in Seventeenth-Century Chinese Painting* (Cambridge: Harvard University Press, 1982), 15.

17. Alice R. M. Ilyland, *Deities, Emperors, Ladies and Literati: Figure Painting of the Ming and Qing Dynasties* (Birmingham, U.K.: Birmingham Museum of Art, 1987), 18.

18. Cahill, *Compelling Image*, 115.

19. Hyland, *Deities, Emperors, Ladies and Literati*, 19.

20. Thomas Lawton, *Freer Gallery of Art Fiftieth Anniversary Exhibition II. Chinese Figure Painting* (Washington, D.C.: Smithsonian Institution, 1973), 82.

21. Pauline Yu, *The Reading of Imagery in the Chinese Poetic Tradition* (Princeton: Princeton University Press, 1987), 191.

22. Ibid., 92.

23. Bal, *Death and Dissymmetry*, 6.

24. Kiyohiko Munakata, "Ching Hao's 'Pi-fa-chi': A Note on the Art of Brush." *Artibus Asiae* 31 (1974), supplementum.

25. Ibid., 8.

26. Cahill, *Compelling Image,* 112.

27. Yu, *Reading of Imagery,* 91.

28. Hans H. Frankel, *The Flowering Plum and the Palace Lady: Interpretations of Chinese Poetry* (New Haven: Yale University Press, 1976), 95.

29. Ibid., 96.

30. Osvald Siren, *Chinese Painting: Leading Masters and Principles,* vol. 2 (New York: Roland Press, 1956–58), 52.

31. David Hawkes, trans., *Ch'u Tz'u: The Songs of the South* (Boston: Beacon Press, 1959), 38.

32. Yu, *Readings of Imagery,* 99.

33. Lawton, *Chinese Figure Painting,* 18–29.

34. Peter de Bolla, *Harold Bloom: Towards Historical Rhetorics* (London and New York: Routledge, 1988), 134.

35. Ibid., 133.

36. Norman Bryson, "The Gaze in the Expanded Field," in Foster, ed., *Vision and Visuality* (Seattle: Bay Press, 1988).

37. For a discussion of this topic in eighteenth-century China, see Martin Huang, "Stylization and Invention: The Burden of Self-Expression in *The Scholars*," in this volume.

38. Benjamin B. Elman, *From Philosophy to Philology: Intellectual and Social Aspects of Change in Late Imperial Chinese* (Cambridge, Mass.: Council of East Asian Studies, Harvard University, 1984).

39. Cahill, *Compelling Image,* 143.

40. For a discussion of the crisis of foreign domination and "discursive displacement" in colonial India, see Gayatri Chakravorty Spivak, "Subaltern Studies: Deconstructing Historiography," in *In Other Worlds: Essays in Cultural Politics* (New York: Methuen, 1988).

41. Ibid., 181.

42. Gayatri Chakravorty Spivak, "The Politics of Interpretation," in *In Other Worlds: Essays in Cultural Politics,* 118.

43. Marina H. Sung, "The Chinese Lieh-nu Tradition," in Guisso and Johannesen, *Women in China.*

44. Guisso, "Thunder Over the Lake," 48.

45. Bal, *Death and Dissymmetry,* 18.

46. Anthony Giddens, *The Constitution of Society: Outline of the Theory of Structuration* (Berkeley and Los Angeles: University of California Press, 1986), 14.

47. Spivak, "Subaltern Studies," 204.

References

Ardener, Shirley, ed. *Women and Space: Ground Rules and Social Maps.* New York: St. Martin's Press, 1981.

Bal, Mieke. *Death and Dissymmetry: The Politics of Coherence in the Book of Judges.* Chicago: University of Chicago Press, 1988.

Baxandall, Michael. *Painting and Experience in Fifteenth-Century Italy: A Primer in the Social History of Pictorial Style.* Oxford: Oxford University Press, 1972.

Bryson, Norman. "The Gaze in the Expanded Field." In *Vision and Visuality,* edited by Hal Foster. Seattle: Bay Press, 1988.

Butler, Judith. *Gender Trouble: Feminism and the Subversion of Identity.* New York and London: Routledge, 1990.

Cahill, James. *The Compelling Image: Nature and Style in Seventeenth-Century Chinese Painting.* Cambridge: Harvard University Press, 1982.

De Bolla, Peter. *Harold Bloom: Towards Historical Rhetorics.* London and New York: Routledge, 1988.

Dissanayake, Wimal, and Bradbury Steven, eds. *Literary History, Narrative, and Culture.* Selected Conference Papers. Volume 2. Honolulu: College of Languages, Linguistics and Literature, University of Hawaii and the East-West Center, 1989.

Elman, Benjamin B. *From Philosophy to Philology: Intellectual and Social Aspects of Change in Late Imperial China.* Cambridge, Mass.: Council of East Asian Studies, Harvard University, 1984.

Fell, Joseph P. *Heidegger and Sartre: An Essay on Being and Place.* New York: Columbia University Press, 1979.

Fong, Mary H. "The Origin of Chinese Pictorial Representation of the Human Figure." *Artibus Asiae* 48 (1989): 5-38.

Frankel, Hans H. *The Flowering Plum and the Palace Lady: Interpretations of Chinese Poetry.* New Haven: Yale University Press, 1976.

Guisso, Richard W. "Thunder Over the Lake: The Five Classics and the Perception of Woman in Early China." In Richard Guisso and Stanley Johannesen, eds. *Women in China: Current Directions in Historical Scholarship.* Youngstown, N.Y.: Philo Press, 1981.

Hall, David L., and Roger T. Ames, *Thinking Through Confucius*. Albany: State University of New York Press, 1987.

White, Hayden. *Tropics of Discourse*. Baltimore: Johns Hopkins University Press, 1978.

Yu, Pauline. *The Reading of Imagery in the Chinese Poetic Tradition*. Princeton: Princeton University Press, 1987.

3

Construction and Insertion of the Self
in Song and Yuan Painting

John Hay

This essay considers the problem of "self and symbolic expression" in the context of visual art, principally painting. This context raises certain problems in relation to the term "symbolism." Although discussions of symbolism have often turned to the visual arts, their conceptual basis has almost always been derived from other areas, especially that of the written and spoken word. There is so much overlap between different media of human communication and expression that such conceptual cross-dressing is often acceptable. The various media have their own constraints and possibilities, however, and for my present purposes I am going to take the term "symbolism" very loosely. Whether or not the functions I shall try to represent should be called "symbolic" may well be a valid question, but it is not one that I shall discuss. Instead, I shall be talking about some of those constraints and possibilities that are especially at issue in considering Chinese painting of the Song and Yuan periods as offering some kind of vehicle for "the self."

There are at least two main aspects to this problem. The first is that of the culture's own explicit conceptualization. The second, my main interest, is that of how visual images, studied in a cultural context, may be seen to work. Both of these aspects, of course, must be approached with some awareness of broader horizons, and during the last two decades a considerable amount of scholarship has been devoted to studying the evolution of self and individuality in Western and non-Western cultures.[1] Most agree that our own notion of the individualistic self is a recent construction, though with ancient and deep foundations, and that the stories of other cultures may be quite different. There has been some degree of agreement on what the corresponding development was in, for example, China. Chinese notions of self are seen as holistic rather than individualistic; they are constructed through part/whole and social relationships rather than through the uniqueness of inner choice and the analogies of divine agency. Among the problems revealed, however, has been the effort necessary to deal with the very powerful sense of individuality that the Chinese tradition clearly exhibits. This same ambiguity is equally noticeable in generalizations about the Chinese people today. They are a cultural mass as yet to be democratically individualized, but there are also hopelessly self-interested individuals. They tend to confound even well-meaning attempts to adapt Western categories. I am not going to talk about this as an issue, but it stands in a conscious awareness as a provocation behind some of what I want to say.

Chinese painting is often seen, in a general way, as dominated by conventions and traditions that were persistently imposed upon some inherent dynamic of development, and eventually they brought the development itself to a halt. For example, in the tenth century, Dong Yuan was a minor official and an admired painter at the Southern Tang court under Li Yu. By the end of the eleventh century, he had been singled out by the exemplary connoisseur Mi Fu as a paragon of literatus virtue in the arts. In the fourteenth century, Huang Gongwang, who devoted much of his life's energy to painting, drew on Dong Yuan as an inevitable source, both for the visualization of his landscape painting and for the technique of its execution. In the late Ming, Dong Qichang saw these two painters above all others as embodying a paradigmatic dialectic of structure and technique, a view that became enshrined among the painters commonly referred to as the "orthodox school." The validity of Dong's formulation, however, was accepted much more widely than among such painters, and is still discernible today.[2] The present is eventually buried under the past.

If one looks at Huang Gongwang's most famous work, "Dwelling in the Fuchun Mountains" (figure 4), there is no difficulty in identifying features such as the rounded, earthen slopes and the long-drawn texture strokes, the "ravelled hemp-fibre" *cunfa* 皴法, and the formulae of motif and brushwork that identify the tradition of Dong Yuan. Such, undoubtedly, would always have been a primary referent for any Chinese connoisseur examining this painting. But the presence of Huang Gongwang himself is no less visible, both in the powerful construction and choreography of the masses and the vigorous activity and rich texture of the brushwork. Any Chinese connoisseur would also have considered this level of identification an elementary stage of engagement with the work. Such relationships can be followed through an enormous number of paintings dating from the tenth century to the present. Much of conventional art history pursues this specifically relevant and indeed essential quest. I use this case only as an illustration. The givens of Chinese art history force one to accept this feature as a primary and deeply significant one.

Both the motifs and the brush strokes of the Dong Yuan/Huang Gong-wang tradition are, obviously enough, categories. There are many analogous sets associated with other painters. There are also a number of other kinds of category, such as subject matter; that of landscape instituted as dominant in the age of Dong Yuan, for example; and that of bamboo, which started to become closely associated with the literati through the painting of Wen Tong, a generation older than Mi Fu. Many categories developed within landscape and several within bamboo. There were other categories, such as those of region and social class. Most of these categories intersected and reinforced each other. Sometimes they were contradictory—but not nearly as often as one might expect. There must have been a Divine Guardian of the Category, carefully guiding the manifold partialities and ambivalencies of the artistic elite who used and produced them.

Attitudes towards this categorical phenomenon tend to differentiate historians of Chinese painting. In traditional Chinese studies, the categories are often foregrounded without question. In traditional Western studies, they may be foregrounded as an esoteric language that will qualify its user for entry into at least the outer sanctum of the mysteries. But, in this latter context, the phenomenon is often seen also as impeding a loftier evaluation of Chinese painting in terms of creative originality. In contemporary studies the categories tend to be slighted as a barrier to more analytic knowledge. In this latter case, however, attention is not usually turned alternatively to the individual painters but redispersed through social history.

Nevertheless, one's understanding of Chinese painting history will be severely disadvantaged unless one has managed to incorporate some grasp of *why:* why categories were so prominent and persistent. I point to this problem here as a necessary preliminary to later discussion. Categorical obsessions are, of course, common in many aspects of traditional China. This circumstance is obviously related, at one level, to the phenomenon of correlative thinking that is so prominent in Chinese cosmology. There seem to be basic cultural orientations involved in this. Manfred Porkert, in a highly systematic analysis of Chinese medicine, begins by stating:

> Chinese medicine, like the other Chinese sciences, defines data on the basis of the inductive and synthetic mode of cognition. Inductivity corresponds to a logical link between two effective positions existing at the same time in different places in space. (Conversely, causality is the logical link between two effective positions given at different times at the same place in space.)[3]

Inductive correlations both require and establish a systematic structure of categories. One of the commonest Chinese terms for the category of category is *lei* 類, and it is common in many fields.[4] *Yang* and *yin* are probably the two most obvious *lei*. Such categories are necessarily holistic. The significance of any single phenomenon within one of the sub-categorizations of *yin,* for example, unfolds only through the structure as a whole. Polar extremes of either *yang* or *yin* are necessarily transient. Most phenomena represent proportional categories, such as minor *yin* in *yang*. The manifold categories of Chinese painting history must be understood holistically, within such a semiotic structure.

Enormously and widely important although such correlative categories are, however, they are not uniformly dominant. A. C. Graham has commented on a misleading impression that has resulted from Granet's pioneering work in this area.

> Granet took it for granted that the mode of cosmological thinking in China was the mode of all thinking, in philosophy of the classical age as much as in alchemy and geomancy. How could Confucius and Mencius, Mo-tzu, and Chuang-tzu fail to exemplify what is by definition *la pensée chinoise?* . . . [but] throughout the classical period correlative schematising belongs only to astronomers, diviners, musicmasters, physicians; the philosophers from Confucius to Han Fei do not engage in it at all. We find different levels of thinking in philosophy and in the proto-sciences very much as in Europe.[5] . . . Any serious inquirer into Chinese thought is on watch for differences between what we are accustomed to call the "conceptual schemes" of China and the West. . . . But to treat Yin-yang thinking as specifically *la pensée chinoise* is in effect to contrast the correlative stratum of thinking which is more fully exposed in China with the analytic upper layer which is thicker and denser in the West, confusing different levels.[6]

This is an exemplary warning both explicitly and implicitly. A searching observation of natural phenomena is one of the primary sources of correlative thinking and not all fields of thinking share this concern. Painting extends both within and without it and is correspondingly complex.

But the obsession with categories also extends beyond the explicitly correlative system, into the powerful and equally persistent models drawn from social hierarchy. The one to which I particularly wish to point is that of qualitative ranking, the *pin* 品 of so many cultural institutions. In literature, a classic exemplar is the *Shipin* 詩品, "Grading of Poets," compiled by Zhong Hong by A.D. 517. Zhong classified more than 120 poets into "upper," "middle," and "lower" *pin*. This practice had long precedents in many areas, traceable back at least to the *History of the Han Dynasty* compiled by Ban Gu (A.D. 32–92). The categorization of people was made primarily for pragmatic and subsequently for aesthetic ends. Politics was rarely far away.[7] Calligraphy and painting followed closely. The issue of such classification in painting remained important through the eleventh century.[8] Huang Xiufu, an eleventh-century commentator on this tradition, approved of four categories. The lowest was *neng,* 能, competent, but of no mean achievement.[9] The work of such painters "vied with the achievements of heaven," and "their formal resemblances have lifelike movement." The middle was *miao* 妙, "excellent": "Painting is done by men, and each man has his own nature"; the quality of such artists is "transferred from the mind to the hand, indirectly exhausting its hidden secrets." An analogy for this category is given as Zhuang Zhou's expert butcher. The upper class is *shen* 神, "inspired" or "divine," in which "the divine force whirls aloft, thought is joined to spirit. [The painter] creates concepts and establishes substance, and their subtleties combine with transformative powers." I will delay reference to the fourth category for a moment. The lowest quality favored with acknowledgment is of the painting itself, as object. The work presents images that are like those produced by natural processes. The upper level, *shen,* is also primarily identified within the work of art. But in this case the work itself does not just imitate the images produced by natural processes; the production itself participates in those very processes. To translate into broader terms: competent works are completed, and therefore fixed and transient actualizations. "Divine" works continue to draw their power from a state of potentiality.

The middle class, *miao,* is the only level into which the individual artist clearly enters. The mode of entry is well established. Zhong Hong's contemporary Liu Xie compared writing to playing chess.[10] This, among much other evidence, demonstrates a performative view of the arts of the gentlemen. This view can be seen already by the end of the Han. In fact, it is highly suggestive in this regard that Fingarette, in his study of Confucius and ritual, emphasizes the performative aspect of Chinese language usage.[11] Ritual, as a subtle phenomenon complexly entwined in Chinese thought and practice, depends upon various forms of performance. In any performance, the way it is performed is crucial to success. The performer, therefore, is inherently part of the product. This does not imply any individuality on the part of the performer; often it is the opposite. But even the apparent absence of any individuality becomes itself a distinctive quality of the performer. Such a performer excels in actualizing the most generic potential. When a ritual is social, the most valued qualities are collective. Rituals and arts derived from them, however, can be socially redrawn, internalized, and even personalized. The collectivity of the performance values embodied can become increasingly restricted, even while the emphasis on performance remains itself undiminished. This does indeed happen in Chinese culture, with crucial shifts occurring during the Song. However, in the eleventh-century text by Huang Xiufu, from which we turned to this topic, the status of the painter is clearly tied to the cosmological status of man. Heaven-earth, *tiandi* 天地, is a cosmological authority in the *yangyin* polarity structure. Heaven equates with potentiality and earth with actuality. Humanity operates between them. In one of many early formulations, Xunzi (ca. 240 B.C.), states this as: "Heaven has time, earth has material. Man has governance; hence it is said that he has the ability to ternate [participate in the two of them].[12] Huang Xiufu's three categories therefore ascend from earth, through man, to heaven. Many different interpretations of this circumstance are possible, of course. Huang Xiufu's formulation allows a major degree of autonomy to the creating-and-transforming processes (*zaohua* 造化) of the universe. But man was increasingly ready to muscle in on this activity. What still needs to be emphasized is that Huang's "marvelous" artist is simply fulfilling his role as a human being, an activity equivalent to the function of *ren* 仁 "humaneness," and not expressing his individuality; and that this *ren*-equivalent has not yet achieved its Neo-Confucian apotheosis.

At this point we must acknowledge Huang Xiufu's fourth category, a category of no-category. This is the *yipin* 逸品 , usually translated as "untrammeled class." Huang writes, "The untrammeled class of painting is the most difficult to group. It is clumsy in the regulated drawing of squares and circles, and disdains minute thoroughness in coloring. Its brushwork is abbreviated yet its forms are complete, being attained through spontaneity *(ziran)*. None can imitate it for it springs from the expression of concepts."[13] The earliest surviving application of *yipin* to painters is in the ninth-century "Record of Famous Painters/Paintings in the Tang Dynasty," by Zhu Jingxuan. Zhu set three men apart in this category, as rejecting orthodox methods. Huang restricted it to only one painter, but placed the class above the "divine." Argument continued over its status, but among critics, necessarily the literati, *yipin* became formulated not only as the highest but even the only category worth mentioning. After this point, of course, it becomes unnecessary to mention category at all. This was part of the social privileging and internalization of the function of performative ritual, taking firm shape during the Song and achieving canonical dominance in the Yuan. The Yuan, of course, is generally seen as the period in which completely personal styles of painting were established. A term often used by later critics to refer to painting of the Yuan period is *sidajia* 四大家, "the four great masters."

But there is another side of the issue. *Yipin* in itself must not be identified with individualism, even though this has been the natural temptation. It has to do, instead, with the dissolution—often ecstatic—of self that has so frequently been the counterpoint to the socialized distribution of self in China.[14] The central meaning of *yi* in "escape" is essentially sociological, as its application to eremietism exemplifies.[15] The ambiguity characteristic of the arguments—where, for instance, the beyond-category *yipin* should be located in relation to the within-category categories—is inherent in the argument itself, an argument that actually belongs to a discourse of categories. This core discourse is usually hidden within an applied discussion, such as that concerning what *kind* of category is in question. Huang Tingjian (1045–1105), for example, described Zhou Dunyi as having achieved a state of mind that was "free, pure, and unobstructed [*saluo* 洒落] like a breeze on a sunny day or the clear moon." As de Bary comments on this description, Zhu Xi adopted it as a quality of sageness, when "It was a freedom of spirit attained by liberating oneself from all selfishness, obstinacy, and rigidity. In this state one's mind was completely impartial and open to reality. Principle inherent in one's nature could then express itself freely and clearly, with no selfish obstructions."[16]

The principles of categorical cosmology require that there should always be another category beyond the presently visible limit. Even with *tian,* the pole of potentiality in its most dynamic state, the question cannot be referred to an ultimate answer. As with the analogous perception of Zhuang Zhou that there is always a beginning before the beginning, the ultimate horizon of this situation is the absence of any creative agent external to the process. A pragmatic response to this as an intellectual problem is to put the problem of origins aside as irrelevant. There seems little doubt, however, that with Neo-Confucianism the boundaries of rational discourse were being pushed further and further into the realm of *tian*. Equivalently, *tian* (never absolutely dichotomizable) was increasingly drawn into the realm of man. Huang Ting-jian's sage is significantly humanized. Huang Xiufu's *yipin* painter belongs to an earlier stratum. Huang Tingjian, of course, belonged to a coterie of literati deeply interested in the activities of poetry, calligraphy and painting and responsible for the first systematic articulation of literatus art theory. At this time, with painting finally adopted into the privileged society of scholar-officials, the already well established belief that the quality of the artist was embodied in the work of art necessarily became canonical.

The vectors of this relationship are complex. A polarity between the subject matter and the artist seems inherent. But if one goes far enough back in time, then the artist is not even part of the equation. As an ontology is articulated, the relationship between cosmological presentation and human representation become critical. And as the social status of the performers, whether in music, literature, calligraphy or painting, begins to demand some acknowledgement of their creative role, this latter is problematized. The dynamics of these various arguments were especially vigorous among the Northern Song literati and within this context the painting of bamboo by Wen Tong apparently roused great interest among his friends. The arguments were not uniform, but one powerful theme is voiced in a poem by Su Shi:

> When Yu-k'o painted bamboo,
> He saw bamboo, not himself.
> Nor was he simply unconscious of himself:
> Trance-like, he left his body.[17]

This implies a dissolution rather than a projection of the self. The painting of the bamboo is so convincing because Wen Tong himself has become invisible. But a Neo-Confucian gloss has crept over an approach probably deriving from Buddhist practice. Su Shi extrapolates Wen's qualities from the bamboo:

> The ink-gentlemen on the wall cannot speak,
> But just seeing them can dissipate one's myriad griefs;

And further, as for my friend's resembling these gentlemen,
The severity of his simple virtue defies the frosty autumn.[18]

This is a categorical, correlational extrapolation. Wen Tong is categorized by a cultural ideal, not identified as an individual.

The dynamics change in another approach that more explicitly projects the artist into his work. This is encapsulated in the term *xinyin* 心印, "print of the heart-mind," which occurs in a history of painting compiled by Guo Ruoxu ca. 1080: "[Personal signatures] are called 'mind-prints.' They originate from the source of the mind and are perfected in the imagination to take shape as traces, which, being in accord with the mind are called 'prints.' If one enlarges on the myriad ways in which activities follow thought, implementing this accord with the mind, they may all be called 'prints'.[19] In the third generation of the Northern Song literati critics, so influential on all later painting, Mi Youren (1086–1165) defined his own painting as *xinhua* 心畫, "painting of the heart-mind."[20] A good painting could only be produced by a good man. A thoroughly good man was necessarily a literatus. Good painting was literatus painting. The rhetoric of linkage between person and artistic performance was now so thoroughly integrated with rhetoric of the literatus cult in general as to remain indissoluble, though still subject to change.

The original significance of terms such as *xinhua* almost certainly must have been closely connected with Neo-Confucian thought. The various developments in the conception of *xin,* the "heart-mind," become a central question in this newly formed aesthetic context. At this juncture, however, I shall change my own emphasis. The conceptualization of painting as "soundless poetry" and poetry as "sounding painting," which emerged in this nexus, inevitably shifted the argument further into its own medium, the realm of literature. The question of how a *painting* specifically could embody the self, for example, although apparently established as a central one, was in fact increasingly marginalized in a discourse of literary values.

Calligraphy, that distinctive conjunction of body and word, was a mediator in this situation. It retained a prominent role, due to its concentration of the performative aspect, its sociological function, and the chronology of its development. For members of the elite group of critics and practitioners such as Huang Tingjian, Su Shi, and Mi Fu, calligraphy was really more important than painting. Important and distinctive although much of the discussion around calligraphy may be, for our present purposes we must limit our remarks to generalities. Calligraphy is at once one of the most controlled of all cultural practices and one of the most spontaneous. When practiced as an art form, it requires a formal knowledge of each individual character to be as deeply internalized as are the words in a spoken language. As these forms are externalized through the activities of the psychophysical body, the brush and ink become the exclusive channel between the interior of that body and the writing surface outside it. The "traces," as they were often called, preserve a record of the physical activity with such sensitivity and precision that not only the physical but also the psychic activity can be read out of it with an accuracy depending upon the reader's own experience of those same functions. At the same time, the practicability and the cultural stability of this script and its practice depend upon a set of rules promulgated and internalized with exquisite precision. The strict maintenance of standards is absolutely essential, not only to sustain the institution but also in order that the standards can be legitimately surpassed. This is another canonical case of the categorical within/without dialectic. If a piece of writing does not attain to the practice, if it is "not calligraphy," then it is useless. If it is not more than its practice, it is worthless. A millennium of criticism in calligraphy, from the Han to the Tang periods, was basically concerned with systematically articulating this circumstance. The Tang was primarily concerned with control, the Northern Song primarily with freedom through and beyond control.

Although calligraphy puts a premium on both physiological and psychic activity, it fundamentally subjects these to the mind as a cultural agency. It thus need have nothing to do with individuality but a great deal to do with identity. That is, the practice has no meaning in the abstract. It must be actualized and the site of actualization is critical. Identity is, in a sense, location. At the same time, it is characteristic of the Chinese tradition that practice is interpretation. This very general circumstance relates most broadly to the lack of any external creator-agent and, correspondingly, to the lack of any articulation of the absolute.[21] Since there was no ultimately authoritative text, instead of a constant effort to "see through the glass darkly" there was an unending process of interpretation.[22] If one were to demand some urtext as to the substance of what is subsequently interpreted, the answer should probably be on the lines of Zhuang Zhou's view of the beginning of the world. Before the beginning there was a beginning. Before that text there was another. The whole of Chinese historiography was essentially an interpretative exercise. Interpretation extended in inherent, specific and unceasing sequence through both time and space. At the same time, each interpretative act remained tied elastically yet inextricably to the textual canon. Each individual is a site of such interpretative practice. Each work of calligraphy was, characteristically, an instance of such practice. The most perceptive, well-structured, and potentially energetic instances became exemplary. Such instances tended naturally to cohere into styles, systematically excellent and therefore exemplary ways of performing this action. Such styles inevitably correlated with individuals, the principal sites of mediation between potentiality and actuality. A style was usually labeled by the name of one patriarchal practitioner. The patriarchal practitioner, of course, was Wang Xizhi (303-79) but the aristocratic, official masters of the Tang, such as Yan Zhenqing (709-85), form the most institutionally canonical—bureaucratic, one might say—group. Although Northern Song masters such as Huang Tingjian and Mi Fu were greatly admired for their interpretative performances in calligraphy, as exemplars they were almost always seen as problematic. This reflects the fact that it was perhaps just at this time, in their own thinking, that the inherent ambiguities of interpretative transmission came under close and sometimes puzzled scrutiny. The debate between differing interpretative strategies became very vigorous and the ideas of men such as Huang Tingjian, Su Shi, and Mi Fu can often be sharply distinguished, even though their concerns were shared.[23]

In a very useful study, Ronald Egan has recently studied the views of calligraphy held by Su Shih and his teacher Ouyang Xiu.[24] He distinguishes three aspects of Su's interests: "seeing the man in the calligraphy, 'lodging,' and stylistic innovation."[25] Su was as convinced of the fact that a man reveals himself in his calligraphy as he was sensitive to the problems in sustaining this view. Egan suggests that the increasingly moralistic concerns of art criticism in this period produced a strongly normative mode, in which the values of the artist were necessarily involved.

In passages where Su brings in both sides of the argument, his implicit conclusion seems to be that the relationship is not fully symmetrical.[26] While it is very problematic to derive a judgment from calligraphy and apply it to the man, the reverse is not only desirable but legitimate. This, I think, demonstrates that the context of a critical judgment is even more important than its inner logic. The degree to which—even the question of whether—a work of art can embody its author cannot simply be a question of how the object of art works. It continues to be constituted in its working context. It comes to depend as much on the reader as on the maker. The interpretative acts of both making and reading have definite location but not fixed bounds; or, if they do, then something is wrong.

The normative aspect of ethical aesthetics is strongly modified by such situational aesthetics. In this period it is countered by a new move, one related much more to the values of friendship than to the ideals of society. Su and his friends differed from earlier calligraphers and critics in the degree to which they believed individual innovation could legitimately transform ancient models. Significantly, the possibility of technical and even physical flaws being transmuted into aesthetic and even moral qualities was accepted and even welcomed for the first time in this field. There is a famous exchange between Su Shi and Huang Tingjian: Su suggested that some brush strokes in Huang's calligraphy looked like snakes hanging from trees. Huang retorted that Su's characters looked like squashed frogs.[27]

One result of this shift is that physical peculiarities of body and gesture can become embodied in calligraphy. Indeed, a sense of immediate physical presence is peculiar to the writings of such critics. Su said of the calligraphy of his teacher, Ouyang Xiu:

> Ou-yang Wen-chung used a fine-tipped brush and dry ink to write squarish, broad characters that exude liveliness and are rich beyond compare. When men of later times view them, it is just like seeing the splendor of the man himself as he used to hurry along, with lustrous dark eyes and full cheeks.[28]

Such responses are glimpsed in Tang criticism and they become conventional after the Northern Song. But in this extreme, I think, they are peculiar to this period. There was a sudden opening up of both practice and criticism, which in its authenticity is later rarely matched. Su's eulogy of his teacher's calligraphy, of course, slips partly into the conventional style of ideal categories. What is most interesting and perhaps remains most distinctive about these critics is the way in which deviation as a privilege of individuality is validated.[29] One suspects that a conjunction of conceptual elasticity and the peculiar society of their friendship was a crucial factor.

Su Shi, among these literati, was most interested in the experience of exteriorizing. With regard to calligraphy, he wrote:

> I have never really found anything easy in my life, except writing: when the force of my brush has to wind and turn in pursuit of where my idea has already reached, I have always managed to follow my idea to its limit.[30]

His own inebriated painting on the wall of a friend's home emerged with an extraordinarily vivid commentary:

Dry bowels take in wine and angular sprouts emerge,
[The energies of] liver and lungs interjecting, generating bamboo and rock.
Flourishing urgency—turning back is impossible—
Writing on the snow-white wall of my friend's home.[31]

One has a vivid sense of Su Shi becoming physically embodied in the surfaces of his calligraphy and painting. It seems possible that painting was seen by Su as less constraining in its formal requirements than calligraphy. There are certainly interesting questions to be asked about the epistemological and ontological status of the images of the script world and the physical world as processed through the mind. Again, however, this is not my interest here, which is more with the nature of the organism that Su Shi projects.

Consistent with so much of what has recently been said about thought and experience in traditional China, Su makes no rigid distinctions between— let alone make separate ontologies for—mind and body. There is a complex system of mutually related functions. A historically specific account of Su's physiological thinking might be partially possible, since his interest in such matters was often explicit. I have not attempted to do this. We can note in general, however, that Chinese medical theory and practice was predominantly physiological and pharmocological, not anatomical. The culturally systematic importance of this distinction has been explored by several authors.[32] Such medical theory was not an eccentric and recondite corner of the culture but a deeply significant area of collective representations. Specific acquaintance with it was probably usual among the literati. Even in cases where specific acquaintance may have been slight, the significance of the collective representation is not necessarily undermined.

We probably will not go far off the track if we see Su's remarks in the generalized context provided by Manfred Porkert's study of the fundamentals of Chinese medical theory. The body in this system is represented as a hierarchically structured set of subsystems processing the transformations of energy, *qi* 氣. Porkert draws especially on the *Huangdi neijing suwen* (Han dynasty) and its Sui dynasty version, *Huangdi neijing taisu,* both well-known texts in the Song.

In this physiology, by *gan* 肝, "liver," is meant the *gancang* 肝臟, the functioning system of energy (*qi* 氣) transmission and transformation specific to the pulse generated by this particular physiological function. It is classified as minor *yang* in *yin* (*Neijing taisu*); it's function unfolds through the sinews and muscles *(Suwen);* its season is spring, and its emotion is anger; and within the integral organism its role is that of the general, *jiangjun* 将軍, seat of the *hun* 魂 *(Suwen)*, "responsible for actively projecting the qualities of the integral personality" (Porkert). It is functionally checked by the *cang* of the "lungs."[33]

The "lungs," similarly, refer to the functional system of the *feicang* 肺臟. It is classified as minor *yin* in *yang (Suwen)*; it unfolds through the skin and hair, which envelop the sinews and muscle *(Suwen)*; its season is autumn; its emotion is sorrow; it stores the energy of the *po* 魄 *(Suwen)*; its "office" is that of the prime minister, *xiangfu* 相傅, responsible for the maintenance of rhythmic order *(Suwen)*. It is checked by the "heart."[34]

The "heart," *xin* 心, has its own *cang* system, unfolding through the hierarchy of arterial pulses and filling the "office" of sovereign, *junzhu* 君主. It maintains the integrity of the person.[35] The medical *xin,* "heart" as psychophysical function, is clearly much more specific — and historically stable — than the Neo-Confucian *xin,* "heart-mind," as intellectual, emotional, ethical, cultural and historical function. But the two are overlapping and compatible. Indeed, the boundary between them may be impossible to draw, because the physiology is an ecological one that cannot even exist without such interconnections. A distinction between "heart" and "heart-mind" may have some use but is arbitrary and ultimately misleading. As with a mathematical function, there are transformations that transpose the function between applications in different areas and at different levels.

It is especially difficult for Western sinology to maintain the visibility of the physiological stratum when dealing with Chinese intellectual history. It is generally visible in the original texts. Even there, however, a very significant problem is sensed. Despite the absence of any canonical mind/body or spirit/matter dichotomy, the Chinese intellectual world was profoundly logocentric. The body was not to be locked up in a separate room, but it was frequently problematic — calligraphy provides a classic case of this ambiguity. Visual art, the production of visual images, once acknowledged in the literatus domain, was one of the very few areas in which the wordless language of the senses could claim a primary value. The linking with poetry characteristic of literati aesthetics surely served the purpose of translating the body back into an acceptable language. But both calligraphy and painting still allowed the body to present itself and be recognized in the organic articulation of brush line and composition.

In a sense, therefore, calligraphy and painting not only allowed but even required the presence of self in a most unambiguous form, the organism of the body itself. Such a body was incorporated by its *shen* 神, the agency controlling the continuous activity of actualizing potentiality. The vitality of the organism was maintained by this connection with potentiality, but Song Neo-Confucians remained deeply exercised about how particularity and the distinct physical nature could be transcended. Physical nature harbors "selfish physical desires." As Zhang Zai wrote: "Therefore in physical nature there is that which the superior man denies to be his nature."[36] The body, however, was not so much to be negated as to be translated and extended. As Zhang Zai also said, "Selfishness means being spatially bounded, *wo you fang ye*" 我有方也 while the heart-mind acts beyond itself, *xin wei you wai* 心為有外.[37]

An act of writing or painting is always physically specific. It results in a physically specific object. Both act and object *"you fang"*—are spatially bounded. In the larger discourse of calligraphy and painting, ways had to be found not only of translating these activities into poetry but also of enlarging them in other dimensions. Connections were extended to incorporate other artists, other places, other periods. This practice became firmly established in the Song and should surely be related to the Song concern with "enlarging the mind," *daxin* 大心. Such connections establish a selfhood in art within the sociology of artistic practice. Philosophically, they demonstrate that such works, in Chad Hansen's terms, are mereological parts of an extended stuff, not atomistic points.[38] Social selfhood can be powerfully constructed in such works.

But still a problem remains, for there was undoubtedly a conscious (at least a culturally conscious) working against the specificity of physical self, the psychophysical self of medical theory, the self evolving in the energy configuration of a specific person's life, the self embodied in calligraphy and painting.[39] The fact that calligraphy and painting provided a field for this "selfishness" meant that their status always remained questionable. It is especially interesting that, in the community of Su Shi and Mi Fu, the term "ink-play," *moxi* 墨戲, is sometimes casually and humorously tossed around.[40] One suspects this represents a realization of deeper powers emerging into consciousness. "Play" can provide direct but protected access to disconcerting depths.

One may also suspect that another psychological function, that of desire, must enter here. As we have noted, Neo-Confucians such as Zhang Zai associated physical nature with energy, *qi* 氣, and the storing of "selfish human desires," *siyu* 私欲. The term *siyu* has links to sexuality, and it would be extremely valuable to have more work done on this psychological aspect. There is a tone to the discussion of calligraphy and painting by literati critics that suggests a distinct, if guarded, awareness of the role of desire. Su Shi's poem, given above, is an example. There were perhaps few acceptable fields for the publication of desire in this society. Calligraphy and painting may have provided one, even if there it was often unrecognizably transfigured.[41] This possibility is related to a much larger question: that of the role of desire in the dialectic between energy and articulation and in structuring an awareness of the self.[42]

The Northern Song literati's knowing engagement with the *qi* in calligraphy and painting coincided, of course, with the development of the quintessential Neo-Confucian conceptualization of *liqi* 理氣. *Li* is not necessarily logocentric. It is sometimes tempting to compare it's conceptualization to the genetic code. But among the Neo-Confucians it was inextricably linked to the logos. Certainly, integral to the self-consciousness of the literati was the idea that culture was coextensive with literacy, that the definition of "being human" was not only a matter of *ren* 仁 (humaneness) but also one of *wen* 文 (pattern/culture/literature). The literati must have been peculiarly sensitive to the irresistible and chronic role of language at that Lacanian juncture where animal becomes culture, and biological "need" is translated and dissolved into the semiotics of "desire," eventually to be transcended by the fundamentally sociological mutuality of a "demand" in which each party "stands for the cause of desire."[43] An enquiry along these lines might make a small contribution to understanding that mundanely persistent but perennially disturbing presence of writing at the boundaries of image and meaning in later Chinese art. It is sometimes in such fissures that problems of self and desire may be glimpsed.

We may bring this set of issues into a particular focus by briefly considering a highly distinctive cultural practice that, on occasion, can embody them all. The practice is that known as *fengshui* 風水, a system of landscape analysis through which potential sites for human activity, primarily building, were identified.[44] Its origins are so ancient as to have become invisible. The two concerns encapsulated in the conventional term "wind and water" are profoundly practical. Referring to weather, access to water, and the state of the ground as mediated by these, they are a succinct summary of the ecological parameters of healthy dwelling, persistent from neolithic times to the present. As such, *fengshui* represents a seemingly seamless evolution of lore and habit from time immemorial.

Fengshui is inextricably linked to a body of cosmological belief, sometimes called *kanyu* 堪輿, "cover and support," and to a systematic physical cosmology, called *dili* 地理, "earth patterns." *Kanyu* and *dili,* which are not in fact strictly compatible categories, are themselves contextualized by even broader horizons of belief. There is a systematically coherent structure embracing all of these areas of cultural activity, such that *fengshui* cannot be understood without the context of the widest horizons. All this is commonplace, but it needs to be reasserted. In relation to cultural history, the status of *fengshui* is comparable to that of medical practice. Neither an eccentric nor a recondite area, it was a very broadly distributed and deeply significant area of collective representations.

Fengshui may be studied as a symbolic set of cultural practices if the assumptions of the symbolic analysis incorporate the reality of *qi* 氣, "matter-energy," and the arterial pulse systems through which *qi* is topologically distributed. Only through such incorporation can one deal realistically with, for example, the analogous systems of *dimo* 地脈, "earth-artery-pulses," and the *xuemo* 血脈, "sanguinary arterial pulses" of physiological theory.

We can say that the representations of Song mountain-water paintings, for example, are *dili* representations. We can say, further, that these representations were of necessity compatible with the practices of *fengshui*. To be precise, discussion of *fengshui* would have to be historicized in time and space. The practice was, however, extraordinarily and persistently consistent. For the purposes of visual analysis, diagrams from a much later period can still sensitize us, at an initial level at least, to the structures of Song *shanshuihua*.

Hong Key-yoon's representation of Korean geomancy[45] has as its source a Korean manual that appears to be essentially identical to Chinese manuals of the seventeenth century. There is a particular diagram which represents a mountain-water topography of exceptionally good quality. It is called "A bright court where the three halls all coalesce in front of the cavity." "Cavity," *xue* 穴, is the term for the functional center of the dwelling site. It is here, as almost always, diagrammed by a crab-like formation, with the *xue* indicated by a circle between the pincers. Undulating wriggles comprising most of the diagram indicate ranges of hills, their crests black and their lowest slopes left white. Watercourses are shown as dotted lines. All hills are included in at least one sequential range, frequently called "dragon-artery-pulses," *longmo* 龍脈. There is, therefore, both a linear system of connections and a circumferential set of relationships. The site is surrounded by encircling phases of hills and watercourses. But the entire diagram is bilaterally symmetrical and the site lies low on the central vertical axis of both the diagram and the topography. It is located at the end of a range of hills that incorporates this axis and intersects each of the circumferential ranges. The hills at each intersection, belonging to two ranges at once, are noticeably enlarged. In this topography, the axial range is the main *longmo*. The topography is cardinally oriented and the main *longmo* is called *Xuanwu* 玄武, the "Dark Warrior" of the north. The lines of hills are paralleled by watercourses, which join in front of the site. The site itself must be on dry land with good soil mechanics and the open area between it and the water is called the *mingtang* 明堂, "Hall of Light." There is a directionality of behind and before. Thus the slopes of the Dark Warrior *longmo* descend behind the site, linking with the enfolding White Tiger and Blue Dragon. Beyond the *mingtang,* across the water rises a lively play of hills, the Red Bird. This directionality is related, on one hand, to that of the body and, on the other, to that of the imperial city. Despite the chronological differences here, we can easily map this topography onto a Northern Song painting such as Li Cheng's "Buddhist Temple amid Clearing Autumn Peaks."

A dominant significance of mountains lies in their embodying of *qi,* matter-energy, in *dili* patterns that are among the grander in our ecology. The Dark Warrior range is the principal articulation of energy in this particular topology. The energy is qualitatively and quantitatively refreshed with each articulation of the range and, particularly, with each intersection across another range. The energy becomes accessible at the point of the cavity, a point that is sometimes compared to a well tapping an aquifer.[46] From the point of view of the site, the main *longmo* is called a "coming dragon," *lailong* 来龍. The particular point of the cavity is access. But its location is both structural and functional, in the settling and coalescence of the dynamic sequences of mountains and waters, in the resulting accumulation of energy in a reservoir where it is protected from dispersal. The *fengshui* specialist's skill is to recognize the quality of energy running through the landforms and to locate the exact spot at the focus of its accumulation.

Multivalence was the norm in this world. We find an aristocratic society in both the diagram and Li Cheng's mountains-and-waters. In traditional terminology, developed before the Song, the central mountain is functionally labeled as a *zhushan* 主山, "ruling peak." It is flanked by assisting peaks. Such a hierarchical social structure is developed throughout the Li Cheng in much more detail than we can show here. At the same time—and as the *dili* diagram makes clear—this is a field of vigorous reproductive activity. The *zhushan* we may discern, is phallic; the flow and collection of water is seminal, and the site appears to be constructed on the model of the female crotch. Descriptions of the dwelling in relation to the site indicate that, at the point of the cavity, individual human life participates or, so to speak, is inserted into the flux of cosmic society. This is an interesting circumstance, with sexuality rampaging through a field from which it is supposedly absent.

Among the points to be emphasized here are (1) the conjunction of a hierarchically social model—the entire diagram can also be mapped on the traditional plan of an imperial city, with the site drawing its functional power from the peak and thereby exercising a sovereign role; (2) the powerfully structured physiological model, in which the site exercises a sovereign role analogous to the *shen* in the human organism; and (3) the major role granted to psychological forces in the desirability of living in a spot that is aesthetically defined. The distinctive conjunction of an individual life and a political power center is mediated by the equally distinctive physiological theory. Although the diagram used here is so late, it is still relevant to emphasize the peculiar role of diagramming per se. In representing a range of issues, including several of selfhood, a visual structure can perform tasks beyond the word.

There is a close correlation between dwelling and desire. Dwelling is a mode of attachment and can be examined through various levels of sublimation. In this respect, we may recall Su Shi again. His third distinctive concern, discussed by Ronald Egan, is the notion of "lodging," *yuyi* 寓意, thoughts and feelings in both objects in the world at large and in works of art in particular. As Egan remarks, [No] one before Su Shih draws the peculiar distinction he does, between "lodging" and "fixing," *liuyi* 留意.[47] The idea is related to Su's description of himself flowing through this world like water, settling in no fixed abode.[48] Some manner of location is necessary for any activity of the self but Su's generative self may be threatened by what, from our viewpoint, we might term a geometrical home. It is clear, even if implicitly, that desire is an issue for Su. As Egan writes, "*liuyi* ('leaving/fixing one's mind upon something') . . . has connotations of obsession and possessiveness.[49] "Lodging" also cannot avoid its links with desire, but there is a difference. It may not only be one of intensity. One wonders whether "fixing" is not comparable to "demand," with its mutual interlocking, and "lodging" comparable to "desire." It is also interesting to note the contrasting attitudes towards dwelling in Buddhism and Confucianism, and their very differing attitudes towards desire. As Irene Bloom writes, "In contrast to the Buddhist ideal of homelessness, Chang Tsai had in the 'Western Inscription' discovered his home everywhere and in everything."[50] Dwelling, indeed, was characteristically a Chinese obsession.

The Chinese heaven-and-earth world, incorporating both mountain-water and society, must be seen as an ecological construction. This has important implications for the position and function of humanity in this context. An ecology is not a background to a player, it is not viewed as a panorama by a functionally isolated observer, it is not even the environment of an autonomous agent. An ecology incorporates all its organisms as agents of mutual generation. The traditional Chinese world of *zaohua* 造化 can be approached in these terms.[51]

To say that the mountain-water world and humanity in traditional China were constructed as an ecological system has important results in the analysis of Song dynasty painting. Amongst these results are implications for conceptualizing space and place that have particular relevance for our present topic. Space, in very general terms, is understood as a dynamic pattern of relationships, necessarily incorporating time. In it functions such as exchange of energy are more important than geometrical constructions. Concepts of place must obviously respond to their spatial environment, but in some ways they may be more difficult to specify. Place is obviously situational but, again, not geometrical. It arises at a center of condensation in the ecological energy. It represents some focus in the pattern of exchange with sufficient continuity to generate an identity, an identity that contributes to, as well as receiving from, the transformational processes of organization. At one level it may be impossible to draw any clear division between the concepts of topological place and human individuality in Chinese thought. Functions of morality and will should perhaps be seen as arising at a different level from the same structural base. There is an indication of this in the various ways of defining self in traditional China, such as in terms of ethics, society, and psychophysiology. Analogously, we might compare the social concept of *guxiang* 故鄉, "ancestral district," with the physiological concept of *xue*, "topological site." The phenomena of landscape and culture in China are closely related to the ecological issues of place, space, and self.

This returns us to the issue of location in identity and interpretation. One finds, running quietly through many Neo-Confucian texts, a discourse of dwelling. Actions are always localized but, in modern parlance, one should "think globally and act locally." If the act is too specific it falls within the rubric or "the self spatially bounded," *wo you fang ye*. But even "the heart-mind acting beyond itself" must still dwell. In Zhu Xi's words:

> When the mind is broad and without the slightest trace of selfishness, having precisely the same compass as heaven and earth, this is "dwelling in the wide house of the world," this is dwelling in *jen*.[52]

As Irene Bloom writes, this impetus toward an expanded self is bound up with Zhu Xi's understanding of the concept of "the oneness of principle and the diversity of its particularizations," *li i fen shu* 理一分殊, and of the mind as relational by nature:

> The mind . . . is thus in every activity. If today you extend it in one activity and tomorrow you extend it in another, gradually it will be fully realized. From one household it will expand to the state, and from the state to the world, and it will be sufficient to preserve all within the four seas.[53]

A man who survived as an anguished remnant of this grand vision of Zhu Xi's was Zheng Sixiao (1241–1318). Under the Mongols he painted orchids deprived of their earth, some of the best-known images of the homeless self in Chinese painting. His poem on one example concludes with the lines, "I opened my nostrils before making the painting, / And there, floating everywhere in the sky, is the antique fragrance undying."[54] He offers here a remarkable abstraction, or interjection, in the senses rather than from the senses; it is a communion of selves in an environment of unselved selves. One of his themes is the relationship between the organism and the ecology. In comparison to Wen Tong and his bamboos, however, Zheng has appropriated the botanical subject for his own purposes.

He was also the author of a remarkable letter to a friend who was embarking on travels to study the earth patterns of the politically dismembered nation. In this letter he transposes Zhu Xi's discourse into another medium:

> Above this person of myself there is heaven. Below is earth. Exactly in the middle there am I. If I look upward from the center, there is the azure canopy loftily suspended. Out of respect I dare not stare. If I look downward from the center, there is the great clod spread around. It is near and therefore I may scrutinize it. Nothing that my leg power can reach and my eye-power can encompass can escape my embosoming. . . . Now whence rises this coming-dragon in the patch of ground under my two feet? If I cannot see the coming-dragon under my own two feet, then I shall not see the coming-dragon at the limits of my eye-sight in the eight directions. If I can not see the coming-dragon at the limits of my eye-sight in the eight directions, then I shall not know each and every coming-dragon of this sub-prefecture, of all the mountains and all the waters, of every hill and valley. If I know not each and every coming-dragon of this sub-prefecture, of all the mountains and all the waters, of every hill and valley, then I shall

not know each and every coming-dragon of the nine regions and the five sacred peaks, of ten-thousand peaks and ten-thousand waters. . . . Finally, finally, I shall not know the one entire and comprehensive coming-dragon of the endless spaces of the boundless great land and great sea. If we wish to know this one entire and comprehensive coming-dragon of the endless spaces of the boundless great land and great sea, then how can I do otherwise than look up and stare, look down and scrutinize, picking out the principles from what is near to compare them with those that are distant?[55]

With all this in mind, let us turn to a physical screen on which is projected both a construction of a particular self of that time and also our own academic constructions: specifically, a painting by Huang Gongwang, which he produced over the period of three years between 1347 and 1350. The painting and its history are well known and I will isolate only those aspects of most immediate relevance.[56]

It is painted on paper, the favored ground of literati artists from this time onwards. As I have suggested elsewhere, I believe that the random structure and the depth of texture of paper, in contrast to silk, provided literati painters with an interface with the exterior world, a screen in which their interior sense of self could be manifested. Such a material stratum is of great import-ance here.[57] Huang's brush technique derives from the Dong Yuan tradition, as I noted at the beginning of this paper. This technique had been singled out for two main reasons. First, the brush strokes themselves are close in technique to calligraphy. This not only invokes the privileges of a literatus art, but also supports a priority of process over product. Second, as a tech-nique in representing forms, it tends to obscure recognition and invites a more active perceptual process. Thus the priority of process is also established in two fields.[58]

Huang Gongwang inscribed this handscroll at the end, describing how he had begun it when "returning to dwell in the Fuchun Mountains." After laying out the entire composition in one inspired sweep, he continued to work it out over three years. In his inscription of 1350 he notes the pain, perhaps the impossibility, of bringing it to completion. The painting clearly displays its growth along the axes of both space and time and is, indeed, an archetypal exemplar of painting as process rather than product.[59]

Directed by the physical format of the handscroll, we must also read this composition through both space and time. But this fact is thoroughly ex-ploited by the artist in a narrative that is a carefully constructed extended image of Huang's dwelling. The format emphasizes what may well be a general truth in the artist's culture: that self-identity can only be understood as a narrative, a configuration of interpretations in both space and time.[60] The painting lost its opening section in the seventeenth century, complicating any programmatic reading. Ignoring the important question of the preface, however, I shall briefly describe three critical phases in the surviving majority of the composition.

Passing as it now opens over a pianissimo of lowlands and water, carefully set with signs of human dwelling and passage, we find a mountain theme building towards the midpoint of a horizontal development with increasing mass and momentum. A massive climax is orchestrated in the form of a dragon-ridge emerging in the far distance, to the right. Rising to a symmetrically overwhelming summit, it then subsides, with sinking slopes spreading and curving to our right. It has shifted its axis through 90 degrees, emerging directly out into the painting's surface and then turning into the lateral axis to meet our own path through the passage of time. Cradled within the lower slopes, where the scenery opens out into the preceding vista, is a village. At the crucial point in this stabilizing pattern is a small, white-empty hut, the site.[61] This is where the coming-dragon settles. Again in the words Zheng Sixiao, who belongs to a generation older than Huang:

> The energy of earth and the configuring of mountains, the coming dragon and the arterial branch, the marvel of the life-extension of true *yang*, finally coalesce here. A cavity where these forces settle without congealing, where [the pattern] moves with life but does not flow away, this is a cavity that brings happiness to men. . . . A cavity is an eye-aperture. . . . When a burial cavity is not an eye-aperture, it is called earth, or stone, or spring, but not a cavity. The meaning of this is in whether the arteries of energy can penetrate from the inside to the outside, . . . whether, at a prodigious point a tiny leakage of creativity's generative powers will sprout.[62]

The immediate ground of the settling dragon is at the scale of the individual dwelling, in the cavity-site. Participation is required to dwell herein but it also links the individual life with cosmic space. Huang's dragon-artery mountain emerges out of the paper's depths, the depths of the creative world, and the still, small house returns us into those depths.

Huang's exploration of place and space, of self and art, continues. Foreground and distance part company across the opening of a great bay. Anglers drift on the nearer waters and a gentleman feeds geese from a pavilion close by. Here, in contrast to the intimate knowledge of touch, the distancing function of sight is reasserted as we look from the here and now of this view point, gazing over there at receding hills. The intensity of the earlier participation in the creative worlds of both art and nature has here been weakened. I would imagine that, from the original opening, this participation was constructed and conducted as a kind of pulse. Here, we shall find, the weakening serves to reintensify the experience.

We move on across flat shoals and slight hills that do not seem to welcome us. Suddenly, out of a sense of repressed unease, a precipitous peak erupts. We find ourselves at a pole opposite to that of the earlier cavity-dwelling. I don't think it inappropriate to say we have moved from a female to a male polarity, from receptacle to phallus.

But it is much more specific than that. An imperial image of ancient, upright splendor, seen in Northern Song paintings such as Fan Kuan's famous "Travelers among Streams and Mountains," has been translated into one of the creative individual. The painting having already established the coextension of space and surface, of optical illusion and tactile medium, this peak emerges from the paper with a sense of overpowering activity. Brush strokes and ink splashes explode in the surface-space. Huang signed this work with a personal name he had chosen himself for deeply symbolic ends, *Dachi* 大痴, "Great Craziness." The name has extensive cultural and political reverberations, especially in the *yipin* category, and it clearly seems to be exemplified in the sudden unleashing of technique in this final section.

Huang's own inscription, lying beyond this final peak, is extraordinarily revealing. It is clear from this confession how he explicitly revealed himself in this painting, in a way that perhaps no other artist had ever done before. The process, he implies, should deny an end. Yet the world demands that the struggle have a conclusion, and Huang Gongwang forces that conclusion out of the participation within. He submits his desire to the socialization of demand, we might suggest, yet objectifies it at the same time.

In the seals that Huang adds after his signature, he uses another chosen name, exemplifying his self-image as a Daoist priest: "One-peak man of the Dao." As the writers on earth-pattern divination said, the hardest pattern to perceive was that hiding beneath the placidity of gentle terrain. But the hardest pattern to accommodate was the heroic isolation of a single peak. For, in *apparently* isolating itself from the fluxing spine of the *long*, it threatened itself with collapse. Like the finished work of art, it must deny its own birth.

Fan Kuan had approached this achievement more nearly than any other and Huang Gongwang, like many other painters of his time, had been enthralled by the monumental imagery of Fan Kuan's epoch. But Huang's own self was the face of the *long,* the power of myth within the life of the self, emerging through the creative struggle of a cultural tradition.

It would probably be impossible to prove, in our usual sense, that Huang actually signed his painting with this single mountain that erupts so abruptly out of its surface. But I'm sure that he did.[63] The vector of Wen Tong's identification with his bamboo has here been fully reversed. The mountain has turned into Huang Gongwang. No houses are found on its slopes—nor could they comfortably survive there. There is no site, no cavity. It is a statement on cosmic axes, a vertical reassertion of the body's being in the horizontal narratives of time—a final participation of quintessential individuality in the cosmological society of mountains and waters. It is followed by Huang's own reinscription, or transcription; the move back into words. We may wonder whether this move explains or obscures, supports or undermines.

Notes

1. The conference revealed an interesting core of such works. Obvious examples that have been particularly influential on this writer are Steven Lukes, *Individualism* (New York: Harper and Row, 1973); Carrithers, Collins, and Lukes, eds., *The Category of the Person: Anthropology, Philosophy, History* (Cambridge: University of Cambridge Press, 1985); Stephen Greenblatt, *Renaissance Self-fashioning: From Moore to Shakespeare* (Chicago: University of Chicago Press, 1980); and Donald Munro, ed., *Individualism and Holism: Studies in Confucian and Taoist Values* (Ann Arbor: University of Michigan Press, 1985).

2. This sequence has been the subject of much study. The best overall account is still that in Susan Bush, *The Chinese Literati on Painting: Su Shih (1037-1101) to Tung Ch'i-ch'ang (1555-1636)* Harvard-Yenching Institute Studies 27 (Cambridge: Harvard University Press, 1971), supplemented by James Cahill, *The Distant Mountain: Chinese Painting of the Late Ming Dynasty, 1570-1644* (New York: Weatherhill, 1982).

3. Manfred Porkert, *The Theoretical Foundations of Chinese Medicine: Systems of Correspondence* (Cambridge: MIT Press, 1974), 1.

4. For the most interesting exploration of this in the context of art history, see Kiyohiko Munakata, "Concepts of *Lei* and *Kan-lei* in Early Chinese Art Theory," in Susan Bush and Christin Murck, eds., *Theories of the Arts in China* (Princeton Univer-

sity Press, 1983), 105–131). For more recent philosophical discussion, see A. C. Graham, *Yin-Yang and the Nature of Chinese Correlative Thinking*, Occasional Paper and Monograph Series no. 6, (Singapore: Institute of East Asian Philosophies, 1986).

5. Graham, *Yin-Yang*, 8–9.

6. Ibid., 23.

7. See John Timothy Wixted, "The Nature of Evaluation in the *Shih-p'in* (Gradings of Poets) by Chung Hung (A.D. 469–518)," in Susan Bush and Christopher Murck, eds., *Theories of the Arts in China* (Princeton: Princeton University Press, 1983), 223–64. Wixted gives a thorough bibliography for the topic.

8. See, for a summary account and basic bibliography of Western studies, Susan Bush and Hsio-yen Shih, *Early Chinese Texts on Painting* (Cambridge: Harvard-Yenching Institute, 1985), 47, 87–92, 99, 100–102.

9. See ibid., 100–101, from which all the translations below are taken.

10. Wixted, "The Nature of Evaluation," 231.

11. Herbert Fingarette, throughout his *Confucius—The Secular as Sacred* (New York: Harper Torchbooks, 1972).

12. For a brief discussion from my point of view of this and other such formulations, see John Hay, "Values and History in Chinese Painting, I," *Res* 6 (Autumn 1983): 99–100. See also the article by Mark Elvin, "Between the Earth and Heaven: Conceptions of the Self in China," in Carrithers, Collins, and Lukes, eds., *Category of the Person*, 156–189.

13. Bush and Shih, *Early Texts*, 100–101. The essential study of *yipin* in early art remains that by Shimada Shujiro, translated by James Cahill: "Concerning the *I-p'in* style of Painting," pts. 1–3, *Oriental Art*, n.s. 7, (1961) 66–74; n.s. 8, (1962) 130–37; n.s. 10, (1964) 19–26. See also Susan E. Nelson, "*I-p'in* in Later Painting Criticism," in Bush and Murck, *Theories*, 397–424.

14. See two publications of 1985: Mark Elvin, "Between the Earth and Heaven," especially 174–86; and Munro, ed. *Individualism and Holism*.

15. See Wolfgang Bauer, "The Hidden Hero: Creation and Disintegration of the Ideal of Eremetism," in Munro, *Individualism and Holism*, 158.

16. Wm. Theodore de Bary, "Neo-Confucian Individualism and Holism," in Munro, ed., *Individualism and Holism*, 342.

17. See Bush, *The Chinese Literati*, 41, for a translation and discussion of this poem, and pp. 37–14 for an extended discussion of Su Shi and Wen Tong.

18. Ibid., p. 35.

19. In the section of *Tuhua jianwenzhi* in which Guo discusses Xie He's "six principles" and the fact that "rare works of the past were mainly those by talented worthies of high position or superior gentlemen in retirement." Translation in Bush and Shih, *Early Chinese Texts*, 95–96.

20. For Mi Youren, see Bush, *Chinese Literati on Painting*, 67–74; and, most importantly, the full-length study in a doctoral dissertation by Peter C. Sturman, "Mi

Youren and the Inherited Literati Tradition: Dirnensions of Ink-Play" (Yale University, 1989).

21. The basic significance of the absence of an external creator has been a sinological theme since F. W. Mote's *The Intellectual Foundations of China.* The issue of absolutes and language formation has been analyzed by Chad Hansen in his *Language and Logic in Ancient China,* an extremely important study.

22. This, of course, is not to say that there were not periodic efforts to leap over all the intervening interpretation. Indeed such *fugu,* "retum of/to antiquity," movements provided a distinctive larger shape to intellectual history. But they were also knowingly interpretation, valorized by a very different context from that attending both historical study and textual fundamentalism in the West.

23. I am relying extensively on the material that Susan Bush presents in *Chinese Literati on Painting* and to a considerable extent upon her analyses. Also very useful is Wen C. Fong, *Images of the Mind: Selections from the Edward L. Elliott Family and John B. Elliott Collections of Chinese Calligraphy at the Art Museum, Princeton University* (Princeton: The Art Museum, Princeton University, 1984), especially pp. 74-129. See also the excellent monograph by Lothar Ledderose, *Mi Fu and the Classical Tradition of Chinese Calligraphy* (Princeton: Princeton University Press, 1979).

24. Ronald Egan, "Ou-yang Hsiu and Su Shih on Calligraphy," *Harvard Journal of Asiatic Studies* 49 no. 2 (December 1989): 365-419.

25. Ibid., 394.

26. For example, ibid., 400.

27. Ibid., 418.

28. Ibid., 402.

29. This is distinct from the categorical *Yipin* eccentricity established in the Tang. We see now a possibility of categories actually dissolving under the force of individuality. Identity and individuality begin to coincide.

30. Quoted in *Chunzhu jiwen* (*Congshu jicheng,* no. 2717), 6:63. Su placed his view of an individual act of calligraphy in an ecological context. Elsewhere he writes that, "My writing is like a thousand-gallon spring that issues forth without choosing a particular site," and proceeds to describe it in terms of a river flowing across plains and twisting through mountains (Bush, *Chinese Literati,* 35). This echoes the phenomenon of *fengshui* discussed below, in a highly individualistic rejection of the individuality of the site in favor of the flux of the entire environment. There is a fascinating exploration of Su's highly distinctive sense of space in Andrew March, "Landscape in the Thought of Su Shi (1036-1101)" (Ph.D. diss., University of Washington, 1964). Egan's discussion of Su's concept of "lodging," *yu,* an acceptable form of temporary connection in contrast to the unacceptable permanence of "attachment," offers another view of this circumstance. The matter of "lodging" will be touched on below.

31. Su Shi, *Jizhu fenlei Dongpo xiansheng shi* 5.11.21b; cf. another translation and commentary in Bush, *Chinese Literati,* 35.

32. For example, most systematically, Manfred Porkert in *The Theoretical Foundations;* the larger horizons throughout Joseph Needham's magnum opus entitled *Science and Civilisation in China,* where the relationships between, for example, anatomy/physiology and geometry/algebra are thematically explored; and the pharmocological aspect by Paul Unschuld, in studies such as *Medicine in China: A History of Ideas* (Berkeley: University of California Press, 1985).

33. Porkert, *Theoretical Foundations,* 117-23.

34. Ibid., 136-40.

35. Ibid., 124-28.

36. Irene Bloom, "On the Matter of the Mind," 307. There is a great deal further on the topic in this very impressive study.

37. Donald Munro, "The Family Network, the Stream of Water, and the Plant: Picturing Persons in Song Confucianism," in Munro, ed., *Individualism and Holism,* 270-80. This study also has been of great use to me.

38. Chad Hansen, *Language and Logic in Ancient China* (Ann Arbor: University of Michigan Press, 1983), 31.

39. Some cultural aspects of a Neo-Confucian engagement with the more individually focussed self are the subject of Wm. Theodore de Bary, *The Liberal Tradition in China* (New York: Columbia University Press, 1983).

40. See Bush, *Chinese Literati,* 70-72.

41. This area remains almost totally unstudied in the Chinese field. For an extremely interesting exception, see Jonathan S. Hay, *Shitao's Late Work (1693-1707): A Thematic Map* (Ph.D. diss., Yale University, 1989), 291-343. This study is, more largely, the most thoughtful and thorough effort so far at analyzing the construction of selfhood in Chinese painting.

42. The psychoanalytic theories of Lacan might be helpful here. I am struck by Lacan's treatment of the phallus as a symbolic function, "the privileged signifier of that mark in which the role of the logos is joined with the advent of desire" (Jacques Lacan, *Ecrits: A Selection,* trans. A. Sheridan [New York: Norton, 1977], 287. Quoted in the discussion by Edward Casey and Melvin Woody, "Hegel, Heidegger, Lacan: The Dialectics of Desire," in Joseph Smith and William Kerrigan, eds., *Interpreting Lacan* [New Haven: Yale University Press, 1983] 83). Leaving aside the phallus for a moment, it is interesting to note how Lacan translates Freud's "energy discourse" of the unconscious into his view that "the unconscious is structured like a language" (Jacques Lacan, *The Four Fundamental Concepts of Psycho-Analysis,* trans. by Alan Sheridan), [New York: Norton, 1978], p. 20; see also Casey and Woody, "Hegel, Heidegger, Lacan"). Lacan's primacy of the signifier in the linguistically structured unconscious is a matter of much debate. Perhaps the Freud-Lacan debate may by analogy be helpful in analyzing the conjunction of a *qi-li* dialectic in China.

43. Lacan, *Ecrits,* 287; see Casey and Woody, "Hegel, Heidegger, Lacan," 83.

44. There is now a considerable amount of study of this question, but I would

note in particular Hong-key Yoon's Berkeley Ph.D. thesis published in 1976, "Geomantic Relationships Between Culture and Nature in Korea," and Steven Bennett's "Patterns of the Sky and Earth: A Chinese Science of Applied Cosmology," published in *Chinese Science* in 1978. "Sitting," as Bennett usefully terms it, was not a monolithic institution, of course. I am generalizing here around a central core, on the basis of an historically appropriate text.

45. Hong-key Yoon, "Geomantic Relationships," fig. 19.

46. For example by the late thirteenth-century scholar and painter Zheng Sixiao, in an essay of farewell to an investigator of *dili* (in *Zhengsuonan xiansheng wenji,* in *Congshujicheng* 7-28). See below.

47. Egan, "On Calligraphy," 403.

48. See above, n. 17.

49. Egan, "On Calligraphy," 403.

50. Irene Bloom, "On the Matter of the Mind," 314.

51. Extremely helpful in this connection is J. Baird Callicott and Roger T. Ames, eds., *Nature in Asian Traditions of Thought* (Albany: State University of New York Press, 1989).

52. Irene Bloom, "On the Matter of the Mind," 314.

53. Ibid., 316.

54. In Sherman E. Lee and Wai-kam Ho, *Chinese Art under the Mongols: The Yuan Dynasty, 1279-1368* (Cleveland: Cleveland Museum of Art, 1968), entry 236.

55. Zheng Sixiao, *Zheng Suonan xiansheng wenji* (in *Congshu jicheng,* no. 2406), p. 10.

56. See the discussion, with associated bibliography, in James Cahill, *Hills Beyond A River: Chinese Painting of the Yuan Dynasty, 1279-1368* (New York: Weatherhill, 1976).

57. See Hay, "Surface and the Chinese Painter: The Discovery of Surface," in *Archives of Asian Art* 38 (1985): 95-123; and "Poetic Space: Ch'ien Hsuan and the Association of Poetry and Painting," forthcoming in publication of *Words and Images: an international symposium on Chinese Poetry, Calligraphy and Painting,* based on the symposium held in 1985 at the Metropolitan Museum of Art, New York.

58. For a discussion of the Dong Yuan tradition and its relation to Huang Gongwang, see Richard M. Barnhart, *"Marriage of the Lord of the River": A Lost Landscape* by Tung Yuan. *Artibus Asiaee supplementum* 27 (Ascona), (1970); for reference to the specific points here, see Hay, "Surface."

59. I examined this aspect of the narrative in this painting in Hay, Huang Kungwang's "Dwelling in the Fu-ch'un Mountains": Dimensions of a Landscape (Ph.D. diss., Princeton University, 1978).

60. For a succinct and key address on the root of this circumstance, see Tu Weiming, "Inner Experience—The Basis of Creativity in Chinese Philosophy," in Christian Murck, ed., *Artists and Traditions: Uses of the Past in Chinese Culture* (Princeton: Princeton University Press, 1976).

61. I am aware that the simple statement, "this is the site," obscures a complicated circumstance. It is a descriptive and analytical statement that implies, in correlation, a conceptual schema and a semiotic and formal construction on the part of the artist. My thesis was, in some ways, an attempt to unpack this circumstance.

62. Zheng Sixiao, *Suonan xiansheng*, 15.

63. One may note a similar inclination in some other famous compositions of Huang's, especially *Clearing After Snow at Jiufeng* (Palace Museum, Beijing) and *The Great Peak of Fuchun* (Nanjing Museum).

4

Stylization and Invention
The Burden of Self-Expression in The Scholars

Martin W. Huang

Traditionally, the eighteenth-century Chinese novel *The Scholars* (*Rulin waishi;* a more literal translation would be "An Unofficial History of the Confucian Scholars") has been mainly interpreted as a novel exposing the seamy side of the suffocating civil-service examination system in late imperial China. This approach, however, has left largely unexplored the novel's subtler contemplations on the cultural dilemma of the Chinese literati (*wenren* 文人) and, especially, its various reenactments of their frustrated attempts to maintain a consistent and viable public identity in a period of rapid change. The issue of self-expression as presented in *The Scholars* is closely related to the identity crisis experienced by China's literati during that time. What further problematized their self-expression efforts was the prevalent sense of "burden": By the seventeenth and especially eighteenth centuries, all traditional avenues for self-expression were so conventionalized that they had become extremely burdensome. Consequently, the literati's anxiety over self-image often resulted in self-stylization, highly stylized attempts at self-invention through careful manipulations of various personae in order to project the desired versions of self.[1] What characterized their self-expression endeavors was their high consciousness of the fact that they had to "stage" their selves

*The author is grateful to David L. Rolston and Robert E. Hegel for their comments and suggestions regarding earlier drafts of this article.

in order to be seen as "unique." They believed or pretended to believe that they could fashion their identity but, at the same time, were frustrated with the extremely narrow range of choices.[2]

In this paper I propose to examine through examples taken from the novel *The Scholars* how the literati identity crisis and the burden of tradition forced many literati to resort to various forms of eccentricity and masquerading for self-stylization and self-invention, and how self-expression had become an increasingly problematic issue in eighteenth-century China.

The Crisis of *Wenren* Identity and the Burden of Self-Expression

At the end of the first chapter of *The Scholars* there is an ominous episode suggesting an impending crisis:

> Holding his cup in his left hand, Wang Mian pointed to the stars with his right [one], and said, "Look! The Chains [constellation] have invaded the Scholars [constellation]. That shows that scholars *[wenren]* of this generation have hard times ahead."
>
> As he spoke, a strange wind sprang up. It soughed through the trees, and made the waterfowl take wing, crying in alarm. . . . Soon the wind dropped, and when they looked again they saw about a hundred small stars in the sky, all falling towards the south-east horizon.
>
> "Heaven has taken pity on the scholars," said Wang Mian. "These stars have been sent down to maintain the literary tradition. But we shan't live to see it."[3]

Thus, at the beginning of the novel, the reader is already told that the main story of the novel will be about literati in crisis (*wenren you'e* 文人有厄). Indeed, many literati found themselves marginalized and alienated due to the important changes that were taking place in the Chinese society during the seventeenth and eighteenth centuries.

The origins of this crisis can be traced back to the mid-Ming period (early sixteenth century) when success in the civil service examinations, especially at provincial and national levels, became more and more difficult because of the rapid growth of population, spread of education, and intensified competition for elite status. Consequently, the traditional and almost sole avenue for social success for the literati, officialdom, never appeared to be so remote.[4] There was a separation beginning to emerge between *wenren* and *shidafu* (士大夫, scholar-bureaucrats), producing a marginalized class of *wenren* who were basically excluded from bureaucratic circles.[5] Those *wenren* could no longer depend on the *shidafu*'s traditional status and social role for their sense of public identity. Direct involvement in state politics could no longer be the immediate concern for many literati, who were becoming perforce "depoliticized." At the same time, by the late seventeenth and eighteenth centuries, the Confucian "sagehood as a goal of spiritual attainment had become almost as rare as had sainthood in the twentieth-century West."[6] Some literati began to question the validity of the Neo-Confucian practice of self-cultivation as an alternative to governmental service. Feeling disoriented, many of them found themselves in an "intellectual vacuum."

On the other hand, commercialization and the rise of the power of merchants seems to have redrawn the map of social classes to a considerable degree. There was a blurring of the traditional boundaries among the so-called *simin* (scholars, farmers, craftsman, and merchants).[7] In *The Scholars* there is an interesting passage that well illustrates the dilemma created by the conflict between the rising power of merchants and the reluctance (whether fake or sincere) of many *wenren* to yield to the pressure of this power:

> "Not long ago Mr. Fang from down river asked me to write a couplet for him — twenty-two characters altogether. When he sent a servant over with eighty taels to thank me, I called the fellow in. 'Go back and tell your master that a price was fixed for Mr. Jin's calligraphy in the prince's palace in Peking,' I said. 'Small characters cost a tael apiece, and big one ten taels. At this standard rate, these twenty-two characters are worth two hundred and twenty taels. You can't have them for a cent less!'"
>
> "After the men delivered this message, that swine Fang, to show that he had money, called in his sedan-chair to pay me two hundred and twenty taels. But when I gave him the scrolls, he simply t-t-tore them up! I flew into such a rage, I broke open his packets of silver and threw the money in the street for salt-carriers and dung-carters to pick up! I ask you, gentlemen, aren't scoundrels like that beneath contempt?" (*The Scholars* 28:306)

Indeed, the integrity of the image of a *wenren* was increasingly threatened as a result of the growing power of the merchant class and the rapid commercialization of culture.

All these factors noted above, among other things, contributed to the crisis in *wenren* identity. Symbolic of this identity crisis, *The Scholars* ends with the story of four eccentrics, each of whom excels at only one of the four arts (zither, chess, calligraphy, and painting), while all of them are supposed to be the essential accomplishments of a traditional literatus. The ideal *wenren* as represented in the character of Wang Mian at the beginning is disintegrated into the fragmented images of the four eccentrics at the end of the novel. They all try to live up to the traditional ideal of *wenren,* but the harsh reality often forces them into undesirable professions such as tailoring for a living.

This identity crisis gave rise to an urgent need among the literati for extra endeavor to fashion their selves and to reassert their public identity.[8] However, their efforts were complicated by the realization that all the traditional means of self-expression seemed to have lost their expressive edge; they were too conventional to be effective. What aggravated their sense of frustration at self-expression was the painful awareness that they had to be unique in a time when uniqueness was becoming increasingly difficult; there was a sense of what Wm. Theodore de Bary has called "the burden of culture" prevalent among the literati in seventeenth-century China:

> Yet they [the Song masters] may have done their work too well for the Ming. Who could compete with such masters? Individuals found the problem too staggering; its magnitude now required large cooperative effort such as was embodied in the massive Yung-lo Encyclopedia (1407). Printing and the dissemination of books, which made education more widely available, rendered mastery more difficult. . . . Indeed the Ming scholar was already confronted by the typical modern dilemma—how to keep up with the proliferation of literature.[9]

In the field of literature, the prevalence of this consciousness of "cultural burden" can be illustrated by the fact that in the late Ming there was an unprecedented flourishing of various poetic theories even though that age saw very few impressive poets, as if the creative imagination of the poets of that time had been overwhelmed by the weight of poetic achievements of previous ages. Lyric poetry seemed to have lost its viability as a major vehicle of literati self-expression. For example, in *The Scholars* Du Shengqing complains, not without justification, that the popular practice of forming poetry societies is "too vulgar a way of showing refinement" (*ya de zheyang su* 雅的這样俗; *Rulin,* 29:400; *The Scholars,* 29:321).

Probably the most eloquent testimonial to this late Ming consciousness of cultural burden is the development of painting during that time. The heated controversies over orthodoxy and unorthodoxy, which found their most articulate expression in the influential theories of Dong Qichang (1555–1636), demonstrate the paramount importance of the role played by the past in the artistic "career" of late Ming painters, no matter which category they fell into, "orthodox" or "individualist."[10] Commenting on the situation in seventeenth-century Chinese painting, James Cahill finds that the multiplication of schools and stylistic traditions made the painter's position extremely difficult during that time:

> The structure of significance that surrounded stylistic choices had become so heavy, in part through the increase in both volume and vehemence of theoretical arguments, that students of painting, must . . . have found it difficult to take up the brush . . . the rules of the game were becoming too cumbersome and confining. In painting a picture, the artist was not committing a simple creative act. . . . He was, in effect, espousing a cause, asserting his status, commenting on the history of art.[11]

It is this kind of pressure of tradition that made efforts at self-expression extremely difficult. Traditional means for self-expression seemed to have been exhausted while the power of tradition was still strong enough to hinder that consciousness of burden from translating into any concrete innovative efforts towards new means. Playing the game of self-expression within the limits of traditional rules, many in the seventeenth and eighteenth centuries took to eremitism, a very traditional mode of self-expression for the literati, only this time with more deliberate eccentricity. The result was often various dramatic gestures of self-stylization and, sometimes, even parodies (often unintentional) of traditional modes of self-expression. In a word, the deep identity crisis of *wenren* and the burden of cultural tradition outlined here, I believe, are the two important factors that created the dilemma of self-expression for the literati in eighteenth century China that is described so subtly in the novel *The Scholars*. Moreover, as we will see in the novel, the literati at that time appeared to be particularly preoccupied with their *public* images—what version of their selves to be presented to the eyes of the public. The "public" nature of their self-expression endeavor receives extra attention in the novel where role-playing becomes an important problematic issue. With this understanding we are in a better position to discuss in detail some related symptoms of this dilemma, such as eccentricity and masquerading as they are presented in the novel.

The Compulsion to Startle and the Necessity to be Eccentric

Historians have observed that there was a vogue of eccentricity among the literati in the seventeenth and eighteenth centuries. First we have what has been called *Kuang chan* (mad *ch'an* or what Julia Ching has termed as "mad ardour"), a phenomenon in philosophy that reached its apex during the late Ming.[12] This *Kuang chan* phenomenon, though usually attributed to a particular trend in contemporary thinking, was certainly associated with the general cultural atmosphere of that period. There was a cult of eccentricity popular among the literati.[13] Not only tolerated but celebrated, eccentricity became an important aspect of self-fashioning in a time when traditional methods of self-expression appeared to have lost their effectiveness. The Ming poet Zhang Xianyi (d. 1604) was said to have taken great pains to collect materials on all the eccentrics of previous ages and carefully classified them for emulation.[14] Another writer, Hua Shu (1589–1643), even compiled a special history of the eccentrics, *Pi dian xiaoshi* (A brief history of the eccentric and the crazy).[15] Almost all the giants of literati painting in the late Ming and early Qing such as Zhu Da (ca. 1626–1705?) and Dao Ji (Shi Tao, ca. 1642–1718) and even Chen Hongshou (1598–1652), were considered to be eccentric in one way or another.[16]

Entering the eighteenth century, the cult of eccentricity reached a new stage. If eccentricity in the seventeenth century still had its effect as a gesture of self-expression, then in the eighteenth century it could no longer "startle" people. It became something rather *expected,* or in James Cahill's words, it became "institutionalized" and "commercialized."[17] Again, the development of contemporary painting, especially the case of the group of painters commonly known as the "eight eccentrics of Yangzhou," can serve as a persuasive index to this aggravated sense of the burden of self-expression among the literati:

> it is not surprising that many painters, while they found themselves under some compulsion to display a marked originality and to create fresh and distinctive styles if they were to be noticed at all, found also it was not easy to do so. Such a situation can easily foster a forced originality, and sometimes did.[18]

To express one's self became synonymous with to startle. Under this compulsion to startle, there appeared some rather absurd twists:

A fastidious anti-commercialism had long been the orthodox attitude for the scholar-artist. Now the deviousness of the age made possible a curious reversal; selling one's paintings could be passed off as simply a new kind of eccentricity. Zheng Xie went so far as to post prices on his door, adding: "If you present cold, hard cash, then my heart swells with joy and everything I write or paint is excellent. . . . Honied talk of old friendship and past companions [are] only the autumn wind blowing past my ear.[19]

Economic necessity was here turned into a virtue of eccentricity, and self-conscious commercialism could be taken up as a desperate pose of self-aggrandizement. Even the grandson of the Kangxi Emperor, who would become known as the Qianlong Emperor (to rule China from 1736–96), wanted to be a part of that fashionable world of eccentrics. He had his portrait painted as a Taoist priest with his own colophon asking the question: "Who knows the true self of this man?" suggesting, according to Nelson Wu, that in another incarnation he might very well have been a Taoist immortal who never would have cared to soil his slippers by touching the human world. Wu further observes that this future emperor "can be classified as another partial eccentric who gained this status by partially renouncing certain privileges of a deity, and reluctantly serving as an emperor."[20] Eccentricity in eighteenth-century China, in Nelson Wu's words, "had been crowned and assassinated."[21] It even had its imperial sanction.

In *The Scholars,* eccentricity is an important avenue to the achievement of "fame" (*ming* 名) for many literati. At the very beginning of the novel, the narrator singles out "success, fame, riches and rank" (*gong ming fu gui* 功名 富貴) as four things that most literati desire from life. Reading through the novel, the reader will realize that it is first of all "fame" that most characters cannot tear themselves away from, even though a quite number of them are "virtuous" enough to get by without success (in the civil service examinations) and even without wealth. The most important thing for a literatus was to achieve fame and to make himself known—the essential aspect of self-expression in the literati tradition. To become a high official through climbing the ladder of the civil service examinations was of course the direct and traditional (also more tedious) way to acquire fame. However, since success in the examinations was becoming more and more difficult, how to make oneself known through other avenues grew to be a major concern among the Qing literati.[22] Recognition as a *mingshi* 名士 ("a well-known eccentric") is something that many characters in the novel fervently covet.[23] There is a revealing description of a conversation on the choice between officialdom and becoming a *mingshi* in chapter 17:

> "Gentlemen," said Jing, "when you choose officialdom, is it for the sake of fame? Or for the sake of profit?"
>
> "For fame," they answered.
>
> "Then you must realize that although Dr. Zhao has not become an official his poems are printed in dozens of anthologies and read all over the empire. Who hasn't heard the name of Zhao Xuezhai? In fact, he is probably much more famous than most scholars who have passed the metropolitan examination." Having said this, he roared with laughter.
>
> This was the first time Kuang Chaoren had heard such views expressed. (*The Scholar,* 17:198)

Basically, what is being argued here is that to be a famous poet might be a better way to achieve fame than officialdom. It is this rationale, so bluntly outlined here, that corrupts the innocent Kuang Chaoren and makes him embark on the pursuit of "fame."

There are many conventional ways to become a *mingshi* in the novel. Writing poetry, as suggested in the above example, is probably a shortcut. Even having a rare book on poetry republished under one's name can bring recognition as a *mingshi:*

> When his grandson heard that there was not another copy of this book in the world, he thought: "Why shouldn't I print some copies in my own name? That would win me fame."
>
> . . . henceforward Prefect Zhu's grandson was known throughout western Zhejiang as a brilliant young scholar *[shaonian mingshi]* . . . he gave his grandson lessons in versification and encouraged him to write occasional poems with other scholars *[mingshi].* (*The Scholars,* 8:94)

Of course, there are other, subtler strategies for self-aggrandizement. Du Shengqing's studied show of his outlandish attitudes toward sex is a good example of achieving fame via eccentricity. Although having great interest in taking concubines, Du Shengqing professes to be a misogynist:

> "You don't know me, Weixiao," said Du. "As our first emperor said: 'If not

for the fact that I was born of a woman, I would kill all the women in the world!' Have you ever met a woman you could respect? I assure you, they affect me so painfully, I can smell a woman three rooms away!" (*The Scholars*, 30:327)

Thus, to be a misogynist is to show that he is above those common souls who are vulnerable to the charms of women. Furthermore, even homosexuality, for Du Shengqing, could become a dramatic pose of self-stylization:

"Weixiao!" he said, and heaved a long sigh. "Since ancient times men have been slaves of love!"

"No love is greater than that between the sexes," replied Ji. "Yet you said just now you had no interest in women."

"And is love confined to that between men and women? No, the love of friends is stronger! Just look at the story of the Lord of E and his embroidered coverlet. And in all history I consider Emperor Ai of Han, who wanted to abdicate in favour of his friend, showed the truest understanding of love. Yao and Shun were no better than this, for all their polite deferring to others. But what a pity that no one understands this lofty love today!"

"True," rejoined Ji. "Have you never had a friend who really understands you?"

"If I could live and die with such a man, I would not be grieving and pining away like this! But I have not been lucky enough to find a true friend, and that is why I so often give way to melancholy!" (*The Scholars*, 30:327-28)

Du goes on to insist that the gay relationship he is seeking is different from what is in vogue among the romantic scholars at that time by, ironically, invoking the powerful idea of seeking "true understanding" (*zhiyin* 知音) from the literati tradition in order to "sanctify" his eccentricity.

A literatus, typically, more strongly feels the need for self-expression when he thinks that he is misunderstood or unappreciated by others. Self-expression has always been associated with the idea of seeking the understanding (*zhiyin*) in a person who can appreciate one's value and virtue.[24] Later Ji Weixiao pokes fun at Du Shengqing by pretending to introduce him to a "beautiful" Taoist priest in the Divine Pleasure Temple (a sarcastic name), who turns out to be nothing but an ugly dunce. A few days later when Ji Weixiao asks him about his encounter with this "beautiful priest," Du Shengqing's reaction is again interesting: "'You dog! You deserve a beating, but I'll let you off because your trick was *not too vulgar!*'" (*The Scholars*,

30:331; my italics). Here he is especially referring to Ji Weixiao's elaborate instructions to him as to how to introduce himself to that *zhiyin*. What is important is style, and a joke or even a trick is acceptable as long as it is played in style (*busu* 不俗 or "not too vulgar"). A Qing commentator on the novel points out with insight that what Du Shengqing is after is not "love" (whether heterosexual or homosexual) but "fame" (*Ruliln* 30:417). To engage in a gay affair or a sexual adventure, which was considered by ordinary people to be "eccentric" (*pi* 癖), was a part of the lifestyle of a romantic (*fengliu* 風流) *mingshi* during the time of the Ming-Qing period.[25]

The contrivance of Du Shengqing's self-stylization is best captured in chapter 29 in the symbolic picture of his walking in the sun chasing his own shadow (a picture of *guying zilian* or "feeling self-pity while looking at one's own shadow," as the Chinese saying goes):

> Then they climbed to the hill top, and gazed at the smoke from the thousands of houses in the city, the Yangzi River like a white silk girdle, and the golden glitter of the glazed pagoda. There was a pavilion at the top of the hill, and here Du strolled in the sun for a long time watching his shadow. (*The Scholars*, 29:322)

As Nanjing used to be the place where Six Dynasties' culture flourished, the scene here seems to have special implications. The period of Six Dynasties has often been considered to be a great age of self-expression, a time when a number of individualist poets wrote unforgettable works. What distinguishes literati self-expression in the eighteenth century from that in the Six Dynasties are, among other things, the high consciousness of "burden" and lack of "political authenticity" in the former (eccentricity was often a form of political dissent in the Six Dynasties). Strolling in the sun on a hilltop that overlooks the city of Nanjing, Du Shengqing is symbolically placed in the context of the tradition of the Six Dynasties. The reader is led to see where Du's self-stylization and self-invention stand in relation to that age when self-expression was not yet so problematic. While Du Shengqing is indulging in chasing his own shadow in the sun, there are two dung-carriers who are also enjoying the sunset from the hilltop. This provokes a bitter remark from Du Shengqing: "Now even cooks and porters have the kind of the Six-Dynasties sensitivity to scenery" (*Rulin*, 402; my translation). Indeed, although unconventional *mingshi* should be normally distinguishable from people of "vulgar taste," so many people were trying to be unconventional that unconventionality appeared to be rather conventional. (This might account for the strange fact that painting pictures for money, a practice previously detested among the literati painters, would suddenly become fashionable with "the eight eccentrics of Yangzhou" in the eighteenth century, as Cahill has observed.)

The presentation of Du Shengqing in *The Scholars* is apparently designed to be compared with that of another important character, his cousin, Du Shaoqing, who appears immediately after him in the novel. Unlike his cousin, as one of the novel's protagonists (if there are any in *The Scholars*), Du Shaoqing is presented as a positive character; moreover, the resemblance between this character and the author of the novel, Wu Jingzi (1701–54), is a known fact. He is praised by a character in the novel as "the eccentric one can rarely find in history since ancient times" (*Rulin,* 34:467). However, in this character the reader can still detect traces of anxiety over self-fashioning.

C. T. Hsia, for example, has found Du Shaoqing's excessive generosity and willingness to be cheated out of money to be a contrived effort at a certain style:

> With all his innate kindness, therefore, Du's militant generosity appears far more a gesture of aristocratic pride. . . . The petitioner has counted on his munificence, and he cannot therefore disappoint that expectation even though he has nothing but the greatest contempt for him. For the same reason, he disdains to look into the accounts of his steward, who regularly cheats him. *It is all a matter of style,* and prudential considerations for self-protection are not just Du's style.[26]

That is to say, Du Shaoqing's generous financial help to others is motivated by anxiety over his own image rather than by any concern for the actual needs of the recipients. His blind generosity has been described by other characters in the novel as *dai* 呆 (foolish). However, this *dai* (which is by no means "innocent") is the very image Du Shaoqing is after, because to be consciously *dai* is often considered an important part of the style of an eccentric.

The dramatic change in Du Shaoqing's attitudes towards Magistrate Wang is another telling illustration of his conscious endeavor to style his self-image. In chapter 31, an invitation from Magistrate Wang upsets him so much that the reader begins to think that his reputation as *mingshi* must be at stake. His explanation for his outright refusal of the invitation is apparently overstated:

> "I must leave it to you, Third Brother, to call on magistrates and pay your respects as a student," replied Du. "Why, in my father's time—to say nothing

of my grandfather's and great-grandfather's—heaven knows how many magistrates came here! If he really respects me, why doesn't he call on me first? Why should I call on him? I'm sorry I passed the district examination, since it means I have to address the local magistrate as my patron! As for this Magistrate Wang, who crawled out of some dust-heap to pass the metropolitan examination—I wouldn't even want him as my student!" (*The Scholars,* 31:346)

However, when later Du learns that Magistrate Wang has been deprived of his official post and is soon to be driven out of his official residence, to Wang's surprise, he offers him lodging in his own house apparently just in order to demonstrate his gallantry:

"As for Mr. Wang, it's lucky for him he knew enough to respect me. To have called on him the other day would have been making up to the local magistrate; but now that he's been removed from office and has nowhere to live, it's my duty to help him." (*The Scholars,* 32:355)

It is the style rather than any specific act or attribute that those *mingshi* are seeking after. The idea of style is a concern of the literati to such a degree that one's personality is often described with the jargon of a style analyst: "Dr. Yu valued Zhuang's *casual tranquility,* while Zhuang admired the doctor's *natural elegance.* They soon became lifelong friends" (*Rulin,* 36: 497; my translation and emphasis). The two terms, *tianshi* 恬適 (casual tranquility) and *hunya* 渾雅 (natural elegance), used here to record the two people's impressions of one another are the sort of expressions a literary critic would use to describe the specific poetic style of a writer. Much of the self-conscious unconventionality exhibited in the behavior of these eccentrics is designed to help them achieve a particular style as suggested by such abstract terms as *tianshi* and *hunya.* Self-expression had become simply a matter of style.

The Publicized Self: Masquerading as Self-Invention

There is a paradox inherent in the enterprise of self-expression, which is first of all a public-oriented act, an effort to publicize one's private self. To express one's self one has to comply with the codes of public communication and even sometimes appeal to the authority of cultural institutions. Acquiring fame through conventional and well-trodden avenues (such as becoming a poet of reputation or an eccentric hermit) is a good example of self-expression being turned into self cancellation.[27] To be an eccentric, when eccentricity has already become a part of well-established social practices, is also an act of self-cancellation, a submission to the authority of cultural institutions.

Eremitism, the refusal to enter into or withdrawal from governmental service, is cherished by many characters in the novel as an assertion of their independent selves. Du Shaoqing would even go as far as faking illness in order to avoid the fate of being "drafted" as an official. However, the reader also finds that eremitism had been a part of the convention of self-fashioning for so long that it had become institutionalized, a mere dramatic gesture orchestrated to catch public attention.[28]

An interesting case of how eremitism intended as an act of self-expression ends up as self-cancellation in *The Scholars* is Zhuang Shaoguang. When invited to offer advice to the emperor, adhering to his eremitic principles, Zhuang tries as hard as he can to resist the offer of public service. When later he is "released," it seems that he succeeds in maintaining his integrity as a hermit. However, the life style of a hermit is so widely admired that even the emperor is anxious to show his appreciation. As if the emperor wishes to see that Zhuang lead a more authentic eremitic life, he grants Zhuang a lake (which has a secluded island in the middle of it) as an imperial gift. Now the hermit has the imperial sanction to lead the more authentic life of a recluse. Eremitism thus becomes imperially sponsored; its usual function as an assertion of the individual self in rejection of the normal social hierarchy is thereby co-opted by the power structure of the society.

Zhuang's self-fashioning efforts through eremitism are further subverted after he moves to the island. The narrator gives us a rather detailed description of this ideal "Peach Blossom Stream," specially emphasizing its seclusion: "A boat was moored at his gate, and to visit any of the other islands he had simply to ferry across; but without this boat, not a soul could reach him" (*The Scholars,* 35:393). However, the moment Zhuang Shaoguang begins to boast of the privacy that the island seems to offer: "We are completely cut off from the world here. . . . Although this is not Peach Blossom Stream, it comes very close to it" (35: 393-94), the island is surrounded by governmental troops, because the guest to whom Zhuang is boasting turns out to be a fugitive. In order to save face, to save the guest, and to be able to continue his own "private" life as a hermit, Zhuang Shaoguang, again, has to come out to the "public" to intervene by pulling strings in the official world, thus seriously compromising his image of hermit. Zhuang's private world of a hermit, built upon the emperor's favor (the ultimate symbol of public incorporation), is inauthentic at its very core.

The reader of *The Scholars* is likely to be impressed with the power of the "public" as it is represented in the novel. No aspect of a character's private life can avoid being "publicized" and being interpreted according to the framework of public implications. The publicity (the public outrage as well as public admiration) surrounding Du Shaoqing's drunken stroll arm in arm with his wife in the Yao Garden is a good example. This private family outing becomes a very important public event among the literati. Those romantically inclined admire its "unconventionality," while the conservative condemn its "dissoluteness." It is the public impact that concerns most people.

Even the ideal hermit Wang Mian at the beginning of the novel, probably the most "private" character in the novel, is sometimes shown to be bothered by concern for the public. Despite his staunch refusal of direct involvement in public affairs, anxiety over the fate of the state is always present in his mind, betraying the Confucian self beneath his apparent Taoist apathy. Wang Mian's role model Qu Yuan (ca. 340–278 B.C.) is certainly a historical figure very much concerned with public affairs.[29] Indeed, the plot structure of the novel itself also seems to be specially designed to keep the reader constantly conscious of the overwhelming power of the "public." The unfolding of the novel's plot is punctuated with literati gatherings, all public events in chapters 12, 18, 30 and 37. Of course, the most important one is the grand ceremony held to commemorate Taibo in chapter 37. Given the importance of the idea of ritual in the novel,[30] the public role of a literatus is certainly one of the author's most central thematic concerns.

Furthermore, the narrator seems to be reluctant to go deep into the private life of the characters. Throughout the novel, the narrator never dwells on one character long enough to allow the reader to forget that this character is merely one member of a large community of many others: his or her existence can become meaningful only when it is interpreted in the "public" context of the community of the whole novel. Thus, *The Scholars* can be regarded as a history of "public" self in Ming-Qing China. The narrative power of the novel seems to come partly from this "communal" strategy. To a certain extent, it is because of the high consciousness of this power of the "public" that many characters in the novel turn to ingenious manipulations of public personae for self-invention. There are many instances of *maoming* 冒名 (masquerade and imposture) in *The Scholars*.

To appropriate a ready-made persona is certainly the easiest way to create a desired public image for oneself. In chapter 20, before dying in a temple, Niu Buyi entrusts two volumes of his poems to the monk and asks him to look for opportunity to have them published—not because he thinks highly of the merits of his own poems, but because these poems are written in exchange with high officials, as carefully indicated in the titles of the poems (*The Scholars,* 20:228). A posthumous publication would insure that he be remembered by posterity mainly as someone who had access to the circle of power. The public image he wishes to leave behind is that of a *mingshi* whose identity depends almost solely on its connections with those big names. It is largely due to the possibilities of "social privileges" (such as fame and access to a higher society) exemplified in these poems that later the young man Niu Pulang conceives the ingenious ruse of assuming the identity of the dead Niu Buyi as a shortcut to "invent" his own public self:

> He also noticed such titles as "To Prime Minister So-and-so," "Thinking of Examiner Zhou". . . .
>
> "These are all titles of present-day officials," thought Niu Pulang. "Apparently a man who can write poems doesn't have to pass the examinations in order to make friends with great officials. This is wonderful!"
>
> Then it occurred to him: "This man's name is Niu and so is mine; and he has only written a pen-name Niu Buyi on these volumes without putting down his real name. Why shouldn't I add my name to his? I will have two seals made and stamp these books with them: then these poems will become mine and from now on I shall call myself Niu Buyi." (*The Scholar,* 21:232–33)

Thus Niu Pulang takes on the identity of the dead Niu Buyi and begins a series of misadventures. The poetic reputation of this "persona" does bring him opportunities to rub elbows with officials who would otherwise never suffer his presence. But they also cause him many unnecessary embarrassments; with this new identity, he is able to commit the crime of bigamy without being punished. Here, an important traditional vehicle of self-expression for the literati, poetry writing, literally becomes a convenient means of self-invention and imposture.

Even the identities of the living can be appropriated for various exploitations. In chapter 9, the imposture of the family of a high official by some boat people is merely intended to insure a privileged route on the river and to allow them to put on airs before others. In chapter 49, a licentiate masquerades as a Patent Office secretary for the simple purpose of making a living: "Because I couldn't make a living at home I started drifting from place to place. If I said I was a licentiate, I should have had to go hungry; but when I said I was in the Patent Office, the merchants and local gentry were willing to help me" (*The Scholars*, 50: 550). Interestingly enough, his deceit is exposed just at the moment when the impostor and his deceived friends are beginning to watch a play:

> The actor in Hong Niang's role came swaying in. . . .
> Hong Niang had just begun singing, when gongs were heard at the gate and guards in red and black caps marched shouting into the hall.
> The guests were puzzled.
> "This is a new way of performing this scene!" they thought.
> Then a steward came rushing over, speechless with horror. And in came an official in gauze cap, jade-coloured gown, and black shoes with white soles. He was followed by two dozen constables. The two foremost strode up to Wan and arrested him, then fastened an iron chain round his neck and proceeded to lead him away. (*The Scholars*, 49:544)

Here masquerading in real life and role playing in drama are juxtaposed, with the distinction between the two becoming not so easy to discern. The description of the dress of the police officer (as if he were in costume) seems to be designed to enhance the illusion that he is also playing a role in the play. No wonder the audience would think "[t]his is a new way of performing this scene." The whole incident is narrated as if it were an episode from some melodrama, which adds to the sense of theatricality that permeates this chapter; here everyone is shown to be playing a role, and in the following chapter the reader will see how the role of knight-errant is played out.

The confusion of role playing in life and in drama emphasized here reminds the reader of the grand performing contest of actors or female impersonators sponsored and conducted by Du Shengqing and Ji Weixiao in chapter 30 (here impersonation certainly assumes added implications). This is not only a contest staged for grading the looks and talents of the actors or female impersonators, but, more importantly, it is a carefully choreographed exhibition of the fine taste of its sponsors. The reader should not overlook the symbolic parallel relation between the sponsors' "performance" off the stage and that of the actors on the stage. For Du Shengqing it is the success of his own "performance" in staging the performance contest that is important: "News of this [contest] travelled from West Water Gate to Huaiqing

Bridge, and the fame of the seventeenth Mr. Du spread throughout the Yangzi Valley" (*The Scholars*, 30:335). Here role-playing in drama is again juxtaposed with that in real life, and everything is, in one way or another, related to "show" business.

Imposture and masquerading, which must have as precondition the concealment of one's true self (which, in a way, like eremitism, is a self-cancellation) and public belief in the assumed identity, can serve as a useful metaphor for the predicament of self-expressive attempts on the part of the literati in the novel. The self reached through the expressing (publicizing) process often turns out to be an invented self, a self that is fabricated for the sake of sheer publicity.

As we have observed above, lyric poetry has been one of the most important literary means of self-expression for traditional Chinese literati. Probably the most subtle reference to the poetic tradition of self-expression and its ultimate dilemma is in chapter 54. There two self-styled eccentrics (both live as fortune-tellers) are arguing over the trivial question if any poems have been written during a gathering of *mingshi* at Oriole-Throat Lake, itself an affected show of self-stylization described with great irony in chapter 12; the two are accusing each other of assuming the air of a *mingshi*. Significantly, one of them is styled (*hao* 號) as Siruan (思阮) and the other is named Ding Yanzhi. The meaning of "Siruan" is rather obvious judging from the frequently-suggested relationship between many *mingshi* in the novel and their Six Dynasties models: here "Siruan" can literally mean "to think of Ruan Ji," the famous individualist poet of the Six Dynasties. The name of the second one has of more subtle implications. His first name *yanzhi* (言志), in fact, means "to express one's heart's intent" as formulated in the locus classicus in *The Book of Documents*—"poetry expresses the heart's intent" (*shi yanzhi* 詩言 志), the most famous dictum in that long poetic tradition of self-expression in traditional China. What makes this symbolic play more ironic is his last name *ding* (丁), which is homophonic with the word in spoken Chinese meaning "most" (頂) and "substitute" (probably also "masquerade," as in the case of *dingti* 頂替). Thus, with a playful combination of the literary and the colloquial, his full name, quite contrary to what he apparently is, may mean something like "the most successful at poetic self-expression"; or very appropriately, it may suggest the meaning of "a replacement of poetic self-expression." Later this Ding Yanzhi, with little money in pocket, has the audacity to go to a fancy brothel in order to discuss poetry with a courtesan, and, as the reader might expect, he is immediately kicked out. (Of course, to discuss poetry with courtesan is also part of the conventional style of a *mingshi* at that time.) Here, by virtue of this comic but profoundly symbolic episode, the poetic tradition of self-expression is placed in a very ironic perspective. It should also be noted that though there are many occasions where writing poetry is discussed among the characters, the author seems to be very reluctant to quote poems in the novel, a reluctance rare among traditional Chinese novelists. This fact may betray Wu Jingzi's own increasing doubts about the validity of poetry as an effective means for self-expression, although Wu himself was considered to be a very competent poet.[31]

Conclusion: the Predicament of Self-Expression

Scholars of Chinese intellectual history tend to see a great discontinuity between the late Ming and the Qing. They find the fascination with self and various radical nonconformist phenomena prevalent in the late Ming disappearing rapidly with the fall of the Ming dynasty. The late Ming has often been characterized with words such as "diversity," "metaphysical," and "liberal," while "uniformity," "empirical," and "conservative" are used to describe the Qing. Or in Jonathan Spence's words, it is "fragmentation" versus "reintegration."[32]

As far as the development of the Qing novel is concerned, there indeed appeared a "conservative" trend in the form of increasing didacticism and of more emphasis on moral retribution.[33] On the other hand, in novels such as *The Scholars* and *The Dream of the Red Chamber* (*Hunglou meng*, also known in English translation as *The Story of the Stone*) we find a surprising development in the growth of an autobiographical tendency, along with an increasing concern with self-expression. In other words, compared with Ming novels, the distance between the creator (author) and the created (characters) in some of the Qing novels is greatly shortened. Pei-yi Wu, in a recent study of traditional Chinese autobiography, observes that the golden age of autobiographical writing in traditional China started around 1565 and ended by 1680;[34] but he also finds that the autobiographical sensitivity manifested in the late Ming autobiography, though no longer welcome in "self-written biography" in later ages, found its full expression in the novels such as *The Dream of the Red Chamber*. Indeed, by the time of the mid-Qing, self-expression as a theme in philosophy and in the traditional genres such as poetry and "self-written biography" seems to have suffered a setback, while some of the novels were becoming more "self-expressive." That is to say, in the eighteenth century the "autobiographical sensitivity," which was supposed to be found in "self-written biography" in the late Ming, "migrated" instead into the novel.[35]

However, self-expression in novels such as *The Scholars* and *The Dream of the Red Chamber* is quite different from that in lyric poetry and other conventional genres of previous ages. In these novels, the world of the self is always framed in a larger context of intersubjectivity; effective self-expression is never taken for granted, as it had almost always been in the works by the individualist poets of the Six Dynasties. The reader feels that the autonomous private world of the self, no matter how much admired and cherished in these novels, is often presented as vulnerable and even illusive (in this respect, the Grand View Garden in *The Dream of the Red Chamber* and, to a lesser degree, Zhuang Shaoguang's garden on the island are two paradigmatic symbols). The lyrical autonomy of the self is always contextualized as well as problematized in these novels. Moreover, it is the urgent need on the part of the novelists, such as Wu Jingzi, for self-expression and their simultaneous awareness of the increasing impossibility of authentic expression that make novels like *The Scholars* and *The Dream of the Red Chamber* so compelling. Paradoxically, *The Scholars* is often most "expressive" when it succeeds in exposing the futility of various attempts at self-stylization and in demonstrating the ultimate impossibility of genuine self-expression. In other words, one important aspect of the novel's success lies in its persuasive demonstration of how problematic self-expression is already becoming. Interpreted from this perspective, the predicament of self-expression as shown in *The Scholars* can be seen as the predicament of traditional Chinese culture in general, which had already reached its final stage in the Qing. The "language" that tradition-burdened culture provides, such as "eremitism" and "eccentricity," after being in "currency" for so long, could no longer be used effectively for self-expression. For those literati, self-expression already became a tremendous burden in the twilight of traditional Chinese culture.

Notes

1. A ready example of self-invention through manipulation of personae in literary writing is probably the famous seventeenth-century writer Li Yu (1610–79?). See Patrick Hanan, *The Invention of Li Yu* (Cambridge: Harvard University Press, 1988).

2. In his *Renaissance Self-Fashioning from More to Shakespeare* (Chicago: University of Chicago Press, 1980), Stephen Greenblatt (p. 3) observes that in sixteenth-century England "there appears to be an increased self-consciousness about the fashioning of human identity as a manipulatable, artful process." However, his detailed analyses demonstrate that this belief in one's power to fashion one's own self is an illusion. As we will see later, certain of his observations about self-fashioning in sixteenth-century England are relevant to the discussion of self-expression in the present study.

3. *The Scholars,* trans. Hsien-yi Yang and Gladys Yang (Beijing: Foreign Languages Press, 1957), 13. All the quotations from the novel will be from this edition, with chapter and page numbers given in parenthesis. For the sake of consistency, when quoted in this paper the transliterations of all characters' names are changed from the Wade-Giles system to that of pinyin. For the original Chinese version, see Li Hanqiu, ed., *Rulin waishi huijiao huiping ben* (Shanghai: Shanghai guji, 1984), 15, hereafter referred to as *"Rulin."* Chapter and page numbers will be noted in parenthesis.

4. Ping-ti Ho has observed: "The enhanced chances for commoners to acquire the first degree did not mean that it was easier for them to reach the final goal in social mobility. On the contrary, the inflated number of *sheng-yüan* resulted in a glut at higher level examinations and engendered an increasing amount of social frustration." See his *The Ladder of Success in Imperial China: Aspects of Social Mobility, 1368–1911* (New York: Columbia University Press, 1962), 182. See also Robert E. Hegel, *The Novel in Seventeenth-Century China* (New York: Columbia University Press, 1981), 14–15, and Paul S. Ropp, *Dissent in Early Modern China: "Ju-lin wai-shih" and Ch'ing Social Criticism* (Ann Arbor: University of Michigan Press, 1981), 22–23. Both Hegel and Ropp consider the surplus of *shengyuan* degree holders to be one of the main reasons behind the rise of social criticism in the Ming-Qing period. Furthermore, according to Ho (*Ladder of Success,* 189–90), this surplus situation, due to the new quota system, became even more serious in the Qing. For a more detailed discussion of this literati identity crisis, see my *Literati and Self-Re/Presentation: Autobiographical Sensibilities in the Eighteenth-Century Chinese Novel* (Stanford, Calif.: Stanford University Press, 1995), 26–44.

5. In the Tang (618–907) and the Song (960–1279) dynasties, the distinction between *wenren* and *shidafu* was not very significant, because most *wenren* were in one way or another admitted into the official world and many of them were actually members of the *shidafu* class. This began to change in the Yuan dynasty (1271–1368), when the Mongolian rulers ranked *wenren* almost at the bottom of the scale of social classes and restricted their role in politics. Although beginning from the Ming dynasty (1368–1644) the social position of *wenren* improved drastically, the intensified competition in the civil service examinations still kept most of them out of officialdom. According to Yoshikawa Kōirō, it is during the Yuan dynasty that the word *wenren* was first used to describe those literati who were not bureaucrat-officials and who

devoted themselves to literature and art while often showing a greater or lesser degree of eccentricity or deviation from accepted norms. See his *Five Hundred Years of Chinese Poetry*, 1150-1650, trans. John Timothy Wixted (Princeton: Princeton University Press, 1989), 84-85; and my *Literati and Self-Re/Presentation*, 29-33.

6. Wm. Theodore de Bary, "Neo-Confucian Cultivation and the Seventeenth-century 'Enlightenment,'" in Wm. Theodore de Bary et al. ed., *The Unfolding of Neo-Confucianism* (New York: Columbia University Press, 1975), 204. See also Ropp, *Dissent*, 47.

7. See Ho, *Ladder of Success*, p. 256 and Yü Ying-shih, *Shi yu Zhongguo wenhua* (Literati and Chinese culture) (Shanghai: Shanghai renmin, 1987), 525-53. For discussions of the relationship between merchants and literati during the mid-Qing, see Vicki Frances Weinstein, "Painting in Yang-chou, 1710-1765: Eccentricity or the Literati Tradition?" (Ph.D. diss., Cornell University, 1972), pt. 1, pp. 4-148.

8. Greenblatt notes (*Renaissance Self-Fashioning*, 3) that "self-fashioning always involves some experience of threat, some effacement or undermining, some loss of self."

9. Wm. Theodore de Bary, introduction to *Self and Society in Ming Thought*, ed. Wm. Theodore de Bary (New York: Columbia University Press, 1970), 9.

10. See Wai-kam Ho, "Tung Ch'i-ch'ang's New Orthodoxy and the Southern School Theory," in ed. Christian F. Murck et al., *Artists and Traditions: Uses of the Past in Chinese Culture*, (Princeton: Princeton University Press, 1976), 113-29.

11. James Cahill, *The Compelling Image: Nature and Style in Seventeenth-Century Chinese Painting* (Cambridge: Harvard University Press, 1979), 185.

12. Julia Ching, "Wang Yang-ming: A Study in Mad Ardour," in *Papers on Far Eastern History* (Canberra: Australian National University, 1971), 91; quoted in Wm. Theodore de Bary's introduction to *The Unfolding of Neo-Confucianism*, 28.

13. Note de Bary's caution (*The Unfolding of Neo-Confucianism*, 28): "Nor is this 'mad ardour' to be confused with the eccentricity. . . . For Neo-Confucians it signified neither world renunciation nor idiosyncrasy, and stood far from either the self-indulgence of many Wei-Chin hedonists or the weird habits of Taoist 'immortals' . . . this was the independence and uncompromising spirit of men totally dedicated to the service of mankind, and mad, like Wang Yang-ming, only because the depth of their human concern set them at odds with a complacent society." While de Bary's caution is appropriate, the cult of eccentricity and development of "mad ardor" are certainly related phenomena, at least in the sense that both are the outcome of the anxiety over being unique and independent under the enormous pressure of the "past."

14. Qian Qianyi (1582-1664), *Liechao shiji xiaozhuan* (Short biographies of the Ming poets) (Beijing: Zhonghua shuju, 1959), 453.

15. Chen Wanyi, *WanMing xiaopinwen yu Mingji wenren shenghuo* (The informal essay and the life of the literati in the late Ming) (Taipei: Da'an, 1988), 81.

16. See James Cahill, *Fantastics and Eccentrics in Chinese Painting* (New York: Asia Society, 1967); see also Judith Zeitlin, *Historian of the Strange: Pu Songling and the*

Chinese Classical Tale (Stanford, Calif.: Stanford University Press, 1993), 61–97, for a discussion of the so-called "obsession with the strange" during that period.

17. Cahill, *Fantastics and Eccentrics in Chinese Painting*, 90. See also his *Chinese Painting* (New York: Rizzoli, 1977), 188.

18. Cahill, *Fantastics and Eccentrics in Chinese Painting*, 90.

19. Ibid., 96. In her study of "the eight eccentric painters of Yangzhou," Weinstein ("Painting in Yang-chou," pp. 305-11) believes that the eccentricity exhibited in those literati painters stemmed from their frustrations at being unable to live up to the traditional ideal of *wenren* and that it is a result of the gap between "ideal" and "reality."

20. Nelson I. Wu, "The Toleration of Eccentrics," *Art News* 56 (1957): 53.

21. Ibid., 54.

22. Interestingly enough, the word *ming* ("fame" or "famous") appears in the couplet titles of the eight chapters of the novel (chapters 1, 12, 18, 21, 34, 36, 50, and 54). The question whether the novel was originally fifty or fifty-five or fifty-six chapters is still an unresolved issue. I will adopt here the assumption that the novel is fifty-five chapters long, though this problem does not directly affect my basic arguments here.

23. Zheng Xie (Zheng Banqiao, 1693-1765), the most famous member of "the eight eccentrics of Yangzhou," once complained that the image of *mingshi* had been "contaminated" and that there were too many people who wanted to be *mingshi* ("the streets are full of *mingshi*"). See *Zheng Banqiao ji* (The works of Zheng Banqiao) (Beijing: Zhonghua shuju, 1962), 25. Here I am adopting Ropp's (*Dissent*, p. 77) translation of *mingshi*, though it may not be the most accurate translation of this term, for which there is no exact English equivalent. Yang Hsien-yi and Gladys Yang, throughout their translation of the novel, render *mingshi* as "well-known scholars." This translation, however, is too vague and too general. Strictly speaking, not all *mingshi* are eccentrics, though they are usually those scholars whose lifestyle has a "bohemian" touch. But what seems to be a characteristic shared by all of them is their high consciousness of self-image. For some information on the earlier history of the concept of *mingshi*, see Qian Zhongshu, *Guanzhui bian* (Beijing: Zhonghua shuju, 1979), 283-85.

24. For a survey of the early development of the idea of *zhiyin* in Chinese history, see Eric Henry, "The Motif of Recognition in Early China." *Harvard Journal of Asiatic Studies* 47 (1987), 5-30.

25. As to the complex issue why there was such a vogue for homosexuality during that time, as far as I know, there have been no convincing interpretations offered yet. However, many of those model *mingshi* in the Six Dynasties (approximately from the third to sixth centuries), whom the Ming-Qing eccentrics tried to imitate, were said to have been homosexuals, such as Ruan Ji (210–63) and Ji Kang (223–62). See Fang-fu Ruan and Yung-mei Tsai, "Male Homosexuality in Traditional Chinese Lit-

erature," *Journal of Homosexuality* 14 (1987): 24; see also Bret Hinsch, *Passions of the Cult Sleeve: The Male Homosexual Traditional China* (Berkeley: University of California Press, 1990).

26. C. T. Hsia, *The Classic Chinese Novel: A Critical Introduction* (New York: Columbia University Press, 1968), 234; my emphasis. I also discuss this aspect of Du Shaoqing from a slightly different perspective in my *Literati and Self-Re/Presentation*, 56-65.

27. Here again Greenblatt's observation on self-fashioning is helpful: self-fashioning "involves submission to an absolute power or authority situated at least partially outside the self" and "any achieved identity always contains within itself the signs of its own subversion or loss" (*Renaissance Self-Fashioning*, 3). In his discussions of six sixteenth-century English writers, Greenblatt details the interplay between self-fashioning and self-cancellation by showing how their self-fashioning had to rely on the cultural institutions (the self's tendency to identify with its culture at the very moment of its apparent resistance). The conclusion suggested by Greenblatt's study (p. 257) seems to be that the self's power to shape an identity is defined precisely by its "captivity" to the authority of various cultural institutions from which the self tries to fashion itself away. However, he confesses in his epilogue, "I want to bear witness at the close to my overwhelming need to sustain the illusion that I am the principal maker of my own identity."

28. Of course, eremitism as an act of self-expression is plagued by its own paradox: here self-expression depends on self-cancellation for success. However, once people begin to suspect that a hermit's self-cancellation (the concealment of his self) is aimed at self-expression, his self-cancellation becomes "consummated." In other words, eremitism is self-expressive only when it is not intended to be so (it should, at least, appear like this to the public). Thus, the moment eremitism becomes an accepted gesture of self-expression, its real value for self-expression is already invalidated and it becomes instead an act of "actual" self-cancellation.

29. For a study of Qu Yuan and his important role in Chinese intellectual history, see Laurence A. Schneider, *A Madman of Ch'u: The Chinese Myth of Loyalty and Dissent* (Berkeley: University of California Press, 1980).

30. For a discussion of the function of ritual in the novel, see Shuen-fu Lin, "Ritual and Narrative Structure in Ju-lin Wai-shih," in A. H. Plaks, ed., *Chinese Narrative: Critical and Theoretical Essays* (Princeton: Princeton University Press, 1977), 244-65.

31. However, despite his increasing doubt and reluctance, Wu Jingzi cannot resist the temptation of using poetry at the end of the novel, when he gives up the persona of a distant narrator and speaks directly to the reader. This testifies to the dilemma many characters in the novel are facing—the limited choices of available means of self-expression (there are only two complete poems quoted in the whole novel). For discussions of the function of verse or the lack of verse in *The Scholars* and its significance in the development of the traditional Chinese novel, see David Rolston,

"Theory and Practice: Fiction, Fiction Criticism, and the Writing of the *Ju-lin Wai-shih*," (Ph.D. diss., University of Chicago, 1988), 841–80; and my "Dilemma of Chinese Lyricism and the Qing Literati Novel" (Ph.D. diss., Washington University, 1991), 120–35.

32. Jonathan Spence, "The Wan-li Period vs. the K'ang-hsi Period: Fragmentation vs. Reintegration?" in *Artists and Traditions: Uses of the Past in Chinese Painting*, 145–48. Of course, Spence is referring to the political aspects of the two periods. However, some scholars began to view the Ming-Qing transition from different perspectives and emphasize the continuity between the two periods; see, for instance, some of the essays in *The Unfolding of Neo-Confucianism*.

33. In novels such as *Xingshi yinyuan zhuan* (A marriage that awakens the world) and *Qilu deng* (Warning light at the crossroads).

34. Pei-yi Wu, *The Confucian's Progress: Autobiographical Writings in Traditional China* (Princeton: Princeton University Press, 1989), xii.

35. Ibid., 236 n. 2. Wu uses the term "self-written biography" to refer to those "autobiographical writings" that are autobiographical in the sense they were written by the "subjects" of the biographies themselves but that lack true "autobiographical sensitivity" or introspective dimension. For discussions of why the "migration of autobiographical sensibility" took place at that particular historical juncture and how it gave rise to certain unique features of some of the eighteenth-century autobiographical novels (including *The Scholars*), the reader is referred to my *Literati and Self-Re/Presentation*.

5

Unseen Lives

*The Emotions of Everyday Existence Mirrored in Chinese Popular
Poetry of the Mid-Seventeenth to the Mid-Nineteenth Century*

Mark Elvin

Astronomers currently believe that most of the matter in the universe is
invisible, that only a small part of it shines as stars. The presence of this
unperceived mass has to be deduced indirectly, mainly from anomalous gravi-
tational effects. It is the same for the lives of the common people in China
before modern times. Unlike the elite, they have almost no one to speak for
them. They are easy to forget. Yet the massiveness of their presence bends
every line that runs through the social space-time of the Chinese universe.
Everything that happens is influenced by their unseen and unheard presence.
If we are not to have a pervasively false impression of China, and Chinese
emotions, we have to find some way of giving them a voice.

There is a poem from the Qing dynasty, *Spring Snow,* by Shen Harn-
guang,[1] that speaks of this division that separates the life and the perceptions
of life of those who live in the cities and those who live in the countryside,
the gulf between those who are fed and those who are not. Formally, it is set
in Tarng times; but this poetic conceit should not be allowed to obscure the
fact that the feelings expressed are those of the later imperial era:

Last night the north wind blew. Through the trees and undergrowth.
Then snowflakes fat as a man's palm came flying in the morning.

113

The old plum in the south yard froze. Its flowers will never open.
Our hungry crows are pecking at the moss-scraps that have fallen.

It's cold in the broken-down homestead, with no meal even by noon-time.
Snuggled in quilts we face the snow, and give long, useless, sighs.
Last year the rain fell again and again. It rotted our wheat till it died.
And ice-melt caused the gushing floods through the village's crooked wynds.

Wells are dry in the Yarngzii Valley. Riverbeds cracked apart.
Here where we are in the North is the water-dragon's domain.
Lordly bullies stun oxen with mallets. Kill their owners in daylight, regardless.
Then, smiling like bows full-stretched, step forth on the Capital's pavements.

The Capital! Painted pavilions piled deep with wool-napped carpets,
Where the golden arrows are hung on high as soon as the chase is done.
Night-time re-echoing with songs. How gay are the flowery lanterns!
And people who find it incredible fellow-humans should suffer from hunger.

These verses come from *The Qing Bell of Poesy* (*Qing shi-duor,* hereafter
QSD, 1:1), a collection of more than two thousand poems about the lives of
ordinary people put together by Zhang Yihngchang between 1856 and 1869.
The original title was *A Bell of Poesy for the Present Dynasty (Guorchaor shi
duor).*[2] It is clear from the prefaces of the compiler and his friends that the
purpose of the anthology was didactic. Its "instruction through poetry" was
aimed both at the authorities and at those literate enough to read it. The
criteria for selection were "concerns with the people's heart-minds, the ways
of the world, government by the officials, and the people's livelihood." The
significance of the word "bell" in the title was to recall the wooden-clappered
bell used under the Zhou dynasty both to summon the people when a new
order was to be announced and to alert the ruler when the people wanted to
tell him something.

The lineage claimed for the collection is somewhat grandiose, though
not entirely unjustified. It includes the ancient *Scripture of Songs,* the verses
gathered by the Music Treasury under the Hahn and later dynasties, and the
poems of Duh Fuu. One of the preface-writers also mentions the Tarng poet
Nieh Yirzhong, who wrote about farmers,[3] and the *Sohng Mirror of Literature
(Sohng wernjiahn)* edited by the philosopher Luu Donglair (Zuuqian), some

of whose pieces touch on the hardships of country life. The professed motive of the 1960 reprint committee was to make available materials that "faithfully reflect the sharp class contradictions" and the "dark phenomena" of mid-Qing society.[4]

Few of the pieces have great poetic merit; and what little there is disappears in a translation that aims at a reasonable fidelity. Nonetheless, they provide a partial answer, even if an indirect one, to our problem. Although they are written by literati they touch on those aspects of life that, so far as we can tell, touched most Chinese deeply. If the reader can be patient with their awkwardnesses, their simplicities, and their sentimentality, they open a window into the heart.

The social contexts in which they were written vary. Some were composed to soften the hearts of officials. Others, like those against female infanticide and child-marriages, were propaganda. This does not mean that the picture they paint is necessarily false; it would not have carried conviction if it had departed too far from reality. But it does mean that we should be cautious about accepting possibly extreme cases as being representative. Other poems were memorials of important events, or descriptions of interesting customs. Many more were probably the simple upwelling of human emotion. The language is workaday literary Chinese, seasoned with a sprinkling of erudite references. Medieval clerical verses in Latin offer a partial parallel. They are not in the diction of the common people.

Many, or most, of the topics treated by these poems have a millennial ancestry; but there is a slight, but inescapable, difference in the treatment that these topics are given in late imperial times. Characterizing this difference is a subtle matter, and not everyone familiar with Chinese poetry will agree with the interpretation that I have found most persuasive. In simple terms, it seems to me that there is a new capacity for *empathy* with the predicaments and the joys of ordinary people, as opposed to the ultimately distant *sympathy* felt by earlier imperial-age poets, and at the same time, but in no sense paradoxically or contradictorily, *a sharper awareness of the reality of the social and political divide* between the writer and the humbler human beings who are his subject matter. The tension between the two aspects quite often produces a duality of tone, that can, for example, be seen in poems like the *Song of the Tightrope Walker*, translated below in the section on women's non-farm work, in which the author plainly relishes a popular spectacle before condemning it at the end in terms of Confucian-physiocratic orthodoxy.

The Technicalities of Translation

Almost all the poems rhyme; and translation without rhyme, the common escape route taken by (I think) every established scholar of the present generation, falsifies their resonant crystalline structure. Faced with the difficulties of the English language, which is as short of rhymes as the Chinese abounds with them, I have used vowel-rhymes on the final stressed syllables as a substitute. The ear quite swiftly learns to hear these echoes, as it does in Gaelic poetry, although they may be inaudible at first. As an illustration of this technique, we can take Zhang Yurn'aor's *Selling a Daughter* (QSD 17:567), with its ABAB pattern:

> The little girl is seven years **o**ld,
> Born and raised in a thatched h**u**t
> Her daddy died a year ag**o**,
> Her mother cannot bring her **u**p.

> Girls sell for several strings of c**a**sh,
> Enough for more supplies of gr**u**el.
> You get some money in your h**a**nds,
> Lose someone who is part of y**ou**.

> The girl's tears fill a palm's ins**i**de,
> Her mother's money two palms, c**u**pped.
> Before her daughter's tears are dr**y**,
> The mother's money's all used **u**p.

No comparably easy technical solution is available for rendering the characteristic effect of the regular structures built of lines containing five or seven syllables, which is the form taken by most poems, although there are some more complex patterns and a very few irregular ones. The combination of stresses replacing syllables and a pause in the flow representing the important fulcrum provided by the midline caesura (usually after the fourth syllable in seven-syllable lines in the Chinese) can however to some slight extent provide a hint of the originals. An example is the translation of the *Tea-plucking Song* of the poetess Wur Larn (QSD 6:179), in which the stresses are accented and the breaks are marked by a double vertical bar '‖':

Dáughter of fólk in the úplands, ‖ her ráven háir cóiled on her témples,
She pícks the néw léaves from the shrúbs, ‖ befóre, and then áfter the
  shówers.
The póols in the róck-bóunded stréams ‖ seem like mírrors that, sháking
  unstéadily,
Refléct, as she wádes through their rípples, her fáce ‖ — like a flówer.

Befóre a fúll básket's been plúcked, ‖ she reléases a lóng-dráwn-out sígh:
To whóm can she spéak of the páin ‖ of these thrée lóng mónths of the
  spríng?
Whenéver she óffers her téa to gránd hóuses ‖ they wón't méet her príce.
Yét for the léaves of one bówl of 'Spríng Snów ‖ she must róam through a
  thóusand hílls.

If a line seems sonically awkward at a first reading, it will in many cases be
because the location of the caesura has been misjudged.

By strict scholarly standards the translations that follow are free, and incorporate, where useful, glosses by the original authors and my own ampli-
fications. The sometimes odd mixture of popular and pedantic vocabulary is,
however, quite close to the originals.

Farmers

The Pattern of Expectation

At the back of each peasant's mind was the ideal of a prosperous normality,
in which seasonal weather and seasonal activities were interwoven with a sequence of festivals. This was buttressed by the concept of a social and political
order that was beyond his power to change in its essentials, and that he accepted, even if with no enthusiasm, provided it was administered with fairness.
Something of this underlying normative vision is expressed, though in the
speech of the educated, by Xur Rorng's farmer's calendar for the southernmost
province, Guaangdong, where crops of some sort could be grown all year
round (QSD 5:150–52). It is a fundamental testament to bedrock Chinese
beliefs about the proper human relationships with nature and Heaven-Nature,
with each other, whether dead, living, or still unborn, and with the many gods:

First Moon

The wind, rising out of the east, takes us into the coming year.
The life-breath, from off of the sea, blows through the leaves' mild greens,
Over the hazy expanse of the coastal salt-rice fields
And the groups of cottages—crouched—under their banian trees.

The thirteenth-day lamps are lit. The neighbors have come together
To drink of the new-warmed wine for those who have newborn sons.
Under the city walls, foretelling this year's harvest,
The elders watch the tossing of beans, and the rice of many colors.
This year the pottery ox is filled with the lucky yellow.
—No need to pick out popcorn puffs to determine the year to come.

We must see the soil by the tree-roots is thoroughly turned over,
Care taken a proper job is made of fixing up the sluices.
Tomorrow a lucky day, from the almanac, has to be chosen
So we know when to send our sons, to enrol at the local school.

We farmers, too, are preoccupied from this time of the year forward.
So swiftly by the days go past they seem to be importunate.

The nature of the "salt-rice fields" *(chaorhua tiarn)* is unclear, but they may have been tidally irrigated (by the rising tide pushing fresh water upstream into a sluice), and grown one of the several varieties of relatively salt-resistant rice.[5] The "pottery ox" *(tuuniur)* or "spring ox" *(chunniur)* was carried in a procession to welcome the spring. During the "Rainwater" period in the second half of the first lunar month rice was roasted in an iron pan, and people would select a puff to foretell their fortune during the year ahead.

Second Moon

The Earth-God's Sacrifice Master moves through the fields in procession,
Not drinking the water pertaining to the clay Spring Ox of last year.
But now, as the dawn is breaking, he tastes the new shower's refreshment,
And in their fullness the hidden springs of the life-force are released.

The lines of pottery basins are laid out in preparation
Now that the moment's come for steeping the seeds in nutrients.
There go the ducks' heads, quacking, across the level lake
And the serried lines of swallows turn above the soft mud in platoons.

When, on the south-facing slopes, the wheat stands ready for reaping,
The high-lying fields must be soaked, to receive the early rice.
Once the spring plowing's over, hand-harrowing's also needed.
Books tell us: already long ago, *this* was what life was like.

Ox of last year, your vital force has still not been destroyed,
But finds an end that is glorious in this surge of life's resumption.
Do you not hear them calling? Those are the wood-pigeons' voices
In accord and concordance, one with the other, among the thick-shaded
    shrubs.

The idea behind the taboo on the drinking of "old water" by the Sacrifice
Master on the day of the ceremony was that this would magically cause it
to rain.

Third Moon

The spring will not be warm—until the equinox.
The rice will not be sturdy—until transplanted out.
How soon the visit to the graves, and the cold-food feast, come on!
In paddy after paddy we transfer our seedling sprouts.

We load up our manure—into the plain wooden tubs.
We carry our rice-plants out, in the trugs of yellow withies.
Each bunch is given a dip, and then is pushed in, upright,
So that the rows lie straight, and faultless in their precision.

Our backs are stooped and bent, like cranes when they are pecking,
At every instant anxious we may strain a joint or a muscle.
Our families come to join us once the noon sun's overhead.
Up floats the fish aroma from the rice that they have boiled us!

The wealthier of our number own several water buffalo,
So leasing a plowteam by the day costs little, and is effective.
Nothing is sweeter than work done briskly, without the need to struggle.
When one eats from one's own exertions, no other taste's so relished.

The spring visit to the semicircular graves high in the hills was the time when
the family reported the year's happenings to their ancestors and ate a meal of
cold food.

Fourth Moon

Once the Plow's and the Pig's Tail stars have set, we sow in the hilly land,
But not in the tidal fields, till the start of the rainy season.
Then the punts, rice-seedlings on board, move down to the flooded paddies,
Hardly come before they've departed, having worked at such a speed.

And even before one household's boiled dry the crystals of salt from brine
Another's scythes will have cleared the shore, where the grasses grew, for hay.
This time of year the limitless skies appear to stretch out on all sides
And the foaming trampling wave-crests seem a thousand acres of snowplain.

The sandfields' tenants' leader, puffed up with his own importance,
Delivers the strictest instructions to govern their activities:
"Keep the land-crabs off by sprinkling lime, at the time the tide's withdrawn.
We can't have the salt-rice damaged by their, or by the molluscs', activities!"

They offer up pig's pettitoes to the Wife of Grains, their goddess,
And, drunk on her afflatus, their spirits are delighted.
Next year, when settling sediment has formed new silt deposits,
They'll sing, and swing their lanterns, to thank her for her kindness.

The two stars were said to be "below Canopus," known to the Chinese as "The Old Man of the Southern Extremity" *(Narnjir laaorern),* which has a declination of South 52°40'. Thus they would only have been visible in south China for a short period early in the year. It was believed that "if the Plow's Tail Star is out, the rice-seedlings will die prematurely, and if the Pig's Tail Star is out, the rice-seedlings will turn yellow."[6] The Wife of Grains was thought by peasants to be the mother of the God of Agriculture, and they set up pavilions and made offerings to her, although she was not an officially recognized deity.[7]

Fifth Moon

The fifth moon is for weeding, so—we make our way out
Between the flowering stalks of rice, all grown to an equal height.
Untroubled by the wind, empty the sky of clouds,
And the water in each field is like a clear glaze shining.

Above us is the sun, that burns upon our backs.
Below us is the mud, that submerges our upper legs.

The colorless rain comes suddenly, giving us a splattering,
And we find our bodies cooked in each others' steam instead.

It is all but beyond my powers to depict for you this scene
Where we don't dare grow weary, our task no matter how hopeless.
From those who pass by on the road we receive no pitying feeling,
Nor would we ask the bureaucrats that they take any notice.

Then one amongst us turns. He says to his eldest boy:
"This field is yours. Your heritage—that your ancestors bestowed.
They wanted nothing more than this: that you get your chance to toil
A lifetime here. As I toil now. *Thus,* at this very moment."

This last verse expresses the sense of the intertwining of an individual's belonging to the land, as well as to both his ascendants and his descendants,
his commitment to a certain way of working, and his acknowledged right to
do so. Property was not the simple commercial commodity it has become in
modern times.

Sixth Moon

Before the mid-point of the year, the first of our harvests' completed.
We can see that our yields this year will be—a little better than usual.
At the confluence of the rivers, where the lychee-trees are sweetening,
Water-chestnuts and lotus-roots are growing in profusion.

No lucre is ever as precious as the gift of a farmland's fruits.
In furrow on furrow on furrow through all the width of our acres
Mild-warmth, and great-warmth rices are flourishing luxuriously,
Each ear is hanging bowed down, half-seen in the haze of daybreak.

We have sickled and gathered in. What joy this labor is over!
We sample our new-cut crop. We can do whatever we like.
The taro-frames that stand by the east-facing wall have been opened.
We focus our thoughts on the taro's taste, eaten chopped up with rice.

It's the honor of modest folk, like us, to know how much is enough.
What need have we for dishes that reek of onions and meat?
Small economy after economy leads to a constant abundance.
Heaven-Nature can more than meet its match in the efforts of human beings.

This last sentence suggests something of the active, even aggressive, attitude taken by the Chinese towards the environment by late imperial times, whatever their archaic philosophies said about restraint and harmony.

Seventh Moon

The best grain's had to be paid away, into the government's granaries.
The second best's been taken so that private granges are stuffed.
The gleanings have been left outside, lying in the paddies,
But when we feed the cranes—why even they grow plump!

Long' an and betel-nuts abound, for the Feast of the Hungry Ghosts.
In village after village, boys shrill harvest-home reed whistles.
But an end to farming labor?—It is *never* really over:
Plowing for our second crop has still to be persisted with.

We soften straw by soaking, we tease apart the rice-shoots,
And savor, too, the cloudless sun that, here, still shines above us.
How soon before the autumn winds come blowing, and their coolness
Does battle with the lingering warmth—our dying Indian Summer?

The resin-scented cypress trees cast their criss-crossing shadows.
The streams flow by for several miles, unmuddied, undisturbed,
While we work on. —And at moments we now relax,
Cold-weather cicadas overhead giving their muted chirps.

In some parts of Guaangdong province the fourteenth of the seventh moon was the Harvest Festival *(tiarnliaao jier)* and the following day the feast for the deliverance of the hungry ghosts. The poem inverts the time-sequence. The exchange of long'ans ("dragon's eyes," a kind of fruit that is close to the lychee) and betel-nut was called "putting an end to predestined fates" *(jier yuarn)*.[8]

Eighth Moon

"The rain that falls in the year's seventh moon is gold.
The rain that falls in the eighth," so the saying goes, "is silver."
The night-time's rain enriches. The daytime rain not so,
For a rain that pours throughout the day will rob the rice of its vigor.

Spreading the paddies with muck is something we've done already.
So now, but not for long, we can take it easy and idle.
We celebrated yesterday the Mid-Autumnal Festival,
Today at our forebears' shrine renew the sacrificial rites.

How long the two generation-lines formed by these forefathers' tablets!
Who gave their trust respectfully to Heaven-Nature's essence.
Modest offerings of meat bring favor from the ancestors,
And spread equitably out upon all of their descendants.

Throughout the sun-filled evenings we hold wine-flushed conversations,
In happiness so perfect it's not easy to describe,
Yet, sadly, family members who've gone to profit from trading
Have deserted our community, and left us—their kin—behind.

Ninth Moon

We do not know the cold here, in our river-basin region,
Where the hills under their cloud-caps are verdant throughout the year.
Once a faint frost has altered the somber hue of the cedars,
We are touched by intimations of the first autumnal feeling.

We step outdoors. We make our way through earthen-colored mists,
The earth itself invisible beneath their immense extent.
The deep-keeled ships are coming in as the tide itself comes in,
Ebb-flow will wash the crawlers back, dazed, into our nets.

The yellow siskins are blown along, by the west wind, in their hundreds,
Transformed from shoals of yellowfish, the legend says, now flapping
Across the crests of countless waves in one unbroken fluttering
To take their chance of feasting on our ears of rain-smirred paddy.

Bird-snarers would trample down our crops. We want our crops abundant.
So, birds, feel free to peck and drink. We'll not catch you in nets.
Once the frost-fall omens are taken, we'll be starting on the cutting,
Having first seen the levelled yards where we thresh and winnow are ready.

The "crawlers" *(herchoong)* are described as having the shape of silkworms, being an inch or two in length, and emerging from the rice-stalks. If a high tide entered a coastal field, they would use its outflow to escape to the sea, but the peasants suspended funnel-shaped nets from rafts to catch them. They were then eaten.[9] As regards the siskins, it was believed that a certain kind of fish changed in the eighth moon into a "yellow sparrow" *(huarngqueh),* and then in the tenth changed back into a fish. A parallel belief was that in Leirzhou, about which the poet was mainly writing, so-called "autumn-wind birds" *(qiufengniaao)* turned into fish.[10] The peasants' representation of their world, as Xur Rorng describes it, was thus a mixture of carefully observed realities to which the modern reader can immediately relate, and of magic, religion, and bizarre natural history like that referred to here, taken almost equally for granted, though the educated person might sometimes be skeptical, as will be shown later.

Tenth Moon

By the onset of winter the principal crop has matured enough to be reaped,
So now comes the time of the year the season's last harvest commences.
We drag behind us field-barrows that teeter on single wheels,
And pole along village skiffs curled up like slices of melon.

We bundle the sheaves up at sundown; then we make our way back home.
We stack them in layers, sweet-smelling, up under the eaves.
Our produce is more than enough. The widows can gather a bonus
From the handfuls of stalks that we've scattered behind to be gleaned.

The upper classes are not alone in having their storehouses stuffed.
We've not suffered a shortfall, either, for stocking our local reserve.
And look at the fields, at how thickly they're covered with stubble,
Which means that our kitchens, till year's end, have plenty to burn.

What good fortune to live in an age so well off!
People's stomachs bulge drumlike. They're happy, relaxed.
Responding with songs and with dance to the blessings sent down by the
    gods,
Nor slow in parading their statues around to show thanks.

Eleventh Moon

"When you travel in a boat, don't overlook the wind.
Don't overlook the tilth when you engage in farming."

Since husbandry's the skill by which we make our living,
Any energy to spare's used to tend the kitchen garden.

First of all there's winter mud that has to be turned over,
And old dikes, likewise, that have to be refurbished.
People prate about the happiness enjoyed by farming folk,
But such happiness we have is based on bitter work.

That neighbor over there. He's an idler and a waster.
His bedding and his clothes are meager shreds of hemp.
This year was the year his land went up for sale.
His children will have nothing left, except what they remember.

At the level of their social class, men and women have to marry,
Then struggle unremittingly to keep their households going.
Do not take exception to our uncouth country manners.
Things have been like this since times remote.

Economic realism breaks for a moment through the idyll, and the Chinese
feeling that in a competitive world the primary duty, and the secret of successful survival, is unremitting exertion. The last line of the third stanza could
also be translated as an admonition: "Children! This is something you would
do well to remember."

Twelfth Moon

How warm the soil's vital force on the southern side of Leirzhou,
Where pestilence-expelling drums throb softly on the eighth!
Its steamed fermented rice for wine's well-suited to the old:
The alcohol's no sooner brewed than it's slipping through the strainer.

How magnificent the fishes from draining dry our pools!
Our oranges, our pomelos, taste sweeter than any outside.
And when sons and grandsons gather, around us, in a group,
How their faces shine with light, as each one starts to smile!

Between Leir prefecture and Qiorng, or so the folklore tells us,
It's *now* that new rice-seedling clumps are taken from their seed-beds.
Why begrudge others their fertile tilth? We put before all else
Tending with diligence the fields our ancestors bequeathed us.

We spend our leisure moments replacing the tiles on rooftops.
Repairs to plows and harrows wait likewise to be started.
And last year's thunder-force moves on—to the thunder of the future,
Auguring that when spring arrives we'll have an autumn's harvest!

A literal rendering of the last line but one is: "Last year's thunder makes the transition to next year's thunder." It was thought to be possible to divine the nature of the coming harvest by the crossover from the "old thunder" to the "new thunder" at New Year's Eve. Foretelling good and bad luck in the future was a Chinese obsession. Finally, it may be noted that the eighth of the twelfth moon was the date of the post-solstice sacrifice made to all the gods. Drums were beaten on or around this day to drive away epidemics.

Thus the time that the peasant lived through was structured, and meaningful as part of an annual sequence that reached far back into the past. It was interwoven with the networks of human society—children, kinsmen, and neighbors, with the half-hidden workings of the natural world—not just rainfall and the growth of cereals and fruits but also wood-pigeons, stars, and yellow sparrows, and with the beneficent surveillance of the ancestors and gods. The vision was fundamentally optimistic. It was quite different from the medieval Western view that, in the words of Pearsall and Salter, "seasonal suffering and seasonal toil were causally related, first and last to the sins of mankind."[11] It had, perhaps, more in common with the earlier vision of the countryside of Virgil and Lucretius and Columella.

The Fear of Disaster

Under the belief, or hope, that Heaven-Nature was ultimately benevolent there lurked the fear that the normative prosperity described in Xur Rorng's calendar might be disrupted, either by natural or by human forces. The commonest concern was perhaps the weather, but the malevolence of tax collectors, landlords, and bandits came not far behind. The weather was perceived as the local interaction of the two basic cosmic forces. The first of these, the *yin,* was dark, cold, wintry, quiescent, and female. The second, the *yarng,* was bright, warm, summery, active, and male. When they became unbalanced, disaster could result. Here, as an example, is Tur Zhuo's *Warm Spell in Winter* (QSD 1:2):

During the brief late winter days, out flew the Golden Crow of the Sun,
Shining on people's faces, till they ran with sweat like curds.
Disordered blossoms in south-facing gardens burst forth from the early plums.
Butterflies wavered unsteadily. Honey-bees roamed and murmured.

In the short-eaved cottages worn-out folk quickly ate breakfast up,
Took off the padded caps from their heads, left their legs gownless below,
And capered in wild melee across streets and markets, like drunkards.
But an aged man among them sighed, and spoke these words of foreboding:

"If the Locked Storehouse be not closed tight, the Bright Force leaks out.
When thunder rouses the insects from sleep, the Dark Force sharply declines.
Everywhere, in the upland fields, break forth fine, thrusting sprouts.
No rain for long days, in winter, nor any snowfall either,
Makes the Two Forces weaken and swell in confused, inappropriate fashion.
I dread that, in the year to come, this thwarts the Spring's reviving.
Don't you recall, in '56, how spring snow caused catastrophe?
How cold killed off the oldest trees, and left hundreds or thousands dying?"

In *The Old Farmer* by Your Torng, who lived from 1618 to 1704 (QSD 6:156), the combined agony of drought and official exactions causes the peasant (as presented in the poem) even to question the benevolence of Heaven. The poet, or his poetic persona, sympathizes with the peasant's suffering but, in a shift of emotional tonality that shocks some readers, ends by looking at it, from the viewpoint of an official, in the wider context of the disorders of early Manchu times, and argues that it really amounts to very little. If this reading is correct, and it is controversial, there is a dramatic tension that is new in late imperial verse and not found in earlier times.

Mantle over my shoulders, I roamed the city's outskirts.
Then I leant on my staff, and asked: "How's the autumn rice?"
The muddy ditches were choked with a rank and useless herbage.
Before me stood an aged man. The tears welled up in his eyes.

"From beginning to end in the second moon, the spring thunder rattled.
The springtime drizzle, in the third, went on and on interminably.
In the fourth, as we trudged along, our hoes across our backs,
The fine-dropped showers kept falling. Down. *Down,* like jades or pearls.

In the fifth moon that followed that, we faced a total drought.
Oppressive weather that would not lift, and went on into the dog-days.
Mile after mile there was nothing but wastes, a sky without a cloud.
Only the red sun burning, high over our reed-thatched cottages.

The bluegreen-colored sprouts turned yellow much too suddenly.
They seemed to be an ocean that had been transformed to land.
I have some fields myself, that I use for agriculture,
But, for the last three years, I've put nothing by in my granary.

Each dawn I'm filled with pity for my sobbing wife and children.
At night I fear the clerks will come, to force me to pay the shortfall.
Once yet again, this year, we are pinched by hunger's misery.
I shiver in apprehension they will hurry me off to court.

Would you be willing, on my behalf, to speak to Heaven-Nature?
To ask why It should play these tricks on the poor and unsupported?
Inflicting on us country-folk our total ruination,
But hardly cutting, if at all, into official resources?"

I answered him: "Such matters as these are not your business to mention.
Why do you think it is that *you* don't sup on fine-hashed meat?
Why are the high officials not accommodating in temper?
Why don't the authorities notice you, their eyes dimmed with grief?

Think! How many acres of farmland does a common person have?
He worries and whimpers about them enough, his forehead puckered with
     wrinkles.
Yet Qirn in the west and Chuu in the south are filled with our battalions.
Robbers and brigands pitch camp overnight in our deserted cities.
Our towns in hummocked ruins are half bleached over with bones.
So who is going to be concerned if your quick and slow millets are growing?

It's a wholly trivial matter if you should perish of hunger.
Be content; at least you enjoy some measure of security.
How can a poem that speaks of the River of Stars above
Be patched with documentation on the fates of displaced persons?"

The reference to the Milky Way is an allusion to its being seen in the
ancient *Scripture of Songs* as an emblem after the Zhou-dynasty emperor

Xuan had quelled a rebellion.[12] The dismissive tone of the second half seems evident enough, but the original text appears to have contained two further lines:[13]

> I came home; sighed in my sadness; and laid myself down to sleep,
> While through the sparsely set bamboos stirred a breath of relieving breeze.

This softens the tone, and it is also worth noting that an alternative version of the line starting "Be content" does not have the contemptuous phrase *goou an,* "undeserved peace," but *an zhai,* "a peaceful home."[14] The import of the historical echoes of the phrase "fine-hashed meat" (*miirouh,* a poetic inversion of *rouhmii*) are elusive. It presumably refers to the remark attributed to the Emperor Huih of the Jin (290–306) during a famine: "Why don't they eat hashed meat?"[15] But whether Huih was really so stupid as this makes him sound is open to question. He had personal experience of food shortages toward the end of his reign.[16] The question for the reader, of course, is not the historical reality but Your Torng's intended implication. Here all that can safely be said is that it reinforces our sense of his sense of the gulf between the classes.

Peasants constantly sought to manipulate supernatural forces to prevent unfavorable weather. Sheen Larn's *Sacrificial Processions for the Fields* (QSD 6:161) both describes what went on and his own skepticism as to its efficacy:

> *Sharp as needle-points in the spring rains, the shoots of rice extend.*
> *But under the downpour of the fall the ears of grain droop bent.*
>
> The Soil God determines the weather, cloudy or clear, that is to come.
> There are prayer-processions in autumn and spring. Sheep and pigs are killed.
> In the morning the Canton Headman calls, to make sure we're all of us
>   dunned,
> So the Soil God's shrine's proscenium is a lofty brocade pavilion.
>
> Puppets arrayed in costumes perform their songs and dances.
> Rival showy feasts are laid for people's affinal relations.
> One would hardly guess respectable ladies would sell their hairpins and
>   armlets
> To squander their cash on a single round of hard-drinking entertainment.
>
> *This fall there will be no rice. The spring fields show tortoise-shell cracks.*
> *So you see, do you not, the potent effects worked by the Soil God's magic?*

Shern's Confucian rationalism, expressed in the ironic closing couplet, marks a fault-line in the belief system of late imperial China. The elite, inclined toward a mixture of hypatotheism,[17] faith in causes and effects driven by the autonomous force of morality, and a humanistic agnosticism, did not really share the religious outlook of the common people, forever seeking personal favors from a multitude of divinities. The Chinese tendency toward syncretism and a relative tolerance of doctrinal diversity tended to hide this cleavage. But it was a hidden source of weakness. Mass enthusiasm and mass devotion were mostly on one side; political, social, and intellectual power mostly on the other. There was an evident contrast in this regard between late imperial China and the worlds of, for example, Islam and Catholic Christianity. Maoist Communism was temporarily to close the gap.

Life in the Countryside

The emotions of the Chinese who lived in the countryside in the late imperial age can only be understood in the context of the society and economy of this age. Since the nature of these institutions has not always been well understood, it is necessary to say a few words about them, even if limits of space mean that the picture has to be an oversimplification of what was a varied regional mosaic.

Chinese civilization was built, almost literally, on mud. In permanently farmed areas a high-density population was supported by a small-scale, labor-intensive agriculture that did not use fallowing but relied on rotations and applications of organic fertilizers to preserve soil fertility. Perhaps half of the cultivated area in the lowlands also depended in one way or another on water control, whether for irrigation, drainage, or defense against floods or incursions of the sea. By late imperial times, the dominant pattern of management here may be described as "family land, collective water." Almost all farming was based on the family, either as small-scale owners or as tenants, or a combination of these statuses, using mainly family labor, though hired workers could be found in a limited number of places. Except for the recently settled southwest, which had a high rate of owner cultivation, the incidence of landlordism varied directly with the productivity of the soil, but most of it was on what was, by European standards, a minute scale. Farmland was normally commercially bought and sold, and not subject to any sort of "feudal" tenure. Water control, in contrast, was the responsibility of collective non-family organizations. These ranged in size from a few tens of households running a small irrigation system up to consortia of villages, working under a general state supervision, to systems directly administered by the state for the very largest projects. In the uplands and many mountain areas, however, inmigrants driven by the pressures of population expansion in the eighteenth and nineteenth centuries, and often without legal title to the land they used, cut down a large proportion of China's remaining forests and engaged in an often locally unsustainable cultivation of crops such as maize and sweet potatoes. Broadly speaking, there was almost nothing in late imperial China that corresponded to de jure "common land" in the West, but the once quite extensive de facto commons where communities had cut their firewood and reeds for fuel, or hunted, gathered wild crops, or fished were substantially reduced or degraded in this period, in part by such developments.

Villages in the sense of collectivities with a certain self-awareness, some self-government, and specified boundaries were relatively weak or even non-existent in North China during this period. In parts of South China where settlements tended to coincide with the presence of a dominant kin-group (such as a lineage), they were much stronger.

Few local notables could be sensibly described as "lords." Most of those who owned more land than they could farm by their own efforts were closer to being rich peasants. In areas where there were large landowners, many of them were absentees who lived in cities and employed agents to collect rents from scattered holdings. Where powerful locally resident landlords existed, their power often had a complex base, such as control of local militia forces and personal and familial links with bureaucrats. Connections with the state were in fact usually critical, and in many places society was dominated by locally resident holders of official rank (some of them retired officials) and those who had won, or in some cases bought, degrees in the imperial civil service examinations. Such persons are conventionally called "gentry" in English-language histories, although the term is in some ways misleading. In later Qing times many of them directed local projects, such as water-control works, as "managers." Entrenched sub-bureaucratic officials, often referred to as "clerks" and "runners," also wielded significant powers, the more so as their bureaucratic superiors were only permitted to serve away from their home provinces, and so lacked detailed knowledge of local conditions. At the lowest level of all were various "bailiffs" and "canton heads" who did much of the footwork for the local bureaucracy and gentry managers, and whose positions were often purchased.

The economy was highly commercialized, and trading was the main route from poverty to wealth. Pawnbroking, with land taken as a security for default, was apt, for example, to be more profitable than simply renting land, with its problems of paying taxes and collecting rents. The continuum of social positions was also so dense, and people moved up and down the social scale so rapidly, that it is misleading, for this period, to talk about sharply distinguished social "classes." The top and bottom of the continuum were of course worlds apart, but there were no obvious points at which to draw major lines of division that would have been meaningful. The formal and informal serfdom of the preceding age was by now a residual phenomenon, and the social distinction between "officials" and "commoners" was blurred by the purchase of titles by merchants, while—across the generations—the recruitment of actual officials largely by competitive examinations meant that no consolidated official "class" could form. Vertical social links were in many respects stronger than horizontal solidarities. A shared place of origin, a shared loyalty to local faction leaders, and membership of bodies like secret societies usually counted for more than belonging to a particular socioeconomic level, or mode of earning a living, loosely described as "class." Especially in the countryside, a conceptual model that closely resembles a "football team" in the broad sense (including financiers, managers, and fans as well as players)— in other words, a fiercely competitive multiclass grouping with a strong local affiliation and its own micromythology—is often a sounder guide to understanding actual conflicts than the nebulous notion of "class warfare." In the towns the merchants did have a measure of potential class solidarity, as shown in occasional "market strikes" against unpopular official actions, but they normally operated through particularized guild structures with a basis in a trade or a regional affiliation.

Except for small groups at the top and the bottom, like the Manchu nobility and certain more-or-less outcaste groups like the Cantonese boat people, late imperial China was thus close to being "classless." It was organized, for the most part, on the foundations of kinship, small-scale private property, an extensive monetized and contractual commerce, and a meritocratic bureaucracy with a strongly civilian orientation. In other words, for a premodern society it could hardly have been less "feudal," at least in its core areas. This, however, is not to say that it was not relentlessly exploitative. To the contrary. The Chinese of this age were remorselessly competitive, and possessed a flair for extracting advantage from each other on the basis of the slightest degree of superiority. This omnipresent exploitation created feelings of insecurity and resentment, especially when the individual and his family

faced government employees or powerful private individuals. These sentiments later formed the psychological basis for much of the revolutionary
mobilization of the countryside, but their essential nature was not usually
that of "class" antagonisms properly speaking.[18]

Labor

Although the peasant lived in a commercialized world, the nucleus of his
economic life was his family, which was not organized according to commercial principles. At any given moment, both basic needs and available labor
power were fixed. Everyone had to be fed; labor could not be laid on or off
as in a factory; and it was profitable for everyone to work, even if they could
not cover their own keep, if the alternative was idleness. The central factor
that determined the economic well-being of a household was therefore not
its ownership—or not—of land, but its supply of labor. Essentially this meant
human labor, though animals were also of importance. The concern with
labor and anguish at its loss runs through many poems. An example is *The
Old Peasant* by Warng Zunmeei (QSD 6:153):

> His son's been conscripted to work in the city. He's left,
>   No more coming home with the evening,
> Obliging his elderly father to tug the door shut by himself,
>   In their cottage beside the stream.
>
> Impatient the wind. Swift the moon that sinks in the sky,
>   As their room fills with frost.
> He strikes on a flintstone to kindle the fire,
>   Then offers their yearling its fodder.
>
> Chill his body as iron, under its thin linen covers,
>   Unquilted, unpatched.
> The atmosphere's heavy with damp. His sick bones
>   Ache as if wanting to snap.
>
> Wine that he dares not taste
>   Brims in the earthenware vats.
> Come the spring he will have to exchange it for grain
>   To settle their tax.

Lii Tianqiarn's *Reaping Wheat* (QSD 6:160) tells how the seizure of men for the nonpayment of taxes has left the women doing most of the farmwork:

> Rambling footloose, as it happened, to the edges of the city,
> I chanced upon some wheatfields, high and low, like ochre mists,
> Where all of those who labored were clustered groups of women,
> Their arms forever moving with their sickles.
>
> Ears of grain lay about, scattered, and waiting the gleaners.
> Piled up in the village ahead there were mountains of sheaves.
> So I laughed though I didn't, myself, own any suburban fields,
> And felt a sudden lifting of ennui.
>
> A man well on in years hurried forward to address me:
> "Sir, since you live in the city, what is it that brings you hither?
> May I speak with you a moment, while you enjoy a rest?
> —How else will you understand these fields, so filled with bitterness?
>
> The drought-parched autumn last year had desiccated the sprouts.
> Weeds grew in the corners of stony acres, which turned into scrubby wastes.
> We filled our bellies with bark from trees, and chalk ground into flour,
> Yet even before our tax fell due they were quick to abuse and chase us.
>
> At dead of night they come to a village. They seize and tie up their victims.
> We tremble like people with fever when we go past the magistrate's court.
> Our guts, burning with hunger, turn round inside like a windlass,
> As we drive our bodies on, on, in terror of being tortured.
>
> How the tears pour down of the women who'd plans to find themselves
>   husbands!
> In the past these "cures for heart-ache" were already not easy to find.
> More than ever these days they must hunt for someone to love,
> Finding no one but stripling lads, barely five feet in height.
>
> See that half-wit begging for rice? Beside that wall? Yammering?
> He's sold himself to a merchant, to drudge for him as his serf.
> Once he'd his hands on the silver, the whole lot went to pay tax:
> Two-thirds to clear the basic sum, "official wastage" one-third.
>
> I'm lucky myself. They've not chased me for tax, not banged on my door at
>   night.

I live on from sun-up to sun-down, though a hollow gapes in my stomach.
So far, I am happy to say, the Lord of Heaven's been kind:
The flour I get from my single plot is enough for savory dumplings.

When I've cut and threshed my wheat, I fear it will turn into moths!
It grieves me that what's in my barn does not amount to much.
Night raids by tax men've already taken every third man of us off,
And the deadline for the next levy is closing in upon us."

On the old fellow chattered, not letting me interrupt him.
Then he tossed back his rough brown cloak, made as if to pursue his
    complaints,
When the hard-muscled prompters smashed in his doorway abruptly,
Trussed him up with black ropes they held in their hands. And led him away.

The loss of a working animal could also be experienced as tragic. Shi Ruhn-zhang's *Cowlad's Song* (QSD 6:153) relates how, with a cow no longer available, farming became all but impossible:

In the fields high up, the fields low down, the valley below the hill,
Three years we broadcast seeds about. But *one* crop came to fruition.

Then when troubled times were past, our old cow bore us a calf.
We rammed down earth in wooden frames, and built her her own thatched barn.

The tax inspectors panicked us, insisting we pay on the spot.
We sold off all our household goods. Our cow, too, was lost.

We still had our cow last year, with which to meet their demands.
Next year the land will lie untilled. I fear we'll have no harvest.

Pipes shrill on the nearby hill. On the further hill drums throb.
The gentlemen feasting there knacker cows as 'twere rats they were knocking off.
Oh, cow, oh, cow! What sort of a place is it to which you've now gone?

It is perhaps worth recalling that many moralists thought the butchering of farm animals created exceptionally evil karma.

The most painful physical labor was treadling the pumps that hauled water up a sloping trough by means of pallets linked together on a chain. This had to be done in the polders of delta lands where the slope was too slight for gravity-driven irrigation and drainage, and the currents too sluggish for water power. Warng Jiafur's *Field Pumps* (QSD 6:169–70) evokes the agony of the human beings constrained to do it:

> Beak-to-tail crowlike pallets rotate about their wheels,
> All around the paddies' banks, making a sound of creaking.
>
> After the fifth moon the sky above has even failed to drizzle.
> On smaller creeks and large alike, fishing nets are forbidden.
>
> Day after day in our fields, we see the rice sprouts wither.
> Plow oxen are exhausted. Human exertions bitter.
>
> Scorching our backs the summer sun. Red cloud banks burn.
> Hands and feet are callus-hard. Bones and sinews hurt.
>
> To feed a spring the farmers' tears are hardly moist enough.
> The streambed holds less water than their eyes hold blood.
>
> It's well that no one talks about the pain of pedaling pumps.
> Having trudged home, we grind stale corn to blunt the edge of hunger.

Peasants welcomed machinery that spared them such agony. Zhou Zhuo's *Song of the Liuryarng Pumps* (QSD 6:171) describes the norias of Hur'narn province. These enormous open-work wheels, with containers fixed to their circumference, were turned by the current in a race below them from which they also scooped up water and then poured it into a flume placed just beyond the topmost point of rotation:

> In Liuryarng *we* use norias, when the water needs a lift
> From the green meandering river, beneath the coiling mists.
>
> Dished wheels that are perfect circles, some ten meters across,
> And the splash! splash! of the water as they turn down past the top.
>
> Away to the northwest, night and day, flow the currents of the Liur,
> Deep channels cut in the high banks wherever low clefts open.
>
> The dished wheels draw the water up, and poured into channels it fills the
> Distributary ditches that take it away to high fields planted with millet.
>
> Turning, turning by themselves, they tax no human strength.
> Year following year they only need the care to keep them mended.

They say in the Yarngzii delta irrigation needs human exertion:
Bare feet pedaling pumps that turn with the caterwauling of urgency.

Where wife and husband, daughters and sons, all share a single pump,
While rain drips or sunshine burns, and they flush the color of sunset.

If you compare our pumps to theirs, one's ease, the other sweat.
Watering high-lying fields with ours does not hold any terrors.

A single family's noria feeds a dozen families' acres,
Leaving these others unconcerned with any tedious maintenance.

So long as the wheel's positioned there, on its axle-tree, securely,
They need not fear, when autumn comes, their grain won't reach maturity.

Chinese peasants and others who did the actual work had a sensitive appreciation of the effort saved by machinery. When one talks about the "cheapness" of labor in the late imperial age—and it was cheap—this is only from the view of an employer who was thus relatively unconcerned about finding or investing in ways of economizing on it as a factor of production.

Oppression

The oppression of a powerful landlord could be worse, on occasion, than that of the tax collectors, although complaints about them are less frequent in *The Bell*. Sheen Larn's *Rent Deadline* (QSD 6:162) evokes the horror that could occur when landlords employed what amounted to a private police:

When the State prompts payment of tax, it lays down a definite limit:
Namely the cold and snowy days after the winter's beginning.

Those who live off private rents have to have their deadlines likewise,
After which their thugs flog tenants, with as little conscience as tigers.

If you pay at the first demand, they'll let you off a tenth.
If at the second asking, at least you do not transgress.

The instant the third is past, the strong-arm boys pay you a visit.
The family's turned upside down, the dogs and poultry scared witless.

If you've curly-haired girls or little sons who try to cling to the bedstead,
Unable to hide, the thugs haul them out, and take them off to sell them.

State taxes are merciful. Private rents are cruel.
How, ever, can Heaven-Nature's eye alight on the homes of the poor?

Small landlords could find themselves squeezed between the demands of the
government for taxes and those of their tenants for relief. This situation is
illustrated in Char Sihlih's *Landlord's Complaint* (QSD 6:158) about an area
in northwestern Hur'narn:

> Lorngshan's county borders touch lakes upon both sides.
> The northeast sinks to marshes. The southwest rises high.
>
> When the upland fields are barren, the lower ones are dry.
> Landlords and tenants, together, join in plaintive cries.
>
> The edicts from officials show the tenants their compassion,
> But the warrants they send flying lay burdens on the landlords.
>
> Landlords are not distressed, they say, whereas the tenants suffer.
> So private rents need not be paid, but official land tax must be.
>
> Landlords buy grain to pay it, but this overstrains resources,
> As tenants demand they be loaned rice, and invoke the state's authority.
>
> They next hear rents are surcharged to fund gruel for famine relief,
> But how can grain be paid for at the cost of selling fields?
>
> A bumper crop the coming year is not at all a certainty,
> And if every landlord sells his fields, who then will want to purchase them?

In those parts of late imperial China that lacked strong village communities, as was the case with much of the northern plain,[19] the surveillance of
maturing crops to prevent theft was often contracted out to bullies, who in
effect ran a protection racket. Liur Shan's *Crop-Watching* (QSD 6:168) conveys the murderous rage that peasants sometimes felt towards these predators:

> The crafty rogues from the market towns, who swagger about in gangs,
> Come to play checkers with empty hands but leave loaded like gods with cash.
> When they go down to the countryside to "watch over the grain in ear,"
> The land's shared out into territories, each run by a separate team.

Their left hands grasp their measures for grain. Their right hands shoulder
    their baskets.
"You'll depend on us for your proper quota of rice and legumes and wheat."
"We'll be taking three bushels of crop," they add, "for every ten you harvest,"
And point out, in advance, the plots they're not going to let us reap.

If we don't concur they'll whistle up a thronging rabble of beggars
Who'll bundle up every stalk and straw, and carry off the lot.
If our old women neighbors interfere, they'll mess them about offensively,
So to sleep in peace we must give them extra, and be sure to take nothing off.

They'll grab much more than their due, if a peck or a pint is short,
Turn back and, for extra measure, rip a field of vegetables up.
It is heartbreak to reach year's end, with hands callused and worn,
To find that you must borrow seed if the tax-grain's to be enough.

Half goes to fill the bottomless pit of that leviathan greed—
The self-important, mincing, canton clerks,
Whose tasseled hats dance above their black gowns, and long sleeves,
So even the dogs wag their tails. And don't bark.

It's their custom, when times are good, to demand of us further sums.
Struck dumb, how can we counter them when they do this all of a sudden?
These canton clerks and market rogues are claws and teeth for each other,
Doing their utmost to ferret and scratch till our flesh and bones are dust.

The market blackguards take our cash for clerks' birthday congratulations.
They dedicate wine and fattened lambs to parades for deities' statues.
Alas! "There are rats on our altars. On our city walls there are foxes."[20]
As scorpions' curved-over tails sting feet, *they* hook the common folks' bodies.

How then can we get our hands onto thorn-spiked brambles of iron
To batter these people to death, to exterminate such tyrants?

This sense of being almost literally eaten alive ran deep in the lower levels of
Chinese society. It engendered various reactions: rage, thirst for revenge, ea-
gerness to organize so as to be able to prey upon others, and, sometimes,
millenarian dreams of the utopia of a Great Well-Being rising out of a disas-
ter-struck world, often exclusively reserved (as with the White Lotus sectaries
at the end of the eighteenth century or the adherents of the Heavenly Kingdom
of Great Peace in the middle of the nineteenth) for the believers in the faith.

Women

The Orthodox Catechism

With few exceptions, women were excluded from participating in the world of public affairs. As adults they were defined in terms of their membership of the family into which they had been married. Insofar as a woman did have any "public" standing it was most likely to be as a widow acting by default as the head of her family.

Among the exceptions were women who acquired independent power as religious leaders, for example in Buddhist or Daohist nunneries, or as entrepreneurs in the world of entertainment and sexual services. There were also a few professions dominated by females, such as midwifery and the arranging of marriages as a go-between. Early female marriage was almost universal, an age close to seventeen being the average for those who were not transferred young to the houses of the parents of their future husband as "little daughters-in-law." There were, however, in the far south sororities of girls who never married and who clubbed together to support each other.

The usual domain of a woman's life was "the inside," the home of her husband's family. Here her life was a progression from relative helplessness to a position of considerable power. As a new bride, she was only a little different from a commodity acquired through a contract in which she had had no say, and to all intents the servant of her mother-in-law. The practice of surname exogamy, and the preference for a certain distance between the location of her original family and her new one, limited the help she could expect from her own relatives if she was mistreated. She also owed deference to women in her new family who outranked her, such as the wives of her husband's elder brothers. If she were widowed young, or her husband's family met with a severe economic crisis, they could sell her and her children. As time passed, though, she forged alliances—with her husband, with the other women in her family, and with those in the community outside. When death removed the older generation and the property had been subdivided, she and her husband would have greater independence. If she had sons, this further increased her standing: she had continued her husband's family line, and the boys, once grown, were both a further physical and social support and the husbands of daughters-in-law, over whom she exercised the same dominion that had once been exercised over her. It seems likely that female suicide rates after the late teens were approximately inversely related to age, and probably reflected a woman's improving status through the life cycle.[21]

Women in late imperial China were restricted by codes of sexual propriety and marital fidelity of a type common to most premodern agrarian-urban societies. These codes served three main ends. The first was to hold the family together as the basic social and economic enterprise, which it was in terms of the ownership of property, the locus of decision making (such as who married whom and who did what tasks), and of consumption. It tended to alternate between a two-generation unit of parents and children and a three-generation unit when grandchildren had been born, the latter phase being relatively short but of some ideological importance. The second purpose was to assure males that there was a high probability that the children in whom they were investing were genetically their own offspring. The physical support that males gave to these children, and often training and education, plus the bequest of property, were of critical importance to the children's chances in life in a society without any serious form of social welfare. The third objective, which was characteristically Chinese, was to ensure, insofar as was possible, that relatives were only related to each other in *one* specific way. Without this there was a danger that the pattern of superordination and subordination might become ambiguous. Hence the importance of surname exogamy. The remarriage of widows was also ideologically undesirable, the wife being defined as someone whose particular quality was to "follow a single person," namely her husband; and popular religion often imagined that spouses would be reunited after death "under the ground," although there were a number of possible postmortem scenarios. Remarriage of course happened nonetheless, but widows who left their late husband's family usually also lost both dowry (if there was one) and children. Widow suicide was morally ambiguous. It was often seen as honorable, even beautiful, but the government and many of the educated deplored it as "treating life lightly," and saw it as an easy option compared to the pains of a long faithful widowhood, caring for parents-in-law, and bringing up orphaned children.

There is a sequence of three poems in the *Qing Bell of Poesy* called *Injunctions to Wives* (QSD 22:786–87) in which Lii Yuhqing—a woman herself—expounds the catechism of orthodox belief about proper female behavior. Through its pieties may be glimpsed many common attitudes: a bleak and submissive stoicism in the face of the loss of one's own family, a self-controlled adaptation to the culturally choreographed conventions of relationships with one's husband's kin, and the view that a woman could only realistically hope to be fulfilled through the lives of others:

I

We leave our homes to marry, and serve our parents-in-law
With the duty we once owed parents. Like parents, in-laws are kind.
You ask, Why do we serve the fathers and mothers of others?—Because
Our existence now consists in being these others' wives.

It is Heaven-Nature's conjunctures that cause our lives to be thus.
Things will go well for us, or ill, as allotted fortune has it.
Men who feel love for their sons will give their sons' wives love,
And, eight or nine times out of ten, will show us kind compassion.

It is normal, as human feelings go, for love to be expected.
And if this love is missing?—That is our own bad luck.
We may not put the question, Do they show us any affection?
But only, Do we obey them, as every son's wife must?

If we've given our all to serve them, given our all to be helpful,
Then, so we may anticipate, no fault will be held against us,
Respectful in all our actions, sustaining our husband's elders,
Unstinting in every way in the care we show his parents.

Reverent, at nuptial ancestral worship, our wormwood and waterplant
    offerings,[22]
And, when we feast his guests, pure the wine in our drinking cups.
To wear herself out in service is the married woman's lot,
And never grow weary—ever—of using the dustpan and brush.

To our husband's elder brother's wives we must show a compliant face.
With his younger brothers and sisters we should not chatter too much.
Careful, in handling our persons, to be frugal and restrained,
Yet, when helping other people, to be generous in abundance.

Obeying father, then spouse, then son, is the emblem of woman's virtue.
Our first concern in all we do must be for filial reverence.
If we act well then Heaven-Nature gives happiness in return,
And the blessings that we stockpile mean wealth for our descendants.[23]

II

A husband guides his wife as the lead rope guides the net,
Yet there is parity as well between a wife and spouse.

Married couples match each other in a balanced complement,
Their feeling affectionate and kind not being in any doubt.

Once matrimony's crimson thread is bound about her foot,
She may not take another man until her life has ended.
Keeping the Sages' teaching, she does everything she should.
Perfect obedience gives her sign "Receptive Earth" its splendor.[24]

What's to be honored in a man is an unyielding firmness.
What suits a woman best, however, is showing soft compliance.
She should urge *him* at cockcrow, "Time to be up and doing!"
Serving him food, she lifts the tray until it's held at eye-height.

But those not ashamed to take worthless wives to serve them as their pattern
Will soon have conjugal harmony jangling and out of tune,
With venomous shrewish fits, with venting of envious angers,
Unleashed without any concern for their neighbors' disapproval.

When in unbroken concord she has happily grown old with him,
She will not, beside his deathbed, be touched by selfish motives,
But shift to the self-restraint that becomes a faithful widow,
Making her nature adamant, till it seems like frozen snow.

Since days now long gone by, great numbers of virtuous beauties
Have bequeathed to us, one by one, their sweet examples showing
That the rise of men of courage, and devotion to moral duty,
Has been half due to the character instilled in them at home.

The span of our human existence is no more than a generation.
A hundred years is the limit that cannot be exceeded.
Only by leaving behind us undying reputations
Can we remain beyond change throughout the uncounted eons.

III

We grieve that our filial obedience is never expressed enough.
We fear in maternal affection that we may go to excess.
Lavishing loving feelings, tirelessly, on the young—
Isn't that simply what birds do, or animals, at best?

Our daughters are made to apply themselves to the task of spinning thread.
Our sons are set to studying the scriptures *Songs* and *Documents*.
Both boys and girls must be obliged to be diligent in these lessons,
And between a father's and mother's concern no difference is proper.

Even a towering building must rise from basement-level.
Nor will it be stable unless, at the start, foundations are truly laid.
When Mencius forgot to study, his mother chided his negligence.
Thrice she slashed at the cloth she wove, and moved to another place.[25]

With firmness, the virtuous mother instills the sense of what's right;
Wholeheartedly determined, her son's moral will develops.
While the boy labors at bookwork, devoted she stands at his side,
And displays in her self-restraint an exquisite female exemplar.

Thus, above, she can answer the ancestors, when they call her to account,
While, in this world below, she makes—her family renowned.

Rather like the Xur Rorng's farmer's calendar translated above, this poem defines an accepted normality against which everything else was implicitly judged.

Killing or Selling Children

A girl's life might be ended before it had properly begun, either as the result of infanticide, or of relative parental neglect. Since she was destined to leave her natal family, popular wisdom saw investment in her, whether nutritional, educational, or emotional, as unlikely to be rewarding. There was, however, an extensive polemical literature against killing girl babies, an example being the *Jieh nihnuu turshou* [An illustrated explanation of the injunctions against the drowning of girls].[26] The practice was said to "break the norms of Heaven-Nature and incur the anger of the spirits and shades of the dead." Among the cautionary tales told in this book are the following. (1) A woman drowned her fourth daughter in succession, whereat the fetus turned into a snake that wrapped itself around her left leg and bit her in the stomach until they both died. (2) A rich man, whose concubines had borne him only girls, forced them to drown the babies. One morning he woke up to find his hands and feet had turned into bull's hooves, after which he died. (3) A husband had all his daughters except the eldest drowned, and lost his wife at the birth of another girl, her intestines spilling out. He drowned the baby. Later his wife told him in a dream that she was in Hell, in the Pool of Blood, and would never escape. He tried without success to confess and repent at the local Buddhist temple, and died the following day "fighting the empty air and apparently resisting [invisible] assailants who were tying him up." (4) "Whenever one of the wives of the servants [of a well-to-do lady from Sihchuan] became pregnant, this latter always required that [the wife] have an abortion. She insisted that infants already born be drowned. This was because she detested the way in which pregnancy stopped [the women] from working. One day she saw more than ten little children, some of them with fully formed bodies, and others with limbs missing, but all of them dripping with blood. They vied with each other to bite her belly. She screamed for several days and then died." Conversely, those who rescued baby girls from death were rewarded by God or Heaven, usually with sons or success in the imperial examinations.

A characteristic anti-infanticide poem in *The Bell* is *The Basin of Water* by Wur Zhaoh, a minor educational official in his home province of Jiangxi (QSD 26:970–71). Interestingly, he assumes the literary persona of a woman:

From that basin of water comes the bleating sound of her cries.
Her baby hair fluffy and downy, her still unopened eyes,
Her pink flesh and her wrinkled skin, hands and feet clenched like fists—
Who could give birth to a baby girl, then have the heart to kill her?

Gentlemen, listen, please, to the words of a humble wife:
The customs of our countryside are only fit for loathing.
That little girl could grow up. There could come a time
When she waits in the women's apartments for news of her betrothal.

How they would boast about her then, her garrulous relations,
Discussing the splendid son-in-law they were going to pair her off with!
"Since the families are fitly matched as regards their social stations,
What need for more comparisons of each one's betrothal gifts?"

Once a lucky day's been picked for the wedding rite's performance,
The many, many things to do can be prepared beforehand."
  "What will she need on her head?"
  "Her hair in two knots, and gold and pearls down to her ears."
  "What will she need on her breasts?"
  "A gown and a skirt of loose silk as chic as can be."

"If, by chance, some detail is not completely perfect,
The groom's family's objections will be irritably urgent.

Once that's fixed, we'll await the groom approaching for his bride.
How the drum-beats of his orchestra stir the villages nearby!"

"On the third morn and the third night we send gifts of tea and soup.
One of the maids accompanying him's a lassie with no shoes."[27]

"Later the groom 'returns the horse.' His wife 'brings back the red.'[28]
So we'll spread out tables lavishly to feast relatives and guests.

Boxed fruits upon their shoulders, they'll throng home tightly pressed.
Each affine with a gift, so the mother-in-law's content!"

"Three hundred days and sixty pass before a year is done,
With a meat feast on the second and the sixteenth, every month.

We'll offer the bridegroom sweet fat pork. We'll toast him in wine as a pledge.
Whenever he comes to visit, he's always an honored guest.

At Dragon-Boat Festival time, when the sun burns at noon,
At Mid-Fall Celebration, when the sky's vault is blue,
We'll rush to send seasonal gifts. And at New Year's, too.

We'll drag boxes, and take along bottles, to meet the demands of each season.
If we don't give her rich-tasting fare, the mother-in-law's not pleased!"

Vexation after vexation occurs on these home-visits made by the girl.
As mother meets daughter across the screen, her teardrops fall like pearls.

She remembers how, when her daughter was young, she cared for her with
    devotion.
But now she's a spoilt young lady. How anger chokes in her throat!

So mothers coldly resolve, when they first give birth to a child
That they will not help another house to maintain its family line.

Even before you've heard me out, or sighed a few times in regret,
In one home after another, girls are no sooner born than dead.

    Oh, grief!
Officials have plastered announcements on every city street,
But who will send the bailiffs out to check on the country people?

Even if the decision had been taken to bring up a child, she or he could still be sold off. The usual reasons for this were to obtain the money needed to pay taxes or rents, or to ensure that the youngster did not starve to death. Zhang Yurn'aor's *Selling a Daughter,* already translated, is an illustration of this custom. Ironically perhaps, girls fetched a higher price than boys. Shehng Dahshih's *Selling Off a Grandson* (QSD 17:570) is one of several poems to make this point, though its chief interest is the imaginative empathy that it shows with the feelings of the grandfather:

> The old man lived by the Huair, his hair falling over his ears,
> His sallow dark features pitted by cold, as death faced him from hunger,
> His son, a hired hand, long since broken in to work's weariness,
> Had one night fallen sick, and not made a recovery.
>
> Two grandsons survived. The elder was just over eight.
> The younger was slung in a cloth, and still strapped on mom's back.
> Through the years, their backlog of debts had grown ever greater.
> Each morning a knocking was heard at the door. Words uttered in anger.
>
> The young one still sucked at the breast. The grandfather couldn't abandon him.
> He put his hand round the elder boy's hand, and led him away to the city,
> Though mother and child grabbed his clothes, blocked his path, screamed in anguish—
> And tears overflowed in the old man's eyes. In his misery.
>
> His mind went blank as he haggled. He could not weigh prices exactly.
> He wanted relief from the whip, from the bamboo's torturing lash.
> He turned, on the point of departure, held the lad once more by the hand
> And fed him a toasted cake, to give hunger a brief satisfaction.
>
> Then they took their roads in different directions, and passed from each others' sight.
> No news came from one to the other, once parted, nor went.
> Over cattle herds in the wastes, over sheep, the sun, then the moon, rose shining,
> While the Huair flowed on, with choking sobs, that tore at a man's intestines.
>
> He lifted his head to watch the birds, as pair after pair winged by.
> But how could they bring a grandson back, to his place at his grandfather's side?

He returned to the shacks where his neighbors lived. He unburdened his
     sickness of heart.
Then he hid his tears, looked them straight in the face, and questioned *them*
     about prices.
They pitied him more, then, having themselves endured the same disaster.
Color had gone from a world made dim by dusk and their lantern's
     brightness.

One family got some thousands of cash, as they were selling a daughter,
Another, who sold their son, mere hundreds in return.
Now they are on their own, being kin who could not give kin support,
Having a son doesn't seem to pay as well as bearing a girl.

If you sell a girl you get a supply of grain that lasts a month.
What you get for a boy, for two or three days allows you to stuff your belly.
Those weak with disease, as the grandfather was, faces all shrivelled up,
Face unavoidable death from hunger, once the year nears its end.

Their hands are shaking, their jaws locked shut. They do not speak very
     much.
Tax men who call to make them pay can't wait to make things unpleasant.

The tragic destiny of parental affection described here contrasts with the
mercenary attitude of some mothers in the lower Yarngzii who, it seems,
deliberately reared children for profit. Shaoh Charngherng's *Sale of Daughters*
(QSD 17:573–74) is another poem with a shift of tone towards the end: from
lip-smacking sensual relish to a sudden Confucian moralism:

The folk of Wur are much attached to giving birth to a daughter,
But not because they're hoping that she'll run a family's house.
They bathe the little darling's face in douches of peach-flower water,
And pray her youthful movements will cause lust to be aroused.

She'll only be eleven when she puts on rouge and powder,
Only twelve when fingers coax the tunes to sing from silken strings.
At fourteen years her tresses will come tumbling down her shoulders
And her moth's antennae eyebrows will bewitch.

Mommy gives herself a smile of happy satisfaction:
The price will reach a thousand taels, of silver, to the ounce,

The highest class of client will now come for matrimony,
And splash out quite a fortune for this beauty from the South.

Just let one of them hear rumors of this sweetheart' s reputation,
And there he'll be, outside the door, to offer his respects.
Out she'll come to meet him, and kneel down in obeisance,
As, steadied by her go-between, she sinks to genuflect.

She'll sweep her skirts back after that, unveil her dainty feet.
The circlets on her wrists will offset her ice-cool flesh.
He'll ask her, Does she understand how to strum the zither sweetly?
Whereat she'll tune the bridges, and play Lii Bor's *Crows at Rest.*[29]

He'll ask, "Have you been trained as well to use the brush and inkstone?"
Like surges breaking over are the verses she'll invent.
"Any good with the pieces?" is the next thing he'll think of,
And facing one another, they will try a game of chess.

The client is enraptured. He assures the young girl's mother:
"No way at all could one regard a thousand as too much!"
Let tonight, he says, become the night that decides a lifetime's love.
He piles the golden hairpins, and the bangles, up and up.

Ecstatically they interlock beneath the red silk canopy,
The tassels at the corners swinging back and forth like pendula.
The scent wafts off her body like the odor of marsh orchids
As she twines herself around him like the dodder-plant's tendrils.

So the master and his purchase enjoy their night-time nuptials.
Next morning child and parent must exchange a last goodbye.
But no affection's entertained by the daughter for her mother.
Nor is the mother different. She is not disposed to cry.

Off they go, then, unconcerned, with no warmth toward their family.
Once a chick's become a grown-up, she makes her own way.
Flesh and blood mean nothing. Money is what matters.
When one's taken this to heart, it fills one with dismay.

But has the mother really done so badly by her daughter? She is beautiful,
educated, and rich. . . .

Premarital sex, betrothal, and marriage

It is not easy today to imagine the horror in which socially unauthorized love-making by women was held by families who regarded themselves as respectable. It was felt to menace the family's honor, authority, and cohesion. Girls some-times committed suicide after a young man had done no more than try to flirt with them, and he could find himself facing the death penalty under such circumstances. The weight of family concern about female sexual indiscipline is evoked by Qiarn Meir's *Mandarin-Ducks Mirror* (QSD 22:823-24).[30] At one level it is a tale of the supernatural: the ghosts of the ancestors still ruling the affairs of their descendants. At another it expresses the deeply rooted Chinese feeling that the sexual impulse was the source of both personal and social disaster. It was so powerful as to be normally only resistible with the utmost difficulty, and by means of social controls; and in the story told by the poem only by supernatural ones. The tale is allegedly based on the real experience of Warng Larnshih, a man from Hur'narn, when voyaging through Jiangxi.

> Mandarin duck and mandarin drake are born among the waters.
> Each pair is male and female, one being matched with one.
> *Wild* birds come flying by them, calling and calling,
> But how can *they* constitute themselves into such married couples?

> *   *   *

> Deep in her cloistered quarters, the girl sparkled in brilliance,
> Versed, since her tenderest years, in rites and fine deportment.
> The look upon her face alone could kindle loving sympathy,
> No date yet fixed for her to take the bands of a fiancée.[31]

> A young fellow who hailed from some nondescript family or other
> By intrigues and insinuation got into the women's apartments,
> Irresponsible, needless to say, and impulsive,
> But practiced, as well, in the secrets of specious palaver.

> "My home's quite near yours," he began. "We're both of us from the same
>   village.
> And the pin in your hair shows your age, and that marriage will soon be
>   envisaged.
> That being the case, there's nothing amiss in our fixing a secretive tryst.
> Just take care that none of your actions arouse foxy-minded suspicions!"

Mutual, lascivious, passion infected them both with its venom.
They waited no longer. They'd meet in the mulberry grove.
"On the east there's a postern," she said, "that leads to our dwelling
Where this tender maiden's imprisoned, in chains made of gold.

A chest is in there. And a mirror. Take it out from its storage
And bind it with double red strands of silk marriage-bond thread,
An affectionate couple of ducks on the back its adornment,
Birds that don't part for an instant but keep close together.

. . . .

This mirror, sir, hold in your hands. Make your way to the temple
Where our Xieh family ancestors sleep. And there enter.

Once night's fallen tomorrow, once everyone's dreaming,
I'll escape, that I vow, from this cloistered part of the house,
Then we'll encounter each other, embrace in a face-to-face meeting,
Agreed in such secret that no one will know the least thing about it!"

* * *

So, on the day they'd decided, as the sun sank down in the West,
A stranger, a native of Chuu, came by, as he passed that way on his travels.
He was flustered, somewhat irresolute, and looking for overnight shelter.
The best he could find was the temple, which he took with scant satisfaction.

He'd borrowed the place to sleep in, but couldn't drift off into dreams.
The moonlight was cold, and a wind—*from the other world*—was blowing.
He saw an old man before him there, and an old woman, seated
In the twin places of honor, both with their mouths slewed open

Angrily summoning two other people to come and appear before them.
These two were prostrate, shrunken with terror, down on the courtyard steps.
"The daughter to whom you gave birth," said the others, "grows worthless
     and insubordinate.
She plots in secret to bring disgrace on the heads of our descendants.

Your wretched home has failed in its duty to inculcate moral tenets.
You have been convicted before the law, and deserve to get a flogging."
Terrifying lictors they seemed, those serried lines of attendants
Who laid the lash on the culprits' backs as they cried out in piteous sobbing.

Below the steps they respectfully knocked their brows for an audience, saying:
"For our degenerate daughter's sin it is right that we be punished,
But we'd wish that she knew that even the souls of those who have passed
   away
Can be covered all over their bodies with weals, and bruises, and cuts.

We should like to shatter the mirror that was part of our bequest.
For only when that mirror's smashed will their passionate cravings break.
And this may atone for the evil we did, we who now are dead,
And, with luck, provide a way of escape from the whips and the bamboo canes."

When the couple sitting in judgment had heard what these two said,
They nodded assent; the grim expressions upon their faces grew bright.
But when the traveler from Chuu had grasped what such words meant
He glanced about and uttered a gasp, because he felt so frightened.

The hairs upon his body stood up, as straight and dense as thickets.
The unearthly light resembled fire that dances on dead men's bodies.
But when, in the common light of the sun, he looked at the household lists
He learned that the temple he was in was Xieh lineage property.

Wild grasses were growing tall outside, toward the front of the building.
Angry screechings came from the back, the hoots of unfilial owls.
No locals were likely to pass that way, at least not in his opinion,
So he'd linger a while before going on, so he thought; and sat down.

But when some minutes had passed, a young man made his appearance.
He held a mirror between his hands, and walked on into the temple,
Where he made two low prostrations before getting back to his feet,
Seeming like someone who deep in his heart is gripped by an obsession.

On a sudden the mirror crashed to the floor.
Its glittering splinters scattered all over.
He'd grabbed at it panic-struck, but—*it was not to be caught,*
And he sank forthwith into a gloomy foreboding.

Then the traveler from Chuu called out, from where he stood to one side:
"It seems as if, in your actions, there's something you've done amiss."
And he told the young man about the events he had witnessed the previous
   night,
Adding, "Truly the dim world of the shades is difficult to trick.

If even the dead may be condemned for wrongdoing in this way,
It's certain the deeds of those still alive are only too well known!"
The hue of the young man's visage had washed out to a muddy gray,
And a horrified shivering seized him that was out of his control.

He kowtowed to the traveler for telling him this, and offered him his thanks,
Confessing that what he'd said was true. True. Only too true!
Nor would he scheme now to do those acts that provoked the spirits' anger,
And he swore that he would set to rights his earlier wrongdoing.

Then he contemplated the mirror that she'd given him for his own,
Its daemonic brightness fractured and scattered about pell-mell,
Fragments tossed hither and thither, on the mosses between the stones,
And a chilling gust of vitality-energy ran through his mortal flesh.

How sad the devoted couple of mandarin duck and drake
Had disintegrated and flown away as though they were weightless dust!
A looking glass filled with light reflects a person's outward shape,
Distinguishing in its clarity the beautiful and ugly,

But spirits, and the ghosts of the dead, can mirror the heart and mind
With candles illumining the depths of the hidden and illicit.
And that young man?—He has my thanks, for having had the kindness
To be my exemplar for this tale of *The Mandarin-Ducks Mirror.*

The denial of social and moral legitimacy to the autonomous expression of love (except to men in second and subsequent marriages) was linked to another possible tragedy: the unhappy arranged marriage. Chern Chunxiaao's *Flower-Seller* (QSD 23:839–40) tells of a heartless and lying go-between who ruined a girl's life:

> The flower-selling lady—
> Though in the autumn of her age, her eyes still sparkle like the waves.
>
> In the latest hair-style and makeup, she goes walking along the pavements,
> Elegant, slender, and graceful, and swaying her southern waist.
>
> Since her youth she's passed, as a matter of course, through great houses'
>   vermilion portals,
> Where her winsome, smiling deportment always makes for a happy euphoria.

By peddling her blooms, it may happen, she can earn herself a few cash,
But it's Old Man Moon, God of Marriage, to whom—she dedicates all of her
     chatter:

> *So-and-so's young lassie,*
> *Her face is like a blossom opening!*
> *So-and-so's young laddie,*
> *His talents justify them boasting!*

Her plausible tongue runs babbling over, like a mouth organ's suasive notes,
But if you're a skilled marriage broker, that's what the job imposes.

For his daughter, muses the family head, to get a groom straightaway's best,
Observing he's heard it be said Madam's skillful at knotting these threads.

So the card of engagement's despatched. Off it goes and comes back—
As in all her three lives arranging a match whose happiness hangs upon
     hazard.[32]

Who'd have thought that our phoenix, in glory, would have to obey a crow's
     orders?
A girl who is joined to a man that's flawed will be crushed by his bullying
     scorn.

The bright pearl on our palm's thrown away. Our daughter, and our mistake.
That matchmaker's self-serving phrases should be spat back into her face.

The marriage we'd hoped to be proud of—corrupted to one that is foul!
But the lady, still peddling her flowers, has moved on to another house.

The marriage ceremony itself was often an expensive extravaganza into
which the two families poured as much money as they could afford, or more.
It was a public expression of their social prestige as well as the cementing of
an alliance. Moralists urged an end to this ruinous habit, but to little effect.
An example of such a polemical piece is Guh Kuirzhang's *Buying Her Costly
False Hair* (QSD 23:837–38):

> *They buy her costly false hair,*
> *A headdress with pearls inlaid,*

> *And pay so she goes with escorting maids,*
> *And a trousseau richly ornate.*

If they've copper cash ready to hand, the locked boxes are bound to be
    emptied.
If penniless, then they'll sell off what's left of the old family farmstead.

The bride's mother's family won't even keep back her "blue-green nephrite salver,"[33]
The mother-in-law's may insist on the gift of the bride's mother's golden armlet.

For a passing moment their nuptial show will be the boast of the street,
With silken banners out in front, and, behind, their subservient menials.

From the "Hundred Children Palanquins" a hundred beauties smile sweetly,[34]
Embroidered hoods and brocaded awnings splendidly prestigious!

Who'd think that white-silk fancy pants would in midcourse drop
    unsupported?![35]
Or a thousand ingots of silver be, in one swift fling, destroyed?

Once they gorged themselves like rats in our imperial granaries,
But now, alas, their storage jars yield fare that's barely adequate.

This princely bridal procession has plunged *both* families into poverty,
Just for celebrating a wedding in a manner by far too opulent.

They should go back to the ancient restraints preached by writers on
    economy.
Why must the customs of today be observed by almost everybody?

In some areas weddings were also occasions for lewd horseplay. One of the
functions of this may have been to convey to the bride the social acceptance of
her new, sexually active status and to break down some of the inhibitions
previously instilled into her. The obscene rough-housing that sometimes occurred is described in Chern Chunxiaao's *Wedding Horseplay* (QSD 23:840).
The region he is talking about is the southern shore of Harngzhou Bay in
Zhehjiang province. The classical references are to Liur Zhen, an official serving
the usurper Caor Cao who looked his master's son's wife in the face at a drink-
ing-party instead of prostrating himself and was duly punished, and to Shurnyur
Kun who maintained, in an argument with the philosopher Mencius, that if it
were wrong for men and women to touch each other's hands, one would be
morally justified in letting one's sister-in-law drown before one's eyes:[36]

They congratulate the new groom.
They congratulate his new bride.
Abashed, groom and bride
Sit inside their room.

The young bucks kick up a shindig. Their behavior is reckless and wild.
Lewd tricks that lack any feeling. Conduct that's loose and unbridled.

Liur Zhen-like they ogle her straight in the eye, causing her limitless misery.
Shurnyur Kun-like they fondle her fingers. Distraught, she forgets who she is.

In couples and triples they wallow about on the bed meant for marital pleasure,
Or snore, their feet placed on the horn-inlaid pillows, sprawling out at full
    length.

The drums' pulsing beat starts up in the streets while the night is still young,
But the guests don't depart till the bright constellations are spangled above.

The newlywed couple, like mandarin ducks, are confined in the quarter for
    women.
By the silver-lit lamp she half turns her back and detaches her sparkling
    earrings.

Speaking softly the two of them, then, have a long whispered natter.
After which what takes place between woman and man is a commonplace
    enough matter.

Oblivious both of the eavesdropping ears pressed tightly against the wall,
But how suggestive the mockery is when the trousseau's inspected next
    morning!

The house is in uproar in daylight.
The house is in uproar all night.

In the fine hall sits the paterfamilias, firmly resolved to say nothing,
Convinced of the bedlam the wilder it is the more it will augur good luck.

But shame and vexation can generate anger, and turn former friends into
    enemies.
These folkways, widespread in Harngzhou and Yuryaor, are a practice that I
    find contemptible.

Once again there is the by now familiar pattern of first relishing the reprehensible, and then, at the end, asserting an orthodox attitude of moral disapproval. The interesting question, though, is how to characterize and then, eventually, explain the interplay of puritanism and prurience in both thought and practice in late imperial China. It should be evident from several of the poems quoted above how inadequate it is to describe the China of this age as simply "Confucian": Confucianism—however one defines this loose term—was always in tension with impulses of a more earthy and sensual nature, some of which had a measure of social recognition and institutionalization, as here.

As an excursus on this theme we can look at *The Blaze of Beauties* (QSD 25:950–51), composed by Hur Been as a polemic to stop women from attending theatrical performances. There is a prose introduction:

> In the fall of the sixth year of the cycle [1749 or 1809], the drama of Muhliarn [the Buddhist paragon of filial virtue who descended into Hell to rescue his mother] was staged at the Stone Ox Stores to the east of the county capital [Xiangtarn in Hur'narn province]. Gaudy multistoreyed theater boxes were lashed up, looking down over the sea of humanity. Not less than a thousand women gathered here to watch from behind curtains. Because no precautions were taken against fire, a fierce blaze broke out in these boxes. The curtains of the women's rooms being of flimsy material, they were tossed into confusion amidst the thick smoke and hot flames. Hotheaded youths treated them with disrespectful familiarity in broad daylight. I know not how many women had limbs broken, hair or skin scorched, hairpins and bangles lost, and clothing ripped. I have therefore written *The Blaze of Beauties* to serve as an injunction against women attending theatricals as spectators.

The verses themselves are too threadbare to be worth translating, but they may be summarized as follows: The Xiangtarn women so loved the unusual, Hur says, and they were so eager to see "the Infernal Regions suddenly appear" on the stage, that they pulled the curtains partly to one side and were thus no longer properly concealed. Most of the men there were so licentious that they were soon ignoring the actors and sneaking glances at the ladies. This lewdness infuriated the God of Fire. He sent the Wind God, followed by the Candle Dragon with fire in his mouth, to "sweep away the miasma of sexual enchantment and the vapors of seduction." This had been the cause of the conflagration. One may be skeptical about the effect of this propaganda on the women's behavior; what it does clearly testify to is the tension.

Finally, there was an alternative mode of marriage, namely adopting a young girl at an age that varied but was always before puberty. She would be brought up rather like the sister of the boy she was destined to marry. It has been suggested that this gave rise to feelings between them akin to those underpinning the incest taboo between true siblings, and tended to reduce both the number of children and the stability of such marriages.[37]

From the point of view of the prospective mother-in-law and father-in-law, however, there were certain advantages in this arrangement. It was cheaper. Only a modest domestic ceremony was needed when the time was agreed to have come for the couple to begin sexual cohabitation. A bride was assured for their son, and the investment in the girl's upkeep and training was not lost. She also provided almost immediately a modicum of useful labor power. It was also easier to establish a moral ascendancy over a youngster than a young adult; and it was perhaps possible for a mother to reduce the risk of her son's affections and loyalty being lost to a glamorous newcomer. Zhehng Xieh's *The Mother-in-law's Hatred* (QSD 25:943) is remorseless propaganda against this mode of marriage, but it must have had sufficient grounding in reality—the mother-in-law's cruelty having its roots in sexual jealousy of the girl's attractiveness to her son—for it to have been persuasive.

The "little wife" is a mere eleven years old.
She's left her home to serve her in-laws' comfort.
Unknown to her the passions that rule conjugal devotion,
She just calls her future husband "elder brother."

The youngsters, both of them, are shy. So bashful
At first they're tongue-tied when they want to chat.
His father tells her to abide in the women's part of the mansion,
Where she can plait replacements for old tassels.

But the mother-in-law insists that chores, of all vexing sorts, be done.
Chopper in hand, she's to go across, into the central kitchen
And slice the meat up into strips, taking care she doesn't cut chunks.
Then she's to stack them, in layered rows, onto the serving dishes.

She concocts a meat-stock broth, but its flavor is insipid:
Neither sour taste nor peppery tang having a sharp definition.
She chops at logs till her soft hands split at the places where they've blistered.
She watches over the blazing fires till all her fingers shrivel.

Her father-in-law observes of her, "She's little more than a kid.
Surely teaching her and training her ought both to be done more gently?"
The mother-in-law snaps back at him: "To the contrary! If we don't break
    her in
While's she's young, who'll keep her in check, once she is past adolescence?

Because of her fierce and, indeed, of her overbearing temperament,
She will begin to deceive us once we are old and decrepit.
If ever we let the reins go slack on her domineering tendencies
Our son will grovel before her, flat, prostrate on his belly!"

Curses rain down on her today. The scoldings come nonstop.
Awaiting her tomorrow morning, already prepared lies the whip.
For five days nothing but torn-apart clothes is all she can put on her body.
For ten in a row she is not even spared to have *one* with unbroken skin.

She swallows her sobs. She turns her eyes to face the wall in the shadows,
Her snivelling only broken by a barely audible muttering.
Her mother-in-law rasps out at her, "Cursing me, are you, you baggage?"
And takes hold of a rod to lash her with, and a blade with which to cut her.

"There are still a few slices left," she leers, "for me to carve out of your flesh!
It hasn't had time yet to waste away, being more than a little plump.
There are even some tresses of hair, still dangling down from your head,
But once I have yanked them out, why then—you'll look like an autumn
    pumpkin!

We can't both of us live in this world. No.—No. That's something that's not
    possible.
If it's *you* that's to survive, then it's *my* fate to be doomed."
The mother's frame is crabbed with age. Her features look demonic.
Her eyes, swollen with rage, bespeak a murderous cruelty.

When her husband-to-be gives his future wife the slightest care and attention,
"How can you be so lacking in shame?" is his mother's curt rebuke.
When her father-in-law encourages her with the mildest intervention,
His furious wife demolishes him as a senile, servile fool.

When, ever so gently, the neighbors make a few enquiries about her,
The mother snaps back at them, "How has this matter got any connection
    with you?"

Oh, grief! Why doesn't this lass, who has come from a penniless household,
Simply end her days by drowning herself in the depths of some river or pool?

True, she'd fatten the fish in the stream, or feed the turtles up.
But she'd also be free from suffering this ill-willed venomous hate.
Alas, if Heaven-Nature ever hears the pleas of the humble
Why isn't it touched by the grievances of which she makes complaint?

If in this, our world of humanity, you must serve as a "little wife,"
You will drown in pain and be the butt of misuse and of mockery.
Each time her stomach is filled, *she pays*—with another cut of the knife,
As they demand she live like their pig, their shorn sheep, or their ox.

Why don't her *own* father and mother come,
Wash away her tears and spruce her up, so that she gives them a smile?
Why is never a question asked by the young men who are her brothers?
Why does she tolerate the pain? Why do the tasks her mother-in-law assigns?

She tugs down the hems of her tattered dress, to cover over the scars.
She explains that her hair is sparse because it was lost through sickness.
If she gives even the least of hints that her mother-in-law is harsh
Before another instant is passed she knows her own life will be finished.

As so often in the old China, the cruelest immediate exploiter of a younger
woman was an older one.

Women's Work on the Land

It is the general view that, apart from those in the far south and the members
of Hakka communities, Chinese women did little farmwork in late imperial
times. It is accepted that they helped in emergencies, especially with the pumping of water in and out of rice fields in low-lying areas,[38] but otherwise female
participation in agriculture is assumed to have been largely of modern origin.
I am inclined to suspect that this view is oversimple, partly because early
modern photographs show numerous women working in the fields in some
other areas,[39] and partly because Qing dynasty poems referring to women
fanners are quite common. It may have been that women's input into intensive
late imperial agriculture helped increase per hectare productivity, for example
by more thorough weeding, applying extra fertilizer, and faster pumping, in

the absence of more than minor technological progress during this period. Whatever the case may have been, and it remains to be investigated, the evidence of these Qing verses is, unfortunately, inevitably ambiguous. Poets may well have written about women engaging in farmwork precisely because they found it surprising (as did Lii Tianqiarn, whose *Reaping Wheat* was translated above), and assumed the same was true for their readers. If the contents of the poems are taken as a guide, they tend to suggest that farming by women was unusual in some areas, and routine in others, but always surprising to outsiders seeing it for the first time. An illustration of the first of these two categories is Guor Jiuuhuih's *Farming Family* (QSD 6:154). Guor, who flourished in the second half of the seventeenth century, was for a time the magistrate of the county of Lirn'an, part of Harngzhou city in Zhehjiang, and the poem probably refers to this area rather than to his native Shanxi:

All night the ageing farmer felt restless with apprehension.
Their prospects of making a living were fading. It turned his stomach queasy.
As the roosters started to crow, he called wife and both children together.
"We'd better talk over a plan," he said, "if we're not going to find ourselves
        beaten.

The fields that are ours to cultivate are but a handful of acres;
The water we have to share among them is drawn from a single pool.
During the time work has to be done, we're vexingly short of labor.
When the crops come to maturity, there is never a surplus of food.

We've a burden of obligations, to the State and to private persons.
It makes me worry, time and again, that if drought or floods cause dearth,
We won't have the means to repay the debts that we've already incurred,
And have no way at all to put anything by towards our own reserves.

I have heard, in years gone by, old farmers express the opinion
That one should never forget to be thrifty and industrious.
So you and I together—I mean both mother and children—
Must all of us sweat our utmost to give each other sustenance."

When she heard this, his wife gave a sigh. A sigh long drawn out and rueful.
Then out of her startled spirit emerged a determined excitement.
So now her hair is disheveled, and both of her feet are shoeless.
Nor does she any more make up her face, as she did when she stayed inside.

Instead, through the middle part of the day, she wields the hoe and the plow.
She totes tubs of manure on her carrying-pole all the long hours after.
Since her younger son doesn't yet possess this sort of physical power,
He sits astride on their ox's back and guides him out to the pasture.

Of a color as lustrous as deepest jade, the meadow grass is verdant.
The ox' s back is as good as a bed, so stable and free from juddering.
The older lad has another task, that of gathering fuel for burning.
He picks up the dried-out stalks of reeds, and the withered branches of
    mulberry.

The wife is out and about in the wind, and under the rain and heat,
With nothing but patches to baste together her tattered jacket and trousers.
Her farmer husband bustles around, fired with new vigor and speed,
Busy non-stop turning over the furrows and getting weeds rooted out.

Neither begrudges, not one nor the other, transforming their sweat drops to
    grain.
What makes them suffer is "cutting the flesh, but merely to doctor a sore."
Their burdensome toil, in my humble opinion, is bitter and distasteful,
But the sting of the whip on the debtor's back is even less easily borne.

It is a moving story, but one cannot avoid having the impression that it was
also meant, ultimately, to serve some sort of polemical purpose, probably to
press for the easing of taxes.

   An example of the second sort of poem is Jih Qirguang's *Farming Women*
(QSD 6:155-56). Jih came from Jiangsu province, and served as an official
in Furjiahn, but the poem is about the environmentally degraded Huair
valley. It unequivocally establishes the reality of the phenomenon of women
engaging in agriculture north of Guaangdong, at least in certain regions such
as this:

On a road beside the Huair River, I met with some farming women.
They stood barefoot, with unkempt hair, on the rising slope of a ridge.
Pointing to where the sun was setting, they told me, a stranger, their history:
"Up there in the western Huair valley, land and climate have always brought
    bitterness.

Only here and there are there farmable patches. It's an arid waste, short of
    streams,
Even if it produced Harn Xin long ago, who helped found the Hahn in their
    glory."[40]
The wind there howls for three hundred miles. Rice in the fields is infrequent,
Though on the veinlike upland ridges grows many a plot of sorghum.

While the well-to-do families offer male servants, and serving-maids, a job,
The everyday work in poorer homes is inevitably farm labor.
The older women lead the way. Those of middle seniority follow,
And toting a plowshare is easy enough for the young ones with rosy faces.

They're accustomed to work at their looms by night, and to drudge in the
    fields by day.
How the north wind blows through the thatch in the roof, through the doors
    of criss-crossed wicker!
They can tell by listening to birds and insects if the day is clear or rainy:
Whole households with bleary eyes come out, to watch if the weather's
    shifting.

In the third night watch they're roused from sleep. They pull on their clothes
    awry.
In the fourth they scrub their hands and hair. The earliest cocks start crying.
During the fifth, with hands clasped tight, they'll pass the crossroads by,
Since it's best they get to the fields by the time the skies are growing light.

From time to time an old man calls out, as they toil at the edge of the
    trenches:
"Store that millet in panniers now!" "Shift that firewood!" "Sickle those
    grasses!"
While their suckling babies grizzle or cry, with only bare earth for their
    bedding.
—They've brought them along, like the stoneware jars, or the woven bamboo
    baskets.

Up-and-over the high field-ridges they clamber. Lower ones they straddle.
Even tough women move with a staggering gait. The weaker ones all limp,
Sickles and hoes tucked in at their waists, infants slung on their backs.
Face after face is running with sweat. Their shoulder blades are dripping.

They cut mulberry leaves. Chop hemp. And for good measure pick the
    melons.
Lofty chestnuts and white-leaved aspens resound to the rooks' sad cawing.
In powerful winds or in passing gusts the dust rises swirling and yellow,
Till every inch of their skins is thick with the moist and sandy soil.

In the sky burns the unforgiving sun, with a heat that seems like a furnace.
Elbows poke through their jackets' holes, though heads are shielded by scarves.
Hands cupped they sip from the stream by the grove, when they're suffering
    from thirst.
Hungry, they munch boiled wheat, sitting down, by the verge of the fields,
    on the paths.

Living since birth in deserted hamlets, suffering's been their lot.
They bow their heads. They look with a smile on the scars that disfigure their
    forearms.
In one body they're bearing a double burden, of plowing and weaving cloth;
And the taste of their patient lives is like—the cabbage stumps they gnaw on.

When you talk of their "bitter affliction," such words give no adequate idea
Of not having *one* extra kernel of corn, not *one single* width of fabric,
Nor the weeds and the rubble of tumbling walls around the beds where they
    sleep,
Nor the tears, nor the moaning autumn storms, nor the night rain, pattering.

. . . .

Not once in the course of their lives have they known either rouge, face-
    powder, or scent,
Nor worn in their hair even one sweet flower.—Is that not a cause for regret?
Why prate of "gold houses" and "pearly apartments" where pampered
    consorts are kept?
Was there ever a time when farming women lacked youthful and lovely
    complexions?"

One of the underlying literary ideas here is old, namely that the beauty of
women who toil out of doors is wrongly underestimated. There is a poem by
Duh Fuu,[41] written approximately a thousand years earlier, about a remote
part of what is now Sihchuan, that runs

The unwed women of Kuirzhou have grizzled hair on their heads.
They've still not entered a husband's home, though some are forty or fifty.
It's more difficult finding spouses now, because of the present rebellion,
So all of a lifetime they'll nurse this grudge, and sigh at their affliction.

By regional custom the men work sitting, and the women must work standing,
So the women's domain is the world outside, while the men stay in, as house-
     husbands.
Almost all of the women stagger home, toting the bundles of faggots
They must sell for money, and so provide a base for the family budget.

Till they're old, the virgins' double plaits still fall against their necks.
For them, wild blooms and hill trees' leaves do duty as silver clasps.
Reckless of life, they quest for profit and boil salt brine from wells,
Their energy spent on climbing cliffs and hauling goods to market.

Rouge and cheap ornaments interspersed with the channels their tears have
     cut,
They are thinly clad in this walled-in land where it hurts to walk on raw rock.
But how can you say these Shaman Hills girls are in any sense unlovely?
North lies the hamlet of Zhaojun, who became the Sharnyur's consort![42]

Just as Duh Fuu was intrigued by the reversal of the usual male and female
economic roles in Kuirzhou, so Jih Qirguang was struck by the unusual fact
that the Huair valley women worked on the land; and both poets end with
a plea that these women's beauty be appreciated. What really concerned Jih,
however, with his extraordinary sense of physical, economic, and social detail,
was much less this unusual fact itself than the suffering that the women's
double burden entailed under environmental conditions that were already
grim. To this extent, since novelty was far from being his only concern, we
can perhaps risk taking his lines as testimony to some measure of generality
of the phenomenon in the Huair region.

A more general point still, to which we shall return, is the extent of the
fascination of the late imperial Chinese poets with the social and emotional
aspects of the work of economic production. Although there are limited
parallels in nineteenth-century English poets such as Crabbe and Hood, and
perhaps elsewhere, it seems that China was probably unique in the premodern
world in the intensity of this interest.

Women's Role in Domestic Textile Manufacture

Another female specialty was the making of textiles, though men also wove and did finishing work such as dyeing and calendering. Many poets speak of the life-saving contributions made to the family budget by the wife's spinning or weaving. Often the man appears as the helpless, or dependent, partner, who stands beside the wheel or loom until she can finish, or who sleeps while she works. (Another theme is the pathos of the woman who has made a length of fabric and then, once it has been sold, does not know who will be wearing what she has made—a form of alienation that touches almost all craftsmen.) An example of such patient everyday sacrifice is *Spinning at Night* by Wang Mehngjuan (QSD 7:207):

> *Her thread becomes long as it's drawn.*
> *Wound back on the bobbin it's short.*

Through the cracks in the paper pane, the wind spies her out. She's alone.
Head bent over, intent on her task. Concerned not to snap the roving.

Her fingers have chilblains from cold. The spinning wheel's squeaking
    urgently.
Getting even a handful of expenses is—unlimited exertion.
Already the oil in her lamp's used up. The last dregs won't burn.

The millet porridge that stood on the stove—every mouthful is eaten.
Nothing is cooked for tomorrow. No cash to buy the ingredients.
She has to be off, yarn in hand, to the market to find a dealer.

The golden cockerels chorus at daybreak. The night-watch drumbeats finish.
She calls to her husband, "Time to get up!" while her son and daughter
    whimper.

Rearing silkworms, and reeling silk off the cocoons, was almost entirely women's work and generated anxieties of a particularly intense kind. It was a race against time and numerous misfortunes were possible. Mulberry leaves could become too expensive or run out altogether; the worms might suffer from shock or cold, or die of disease, or be eaten by rats. The production process was, understandably, surrounded by superstitions and taboos. During the period when the worms were feeding and sleeping, for example, it was forbidden to utter the word *suun,* meaning "a bamboo shoot," since it had the same sound as the word for "damage." Women often kept silkworm eggs warm with the heat of their own bodies, and were sometimes even said to look after them more carefully than their own infants at the breast. The atmosphere of the decisive weeks is evoked by the jerky and irregular lines of Xur Zhuo's Grief at *Continuous Rain during the Silkworms' Month* (QSD 7:181):

I

> The steady downpour does not cease.
> —The worms are starting their third sleep.
>
>> The gathering of fuel has stopped.
>> Lighting cooking-fires is barred.
>> In fields, the wheat and broad beans rot,
>> And on the farms the farmers starve.
>
> Starving is all right for men,
> But if our silkworms starve, what then?

II

> The water clock resounds plink! plink!
> The rain sounds insignificant.
> Now the water clock has stopped,
> But the falling rain has not.
>
>> The farmers' ankles sink in mud.
>> The silk-wives' eyes are shot with blood.
>> Yellowing plums before their eyes,
>> What hope to see cocoons grow white?

III

> Without restraint the rains pour down.
> Around us night-time grows profound.
>
> Rain beats only on our faces when the day is light.
> Night-time rainfall falls in the mind.
>
> Human hopes do *not* demand that Heaven rain down rice,
> Or precious metals, in largesse, fall on us from the skies.

Only that the Sun-Bird should let his pinions beat
And briefly warm the mulberries, so that our worms may eat!

IV

We return, dressed in grass raincoats, every leaf stripped off the mulberries.
No neighbor anywhere around has gathered a sufficiency,
Damp in the straw-clad trestles has to be a source of worry,
And also that the silkworms may perhaps be feeling chilly.

If a roof is leaking, we'll in due time get it fixed.
But if the Heaven springs a leak, can we ever get it dry?
Who are we to have the goddess Nüügua's skills,
And with a single effort repair a dripping sky?[43]

Upon the wutong trees' leaves drips the never-ending rain.
All through the night it irritates. One wishes one were deaf.
Up early, we light incense, to give Heaven our obeisance,
Then hang gay poppets bearing brooms under eaves to bring fine weather.[44]

Little urchins block the streets. They curse the stupid dragon:[45]
"Can't you *see*, like strings of pearls, our cocoons still unremoved?
It's us that have to find the tax, and the loans to be paid back.
Bare truncheons and the yellow thorns are not going to land on *you*!"[46]

For a more detailed account of the almost awesome intensity of the involvement of women in sericultural work, and a desperation whose ultimate origin was the inadequacy of the natural environment to provide all the resources demanded of it, we may turn to Zhu Yihzeng's *Song of the Silk-wives* (QSD 7:184):

The third of the third lunar month: the sky's aethers are fine.
Along Tecoma-Flower Stream girls follow each other in lines.[47]
They don't mind the square baskets and circular panniers being a heavy burden.
Their purpose is gathering mulberry leaves to nourish the unhatched
    silkworms.

How thin the worms when they first emerge, like filaments of silk.
The fine-bladed knives that cut the leaves sound like a chop! chop! chop!
The worms take their first and second sleep on frames of bamboo splints,

While little by little price of the leaves reaches almost what yellow gold
    costs.[48]

For the purchase of extra mulberry leaves, they pawn both hairpins and
    clothes.
Being only concerned about the leaves, they take no account of expense.
Senior sister-in-law has disheveled hair, unkempt, untouched by a comb.
The junior forgets, in her distress, to redden her lips with cosmetics.

The elderly wife gives the worms their food, her hair knotted up in a bun.
She never removes this outer garb. Her body is never relaxed.
Daring daylight hours she takes good care her worms don't suffer from hunger,
And she keeps a lookout the long night through, to see they're not bitten
    by rats.

They take care of the worms like babes, at suck on the breast, so cherished
They won't leave them alone a moment, while they themselves go off.
After their third sleep's over, the worms will wax strong and heavy.
The women burn paper money, and pray, begging their worms will prosper.
To buy beasts for sacrifice, and wine, they go to the moneylenders.
Whole families down on their knees beseech these favors from the gods.

In the period Swelling Grain, the worms mount the straw-capped trestles.
People lift their emaciated faces. Worms coil themselves in threads.
Charcoal heats water sizzling hot inside the stoneware vessels.
The tight cocoons show their varied hues, both the male and female sexes.

Then—the reeling-machine turns round like a spinning wheel, rotating its
    frame wound with silver.
In hundreds of bubbles the boiling froth tumbles cocoons around in its vat.
Elder sister-in-law, with her delicate fingers, teases loose the free end of a
    filament,
And the length that pulls out from this one single strand extends for a
    thousand fathoms.

No sooner they're happily looking at silk, come newly reeled from their
    caldrons,
Than red imperial warrants for tax arrive from the government offices.
The grain's to be paid by the specified date. No time for delay is accorded.

When sub-bureaucrats pounce on the countryside, they have a tiger's
   ferocity.

The wives have entrusted their silken skeins to the master who rules their
   family.[49]
And the master has taken the skeins away to be sold in the walled county
   capital.
Most years the silver they earn in return will pay the official taxes.
It's a heartbreak that, *this* year, all their slaving has only left them bankrupt.

With bitter tears the silk-rearing women explain why they have a grievance:
It is hard to accept that caring for worms is *worse* than a waste of effort.
They've had no return for their gifts to the gods, nor the cash spent buying
   leaves.
Nor have they been left with an inch of thread, or a foot of plain silk, for
   themselves.

The head of the household breaks into tears. He tells the silk-wives what's
   happened:
"The thread that I've marketed's not fetched enough to meet the official levy.
The higher authorities, once again, have prompted the payment of tax.
So it's on the sale of next month's grain that we'll have to wager everything."

The Jesuits who wrote their observations of China in the eighteenth century
were of the opinion that the economic competition was more relentless than
it was in the Europe of that date.[50] This poem gives some substance to their
remarks.

    Economic and environmental pressures forced some families to abandon
agriculture and earn their living in more precarious but perhaps more interesting ways. Women entertainers were common, as may be seen by the
popular woodcuts showing them practicing their arts.[51] The poets were as
fascinated by their displays as was (almost) everybody else, even if they felt
obliged to preserve appearances with a few disapproving physiocratic plat-
itudes once the fun was over. Here is Zhu Perng's *Song of the Tightrope-
Walker* (QSD 25:951):

Her husband leads the way in front. He beats a bronze gong, ear-shatteringly.
At his shoulder behind, his missus bends, under her trussed-up pack.
Where three roads come together, he bellows: "Tightrope acrobatics!"
And boys tumble out to welcome them, delightedly clapping their hands.

Keen for the show, folk gather around. Fees are collected swiftly.

Onlookers perch themselves on walls, as they try to press closer together.

She appears from one side! The crowd's all about her. She takes a hold on the
cloud-rings,

And seeming about to soar skywards, turns head-over-heels, and stands there,
erect![52]

She glances about her. She leaps in the air, like a spirit with powers unequaled,

Evoking a chorus of gasps, from the disbelieving spectators.

Only she, of all there, seems composed, with her calm, disdainful demeanor.

Then, with the movement of willows in wind, she lightly sways her waist.

Next, with high-stepping gait, and lofty carriage, she walks as on a straight
path,

And during this time she seems unaware there is any rope beneath her.

Then, back and forth, in continuous motion, she speeds as though Zephyrus
startled,

When one loss of balance, when one foot put wrong, would be certain to see
her go over.

She hand-stands. Then hangs upside down, as a monkey would from a tree
limb,

With the merest half inch of tapering foot, suspending her, hooked round
the rope.

She seesaws in space. Like a pulley, she suddenly spins!

Gyrations merge into a blur. One's eyes are glazed over.

Others admire this consummate skill, this technique that admits of no rival.

They do not agree with the view that I take, namely, that it's regrettable

Plowing and weeding, and spinning of thread, are all put away to one side,

While she thinks that the risk of her life for gain has very much more to be
said for it.

She answers me: "Most respected official, don't scorn me, and don't rebuff me!

An acrobat's wandering mendicant life is not what I aspire to.

Our fields by the riverbank yield little rice. Once taxes are levied, we've
nothing.

Our food, our clothing, all, all depend—upon this length of tightrope."

In approximate terms, both the necessity and the acceptability of the public
display of a woman's person, even in the most modest fashion, as for shop-

ping, were inversely related to her social class. Physical performance before the eyes of often rowdy spectators in the manner of the tightrope-walker implied that she belonged to the lowest level, that of the "wandering beggar" *(xirngqii).* The closing lines of Liarng Yuhsheeng's poem on the same theme (QSD 25:949) are even more explicit:

> She recalls how in her early days, when she studied the routines,
> Father and mother, morning and night, urged she care for her moral health:
> "If your dream is to tread the tightrope, and fare forth on the endless streets,
> Your life will be a life of shame, and worthy of no one's respect."

Domestic Love

We turn now from the public world to the private one. There is a darkness—a warm, self-absorbed and self-absorbing darkness—at the heart of every family, into which not even the closest outside friend can really penetrate. For the ordinary Chinese, unless he or she had found another relationship with life through Buddhism or Daohism, this was something infinitely precious; and it was a state that many believed perdured after death.

At the center of every such family nucleus was the woman who had created it as a wife and as a mother. Psychologically, she was apt to be its strongest member. Something of this is conveyed by Lii Furqing's *Ballad of Date-Tree Lane* (QSD 26:963):

> The time for rearing silkworms had not run its course in full
> When the red warrants demanding tax were sent to the countryside.
> In the morning, people were pressed to pay, no hen or pig overlooked.
> They were pressured again, late in the day, and the weak and the elderly died.

> A poverty-stricken married couple, then living in Date-Tree Lane,
> Set off to the county capital market, to dispose of their only son.
> To feel affection for one's child is only human nature,
> But when taxes have to be paid to the State, what else is there to be done?

> When halfway there, their hunger—stopped them going on ahead.
> She felt exhaustion crushing her, but her heart still stirred with resolve.
> So she could purchase from an inn two leftover loaves of steamed bread,
> She handed in her own torn clothes, as a pledge, at a pawnbroker's shop.

"To look at my husband's tragic face devastates my own feelings.
To see that my son is crying cuts at something in my guts.
These loaves are for husband and son to eat. They're easily conceded.
Taste them myself? No, that's an act for which I have no stomach.

If I am to have no son, our lineage comes to an end.
If I am to have no husband, then I shall be left by myself.
A wife must grow accustomed to never being fed,
Unmoved by any protests that may stir in her empty belly."

So, she spoke to her husband, using gentle words to urge him:
Let him and the boy, she intimated, go on a little in front.
There were excellent mulberry trees just here, along the roadside verges.
She'd stop, herself, and pick some leaves; then, later, catch them up.

Agreeing, he took their son by the hand. They went off in advance,
The two of them strolling on ahead, for a third of a mile, together.
But he saw no sign of his wife, once the evening was growing dark,
So they turned to return to meet her, swiftly retracing their steps.

They soon got back, one leading the other, to where they'd seen her last.
Here, too, as before, they could catch no sound from any human throat,
Though from a grove of trees there came rooks' voices cawing harshly.
They found her there. Already hanged. At the end of a silken rope.

Sick with his grief, he hugged and hugged his motherless son in his arms.
Without restraint their tears poured down. Not a word passed between them,
To be with *her*, in their final home, the two of them also departed.
Three bodies hung there, from the branch, under the mulberry trees.

Like wings that support each other in flight they soar now in Heaven above.
On this Earth beneath they are linked, each with each, like intertwining
    branches.
The physical souls of their essences keep, forever, in touch with each other,
Which far surpasses living on, if they'd had to live apart.[53]

It is difficult for the Western mind to empathize with the feeling that under
such cruel circumstances suicide can be affectionate, gentle, and even beautiful. We have been reared on different metaphysical beliefs. But empathize
we must, if we are to understand China.

At the end of the road was widowhood. Everyday widowhood is not treated in *The Bell*. Faithful widows, however—that is, those who were bereaved when still young and remarriageable, but who refused to remarry—were objects of respect, admiration, and even awe in late imperial times. Many of those whose lives were regarded as having met the prescribed conditions, notably the number of years during which fidelity had been maintained without a blemish, were honored by imperial awards. Inscriptions were placed on their houses; and stone arches bearing their names graced the countryside. Their names were recorded in official shrines, in local gazetteers, and in the registers of their lineages. To have such a widow in one's family was a source of social prestige, although it was less profitable than selling her off to a second husband; and of course canonization fell disproportionately on those who were socially visible.[54]

The seemingly miraculous powers of a widow's fidelity are recounted in Ferng Jiing's *Cutting Off Both Ears* (QSD 20:711). It refers to a widow who came from the scholar-gentry stratum and lived in Furjiahn during the eighteenth century. There is a prose introduction:

> She preserved her fidelity after her husband had died. His younger brother, Wernfang, made sexual advances to her. In her anger she cut off her left ear and denounced him to the head of their clan, who had him flogged. Wernfang then fabricated a libel about her, and put it into her son's document-case. She was outraged, and further cut off her right ear. Her father sued Wernfang in court, and the governor commanded that the miscreant be lashed. He was displayed in public, his buttocks pouring blood, and wearing a cangue round his neck. This took place at the time of the summer heat, but on this day there was a heavy fall of rain, *and both her ears suddenly regenerated themselves*. The reason for this was that Heaven-Nature was making manifest her exceptional fidelity. . . .

> Just as the Five Human Interactions match the Five Phases of Matter,
> It is of the greatest importance we have proper ritual behavior.
> The people of this world-age are not quick of understanding.
> When obliged to be concerned with it, it makes their ears feel painful.[55]

> Those like warrior-general Lady Xiaan, who ruled the South long ago,
> Counted it shame to meet with words they found offensive or foul.[56]
> How much truer of this lady, then, nature chaste as ice or snow,
> When maligned by vindictive libel, alleged on baseless grounds!

More than a thousand characters filled that false, defamatory document
—The hooting of unfilial owls, the hubbub of jackals baying—
But the flash of her blade from its scabbard was like that of Night-Flying
    Frost,
As her surging moral energy spread through the empyrean's space.

She chopped off an ear, first of all. Then a second ear was chopped.
She let them drop, much in the way she might have dropped two turnips.
Her sincerity was mirrored in the shades' and spirits' response,
While to ease her anguish the river gods both put their help at her service.[57]

But the flesh that had been severed on a sudden grew anew.
Was the past, then, preeminent in virtue? Or is, rather, the present day?
Think back on the wife of Warng Nirng. Or the widow of Huarn of Luu.
Both of these ladies were engaged in adulterous liaisons.[58]

She placed her trust in a blade of steel, refined one hundredfold.
The passion of her anger stilled the hearts of the mob with awe.
The life force drained away from those who were poisoned with lust, like toads,
And the hundred bones of their skeletal frames functioned for them no more.

Virtue was perceived as having a powerful causal force, and by its influence on Heaven-Nature and on matter-energy-vitality, the basic stuff of
the universe, it could bring about what seemed to be miracles, but which
were not in fact accidental or dependent on something like grace. This episode may seem a mixture of the ludicrous, the pathetic, and the macabre to
a modern reader. It was certainly not so to a Chinese of late imperial times.

The feelings of faithful widows who committed suicide may be seen in
the lines written by Zeng Rurlarn, from Furjiahn province, when she was
about to destroy herself (QSD 20:726-27). She had previously made two
unsuccessful attempts at suicide in order to keep the vow she had made to
her husband on his deathbed. She had desisted from further attempts at the
order of the county magistrate, who had told her to have a son adopted as
the successor of her late husband, and to take care of her father-in-law for
the rest of his life. After the old gentlemen had passed away and she had
performed mourning for him, she told her sisters-in-law that now at last she
intended to keep her promise. She "bowed in farewell to Heaven and Earth,
and to the Ancestors." Seating herself, faultlessly dressed, she composed the
poem that follows, so earning herself a share of immortality—because you

are reading her lines now. In a strange way, it is almost a love poem. This done, she flung away her brush, swallowed a little metal ball prepared beforehand, and so died:

> Like the water-chestnut's blossom, cold my face in the looking-glass,
> And never, through these last three years, have my tears been dried away.
> In the fullness of old age, my parents-in-law have departed:
> Once more I taste the frost and snow, the chill of the widow's estate.
>
> But now I, myself, am returning, to that place for all time my home.
> You, whom I leave behind me, don't think I'm heroic. Not so.
> Under the faith-keeping pines and cedars that rise on the Western Slopes,
> Husband and wife, we roam together, where delight has bidden us go.

This is an emotional domain that has been unfamiliar to Westerners and is all but inaccessible to them.[59]

Last of all we return to "normal" life. Xuu Zongyahn's *The Late Lady Warng, Faithful and Filial Mother to the Zhang Family* (QSD 20:721–22) is mostly as plodding as its title, but it is also a celebration of the rewards of patient merit, and so human, heartwarming, and in its own way revealing:

> The waters of the Maple River
>   flow by clear, and over-brimming.
> Maple River's a locality
>   of faithfulness and filiality.[60]

> There was once in this township a mother, whose conduct was lofty and
>   lovely.
> She came alone, young, from the Warngs to the Zhangs, whose family
>   brought her up,
> Like the dodder that climbs and entwines itself on a pine's or cedar's trunk.

> She gave way to the main wife, as being her senior,
> She offered her parents-in-law obedience.
> When told to serve as another's helper,
> She was filially humble, and conscientious.

> She waited respectfully on her husband. Nor did she presume on her beauty.
> In rearing and teaching their sons and daughters, she found the right
>   methods to do it.

When sickness took hold on her husband, and seemed sure to afflict him
    fatally,
She offered up prayers that death take away her own life, instead, in his place.
But the demon chieftains, as she related, came in no lesser numbers,
"And the blow that fell when he expired left my own heart-mind crushed."

Above her was her old mother-in-law, her white hair tossed in disorder,
While the senior wife was confined to her room, being utterly exhausted.

    By her the family was maintained.
    Her perseverance never changed,
    A person no one could replace.

Whenever she endured a pain, she just intensified her efforts,
Seeing to what was necessary, offering dainties to her elders.

    When her mother-in-law reached ninety
    How her heart-mind felt delighted!

Wasn't she beyond compare, this mother as faithful and filial
As Lady Jihng Jiang, the widow, who lived long ago in antiquity,[61]
Toiling in coarse linen clothes, at her woman's duties with diligence!

    The senior wife's offspring received her affection
    As much as did those she gave birth to herself.

The departed she served just the same as if they were living,
With exquisite offerings to ancestors summer and winter.
So, too, in the fall and the spring, she would go to the graveyard
As though paying a call on her husband's mother and father.

    She took care of her husband's burial rites,
    And likewise those of his senior wife.

The grave mound where they were interred was a tumulus high as a dike.
She dug out a space in its earth where she, also, could lie at their side,
So showing her righteous intent to be buried there too as his wife.

A nonpareil, then, without doubt, was this mother so filial and faithful,
Bereft of her spouse when she'd reached the twenty-ninth year of her age.[62]
She kept herself flawless thereafter, unblemished as gold or as jade,
A painful fidelity blessed by compassionate Heaven-Nature

Which, in recompense, granted the rare and quite exceptional favor
Of seeing before her, living together, no less than five generations!

In this world of ours it rarely happens that anyone lives beyond eighty
With such numerous grandsons and sons, or so thriving a family estate.

> Whenever one called at *her* home, it would seem that a load
> No longer weighed down as it had done before on one's shoulders.
So I've written this song for the Empresses' Scribe, to make sure that her tale
is told.[63]

This is a characteristically Confucian glorification of the mundane, an exaltation of normal life lived with a far from normal excellence, and an affirmation of the family as giving human life its central meaning.

The Semihuman

At the bottom of society were those directly prevented by their fellow human beings from leading a fully human life. These people were allowed little or no choice as to their movements or activities. Often they could not live with a wife or a husband. They rarely enjoyed protection from the legal-disciplinary system.

The extreme form of this semihuman existence was that endured by the jailhouse prisoner, who was not always a person who deserved to be incarcerated. The next category up was that of the labor-conscript. Young men were constantly being recruited by bureaucratic force for a variety of tasks: to haul army and government barges, to dredge waterways, to build dikes, roads, and fortifications, even ships, and many other such tasks. These assignments were for a limited period, but discipline was so harsh, and the working conditions often so foul, that many died or suffered damage to their health. Most of the poems that treat of this subject are from the earlier part of the dynasty, and it may be that the situation gradually improved, if this distribution in time is not just due to the accidents of selection. In contrast to the conscripts, serfs and hereditary servants, though not a large group in this period, were bound to their condition for a lifetime. Their fortunes were extremely various, depending on the position and disposition of their master, as well as on their own resourcefulness and strength of character. Last of all, rank-and-file soldiers had an ambiguous status. They were subject to a peremptory discipline, suffered the rigors of campaigning, and had only limited opportunities for family life, but they preyed, when occasion offered, on the civilian population. The poems that follow give a first impression of these worlds, whose existence is usually forgotten, and the emotions that characterized them.

Prisoners

Jin Shih's *Lament for the Prisons of Shandong* (QSD 10:267) describes how the prison warders bound the inmates to wooden boards at night, which prevented them from turning on their sides when they tried to sleep:

> I grieve for the Shandong prisons,
>   Where the warders are so vindictive
> That once the trussed convict enters in, he's no more than salted mincemeat.
>
>   In Shandong, it's jailhouse practice
>   For wooden planks to be used as straightjackets.
> So night after night the plank-bound men have the look of demonic rakshas.[64]
>
>   "Though *your* offense may be light,
>   And *your* offense is frightful,
> We're strapping both of you to the plank, too stiff to stir even slightly."
>
>   The prison warders' anger
>   Puts the inmates in a panic,
> With "Heaven pressing them from above, and Earth from below," so cramped
> That they believe there *is* a hell, right here, among humanity.[65]
>
> The prisons in antiquity were no more than simple lock-ups.
> All that security required was that jail walls be lofty.
> *These* warders take life easy at nights, or go out for a little jollity,
> So they claim they have a need to stop the inmates from making off.
>
>   Alas!
> Their pretext is the need to stop the jailbirds from making off,
> *But they never hear the midnight cries that rise in wild cacophony.*

The circulation of poems such as this may well have served as the premodern equivalent of newspaper exposés of malpractices. The author implies in his prefatory note that it was his intention to bring the horror to outside attention.

A more detailed picture of the jail regime is provided by Lii Luarnxuan's
Verses of a Superintendent of Prisons (QSD 10:276–78). Lii, who was born in
Shanxi in the late eighteenth century, served first in the board of punishments, and was then governor of Yurnnarn province. He was a would-be
prison reformer, though it is unclear how much he actually accomplished.
What is interesting, in the context of the present broad-ranging sketch of
emotional attitudes, is that he was driven by a deep Buddhist compassion:

I

Poverty and low status were my heritage at birth.
For one year after another we suffered from cold and hunger.
The year before last I graduated: Academy Doctor of Learning.
Last year I was appointed to serve in the Board of Punishments.

This year I've been given the management of its disciplinary officers
Who have the responsibility for supervising our jails
—An ocean that is vast and black, whose depths sink down bottomless,
Such that one never expects to see any stir or swell of change.

How utterly dispirited, these multitudes locked in prison,
Iron fetters clamped on their bodies, dragging themselves along limping.
There are even a few among them, some ten, say, maybe a dozen,
Strung up in the air spreadeagled, between a couple of ridge-beams.

They've no way to get their buttocks to support their weight on the ground.
Their heads, like a ram's in a thicket, can't move either this way or that.
They choke with asphyxiation, their life-breath almost out,
And hardly an inch unlacerated, anywhere on their skin.

These disciplinary tortures are all unspeakably cruel,
Sights that indignant pity turns its eyes from in aversion,
So I called the warders together, and told them that in the future
They were forbidden, and none of them was to practice such perversions.

I had them get busy unlocking, then, the manacles and fetters,
To give the convicts' spirits some slight respite from their troubles,
Since the reason the True Kings instituted the five traditional penalties
Was to root out evil-doing and disobedient stubbornness.[66]

Show them pity. Like us they are children who were born of human beings.
It's a cause for regret that they've been caught in the meshed nets of the law.
They should be fed on thin porridge, made from a gruel of cereals,
And settled to rest on mattresses stuffed with rushes and straw.

> All those immured in prison weep, letting their heads droop sadly.
> I likewise feel my courage sink when thinking on their tragedy.

II

As the sun was rising, I went to a prison, bypassing the formal procedures.
The rations were just about to be cooked by the menials there on duty.
Once the rice was ready they piled it up, on bamboo baskets, in heaps.
I went myself, on the prisoners' behalf, to see to its distribution.

The keys were turned to open the doors, and the jailbird rabble came out,
Linked together with lengths of chain around their necks and wrists,
In several groups of five or ten, or something thereabouts,
Walking behind each other in file, like so many strings of fish.

One bowlful of cooked rice per man. That was the portion dispensed.
The screws looked on with glaring eyes. Their attitude was vicious.
Artful old lags got their porringers filled, or at least more or less;
But they only doled half-helpings out to those who were slow-witted.

I wanted to stop this villainy. It lacked principle and fairness.
So I watched each portion being served, as the bowls passed before my eyes,
Then without giving warning I picked up a mouthful, to see if it had any
    taste,
And within me welled up, though unintended, the deepest of heavy sighs:

In Our Imperial Majesty's granaries, chests in their tens of thousands
Hold rice within that sparkles in the whiteness of its purity.
Since prison rice is also grain from our imperial storehouses,
Why should it be, unlike the rest, so grimed with mold, so dirty?

A prisoner pushed forward then, and gave me their complaint:
"Your Honor, these corruptions are matters for you to judge,
But gouging and fleecing are habits to which these sly warders give rein.
They use neither coal nor charcoal, when they're boiling our rations up.

Instead they jumble together some horse dung, or rotten firewood,
Which if combustible at all, does not give a flame that burns freely.
Then, when the time approaches they should finish with cooking our rice,
They give it a thorough sousing with water that's not been heated.

Why do they give it this sousing, you ask? There's a reason for it. It's this:
Every kernel of grain weighs double when put on the scales for reckoning."
When I'd heard what he had to tell me, my heart-mind filled with pity.
Rules are made a mockery of, if we supervise them neglectfully.

III

How protracted is their agony through the blazing days of the summer!
The sweat pours off their bodies more copiously than broth.
The jailhouse in every corner is filled with bluebottles buzzing,
A din too loud to fight with for continuous talk to be possible.

They're crushed more tightly together at night, side pressed up against side
Than the short-legged *beih* who has to squat propped up on the rump of a
    wolf.[67]
Across their bodies, dragging long tails, crawl hungry jailhouse lice
Sucking their blood as one might sink one's teeth into the pulp of a gourd.

In pain and mortification at being trussed up with cords,
They long for sleep but sleep, for them, is a land that they cannot find.
Convicts! What crimes in a previous life are you now paying for?
Wherever I look I see only souls that stumble in ignorant blindness.

"Come out!" I called to the prisoners. "Wait there on the walkways outside!"
Then I told the warders to take their brushes and beat out the inmates'
    bedding.
This done, to use their brooms to sweep their accommodation tidy.
Dustpans and besoms rose and fell, like the flails of harvesters threshing.

Freshly cut lumps of ice were placed in a box for keeping them cool.
Steam from the teacups drifted up in wavering, unsteady wisps.
Twigs of pine were burnt in the prison cells to clean them out with the fumes,
Which mixed with the scented smoke given off from the roots of the
    mountain thistles.

How can we enlighten them, without wasting another moment,
So Mercy's Boat float them on dharma's rains across to the Other Side?

So all the three thousand realms of which our universe is composed
Be pure and calm through motionless space and through onward-moving
    time?[68]

IV

The shortness of the winter's days is also a source of grief.
The different sorts of flowers, that grew by the steps, have withered.
The wind, out of the north, sucks the cold snow into vortices,
And howls, in its crazy dementia, round the corners of the buildings.

Alas, for you who are prisoners, locked up here in detention,
Your fingers splitting with chilblains, your flesh raw and chapped,
Unable to cover your naked frames with a single twist of thread,
Stripped bare, but still erect, the way dead tree-trunks stand.

And some of you have expired—toppling over as you died,
Then lying there stiffly a long, long time, and never coming back.
Since it's my responsibility to be prison supervisor,
If things like this are occurring, I must make an urgent plan.

I take my brush in my hands—and paper—I beg my friends
To send me, for my prisoners' sakes, financial contributions.
"A hundred copper cash will buy a single pair of leggings,
A thousand on a string acquire one inmate's short-hemmed tunic."

We'll heap up straw in bundles till their beds are plumply stuffed,
And set the ardent coals a-glowing, brimful in their braziers,
Make sure that those who are frozen have clothes on their backs, from us,
And the nourishment that we provide will stop their stomachs' cravings.

Throats will be moistened by the taste of ginger-flavored soup.
Their famished bellies will rotate, like capstans, as they digest.
But Hell's demonic legions will feel compassion for *you,*
As night falls you will hear them sob, with sharply drawn-in breath.

Lii's poem was thus a begging letter, couched in terms of his friends' own postmortem self-interest, but there is no mistaking his own passionate concern with charity. In later stanzas he describes his efforts to provide medical care for the convicts and to arrange the twice-monthly visits permitted the families of those serving long sentences. His outlook illustrates one aspect of the contribution made by the Buddhist faith to the emotions of the late imperial world: the fulfillment of the soul through charity.

Labor Conscripts

The sufferings of those impressed for labor services are summed up in the opening lines of Liarng Qinbiao's *Boat-Hauling Song* (QSD 8:226), written some time in the seventeenth century:

> On the official haling-way, the dust comes off best.
> On the official haling-way is no place for men.
> The dust gets trampled on once, but then has the time to rest.
> Men's strength gets exhausted, their bodies done to death.[69]

Skilled artisans were sometimes conscripted for the state's purposes, as well as the relatively unskilled. There are two poems by Qiarn Cherngzhi, the Mirng-dynasty loyalist who lived in seventeenth-century Suzhou, that give a description of these two kinds of labor levy. The first is entitled *Seizing Artisans* (QSD 8:225), and the word for "seizing" is that commonly used for the arrest of criminals. The date of composition is unfortunately unclear.

> So many ships were built this year in the lower Yarngzii valley,
> The officials press-ganged artisans. Their underlings raked in cash.
> The clerks went down to the countryside with utterly villainous attitudes,
> Arresting those skilled in working wood as if they were seizing bandits.
>
> Since the matter concerned the military, nobody dared to hide.
> Axes and chisels were ferreted out like robbers' stolen spoils.
> For every ten workers they dragged away, nine of that number died,
> Since throughout their stint they hammered and chipped standing deep in
> water.
>
> Their legs, from their waists on downwards, were all infested with worms.
> At random fell the leather-thonged lash, with never the slightest let-up.
> Even conscience-stricken officials could find no way to avert it,
> Only holding their noses because they objected to how the corpses smelt.
>
> Just yesterday a youthful tradesman, and only just recently married
> Having come from some way away to join his betrothed for their wedding,

Was whipped in the daylight hours, and at night-time clapped into manacles,
So he swiftly sold his newlywed bride in order to save himself.

As this story shows, it was usually possible to buy oneself out of labor conscription, if one had enough money.

The second poem is called *The Boatmen's Ballad* (QSD 8:225):

The boatmen live, along the banks, beside the Yarngzii River,
Year after year conscripted, for the transport of the military.

They've been upstream, they've been downstream, too often to be told,
And all they see is vessels come, conscript a crew, and go.

From each ten households, for one trip, one boatman is assigned,
Not grumbling at what lies ahead, whether it's death or life.

Why fuss if they must search his clothes, why make it a cause for grievance?
If they find no money on him, they'll tie him up each evening.

He may be lashed, or beaten, until his skin is broken.
For slow progress with the boat, their swords and arrows goad him.

Swords tucked into their belts, their quivers gripped in their fists,
They've as much respect for a human's life as they do for a dog's or pig's.

Those shot to death lie scattered about, their corpses blocking the path,
But who they are is the question that no one dares to ask.

Your fathers and mothers brought you up, till adult strength was acquired.
They saw you off when you went away. They leant on their doorposts, crying.

Though it's now long past since your rotting flesh fed the crows' and the
  kites' voracity,
Hope in their hearts, they still keep watch, for their boatmen corning back.

Sometimes conscripted artisans were taken to the frontiers. Yaor Shujih's *Song of the Artisans' Carts* (QSD 9:29) evokes the Chinese horror of having to leave not just one's home but one's homeland and the fear that if one dies in some faraway spot one may not be able to have a quiet existence even in death:

As the carts with the artisans went by
Their wheels were creaking like cicadas crying.

I heard them at the roadside, and the sound made me sigh.
Hoofbeats clattered to a stop. When I questioned one inside,
His voiced choked but, reluctantly, he gave me this reply:

"There is a stubborn little state giving civilized rule resistance,
So our task-force crossing the frontier must at once be made amphibious.
The way is long, over wind-driven waves, across the Yaluh River.
Constructing vessels of war, and skiffs, takes more than days to finish.

The commanders gave instructions for conscripting artisans.
Though, to the contrary, our skills, in that sort of craft, were lacking,
The clerks enrolled us even so, through their records for people and land,
Exempting from duty only those with pregnancies in their families.

I've met a man who's been there, for his tour of garrison service,
And yesterday he told me: not one of their seasons is summer.
Ice and snow, uninterrupted, have reposed there since time eternal.
When the spring thaw quickens, the topsoil floats. Often horses go under.

The sunbeams fall in the depths of the forests, unable to reach the earth,
Bears are heard roaring in open daylight across the desolate uplands.
While the sun was up they had to march with wolves and tigers among them.
Once it was dusk they hid themselves under the tangled shrubs.

He alone, of those who'd campaigned with him then, has managed to make it
    back.
Even now, when he speaks of their hardships, his teardrops fall and splatter.
My heart started pounding on hearing his words. It beat up and down, like a
    ram,
As I imagined those three thousand miles, through overgrown wastes,
    companionless.

When my father and mother gave me birth,
They dreamed I'd be skilled at my craft, that I'd make their old age happy.
    Today I've no prospect of return,
Leaving them while they are living, afflicting those who once carried me.

Who will there be, from my home-place, I can trust to carry word back
To tell them I've long ago perished, under the Mountains of Shadow?[70]

Alas, I've no wish, while alive, to go north through the Pass of Elms.[71]
My desire's to escape, when I'm dead, from the flux of cause and effect.[72]
In the realm beneath earth, will the day ever come when my grievances get a
   hearing?
How can it? For year after year, my ghost-fire will glimmer out there, on the
   frozen frontier."

It was commonly believed that what was called "old blood," especially that
of dead soldiers, gave rise to restless will-o'-the-wisps called "ghost-fires," and
the conscript is haunted by the possibility that this will be his fate. His spirit
will be trapped in limbo, unable even to present his case to the court of the
underworld.

Servants

Permanent family servants in late imperial China were often in a position of
dependence that made them closer to domestic serfs than employees. Some
of them were in a bound status that was the result of indebtedness or inherited from a parent who had been forced by debt to sell himself into service.
The poem *Servants* (QSD 26:976) by Chern Yirn, which was probably written toward the end of the eighteenth century, expresses a disapproval of this
institution that may have been becoming more widespread among the educated classes at this time—a matter that still needs enquiry.

The position of servants is an understudied theme in Chinese social history, and Chern shows that they present a certain paradox. While in an inferior
and exploited status vis-à-vis their masters, they could dominate many other
members of society if their master's family was a powerful one. Servants' fortunes and characters thus tended to reflect those of their masters and employ-
ers. As a group they do not fit easily into any conventional analysis based on
the concept of "class." What follows is about half of the original poem:

When the Creator of Things bore humans, they were, at first, of one kind.
When did those of "honor" get access to Court, unlike the "base" who
   did not?[73]
Both share the same body structure. Their five senses are all alike.
Yet male and female servants are both designated "helots."[74]

They enter their masters' homes through contracts, signed in a single day,
But must, till death, give others the toil of their hands and feet,
Generation after generation, sons and grandsons still in this status
—Something our laws on family life have banned as being illegal.

The satisfactions of servants are like clouds that follow a breeze.
How else did a menial of Huoh Guang grow mighty all of a sudden,
Or whiskered minister Huoh himself treat rulers with cruel deceit?[75]
Yet great families need these persons' power to make the masses look up
    to them.

Few of their base associates, then, will be able to keep their acquaintance,
With their bulging eyes, distended guts, and disdain for other folk,
Abusing position and pocketing bribes, of which they never grow sated,
Promoting their kinsmen by leaps and bounds, until they resemble nobles.

A fated distinction in "Heaven and Earth," like the hexagrams "Break-
    through" and "Thwarted"
Applies to the less well off. *Their* serfs have no way to compete.
—Those half-starved lads with sallow faces who act as gatehouse porters,
Those housemaids out on their shopping rounds in tattered clothes and
    bare feet.

Of all sights the sight that's most piteous is the whiplash cutting their flesh.
The flogged slave could not desert general Xiaao, whose talents he so much
    admired.[76]
How much more is this so for great households, whose retainers number so
    many,
And upon whom they trample like mud, and decide—to allow them to live,
    or to die!

This recalls lines written by Duh Fuu a millennium earlier at the beginning
of his poem *Describing My Feelings.*[77]

Were honor and status abolished, the serf would feel no disgrace.
Without the rich the poor would relish their poverty-stricken estate.
From times remote we have all of us shared a similar bodily frame;
Happy songs shift from house to house, and so do tearful complaints.

But Duh's humanism is relatively remote and reflective, accepting what goes
on in the world, whereas Chern Yirn, writing in a different age, is both
philosophically and emotionally hostile to servitude. *Tempora mutantur* . . .

In the Chinese view of things, if a human being were to live a properly
human life, he or she had to marry. The masters of female servants were
therefore meant to find them husbands once they had reached nineteen Chinese years of age (or approximately eighteen years, by Western reckoning).
This was not always done and some servants were obliged to live and die
without the fulfillment of a family. When Lirn Yurnmirng, who lived in the
seventeenth century, found this happening in Xiunirng (or "Haaiyarng") in
Anhui province, he described his dismay in his *Old Maid's Song* (QSD 26:
972). There is a short prose introduction:

> It is the custom of many men in Anhui to trade away from home. The wives
> manage the family's affairs. They think it unacceptable to have male servants in
> the house, so they provide support for their female servants but not for any
> husbands [for the latter]. It even happens that these women do not marry their
> whole life long. There is an ancient verse that says

> *If an old maid be not wed,*
> *She stamps the Earth,*
> *She cries to Heaven!*

> Resentment always gives rise to anger. I have written about what I have
> seen, so making a song of a matter that deserves tears.

> Daybreak over Haaiyarng. — A woman was drawing water.
> Her feet were naked. Around her, her skirts were hanging torn.
> Hands kept a grip on the well-rope, as she leant on the winch for support,
> Head bent over the icy spring, covertly letting tears fall.

> I held back the whip from my horse. I asked her why she was grieving.
> She answered me, "I was a daughter once born to a family of freemen.
> But when I was twelve, I was sold. To my present master. Since then
> I come, mornings, to draw them the water they need for cooking the
>   breakfast.

> All day I shoulder their firewood. I don't get given time off.

Shuttle flying, I help with the weaving. And, so, my toil grinds on.
How pitiful are my tangled tresses. I am twenty-nine years old.
The moon, my companion, wanes above. I lie in my bed alone.

I recall in the past (and my master, then, was with us here, at home)
That his wife'd say 'Smarten your "piled-black" hair!' and give me a little
    scold.[78]
She's swear, year by year, she'd be finding the *handsomest* husband for me,
While my spring charms slowly faded away, like dried-out blossoms falling.

Oh, blossoms! they burgeon and drop away, swift as water flows in the
    stream.
The girl next door is still at the age when she's got her baby teeth,
But yesterday a suave matchmaker urged her: 'Dab on some makeup, and
    prink!
Show them your broad, gosling-yellow temples. Step forth in your slippers
    of silk!'

Oh, the swallows! they make their nests in our beams. That's what I'd like
    to be,
As each with her mate, pair following pair, flits through our hall roofed
    high.
Or else, with my trail of bubbles behind me, I'd like to be a fish
Who appears and disappears with her spouse, out of then into the silt!

But, in human form, all I want to be is building timber and plaster,
My feelings extinguished, and conscious no longer of pain that wounds my
    heart."
She had finished speaking. She choked on her sobs. Tears dewed her
    kerchief wet.
My brows had creased in a sudden frown, at sorrow like hers, on my forehead.

Nine years' neglect and maladjustment, when she's fit for married relations.
How will she ever find a husband? *Will she weep for ten decades?*

Soldiers

The last sizeable group of people whose lives were largely determined by the
decisions of others were the soldiers. Gao Zhuo's *Listening to the Words of*

the Old Soldier (QSD 12:381) brings out clearly this condition of being at the beck and call of superiors, tossed this way and that by circumstance. The veteran of the Manchu forces who speaks refers back to the rising in Shuuixi, which took place in 1664, as occurring "last year," and this gives an approximate date to the poem as some time in the late seventeenth century. Overall, it is a good example of something that the Chinese liked doing, namely, to pass a person's whole life in review from beginning to end in a single sweep:

Distance. The mountains were rising up. Layer on layer of autumn colors.
Chill the wind that was blowing by. A sound like wings beating swiftly.
The cloud banks frozen in earthen hues, at the life-killing aethers' touch.
Face grimly sober, I journeyed forward, feeling no joy in my spirit.[79]

A veteran accosted me, and these are the words he said
As we sat on the boulders together, relaxing a while from our business:
"A stripling of twelve was all that I was when we came to the frontier to
     settle.
I was fourteen when we moved again, into the Liaordong peninsula.

I was fifteen when I was recruited, joining the ranks of the army.
At sixteen I served in attendance upon some important officials.
For ten years I never ceased wearing my suit of defensive armor,
While fending off barbarian raids on the great north loop of the River.

I've seen combat in war, and suffered from it, for all of thirty years.
The only son I've had was drowned. He fell in the Sanggan river.
My wife's dead, too, but where she perished I still have no idea.
My mother's passed on. Her lonely grave is crumbling into bits.

I was middle-aged before I saw the splendors of the capital.
But after that I was moved again, to guard the Harnguu Pass.[80]
I stayed hardly long enough in the west to 'impart some warmth to my mat,'
Being almost at once sent off to fight with the northern and southern savages.

Last year came a tribal revolt in Shuuixi.—So we smashed it.
This year we went to the bend where the Lur empties into the Yarngzii.
Mornings we'd make our way stumbling, over the pebbles and mudflats.
At night find a place in the swamp plants, where we could pitch our bivouac.

We used up the last of our strength to gather our firewood, wearily.
For many a long succession of days we went without a cooked meal.
Through the waterlogged dunes we trudged, with no complaint of exhaustion.
We earned scars from arrowhead wounds, to uphold the emperor's authority."

I listened to what he had to tell me, but even before he had finished
My mind and my courage felt shaken, with sympathy and with pity.
Though generals' strategic achievements may earn them exceptional merits,
It's the rank and file who've got the guts to face the hard slog and the terrors.

Their pictures don't hang in the gallery 'Transcending the Everyday World'
Towering up to the last azure clouds of the highest official preferment.[81]

Is there a sea-change here? A slight but subtle shifting of attitudes that now
at times can see the "ordinary" people as the real makers of history? The
evidence is still too slight to come to any conclusion, but it would be consistent with the focus of interest in many of the poems translated in the
foregoing pages.

Conclusions

I have tried to sketch, with the broadest of brush strokes, a panorama of the
everyday emotional life of the Chinese during the centuries that immediately
preceded the modern era. The two questions that I have always had in my
mind have been, What moved people, and Why? Poetry is apt to be used to
crystallize intense emotion, and poetic subjects are therefore quite useful preliminary indicators of what might be called "emotional foci," even if, evidently, the antecedent literary tradition had an immense effect in shaping
both concerns and concepts. That is less, though, perhaps, at the rather low
level that we have been examining than at loftier and more self-consciously
artistic ones.

I have tried, so far as is possible, to let the material speak for itself—
though well aware that an author's semiconscious predispositions (in this case,
my own) are always at work both on the process of selection of the poems
to translate and on the vocabulary of the translations. Hence I have tried to
avoid direct involvement with theory and polemic. Nonetheless, it must be
evident that while I think both class and gender important aspects of human
life, I regard both Marxist doctrine (in the past) and feminist doctrine (in the

present) as incapable of encompassing in satisfactory fashion the complexities of late-traditional Chinese society. (They cannot, to take two modest examples, make serious sense, in terms of the evidence presented here, of, servants and mothers-in-law respectively.) I also hope that these poems will make readers wary of the kind of generalizations recently offered by Shulamith Potter.[82] Professor Potter argues that "Chinese culture does not recognize itself as utilizing the emotional life of individuals in the service of the social order," and that "the Chinese assume that the existence of a continuous social order . . . requires no affirmation in inner emotional response, but only in behavior," and that hence "[e]motional experience has no formal social consequences." That a well-regarded social anthropologist (and one for whom I have much respect) could write such nonsense seems to indicate that the poems and the analysis given in these pages, and what they imply (which is approximately the opposite of what she says), have an important part to play in our conceptualization of emotion in Chinese society.

Notes

1. Chinese words are transcribed here into tonal pinyin: *r* following the vowel(s) to show the second, or rising, tone, and *h* after the vowel(s) to mark the fourth, or falling, tone, while a doubled main vowel indicates the third, or low-dipping, tone, as in the standard form of the name of the province Shaanxi.

2. The 1960 Mainland reprint by the Zhonghuar publishing house is missing a few of the original pieces, removed by the unnamed editors lest they "prove disadvantageous to national unity."

3. *Nieh Yirzhong Duh Xurnher shi* (Poems by Nieh Yirzhong and Duh Xurnher) (Beeijing: Zhonghuar, 1959).

4. *Qing shi-duor,* introductory matter, 1.

5. E. S. Rawksi, *Agricultural Change and the Peasant Economy of South China* (Cambridge: Harvard University Press, 1972), 42; and J. L. Watson, *Emigration and the Chinese Lineage* (Berkeley: University of California Press, 1975), 31.

6. Qu Dahjun, comp., *Guaangdong xinyuu* (New comments on Guaangdong) (circa 1690; reprinted Hong Kong: Zhonghuar, 1974), 1:7–8.

7. Qu Dahjun, *New Comments,* 6:210–11.

8. Qu Dahjun, *New Comments,* 10:20.

9. Qu Dahjun, *New Comments,* 24:606.

10. Ibid., 22:551–52.

11. D. Pearsall and E. Salter, *Landscapes and Seasons of the Mediaeval World* (London: Elek, 1973), esp. chapter 5.

12. B. Karlgren, *The Book of Odes* (Stockholm: Museum of Far Eastern Antiquities, 1950), 190–92.

13. Xue Ruohlirn, *Your Torng luhngao* (Draft discussion of Your Torng) (Peking Zhongguor xihjuh chubaansheh, 1989), 128. I am grateful to Dr. Warren Wan-kuo Sun for drawing this to my attention.

14. Ibid., 128.

15. Farn Xuarnlirng et al., eds., *Jin shu* (History of the Jin) (ca. 635; reprinted Beeijing: Zhonghuar, 1974), Dihjih 4, p. 108.

16. Ibid., 103.

17. The belief in a dominant but not unique deity.

18. See M. Elvin, "Early Communist Land Reform and the Kiangsi Rural Economy: A Review Article," *Modern Asian Studies* 4, no. 2 (1970).

19. Hatada Takashi, *Chûgoku sonraku to kyôdôtai riron* (Chinese villages and collectivity theory) (Tokyo: Iwanami, 1974), especially chap. 5. See also S. Gamble, *North China Villages: Social, Political, and Economic Activities* (Berkeley and Los Angeles: University of California Press, 1963) for the first third of the twentieth century, when village-based crop watching and contracted-out crop watching were often uneasily combined.

20. This phrase usually implies that it is hard to remove such pests without damaging what is valuable underneath; but here it just seems to mean "in the heart of the system."

21. Margery Wolf, *Women and the Family in Rural Taiwan* (Stanford, Calif.: Stanford University Press, 1972), 163. On the life-cycle in general, see M. C. Yang, *A Chinese Village: Taitou, Shantung Province* (London: Kegan Paul, 1947), chapters 6 to 11.

22. Probably white artemisia and *Marsilea quadrifolia*. These humble plants were traditionally offered to the spirits. (See the *Zuuozhuahn* [Commentary of Zuuo], Yiin-gong, 3.) Bor Juhyih's poem *Drawing up a silver bottle from the depths of the well* contains the line: "Betrothed she is a principal wife, wed in irregular fashion a concubine. / If unworthy of the full sacrifices, an offering is made of Marsilea and white artemisia." (*Bor Xiangshan shijir* [Anthology of poems by Bor Juhyih] [Tairbeei: Zhonghuar, 1963], 42.)

23. The Wernyarn commentary on the *Book of Changes* says: "Families that stockpile good acts will always have a surplus of good fortune, whereas families that stockpile acts that are not good will always have a surplus of misfortunes." (*Zhou Yih Yaor-shih xuee* [Mr. Yaor's study of the *Changes of the Zhou*] [Tairbeei: Shanghwuh, 1965], I, 53.)

24. This refers to the hexagram Kun, which "represents nature in contrast to spirit, earth in contrast to heaven, space as against time, the female-maternal as against the

male-paternal. The Receptive must be activated and led by the Creative; then it is productive of good." (R Wilhelm, *The I Ching or Book of Changes,* trans. C. F. Baynes [New York: Bollingen/Pantheon, 1950], 1:10–11.) Likewise, "the Earth must receive the Heaven, the wife must follow her husband" (*Mr. Yao's Changes,* I, 40 [kun, commentary].)

25. The sage's mother cut the fabric to symbolize the destructive effects of weakening in one's continuity of purpose. She moved house in order to find a neighborhood that had a better influence on him. See J. Legge, *The Chinese Classics,* vol. 2; *The Works of Mcncius* (London: Trubner, 1861), prolegomena, 18–19.

26. Reprinted in 1812 by the Liuryur Bookshop from an original said to be preserved in Guaangzhou. A copy is held in the library of the School of Oriental and African Studies, London (call number c.804.c.29).

27. The significance of this is not clear.

28. Returning the horse was an archaic custom by which the horse ridden by the girl to her new home was kept there until it was accepted that the marriage had been established. The implication was that if she had not been found suitable she would have ridden it back. At this period this is almost certainly only a literary reference, not a description of what actually happened. "Bringing back the red" means the visit home made by the bride within the first month of her marriage.

29. This celebrated poem describes the beauty Xishi and her lover, the king of the state of Wur, on the night before the ruin of his kingdom by the armies of Yueh They take their pleasure heedless of the doom that awaits them. The crows were birds of ill omen.

30. Mandarin ducks were traditional symbols for marital fidelity.

31. The neckbands of a fiancée *(ying)* were brightly colored, and probably originally signified her dependency on and service to her future in-laws. See Kurihara Keisuke, *Kodai Chûgoku no rei—rinen to keitai* (The concept and form of marriage ritual in ancient China) (Tokyo: Tōhō shoten, 1982), 148.

32. The three lives are her past, present, and future incarnations.

33. A reference to *The Four Griefs* by Zhang Herng, a poet and scientist of the later Hahn. See the *Wernxuaan,* 29, translated by E. von Zach, *Die Chinesische Anthologie* (Cambridge: Harvard-Yenching, 1958) 1, 523–25. The theme is giving presents in return for favors received.

34. Probably a reference to the so-called Hundred Children Pictures displayed at weddings to express the hope the couple would have numerous offspring.

35. "White-silk trousers" was a term for well-to-do young men intent on having a good time. The trouser-dropping pun is in the original.

36. *Zhongguor rernmirng dah cirdiaan* (The large Chinese biographical encyclopedia) (Hong Kong: Taihxing, 1931), 1473; and Legge, *Mencius,* 4.1.xvii, p. 183. The modern reading of the second name is "Churnyur" but I have followed Legge for the sake of consistency.

37. A. O. Wolf and C-S. Huang, *Marriage and Adoption in China, 1845–1945* (Stanford, Calif.: Stanford University Press, 1980), chapters 7 and 11 to 13.

38. Fei Hsiao-t'ung, *Peasant Life in China* (London: Routledge and Kegan Paul, 1939), 170–72. See also the remarks on the lower Yarngzii area in Zhou Zhuo's *Song of the Liuryarng Pumps,* translated above.

39. For example, those in Rural Reconstruction Commission of the Executive Yuahn, *Zhongguor norngcun ziliaoh wuuzhoong* (Five sorts of materials from investigations into farming villages in China) (1933 [?]; reprinted Tairbeei: Xuerhaai, 1971) volume 1, on parts of Jiangsu and Zhehjiang.

40. Marquis of Huairyin, and one of the generals who conquered China for the Hahn dynasty.

41. *The Song of the Firewood Carriers,* in Chour Zhaoh'aor, ed., *Duh Shaaolirng-jir xiarngzhuh* [Collected Works of Duh Fuu with detailed notes] (Beijing: Wernxuer guujir, 1955) 15:110–11.

42. The Shanyur was the khan of the Xiongnur people who lived north of China during Hahn times.

43. Nüügua is said to have mended a black hole in the sky after the rebel minister Gohnggong had pulled down one of the pillars of heaven. See E. T. C. Werner, *A Dictionary of Chinese Mythology* (1932; reprinted, New York: Julian Press, 1961), 334–35.

44. According to ibid., 406, figures cut out of paper to represent the Sky-Sweeping Lady, who was also the Spirit of the Broom Star, and holding a paper besom, were hung up under the eaves of the women's quarters to bring an end to rain.

45. Dragons make the rain, according to Chinese folk belief.

46. The "bare truncheon" was a thick club. The yellow thorn, a shrub, was presumably used to make canes for flogging debtors.

47. The third of the third was the Fairy Peach Festival, held in honor of the Queen Mother of the Western Heaven. Tecoma-Flower Stream was in Zhehjiang province, and took its name from the white flowers that were said to look like snow on its surface in the fall.

48. "[S]plit bamboo screens equipped with straw cocks are placed on wooden supports . . . under which braziers of burning charcoal are placed. . . . As the worm starts to spin out the silk, he is induced by the warmth of the fire to stay on the same spot instead of wandering around." Sung Ying-hsing [Song Yihngxing] *T'ien-kung k'ai-wu (Chinese technology in the seventeenth century),* trans. E-T. Zen Sun and S-C. Sun (University Park: Pennsylvania State, 1966), 42. According to F. H. King, *Farmers of Forty Centuries, or Permanent Agriculture in China, Korea and Japan* (London: Jonathan Cape, 1927), 275–76, more than a hundred pounds weight of leaves were needed for each pound of silk.

49. The term used here, namely *zhuugong,* is normally applied to the master of servants, but the context makes this sense relatively unlikely.

50. *Mémoires concernant les Chinois,* 30:53.

51. For an example, see the picture of the female tightrope-walker of 1609 reproduced in M. Elvin, "Tales of *Shen* and *Xin:* Body-Person and Heart-Mind in China during the Last 150 Years," *Zone* 4 (1989): 266.

52. Cloud-rings were probably bronze rings used to make the rope taut. They are mentioned in a poem with the same title by Liarng Yuhsheeng (QSD 25:949).

53. The "physical" soul *(jingpoh)* was linked to the body as its form or essence, and remained with the body after death. The "spiritual" soul *(hurn)* was part of the vitality-energy *(qih)* of the person and was liberated from the body when the latter perished.

54. M. Elvin, "Female Virtue and the State in China," *Past and Present* 104 (August 1984).

55. The Five Interactions were facial expression, verbal expression, seeing, hearing, and thinking. The Five Phases were earth, metal, water, wood, and fire. The point about ears is presumably that they redden with shame.

56. Lady Xiaan, who flourished in the sixth century, came from a line of Viet tribal leaders. She married a Chinese official but was a military leader in her own right and put down two rebellions. She rallied to the Suir dynasty, who conferred honors and position on her. See the *Biographical Encyclopedia,* p. 669.

57. The Yarngzii and the Yellow River.

58. Wern Jiang, wife of Duke Huarn of Luu, committed incest with her brother, Duke Xiang of Qir, which led to her husband being murdered. Warng Nirng (an abbreviation for Nirngzhi), who lived in the fourth century A.D., was such an imbecile that his wife, Xieh Daohyuhn, deserted him. He died after trying to defend the city of Guihji (modern Shaohxing in Zhehjiang) by magic, but she rode out and killed some of the enemy herself, bravery that moved the conqueror, Sun En, to spare her. See *Biographical Encyclopedia,* pp. 148 and 1682.

59. The references may perhaps need a word of explanation: the term "a water chestnut-flower mirror" was used for a lady's vanity glass, and though the original speaks only of the flowers reflected in the mirror being cold, the writer's face is almost certainly implied; the Western Slopes were the land where, in the dawn of the Chinese race, the Yellow Emperor married his wife Leirzuu.

60. Fengjing in northern Zhehjiang. Strictly, "maple" should be "liquidambar."

61. Mother of Gongfuh Wernbor Zhuo, prime minister of Luu. Confucius commended her for her view that diligence was the source of virtue and idleness of vice.

62. This age marked the upper limit for the permitted start of an officially recognized faithful widowhood.

63. There was a special clerk to record the doings of the empresses. The use of the term here is evidently metaphorical.

64. The swift-flying, man-eating devils of Buddhist demonology.

65. When Guaan Zhong, first minister of the state of Qir in the Springs and

Autumns period, was imprisoned, he is said to have said: "Why is high Heaven so low, and the generous Earth so confined?"

66. In ancient times the five penalties were branding, cutting off the nose, removing the feet, amputating the penis, and putting to death. In late times the first four of these were replaced by fines, floggings, imprisonment, and banishment to the frontiers.

67. The *beih* was a fictitious animal with such short forelegs that it was thought it could only move by straddling the back of a wolf, which, it was alleged, had correspondingly short hindlegs.

68. The Boat of Mercy ferried souls across to the Buddhist paradise. The Buddha's teaching of right conduct, that is *faa* or dharma, was likened to the rain that fell equally on all.

69. "Haling-way" is the old fenland term for a tow path. The original says, literally, "official road," but the translation gives its actual meaning.

70. The Mountains of Shadow, or Yinshan, run across Inner Mongolia to southern Manchuria.

71. Another name for Shanhaai-guan, the gateway into southern Manchuria.

72. *Xiaoxir chuarn* indicates something like the transmission of the alternating swelling and weakening due to the *yin* and *yarng* forces.

73. The reference here is to the Portal Register *(mernjir)* of the Hahn dynasty, which listed those allowed entry into the palace.

74. The old Spartan term conveys something of the flavor of *carnghuoh,* which originally implied enslavement for a crime.

75. This refers to Ferng Ziidu, the majordomo of Huoh Guang, who served the emperor Wuu of the Former Hahn but arrogated excessive power to himself during the reigns of Wuu's successors. Ferng was later said to have had illicit sexual relations with Huoh's widow, but this may have been a covert way of attacking the servants of General Douh Xiahn's family during the later Hahn. See Beeijing University Literature Office for Instruction and Research, *Liaang Hahn wernxuer-shii cankaao ziliaoh* (Reference materials for the history of Chinese literature under the two Hahn dynasties) (Beeijing: Gaodeeng jiaohyuh chubaansheh, 1959), 486 and 536. I am grateful to Sam Rivers (Chiang Yang-ming) for this reference.

76. Xiaao Yiingshih of the Tarng dynasty. He is said to have beaten one of his slaves so cruelly that an acquaintance urged the latter lo run away, but the slave refused, saying "I cannot, I so love his ability." *Biographical Encyclopedia,* p. 1659.

77. Chour Zhaoh'aor, ed., *Collected Works of Duh Fuu,* 20:98.

78. 'Piled black' *(duiya)* was a way of dressing women's hair.

79. Once the autumn had started it was believed that the "killing aethers" *(shaqih)* of the Dark Force began to dominate those of the Bright Force.

80. In the southeast of Hur'narn province. It is said to have spectacular cliff walls.

81. In 643 the emperor Taihzong of the Tarng had the portraits of twenty-four outstanding officials placed in this building in Charng'an as an exceptional honor.

82. Shulamith Polter, "The Cultural Construction of Emotion in Rural Chinese Social Life," *Ethos* 16 no. 2 (June 1988), esp. pp. 181 and 185. I am grateful to Dr. David Kelly for drawing this article to my notice.

—— *6* ——

The Self in Transition:
Moral Dilemma in Modern Chinese Drama

Kwok-kan Tam
Terry Siu-han Yip

The self is defined in traditional Chinese culture, according to Confucianism, as "the center of relationships" in the family as well as society; it is the basis of the cultivating process in which persons exist and cultivate themselves for the purpose of perfecting the self to better serve others (Tu, "Selfhood," 231). As succinctly summed up in the statement in the *Great Learning:* one should "cultivate oneself, regulate the family, govern the state, and bring peace to the world." It is in this socio-moral context that one sees oneself as the point of departure and the serving of others as the end of the cultivating process. Such a Confucian view reveals the strong sense of collectivism in traditional Chinese culture in which the self is a relational self but seldom an individual self. In other words, the traditional Chinese regarded the self as primarily a role-self, expressed in familial and social relationship. This role-self is ideally expressed in Confucian thought as follows: "Let the ruler be ruler, the minister minister, the father father, and the son son" (*Analects* 12.11). In this relationship persons are not completely individuals, for they have little individual identity or individuality, and exist only to fulfill dutifully the various roles expected of them. Individuality is allowed within the limits of roles. Self-awareness in traditional Chinese culture, if there is any, is therefore presented mainly as role-awareness, and identity crisis is seldom a problem in traditional Chinese consciousness.

May Fourth Iconoclasm

Such a Confucian system of morality was the dominant mode of thought in Chinese culture until the downfall of the Manchu regime in 1911, which marked a new chapter in modern Chinese history. The political changes further brought about an ideological crisis, which culminated in the May Fourth 1919 cultural movement, in which "democracy" and "science" were considered the two most important aspects of the modern attitude of the individual (self) toward others in the social world and physical world. To the May Fourth intellectuals, "science" was not merely technological advances, but a "Mr. Science" that had to be treated as a new, modern way of thinking and an attitude toward life. Being scientific was taken to be the first criterion for measuring the validity and progressiveness of things. The same attitude applies to democracy, or "Mr. Democracy," which stood not only for ideal political institutions but also more revealingly for an attitude toward the relationship between the individual and society, between the self and others. Hence, democracy was considered as both the opposite and the remedy of Confucianism, as it advocated a completely new view of familial and social relationships to the Chinese. This was the central idea of Chen Duxiu's program of democracy as delivered in the leading intellectual journal *Xingqingnian* [New youth] in 1918.

The zeal for science and democracy in China since the May Fourth Movement can be accounted for as a conscious reaction against the decaying Confucian order in traditional Chinese society. Although in principle Confucianism with its view of social and familial relationships may not be as undesirable as it was regarded during the May Fourth era, unfortunately in practice it was associated with a backward and disintegrating sociopolitical system supporting the Manchu regime. Perhaps for the first time in Chinese history, the essence of the Confucian order, which emphasizes the reciprocal ruler-subject/father-son relationships (Tu, "Selfhood" 234), was questioned. It lost its meaning and appeal for the people. The emperor of Qing was regarded as a usurper, whose previously "well-established, permanent, and pivotal locus" within the traditional cosmic order was challenged (Schwartz, "Chinese Perception" 283). The sociopolitical change was also reflected in the family when the family authorities were suddenly viewed by their newly "awakened" sons and daughters as puppets of a crumbling system, or as ineffectual intellectuals, or even as "reactionaries." Examples of this revolutionary attitude can be found in abundance in early modern Chinese drama—

the so called *wenmingxi* (enlightened drama) — in which the new intellectuals are portrayed as awakened individuals struggling for a free life against the stranglehold of sociofamilial relations.

In the midst of these upheavals, the self lost its fixed moral and social focus and its well-defined roles, and became confused in life. It must be noted that the sense of selfhood and otherness, central to one's understanding of one's self, might not come naturally to many people who were assigned fixed roles upon their birth and accepted their roles without questioning. Only when the roles of others were changed or challenged would they then reevaluate their own selves in relation to others. For a reflective person, however, the situation was conducive to a rethinking of oneself as an individual and a readjustment of one's relationships with others. This conscious act very often caused newly awakened persons a great deal of hardship in their struggle for freedom and readjustment of their roles with others and in society. In this process of moral and cultural reevaluation, Chinese intellectuals of the new generation turned to the West for direction and/or for some resolution to their identity crisis.

Awakening to Individualism

Lu Xun was among the early few who introduced the revolutionary spirit of European romanticism and individualism as an antidote to the diseased morality of the Confucian order. He did so in his seminal essay, "Moluo shili shuo" (On the power of Mara poetry), in which Ibsen's ideas of individualism as represented by the iconoclasm of Dr. Stockmann, the protagonist of *An Enemy of the People,* was admired by Lu Xun as a principle of upholding truth against the prejudices of society. This Stockmann-style individualism and courage appealed to the young Lu Xun as a moral remedy very much needed by the Chinese at the beginning of the twentieth century. He thought the Chinese needed a rebellious spirit and a determination to face one's self as well as the world alone, that is, "to face the accusations of a thousand men with indifference and cold eyebrows" *(Hengmei lengdui qianfu zhi)*. This was a message Ibsen's characters conveyed to Lu Xun: "to believe in the strength of reform and struggle and not to be afraid of being opposed to the majority" (55). Lu Xun further affirmed individualism as one of the greatest achievements of Western culture in his essay *Wenhua pianzi lun* (On cultural extremities), and introduced to the Chinese the sense of the individual as an existential self. Thus he later wrote many short stories, including the masterpiece *The True Story of Ah Q,* with the purpose of ridiculing the evasive attitude of the Chinese and their lack of individuality.

With the launching of the Literary Revolution and the call for the introduction of Western thought to replace traditional Chinese ethics during the early days of the May Fourth era, the Chinese intellectuals were eager for a complete revolution in culture in the late 1910s. Hu Shi, the spokesman of the May Fourth cultural movement, strongly attacked the Confucian moral order as a dying institution in China in his revolutionary manifesto "Yibusheng zhuyi" (Ibsenism) in *New Youth* in 1918. To Hu Shi, traditional Chinese institutions of law, religion, and morality were regarded as social evils, and the family system was considered nothing more than a perpetuation of selfishness, slavishness, falsehood, and cowardice. The individual was always suppressed by society, and only when society collapses will the individual be free from all bondage. Hu Shi admired the uncompromising courage and determination represented by Ibsen's characters who, like Dr. Stockmann, chose to be among the lonely minority in their fight for justice, truth, and self-fulfillment. Hu Shi was eager to introduce this concept to the Chinese, for he thought that the majority principle was anti-individualistic. Like Lu Xun, Hu Shi held that the courage to stand alone was the most noble and that it was necessary for the newly awakened self to assert itself in opposition to traditional social practices in order for social and cultural revitalization to take place in China. With the propagation of Western-inspired notions of self by the awakened Chinese intellectuals, a new morality combining iconoclasm with individualism, which explicitly stated that the self as an individual must not be considered subordinate and secondary to others, became the milestone marking the difference between the old morality and the new. The iconoclasm promoted by both Lu Xun and Hu Shi led to the massive introduction of social and political anarchism during the May Fourth 1919 Movement, which aimed at completely undermining any authoritative social order, particularly the Confucian order of human relationships, and freeing the human desires of the individual self from repression. Evidence of this radical attitude is found in abundance in such leading journals of the period as *New Youth, Xinchao* (Renaissance), and *Qinghua* (Tsing Hua) *University Journal.* This is the essence of early May Fourth literature and culture. As Zhou Zuoren, a well-known essayist and Lu Xun's brother, clearly pointed out in his May Fourth manifesto, what China needed was a "Literature for Man" (Ren de wenxue) that discusses the conflicts between the individual and society, free will and environment, and heredity and personal temperament, and that promotes such individualistic beliefs as freedom, which means "to have the will to be responsible for one's self" (19). As a result, a great number of literary works at that time presented the individual as a lonely fighter against society. A Western play like *A Doll's House* became very influential, for it offered a ready solution to the Chinese intellectuals as to how they could face the immediate problem of breaking from their family fetters and fulfilling their self-responsibilities as human beings. The younger generation in China was awakened to a new world of experience and ideas grossly represented as individualism.

In the early years of the May Fourth era, particularly those between 1917 to 1927, Western ideas of individualism were taken as a force countering Confucian collectivism. One effective and lively means to appeal to the intellectuals was drama, which suddenly became a widely adopted mode of mass media. Many Chinese intellectuals resorted to playwriting to reveal the moral disease of the Chinese majority and to advocate ideas of iconoclasm and individualism as necessities to progress. There was a vogue among the playwrights to depict the minority as young heroes or heroines in defiance of tradition and all kinds of moral bondage that pose as obstacles to their pursuit of individual freedom.

The three leading playwrights of the time—Guo Moruo (1892-1978), Tian Han (1898-1968), and Cao Yü (1910-1997)—represented this tendency to treat drama as an artistic expression of contemporary moral and social issues. Of immense interest to the reader is the different resolutions in their plays, which reveal their own ideological inclinations, moral visions, and dramatic choices. Their plays can thus be regarded not only as dramatic expressions of their view of the self in relation to social change but also as manifestations of the young Chinese intellectuals' moral dilemma and self-searching in transitional China.

Guo Moruo and the Romantic Revolutionary Self

In Guo Moruo, the historian, poet, and playwright, the moral dilemma and conflicts the self faces in social transition are presented in a way different from that in Cao Yü and Tian Han. Guo considered the study and rewriting of history as his mission; he wished to rectify the wrong concepts in the traditional morality represented by Confucianism and to free the self from its historical and cultural fetters. Taking Goethe and Ibsen as models,

Guo began his career as a writer of history plays. He aimed at breathing fresh air into modern Chinese literature by introducing new ideas, progressive thoughts, and the romantic revolutionary spirit to his readers during the May Fourth era.

With a strong romantic impulse for self-expression and self-exploration, Guo used literature to define his own existential experience. Like Goethe in his use of the Faustian legend to voice his own ideas and depict the spiritual crisis of the Renaissance, Guo employs mythological settings and legendary figures and situations in order to express his own feelings and opinions, his hopes and ideals. In his verse drama, *Nüshen zhi zaisheng* (The rebirth of goddesses, 1921), the audience finds the influence of Goethe, particularly in the romantic pursuit for individualism and personal freedom against social and political bondage. His second play, *Guzhu jun zhi er zi* (The two princes of Guzhu, 1922), again celebrates self-liberation. Traditional Chinese social and cultural practices, especially those moral observations and manners prescribed in *Liji* (The book of rites), are taken as inhumane customs. As the unnamed female protagonist who represents the collective voice of the enlightened new individuals in China, says:

> Oh, pitiful men, you don't even complain!
> They teach you to be obedient and loyal,
> They teach you to respect and observe your roles,
> They teach you to sacrifice yourselves,
> And they tell you this is morality and civilization.
> But let me tell you, take off you hypocritical human mask immediately,
> And return to Nature.
> . . . .
> Wake up, wake up, pitiful, quiet men!
> I welcome you, in Nature and on this great moral road,
> To sing the victorious song of human nature! (67–68)

The godlike female hero-speaker in the play even urges her audience to be their own god and master of their lives. Compared with Cao Yü and Tian Han, Guo was the most radical of the three in suggesting drastic changes in his country. Although Guo was less mature in dramatic technique and his plays were full of revolutionary slogans, he was nonetheless the most radical in his advocacy of individualism in the spirit of revolution, which combined the concepts of iconoclasm and rebellion. Guo seldom depicts his heroes or heroines as victims. Instead, he presents to the audience disturbing images of courageous moral rebels and fighters.

A prime example of a Guo-style rebellious heroine can be found in his historical play *Zhuo Wenjun* (1923). Guo purposely set the play in a traditional society some two thousand years ago in order to put his heroine in sharp conflict with the moral system of the time. The play centers on her struggles for individual freedom, as she rejects the roles assigned to her according to conventional Confucian morality. Although Zhuo Wenjun is a historical figure, in the play she advocates an attitude of individualism that Guo believed to be thorough and revolutionary. Like Nora in Ibsen's *A Doll's House,* Zhuo Wenjun considers her duties toward herself as the most important matter in her life. On the issue of her freedom to remarry, she insists on her rights as an individual human being, whose duty to her self should come before role-responsibilities as a daughter and a daughter-in-law:

> ZHUO WENJUN: In the past I was a daughter and a daughter-in-law to you, but now I am speaking to you as a human being.
>
> ZHUO WANGSUN [ZHUO WENJUN'S FATHER]: Ah, terrible! Terrible! This is a rebellion, a rebellion! *(Tries to hit Zhuo Wenjun.)*
>
> ZHUO WENJUN: One of you says that I am immoral, while the other asks me to die [to save the family from humiliation]. This is what you should say to yourselves.
>
> ZHUO WANESUN: Rebellion! Rebellion!
>
> ZHUO WENJUN: I hold that what I am doing can serve as an example of good morality for later generations. The old moral order set by you men and old people can no longer confine us awakened youths and enlightened women. (117–18)

Knowing that he cannot stop the awakened and determined Zhuo Wenjun from remarrying, Cheng Zheng, the father-in-law, resorts to appealing to her moral conscience and reminds her of her other family obligations and roles in life. To the enlightened Zhuo Wenjun, these social and familial roles and duties are rooted in the foolish beliefs of the old morality, which she refuses to accept. She rebels against the normal expectation and practice of having her life (self) run by other people and bound by outdated and outmoded morality:

> CHENG ZHENG: Wenjun, you are too radical. You can discuss with us calmly. You don't have to be so hot-tempered. . . . You have a younger sister and brother, you have to show them a good example.

ZHUO WENJUN: I am a good example!

CHENG ZHENG: Are you so hard-hearted as to leave your younger brother and
   sister? When you wake up, they will cry and look for you!

ZHUO WENJUN: When they wake up, you can tell them to go to the pavilion
   [her lover Sima Xiangru's place], where I will introduce them to their new
   brother-in-law.

CHENG ZHENG: Can you neglect your duties as a daughter?

ZHUO WENJUN: I have my own duties as a human being! To follow you old
   people blindly is not filial piety at all! (119)

Guo depicts in the play an awakened individual who seeks fulfillment of her
own desires and aspirations, and bears responsibility for herself and her deeds.
In short, Zhuo Wenjun is portrayed as a rebellious character in line with the
feminist in spirit. Seldom in the history of modern Chinese drama does one
see such a harsh and explicit attack on traditional role-morality. The most
apparent contribution of Guo's play in the presentation of the revolutionary self
is the message that one should seek one's true identity by being fully responsible
for one's self: one should never sacrifice one's duties toward oneself when such
duties are in conflict with the duties of one's other roles in life. The play *Zhuo
Wenjun* can thus be read as an artistic expression of Guo Moruo's determined
and revolutionary attitude toward traditional morality, for the moral conflicts
in the play are described as conflicts between characters representing different
systems of morality and value. The play can further be regarded as a manifesto
of individual self-assertion in a conservative Chinese society and an "outcry" on
the playwright's part with the wish to quicken the pace of change in the country.
Thus Guo's historical play is in fact ahistorical in its message.

Tian Han and the Sentimental Lonely Self

In Guo Moruo, the contradiction between traditional morality and the new
morality is presented in the form of clashes between the individual self governed by personal wishes and the sociofamilial self governed by the public
roles assigned to the person. While reflecting the sociopolitical unrest in
China, Tian Han also depicts the quest of many young people for selfhood
during the May Fourth era in his early one-act play *Kafeidian zhi yi ye* [A
night in a café, 1920, 1932]. It portrays three different images of the self in
a transitional society. Each person is caught in a moral dilemma and suffers
the crisis of self-identity and self-definition.

Set in the winter of 1920, the play delineates the struggles of two young people, Bai Qiuying and Lin Zeqi, for selfhood in a conservative Chinese society. Bai is presented as a nonconformist who refuses to accept the socio-familial role assigned her. She openly defies her father by rejecting the "ideal" marriage her father arranges for her. She would rather leave the security of home for the indifferent, if not hostile, city in order to realize her own self—a self that is defined not by her own social role but by her personal desires and goals. Indeed, she represents those young Chinese of the time who were in quest of another ideal based on love, free will, and the fulfillment of the private individual self.

Bai's decision to leave her family, which provides social and economic security to its members, indicates her firm determination to seek self-fulfillment and personal happiness and her rejection of the entire Confucian culture and tradition. She typifies the Chinese young people in that period, who were for the first time aware of themselves as individuals with desires and aspirations and who refused to deny their individual self for the fulfillment of social expectations. In short, Bai makes a choice to follow her free will and her desire to be true to her self even if such a choice demands a self-imposed exile on her part to a lonely but free life in a cold and indifferent world. She supports herself by working as a waitress in a café, which is in itself a symbol of Western culture and influence in China and a refuge for Bai, the lonely fighter in her battle against tradition and conventional morality.

While Bai is presented as a nonconformist who is courageous enough to assert her self in defiance of a conservative society represented by her father, an upholder of traditional practice and Confucian ideology, her childhood lover Li Qianqing is portrayed as a loyal follower of Confucianism. Li's decision to marry a socially acceptable lady reveals his conforming character. He represents the compromising and submissive type of young men who are willing to trade their happiness and ideals for material gain and social security. Although Li Qianqing has a glimpse of Western individualism through his education, he still chooses to conform to the Confucian practice of effacing one's self before authority and obediently observes the social and familial roles expected of him.

His choice to compromise is in direct contrast to Bai Qiuying's determination to exercise her free will and to assert her self in a society governed by Confucianism. Her chance reencounter with Li Qianqing enables Bai to view herself in a new light as a lonely fighter in the battle for self-realization. Her self-autonomy, however, is achieved with the termination of her relationship with Li Qianqing, her last link with the Confucian tradition, her past self, and her cultural background. Through Bai's unfulfilled love with Li, Tian Han affirms the price one has to pay for individual freedom and self-independence and emphasizes the alienation and feeling of loneliness experienced by the young people who strive hard to attain self-identity and achieve selfhood through courage and determination in their moral and existential battles.

Besides depicting Chinese young people who take different paths in life in *A Night in a Café,* Tian Han further presents another image of the self through the character of Lin Zeqi, who is a young intellectual at a crossroad, and who feels uncertain amidst all the changes in transitional China. Like Bai in the past, Lin is troubled by the prospect of a marriage arranged against his wishes. And he often indulges himself in excessive drinking as a means of benumbing his senses so as to forget his immediate trouble. What causes his sorrows, as revealed in the play, is his moral dilemma between total submission of one's self to family authority based on Confucian teachings and filial piety, and a determined rebellion against tradition in order to lead a life based on Western notions of individualism. As Lin confides to Bai, "[My] situation now is comparable to that of a lonely traveler in a desert with no sight of a shade, and anxiety is driving him crazy" (11–12). Unlike Bai, who has forsaken everything for her wish to achieve an individual self independent of all forms of familial and social bondage, Lin is torn between his familial role as a son who should dutifully take the advice of the father and accept the arranged marriage, and his private individual self who rejects any form of compromise or subservience to one's social or public duty. In this light, Lin typifies the majority of young people of the May Fourth era who had no courage to openly defy the authorities, yet they had no intention of submitting their selves to the older generation, either. As Lin succinctly states:

> It would be a good thing if one could really be a dutiful son who sacrifices himself for his father. However, my weak character does not allow me to bear such sufferings. I can neither break through all the social shackles in a devilish way and love my true love, nor can I humanely force myself to love someone I have no feeling for. That is why I must suffer forever. (14)

It is in this state of mind that Lin often frequents the café where Bai works, and it is through his association with Bai and his subsequent knowledge of Bai's relationship with Li and her final rejection of the latter that Lin changes his attitude towards life and adopts a new view of his self in relation to society.

He is "enlightened" by Bai's determination to seek self-fulfillment in life. At the end of the play, Lin and Bai pledge to support one another as companions in the struggle for selfhood. Both Bai and Lin come to realize the importance of the individual self, and their self-awareness is achieved after much suffering and struggle over the moral dilemma of choosing between their individual self and their social role-self. In the play, Tian Han characterizes three images of the self in the May Fourth era and reveals his personal inclination to side with young people like Bai and Lin who are determined to develop their romantic individual self in a society in which Confucianism with its collective behaviorism prevails. Bai's and Lin's ultimate choice to seek self-fulfillment and assert their self-identity is basically a moral choice that inevitably places them outside the security of the established social order. They are indeed presented as the true disciples of Lu Xun and Hu Shi—young people who confront society with courage and determination.

In Tian Han one sees that the conflicts between a person's individual choice and one's moral duties toward others are presented not only as outer conflicts between the self and others, but also as inner conflicts (or moral dilemmas) in the person. It is also in Tian Han that one notices a change of attitude from indecision and moral uncertainty to determination, self-assertion, and self-definition on the characters' part, and a more mature and subtle treatment of the conflicts between individual desires and moral-roles that not only offers a view completely different from Guo's emotional outbursts in *Zhuo Wenjun* but also shows the complexity of the post–May Fourth mentality.

Cao Yü and the Indecisive Self

Cao Yü's *Leiyu* (Thunderstorm, 1934) is a play set in the 1920s, using the gradual disintegration of an old Chinese family, together with its social and moral system, as its background. The play moves back and forth in time, exposing in retrospect the conflicts between the characters. Hidden in this temporal structure is the message that the present will replace the past though it is haunted by what has gone before. The plot of the play revolves around the authority figure Zhou Puyuan and develops to show how his moral falsehood causes catastrophes not only to himself but also to others in the Zhou and Lu families.

As head of the family, Zhou Puyuan considers himself responsible for the order of the family and for making sure that the roles of the family members are fulfilled as expected. Thus Zhou Puyuan says, "I believe my family is the most perfect and well-behaved, and I think my sons are both good, healthy lads. I've brought the two of you up, and I won't have you giving anybody an excuse to gossip about you" (66). Zhou sees himself as a model of Confucian order according to the principle of "cultivating oneself, regulating the family, governing the state, and bringing peace to the world." Through his relationship with his family members, he conceives his self in the role of a father, a husband, and a moral authority. He emphasizes this role as being most important in maintaining the order of the family—society in miniature. And the play focuses on developing the conflicts between the familial-public role-self and the individual-private self of the characters.

Zhou Puyuan's bizarre insistence on arranging the furniture in exactly the same way as it was thirty years ago shows not so much his love and memory of his supposedly dead first wife as his conservative and traditional attitude toward life, unshaken by time or circumstances. He is regarded by his family members, especially his sons, as a man of high moral standards. When he reminds Zhou Ping, his eldest son, to mend his ways, Zhou Puyuan requests him to do so out of respect for Zhou Ping's mother. In other words, Zhou Puyuan also adopts and fulfills the maternal role of his "dead wife" in bringing up the children. And it is through his assumptions of the role of the absent "dead" mother, as well as his assertion of power and authority as the father that he "rules" in the family. Zhou is never aware of himself as an individual but always as a role player with absolute power over others (sons, wife, and employees). Yet this authority of Zhou Puyuan, which is instrumental in maintaining the order of the family, is soon shattered when Shiping, his supposedly dead first "wife," appears and reveals the secrets of his true self in the past when he seduced her, then his maid, an act which violated the established master-servant roles. In the eyes of the sons, the self-built image of Zhou Puyuan as a respectable authority is ruined, for he fails to live up to the moral principles he "advocates" and imposes upon others. Zhou Puyuan's tragedy lies in his inability to recognize his individual-private self governed by instincts and free will—a self that is foreign to his moral consciousness and his traditional beliefs. His succumbing to the role-morality that considers it wrong for a master to marry a maid brings not only suffering to himself but also disaster to others. Zhou Puyuan was relying on Confucian morality as the guiding and ruling principle in his family, and the revelation that there exists an individual-private instinctual self that works contrary to his familial-public role-self inevitably leads to the collapse of Zhou's family. This represents the disintegration of the traditional Chinese society governed by Confucian collectivism.

Zhou Ping finds his familial-public role-self in conflict with his individual-private self in moral matters as well as in family affairs. His public self tells him that Fanyi is his stepmother and he should treat her in a respectable and "appropriate" way. Yet his secret and dangerous "liaison" with Fanyi shows that the principle of behavior and order based on the Confucian moral code and imposed upon him by his father Zhou Puyuan does not work, for he actually follows his own desires, sexually and emotionally. In short, he is portrayed as a character who defies and transgresses the world of tradition and Confucian morality with his youthful passion. Zhou Ping's love affair with Sifeng is Zhou Puyuan's past history with Shiping repeated, the consequence of which is half-sister/half-brother incest committed out of ignorance. Zhou Ping's attitude towards Fanyi and Sifeng reveals his indecisive and cowardly character. Instead of altering the suffocating environment in which he dwells by openly challenging it, Zhou Ping resorts to self-pity, self-condemnation, and self-destruction. The revelation of his father's past guilt and his blood relationship with Sifeng confirms his view of moral decadence and spiritual sterility in the family.

While Zhou Ping is described as a young man uncertain about life and indulgent in sexual affairs as a temporary respite from his moral and identity crises, Fanyi, the stepmother, epitomizes the frustrations of a young woman in a transitional and conservative environment. She is trapped in the conflict between her public self as mother and wife and her private self who passionately loves Zhou Ping, and not Zhou Puyuan, her husband. To observe the moral code and maintain her public self, she is forced to act as a puppet mother and a "sick" wife. Being a woman with a strong desire to be an individual true to her self in private and in public, Fanyi finds it impossible to realize her self in the Zhou family. When the reality is revealed and the individual-private selves of all the characters are exposed, Fanyi clings to Zhou Ping, her only hope for a new life and a new role. As she says at the end of the play, she is a human being the same as the others and she cannot sacrifice her private self for the familial-public role she finds herself ridiculously caught in. This can be considered as one of the earliest signs of the growing awareness of the self in a married woman treated in Chinese literature of the 1930s. Unfortunately, Fanyi's hope to free herself from her familial-public role to become her true self is destroyed with the suicide of Zhou Ping, and this turns out to be so much a blow for her that she suffers a mental breakdown as a result.

A closer look at the play shows that the characters' tragedies are constructed on the principle of discrepancy and conflict between the appearance of surface relationships and the reality of hidden relationships, between the familial-public role-self and the individual-private instinctual-self, between the old morality-run family and the newly awakened individuals living in it, as well as between Confucian collectivism and Western individualism. *Thunderstorm* is a play with a tragic theme heavily based on the impossibility of self-definition and self-realization under the old moral system in which everyone has to act according to the roles of one's public self. In other words, Zhou Puyuan himself is not to be blamed for causing the sufferings of others. Rather, it is the system of role-morality he supports that has caused all the suffering and disturbances. In this light, Zhou Puyuan is also a victim of the traditional role-morality that prevents him from recognizing and realizing his self. Throughout his life, he sees himself as a moral icon and suffers as a consequence. Yet, he is actually the symbol of the crumbling moral and social order in a China inflexible to changes.

Thunderstorm is thus an indictment of the traditional role-morality whereby all the characters are unfulfilled selves and can only lead the life of the living dead. Showing the sufferings of the awakened but helpless individuals in the turmoil of social change from the old to the new, Cao Yü is rather pessimistic compared with Guo Moruo and Tian Han in his view of moral transition and self-assertion when he resorts to "cosmic cruelty" as an explanation of the tragedy. His characters are victims of their own frailty and weakness, and lack the courage to rebel against traditional morality. The conflicts between individual desires and role-morality are depicted in the play as the characters' moral dilemmas (or psychological/inner conflicts). Zhou Ping thus is a personification of all the conflicts that occur to a weak and indecisive young man of the time caught between the traditional sense of moral responsibility and self-evasion and the Western notion of individualism and self-assertion.

From Outcry to Hesitation: Post–May Fourth Uncertainty

Portrayed in the plays discussed above is the self as an awakened individual, a lonely fighter who becomes increasingly aware of his/her individual self in relation to others in the family and society. Of particular interest are the changing images of women characters presented in relation to others in the world of men. Guo Moruo, Tian Han and Cao Yü are three modern Chinese dramatists, whose representative works, specifically in respect of the changing roles of the self in relation to others, can be seen as a "trilogy" dealing with different representations of the self as the romantic revolutionary nonconformist who faces opposition with courage and determination, as the lonely fighter, and as the tragic victim of old moral falsehood. In their plays, one is conscious of the various choices made by the young generation of the period who either submit to authority in exchange for financial gain and social security, or rebel strongly against any form of moral and spiritual constraint confining the emerging self. The majority are the uncertain and indecisive youths who feel confused and frustrated at the crossroads.

The three playwrights discussed above can also be viewed from a broader perspective in relation to the general and popular trends that treat literature and the performing arts as experiments of social ideals. Hu Shi's topical play, *Zhongshen dashi* [The greatest event in life], Tian Han's *Huo hu zhi ye* [The night a tiger was captured], Cheng Fangwu's *Huanyinghui* [The welcome party], Ouyang Yüqian's *Pofu* [The shrew] and *Hui jia yi hou* [After returning home], Guo Morou's *Nierong*, and Cao Yü's *Richu* [Sunrise], are a few typical examples in which the protagonists are treated as embodiments of individualistic ideas, and the plays delineate their revolt against conventional moral practices in their quest for individual freedom in love, marriage, education, or career. These plays are constructed on the principle of having two sets of diametrically opposed characters to represent the two forces in the struggle: the conservatives are repressive authority figures and the iconoclasts are awakened young individuals. In the early years of the May Fourth era, the general resolution was that the iconoclastic individual would win in the struggle over the conservative and repressive authority figure. In this way, the ideas of individualism and iconoclasm were often presented in modern Chinese drama as an alternative to social conventions and a counterforce against traditional morality. With the gradual fading of the revolutionary spirit in the later days of the era however, the intellectuals began to reconsider the tradition with a more sober mind. As Chow Tse-tsung points out,

> As time went on, the ideological issues were examined in more detail. Those who were trained in modern thought found the problems of the intellectual tradition and transplantation of Western ideas more complicated than as first imagined, and in many cases they were driven to take divergent and controversial stands. In theoretical debate, opposition to the new thought grew stronger in the latter period. The main currents of iconoclasm and the critical spirit still prevailed

among most of the new intellectuals but their minds were occupied by more controversial issues than those conceived previously. (*May Fourth Movement*, 314)

Thus the unsurpassed revolutionary spirit begun in Guo Moruo's plays and picked up and further developed by Tian Han can be seen as a step toward self-searching and intellectual maturity and thoughtfulness among the young intellectuals of the May Fourth era. Cao Yü's notion of "cosmic cruelty" as fate and his depiction of troubled young characters entangled in various forms of familial and social relationships reveal the complexity of the problem and a general feeling of frustration and helplessness among the young intellectuals in their quest for selfhood and self-realization amid the strong torrents of tradition and convention. Instead of the naïve belief that self-fulfillment can be attained through personal battles and perseverance, the Chinese intellectuals in the post-May Fourth period came to realize that there was still a long way to go and countless battles to fight before they could stand up and be recognized in society as individuals with self-identity and dignity. In this respect the plays discussed above capture succinctly the spirit of the time when China's youths, overwhelmed by Western notions of individualism and self, were groping for the means to shed their old role-selves for a new identity governed by freer expressions of the self. The plays further portray the sacrifice, sufferings, and ordeals involved in the struggle for self-responsibility of the individual.

Works Cited

Cao Yü. *Leiyu*. In *Cao Yü wenji*, ed. Tian Benxiang, 1:1–223. Beijing: Zhongguo xiju chubanshe, 1988.

Chow, Tse-tsung. *The May Fourth Movement: Intellectual Revolution in China*. Stanford, Calif.: Stanford University Press, 1967.

Guo, Moruo. *Nüshen zhi zaisheng*. In *Moruo juzuo quanji*, 1:26–34. Beijing: Zhongguo xiju chubanshe, 1982.

———. *Guzhu jun zhi er zi*. In *Moruo juzuo quanji*, 1:59–83. Beijing: Zhongguo xiju chubanshe, 1982.

———. *Zhou Wenjun*. In *Moruo juzuo quanji*, 1:84–121. Beijing: Zhongguo xiju chubanshe, 1982.

Hu Shi. "Yibusheng zhuyi." *Xinqingnian* 4, no. 6 (June 1918): 489–507.

Lu Xun. "Moluo shili shuo." In *Lu Xun quanji*, 1:63–115. Beijing: Renmin wenxue chubanshe, 1981.

————. "Wenhua pianzi lun." In *Lu Xun quanji,* 1:44–62. Bejing: Renmin wenxue chubanshe, 1981.

Schwartz, Benjamin. "The Chinese Perception of World Order, Past and Present." In *The Chinese World Order,* John K. Fairbank, ed., 276–288. Cambridge: Harvard University Press, 1968.

Tian, Han. *Kafeidian zhi yi ye.* In *Tian Han juzuo xuan,* 1–32. Beijing: Renmin wenxue chubanshe, 1981.

Tu, Weiming. "Selfhood and Otherness in Confucian Thought." In *Culture and Self: Asian and Western Perspectives,* Anthony J. Marsella et al., eds., 231–51. New York: Tavistock Publications, 1985.

Zhou, Zuoren. "Ren de wenxue." *Xinqingnian* 5 no. 6 (December 1918): 317–34.

Part Three

Self as Image in Indian Theory and Practice

INTRODUCTION

Wimal Dissanayake

The five essays included in this section on India deal with self as image in terms of a number of representational practices and symbolic discourses of great importance in Indian culture. In the construction of selfhood, the role of signifying practices is of crucial importance, and what the ensuing chapters underline is the complex ways in which the idea of image is related to it. These five essays thematizing poetry, fiction, autobiography and cinema in terms of the entwinement of self and image foreground the fact that self is neither totally autonomous and self-present nor a passive product of discourse, but that there is a dynamic and incessant interplay between these two extreme positions advocated by some theorists. Selfhood is embodied, historically situated, and culturally constructed; but at the same time it seeks to acquire a sense of agency. And the interesting ways in which this effort is imbricated with the notion of image is indeed significant, as the following essays demonstrate.

Images are central to the understanding of Indian culture. They subtend discursive writings ranging from religious and philosophical texts like the Upanishads to works on medicine and physiology. Imagery plays a crucial role in classical Indian poetry and drama, and aestheticians like Vishvanatha have taxonomized in detail the various types of images that find articulation in literary texts. In architecture and sculpture, just as in painting, images generate a plurality of layers of meaning relating mundane experiences to transcendental and cosmological phenomena. In classical poetry and drama, the projected image of the hero had to conform to certain specifications handed down by tradition; he had to be of noble birth, handsome, fearless, intelligent, generous, and so on. The relationship between self and image as found in classical Indian literature generates a multiplicity of complex issues bearing on literary hermeneutics. Let us, for example, consider the following verses from Kalidasa's "The Cycle of Seasons," a poem that, in my judgment, is grossly underestimated. Kalidasa is justly regarded as an extremely gifted poet who captured the beauty and sublimity of nature in his own distinctive way. "The Cycle of Seasons" gives figurality to the six seasons, and what is interesting about his textualizations is the way in which human beings and Nature interact in an eroticized representational space and the way nature is anthropomorphized.

> With streaming clouds trumpeting like haughty tuskers
> with lightning-banners and drumbeats of thunderclaps
> in towering majesty, the season of rains
> welcome to lovers now comes like a king, my love.
>
> Clouds burst with terrifying peals of thunder;
> lightnings flash. Women shrinking in fear
> cling closely in bed to their loved husbands,
> guilty though these men may be of philandering.

In his nature poetry, Kalidasa projects a distinct image: that of a poet with a transpersonal vision, who is able to see from a distance the drama of human beings and Nature. Being a steadfast devotee of Siva, this drama takes on added significance. For Kalidasa, Nature is not a mere objective entity or a backdrop against which human beings act out their day-to-day lives. For him Nature displays the cosmic unity that is the hallmark of Siva, and he is able to see this and capture it in words from a transcendental viewpoint. This is indeed the image that Kalidasa wishes to transmit of himself through his nature poetry. What this example shows is the multifaceted relationship that exists between self and image in poetry. In order to appreciate the plenitude of meaning and the depth of intensity inscribed in his poetry we need to pay close attention to the idealized image of himself that the poet seeks to project.

Images play a central role in Indian culture and are inseparably linked to thought. The term, *darsana* that references both visuality and intellection underlines this point in an interesting way. The visual perception of the image constitutes a predominant element in Hindu worship, and the widespread habit of image making and the high esteem in which this activity was held attests to this fact. To see an image of a god, whether it be Siva or Visnu or Durga, and to be seen by the divinity in turn counts as a highly significant religious experience to the Hindus. And the notion of *darshan* does not enjoy this kind of esteem in the Western tradition.

Very often in the West, classical Indian forms of spirituality are discussed in terms of a vocabulary of transcendence and mysticism. However, we need to bear in mind the fact that there is countervailing force that emphasizes the phenomenality and materiality of things, and images serve to exemplify this dimension of Hindu thought and practice. Philosophers like Susanne Langer have persuasively argued that images are vital to conceptual thinking and this is clearly in evidence in Indian culture. Images are ubiquitous in India: in temples and houses, in bazaars and shops, in walls and compounds, in taxis and public buildings; and many of these carry deep religious connotations. Images seem to open a particularly interesting window onto Indian thought and imagination. Diana Eck says, "The very images of the gods portray in visual form the multiplicity and the oneness of the divine, and display the tensions that are resolved in a single mythic image."

In Hindu culture, we find both iconic and aniconic images, the former emphasizing mimeticism and representationality, while the latter emphasize symbolicity. And both types serve to establish a deep emotional bond between the devotee and the divinity in question and facilitate a close identification. Very often these images are not only gazed at but also associated with various forms of rituals of caring, such as offering flowers and incense, celebrating in song, and bathing and offering food. Hence, it is very clear that there is a close personal bond between image and worshiper. The ways in which images function in Indian culture are many and complex, and one cannot do full justice to the full range in a subsection of a book. Hence, we have sought to focus on a few select areas dealing with self as image in Indian culture, focusing heavily on the contemporary.

In the first essay, Wimal Dissanayake compares the nature poetry of Kalidasa, who is generally regarded as the greatest Sanskrit poet, with that of Du Fu who, in the opinion of most discerning critics of Chinese literature, is the foremost classical Chinese poet. By comparing the two distinctly different images of poetic selfhood that emerge from their poetry, Dissanayake has sought to focus on the relationship between self, image, and poetry. The first essay, then, deals with classical literature, while the rest of the chapters

in the section on India address issues pertaining to contemporary representational practices and symbolic economies.

In the second essay, Vinay Dharwadker discusses late colonial and postcolonial selves in Hindi and Marathi poetry. Literature is a product of a wider
cultural discourse, and the construction of self in poetry can best be understood in relation to those wider cultural discourses. Dharwadker points out
how some poets writing in Hindi and Marathi experienced a general disillusionment with the nationalist freedom movement and the elitist politics of
India, and how this disenchantment was expressed in poetry and self-making.
Rather than seeking to develop a single, unified master narrative that would
capture the story of modern Indian self and the way it is articulated in
literature (which is an impossibly arduous task, given India's social and cultural pluralities), the author has chosen to focus attention on eight poets
writing in two different traditions in two different periods as a way of calling
attention to the emergence of newer selfhoods.

The third essay, titled "Communal Self and Cultural Imagery: The *Katha*
Performance Tradition in South India," by Gayathri Rajapur Kassebaum,
deals with music and performance. Here the focus of attention is not on the
individual self but the collective self. In this chapter, the author explores a
form of performance, distinctive of certain geographical areas and collectivities in South India that integrates music, drama, poetry, and narrativity producing a complex communal image characteristic of the region. The particular performance that Gayathri Rajapur Kassebaum focuses on can be usefully
regarded as a symbolic articulation of the autobiography of the community
presented through images. The intent of these performances is inextricably
linked with the notion of self as communal image.

In the next essay, titled "Carving a Self: Feminist Consciousness, the
Family, and the Socialization Process—A Study of Ashapurna Devi's Trilogy,"
Shivani Banerjee Chakravorty explores questions of feminist consciousness,
the family, and the socialization process in terms of human subjectivity. In
patriarchal societies—and India is clearly one—the selfhood of women has
been largely marginalized and silenced. At the same time, literature produced
by women offers tantalizing insights into the social and cultural formations
that influence the subservience of women. In this essay, Chakravorty seeks to
examine the complicated relationship that exists between social and cultural
discourses and the construction of gendered selves by investigating three novels by Ashapurna Devi. The central impulse behind much of feminist think-

ing is the need to deconstruct the male hegemonic discourses, and Shivani Bannerjee Chakravorty's paper serves to underline this fact.

The final chapter in the section on India has been written by Ashis Nandy and deals with the work and the projected selfhood of the celebrated Indian filmmaker Satyajit Ray. Nandy is concerned with exploring the general personological issue of partitioning the self that seems to surface in many guises in South Asian societies. As he observes, the partitioning of the self we see in Ray and others is representative of a larger social dynamic. He says that, "It allows a greater play to the internalized aspects of social processes which would have been otherwise irreconcilable." Through an examination of Satyajit Ray's creative works, Ashis Nandy has foregrounded an issue that is imbricated with self, image, and cultural discourse. His essay throws an interesting light on a significant dimension of Ray's life and art and the wider cultural formations with which they were constantly and fruitfully in dialogue.

These five essays, then, with their different thematics and from their diverse vantage points call attention to some important issues related to self and image in Indian culture. They serve to underline the multifacetedness and multivalence of the concept of self as image.

Self as Image in the Nature Poetry of Kalidasa and Du Fu

Wimal Dissanayake

How does a poet win a sense of authority for himself and persuade his readers? What is the nature of this poetic authority that enables the poet to carry the readers along with him? These are questions that are as complex as they are fascinating. There are a number of dimensions of poetic selfhood that enter this calculus. One important consideration, it seems to me, is the interplay between the historically constructed empirical self and culturally sanctioned normative self. It is through the power of this normative self that the poet seeks to give order and significance and to legitimize his observations, musings, and commentaries. The interplay between the empirical self and the normative self produces a complex image of the poet. Each time I return to Kalidasa and Du Fu—two of my favorite classical poets—I find this conjecture of mine repeatedly strengthened and reinforced. The objective of this essay is to explore this facet of poetic authority a little more deeply, and in the process to illuminate the concept of self as image in terms of literary creativity.

Kalidasa, by common consent, is the greatest Sanskrit poet and playwright, and was referred to as the "Supreme Poet" *(kavi kula guru)*. He had a profound and far-reaching influence on subsequent writers and commentators. Like the Chinese poet Du Fu, whose work I will discuss in the latter part of this paper, Kalidasa displayed a rare poetic imagination and mastery of language and form. Although Kalidasa was an indubitably gifted and influential poet and dramatist, very little is known about his biography. His name literally means "servant of the goddess Durga." Kalidasa is the author of seven works—four works of poetry and three plays. The poems are "The Cycle of the Seasons" *(Rtusamhara),* "The Cloud Messenger" *(Meghadutam),* "The Lineage of Raghu" *(Raghuvamsa),* and "The Birth of the Prince" *(Kumarasambhava).* The plays are *Malavika and Agnimitra (Malavikagnimitra), Vikramorvasi (Urvasi Won by Valor),* and *Sakuntala and the Ring of Recollection (Abhijgnana Sakuntala).* In this chapter, I wish to focus on his two lyrical poems, "The Cycle of Seasons" and "The Cloud Messenger," that capture the beauty and grandeur of Nature.

The exact dates of Kalidasa's life are a matter of doubt among Sanskritists and Indologists. However, the generality of opinion seems to favor the view that he lived in the Gupta period (A.D. 300–650) and that he was associated with the royal court of Chandragupta II, who was the ruler from A.D. 375–415. Although it is difficult to affix dates with any degree of certainty, an inscription dated A.D. 634 provides us with an upper limit in that it describes Kalidasa as a distinguished poet. Kalidasa was essentially a court poet who chose to celebrate the royalty in grandiose terms. Kalidasa was also a devotee of Shiva and passages from his work, as well as various legends that have grown around his name, testify to this fact. The benediction of his most famous play *'Sakuntala,'* refers to the mysterious powers of Shiva.

This fact of Kalidasa being a votary of Shiva is important in understanding his attitude to Nature and the way he textualized it in his poetry. In this essay, I wish to focus attention on his nature poetry as found in "The Cycle of Seasons" and "The Cloud Messenger." "The Cycle of Seasons" consists of six cantos, and each canto is devoted to the thematization of one season: summer, rainy season, autumn, frosty season, winter and spring. In each of the cantos, the poet describes the incessant interplay between human beings and Nature in a highly eroticized aesthetic space. "The Cloud Messenger" is a lyrical poem consisting of 121 stanzas, and consists of two parts: the *purvamegha* and the *uttaramegha.* The poem describes the sentiments of a certain yaksha who is banished by his master Kubera, the god of wealth, for neglecting his assigned duties. He now lives in exile in Ramagiri in the Vindhya mountains, where he spends his days in solitude. After about eight months, one day he happens to see a cloud resting on the top of the mountain. Realizing that the cloud in its northbound course would almost certainly pass over his home Alaka, where his beloved is living, he sends a message to her through the cloud. This is the essence of the poem. This allows the opportunity to the poet to describe the

beauty of Nature—mountains, valleys, forests, gardens, rivers, and so on—
from high above.

Kalidasa is justly regarded as a poet who sought to capture the beauty
and sublimity of Nature in his own unique way. "The Cycle of Seasons"
describes the six seasons, and what is distinctive about his descriptions is the
way in which human beings and Nature interact in an eroticized discursive
space and the way in which Nature is anthropomorphized. This is how he
opens his description of the summer:

> The sun blazing fiercely,
> the moon longed for eagerly,
> deep waters inviting
> to plunge in continually,
> days drawing to a close in quiet beauty,
> the tide of desire running low:
> scorching Summer is now here, my love
>
> Night's indigo-masses rent by the moon,
> wondrous mansions built on water,
> cooled by fountains; various gems
> cool to the touch; liquid sandal;
> the world seeks relief in these
> in Summer's scorching heat, my love.
>
> Palace-terraces perfumed, luring the senses,
> wine trembling beneath the beloved's breath,
> sweet melodies on finely tuned lutes:
> lovers enjoy these passion-kindling things
> at midnight in Summer, my love.[1]

Similarly, he begins his description of the rainy season in the following
manner, employing the same rhetorical strategies:

> With screaming clouds trumpeting like haughty tuskers
> with lightning-banners and drumbeats of thunderclaps,
> in towering majesty, the season of rains
> welcome to lovers, now comes like a king, my love.
>
> Overcast on all sides with dense rain clouds, the sky
> displays the deep glow of blue-lotus petals,

dark in places like heaped collyrium, smooth-blended,
glowing elsewhere like the breasts of a woman with child.[2]

Kalidasa follows the same representational strategy in his description of the beauties of Autumn.

Robed in pale silk plumes of Kasa blooms,
full-blown lotuses her beautiful face,
the calls of rapturous wild geese
the music of her anklet bells,
ripening grain, lightly bending, her lissome form:
Autumn has now arrived, enchanting as a bride.[3]

And this is how Kalidasa begins his description of Winter:

Stacks of ripe rice and sugarcane cover the earth;
the air rings with the hidden calls of curlews;
love grows exuberant: dear to lovely women
winter is now here; hear now, my love.

People close their windows tight, light fires,
keep warm in the sun and wear heavy garments:
men find the company of youthful women
pleasing at this time of the year.[4]

As these passages clearly indicate, the entire poem glows with a pervasive eroticism. The impact of Nature on human lives, human behavior, and human emotions is charted through erotic imagery. At the same time the perspective of the poet is one of transpersonality. He observes the interaction of Man and Nature not from within that interplay but from outside, adopting a supramundane angle of vision. This same epistemology and representational strategy is to be found in "The Cloud Messenger."

its slopes covered by the glow of ripened mangos
and with you poised on its crest, darkly shining
like a braid of coiled hair, the mountain seems
a great breast of earth, dark at its center,
pale gold around, a vision
right for a loving pair of immortals.

On your way, when you meet the Nirvindhya River,
whose stumbling glide is filled with grace, whose eddies
make her a navel, whose belt is a clamoring row
of birds on her swaying billows—be sure you fill yourself
with her waters, for the first show of women's love
for their favorite is surely in tempting play.[5]

Kalidasa's nature poetry bears the distinct stamp of his adoration of Shiva. He perceives the omnipresence of Shiva in the phenomenal world. For him Nature is not an object to be seen or against which human beings lead their daily lives. For him, Nature is imbued with a different order of significance, displaying as it does a cosmic unity that is indeed the hallmark of Shiva. As Barbara Stoller Miller points out, Shiva's creative nature is articulated through the eight essential principles of empirical life: water, fire, ether, earth, air, sun, moon, and the ritual sacrifices integrated into the cosmic system.[6] Chandra Rajan says that, "The word 'samharam' (gathering in, or collection) in the title of the poem has a specific metaphysical meaning, of universal destruction when all creation is drawn in at the end of time into Shiva, its ground and source. The mystery of Shiva and his presence is never far from any of Kalidasa's works."[7]

The nature of the poetic self that emerges from Kalidasa's poetry is one of transpersonality that functions as a celebrant of the power of Shiva. The poet's attempt is not to portray Nature in a partial, provisional, or dimly understood way as in the poetry of Du Fu that I will discuss shortly, but from the perspective of a person in full command of the subject with a totalizing awareness. For this to materialize, the poet's self has to be constructed through his rhetorical strategies as an omniscient and transpersonal one. Kalidasa constructs a complex and multifaceted image of his poetic selfhood through his poetry, and this effort is related to questions of epistemology, ontology, aesthetics, cultural memory, and tradition. There are a number of important dimensions related to this composite image that merits our close attention. The constructed image of self that emanates from his poetry is one of transpersonality that is above the contingencies of history. The poetic narrator is self-possessed, self-certain and has access to a totalizing vision. Elements of self-doubt and self-limitations do not find articulation in the poetic selfhood of Kalidasa in the way that they do in Du Fu. The sense of eroticism and specularity that pervades his poetry is closely related to this idea of a transpersonal self. Kalidasa's poetry is energized by a sense of wonder—wonder of the functioning of the universe—and this has a direct bearing on his trans-personal poetic self as well as on his being a devotee of Shiva. Passages such as the following illustrate these points vividly:

> And you must visit there the only shrine
> of the Master of the Three Worlds, Chandi's Lord,
> His groves ruffled by breeze from the Gandhavati,
> heavy with pollen and fragrant from the perfume girls
> at play in water. There, Shiva's attendants, amazed
> at your sight, will see in your hue the dark of their own Lord's throat
>
> O Cloud, being in Mahakala
> then, though it's early still, you should rest
> until the sun sets, and then perform
> the high office of drums for the Lord's
> twilight service, and you will receive
> the full reward of your mellow thunder.
>
> The dancing girls there, belts clinking
> as they place their feet, weary hands elegantly
> flicking those fly whisks with gem-studded handles,
> feeling your first drops so soothing
> to scratched skin, will send you, like a flight
> of bees, long sidling looks.
>
> Then, resting as a sphere on the tall forest
> of Shiva's arms, and taking luster from the twilight—
> red as just-blooming china roses—offer yourself
> to Shiva for the elephant's bloody hide
> He wears in His dance, your devotion observed
> by Bhavani with steady eyes, her terror now calmed.[8]

The tone of these poems as well as the tropes that undergird the thoughts and sentiments bear the distinct imprint of those qualities that I referred to in the earlier paragraph. The persona of the poet is one that is exceedingly alive to the eroticization of life and is in full command of his all-encompassing gaze.

Let us now consider the poetry of the renowned Chinese poet Du Fu, as a way of pointing out an entirely different outlook on nature from that of Kalidasa. Du Fu, in the opinion of most knowledgeable Chinese literary scholars and critics, is the foremost Chinese poet. Du Fu was born in A.D. 712 in Honan in the region of La-yang. He had an elite family background. His father was a district magistrate; his grandfather was one of the illustrious poets of the seventh century. He was considered to be a thirteenth-generation descendent of Tu Yu (222–84), famous for his commentarial work on Confucius. Despite the fact that he hailed from a cultured, literary family and had important social connections, his initial attempts to obtain a position in the government through the established examination system did not meet with much success. It was only in A.D. 755 when Du Fu was forty-three years old that he succeeded in gaining an official position as registrar in the palace of the crown prince.

Du Fu had matured to be a man of character imbued with Confucian ethics. He was a devoted family man concerned very much about the members of his family. He was intensely loyal to the state and had resolved to serve it to the best of his abilities. He was warm to his friends and cared deeply about the misery and tribulations of the poor and the dispossessed. All these aspects of his personality find creative expression in his poetry and go to form the image of his poetic selfhood.

Emperor Hsuan-tsung distinguished himself as an able ruler in his early years; but when he was in his sixties he fell in love with the attractive Yang Kue-fei, resulting in his losing interest in the control of state affairs. The court was riven by internal quarrels and military leaders in the outlying regions grew more and more powerful. One such leader, An Lu-shan, who was in the Northeast, instigated a rebellion. The emperor abdicated in favor of his son. Amidst this turmoil, Du Fu and his family, in order to get away from the rebel armies, fled north. He left his family there and sought to rejoin the new emperor at Ling-wu. However, he was captured by a band of rebels and was held in prison for about eight months, during which period he wrote some of his most memorable and moving poetry.

> Tonight the Fu-chou moon
> In her chamber alone she watches.
> From afar I pity my little children
> Who know not enough to remember Ch'ang-an
> With fragrant mist his cloud-hair-knots damp;
> In the chill moonlight her jade arms are cold.
> When shall we lie within the empty curtains
> And it shine on both, our tear-traces dry?[9]

In A.D. 757, in the early Summer, once a modicum of law and order had been reestablished, Du Fu escaped from his captors and joined the royal court once again. However, before long Du Fu offended the emperor and was demoted to a minor position. In the Fall he reunited with the family. In A.D. 759 Du Fu left his official position and the remainder of his life was given over to travel throughout the country. During the last remaining years of his life Du Fu overcame illness and fatigue and traveled down the Yangtze with the intention of arriving at his old home in the East, but died on the way.

Du Fu's impact on later generations of poets was both profound and far-reaching. He left behind nearly one thousand five hundred poems, and they bear eloquent testimony to his many-sided genus. He possessed a powerful poetic sensibility, facility with language, and a technical mastery that many scholars of Chinese literature maintain are unrivaled. Interestingly, these are the very qualities and attributes that distinguish Kalidasa's poetry as well. However, in terms of thematics, rhetoric, representational practices, and vision the gulf separating the two poets is enormous. Du Fu was an intensely personal and confessional poet in a way that Kalidasa was clearly not, so much so that his poetry is perceived as the most reliable source for the construction of his biography. The following are some characteristic examples. Immediately after arriving at Sichuan he was able to build a home, the comfort of which he had not enjoyed for years. He captures this mood in the following way in his poem titled "Siting a House."

> By the flower-washing waters, by water's edge
> as master, I have chosen this secluded wood and pond.
> Well I know: leaving a city decreases dusty business;
> What's more: pellucid river dispels a wanderer's woe.
> Innumerable dragonflies together rise and drop;
> A couple of wood ducks facing me bob and dive.
> Myriad leagues away east, riding on high spirits,
> I ought to head for Alpshade abroad a little skiff![10]

Similarly the following poem titled "A Stranger's Night" recaptures an intensely personal experience.

> Stranger's night, why can't I go to sleep?
> These autumn skies just won't get light.
> Entering my curtain, fading moon shadows;

Propped on a pillow: distant river sounds.
My plan's are clumsy—no food or clothing;
My path is blocked—rely on kind friends.
Poor old wife has written several pages—
She must know my feelings far from home.[11]

Du Fu's intensely personal poetry, in keeping with his Confucian cast of mind, is inflected by a deep concern for his fellow human beings. The following poem, which is also highly personal, is inscribed by a sense of social consciousness.

Darkling hues march up an alpine path;
My steep study camps by the water gate.
Tenuous clouds bivouac bordering cliffs;
A lonely moon tumbles among the waves.
Troops of cranes in silence fly pursuit;
A pack of wolves clamors to find a kill.
I'm sleepless, worrying about battles,
All powerless to right heaven and earth.[12]

The following passages of poetry, too, bear the imprint of the union of private and public experience:

I came through the gate, I heard a crying out,
my youngest child had died of starvation
. . . .
And this thought obsesses me—as a father,
Lack of food resulted in infant death;
I could not have known that even after harvest
Through our poverty there would be such distress.
All my life I've been exempt from taxes,
and my name is not registered for conscription.
Brooding on what I have lived through, if even I know such
suffering the common man must surely be rattled by the winds;
then thoughts silently turn to those who have lost all livelihood
and troops in far garrisons.
Sorrow's source is as huge as South Mountain,
a formless, whirling chaos that the hand cannot grasp.[13]

At times Du Fu was capable of combining introspective analysis and self-mockery in a way that few other Chinese poets were able to do. And this certainly is not a characteristic found in Kalidasa's poetry. The following passage illustrates this aspect of his poetry:

> As a man in my nature's lopsided and addicted to lovely lines
> If my lines don't startle others, in death I'll find no rest.
> And now in old age my poetry is really getting relaxed.[14]

Commenting on this passage, Stephen Owen remarks that, the easy going, colloquial tone of these lines was characteristic of Du Fu's Ch'eng-tu years and mockingly reflected the self-image of the eccentric.[15] A strong humanitarian impulse runs through most of Du Fu's poetry, energizing it with compassion and generosity of spirit. He saw only too well and disconsolately how the war levies had placed unbearable burdens on the poor and oppressed them. In the following poem titled, "Another Note to Master Wu," he writes to his nephew Wu requesting him to permit impoverished neighbors to steal their dates:

> Let our western neighbor knock down dates before the hall
> Bereft of food, bereft of sons—a solitary wife.
> If she weren't at wits end, would she have come to this?
> Just because she's terrified, we've had to turn more kind.
>
> Although her wearying a stranger was quite necessary,
> Yet your building a fence would actually prove her fears!
> She sued that cruel exactions beggared her to the bone,
> Now as I think of war-horses, my kerchief soaks with tears.[16]

Du Fu represented the interrelationship between human beings and Nature in their manifold interactions with remarkable sensitivity and depth of understanding. The objects of nature often become signifiers of his mental states and emblems of moods in his poetic discourse. Some of his most memorable poems reconfigure the beauties and anxieties of the night. McCraw says that, "By habit Du Fu was well suited to nocturnal composition; he often slept late and took afternoon naps. Moreover, his days were taken up with occasional jobs and family and social obligations. Nights were his only chance for solitary reflection and undisturbed 'intoning.'"[17] The following poem titled, "Night" draws our attention to his preoccupation with nocturnality.

> Dewdrops fall, the sky soars, autumn's air clarified:
> Empty hills, a lonely night, my errant soul startled.
> A faint lamp illumines itself, the lone sail rests;
> The new moon suspended still, paired pestles pound.
> Southern chrysanthemums met again, as I lie in sickness;
> Northern letters don't arrive, geese are heartless.
> Along the veranda, I lean on my cane, watch Ox and Dipper:
> Silvery River, far-off, should connect to Phoenix Town.[18]

Politics formed an important theme in Du Fu's writings, and it was not politics in the abstract but politics as felt on the pulse that captivated his interest. In his poetry, political themes and personal emotion are conjoined in interesting and complex ways. The following poem titled, "Midnight," mirrors this penchant

> It is midnight, jiang and alps are stilled;
> In a steep tower I gaze at the North Star.
> Long have I been a myriad-league wanderer,
> Much ashamed of this "hundred-year" frame.
> O'er my old land, vapor of windblown cloud:
> Round the high hall, dust from waging war.
> The alien chick betrayed generous boons:
> Alas! All of you men from a peaceful time![19]

Clearly, Du Fu's poems dealing with Nature are very different from those of Kalidasa. He situates man in the natural world and there is often a perceptible tension between the two. In his later poetry, this aspect of his poetic discourse on Nature becomes more prominent. The poet is constantly struggling to make sense of the phenomenal world, making human agency a vital factor in this effort, not always with staggering success. For example, in his poem "Facing the Snow," which is a relatively early poem, we see a relentless effort to impose meaning and order on the natural world:

> In sorrow reciting poems, an old man all alone,
> A tumult of clouds sinks downward in sunset,
> Hard-pressed, the snow dances in whirlwinds.
> Ladle cast down, no green lees in the cup
> The brazier lingers on, fire seems crimson.

From several provinces now news has ceased—
I sit here in sorrow tracing words in air.[20]

Commenting on this poem Stephen Owen remarks that,

> The title, "Facing the Snow," involves a primary opposition between the poet and the winter world outside. Indeed, Tu Fu's treatment of the topic has strong echoes of the formal amplification of seventh-century poetic rhetoric. The first couplet repeats the primary opposition in nominal terms: out there, on the battlefields beyond the horizon, many "new" ghosts, the young dead slain unnaturally before their time; within is the "solitar" survivor, the old man for whom death would be appropriate. The city disappears in the poem; there is only the poet who "faces" and the snow world that is "faced," the world of death and winter. What this poem illustrates is Tu Fu's characteristic attempts to make sense of the hostility, desolateness, antipathy of the natural world. Interestingly, for Tu Fu Nature in all its bewildering complexity and contradictory manifestations stood for order and stability as opposed to the ephemerality of human affairs.[21]

Du fu came to maturity when the Tang empire was in decline. This was a period characterized by mutinies, rebellions, the activation of fissiparous and centrifugal forces. Du Fu, with his Confucian bent of mind, was loyal to the state and what he saw around him disturbed him intensely. He was a compassionate man who was troubled by the overwhelming burdens that the poor had to bear in their day-to-day lives.[22] The Confucian self thrives in an atmosphere of harmony when it is fully realized in its relations with the family, clan, state, and Heaven. Du Fu lived during a period of turmoil when this appeared to be a distant dream. Hence it is hardly surprising that his poetic self mirrors these anxieties and worries. The epistemology and signifying economies that subtended his poetic self served to fashion it as fissured, conflicted, at times morally outraged, occasionally questioning his very poetic authority. And these traits are vitally related to the historical context in which he lived and the cultural discourses that inflected his thought.

Kalidasa and Du Fu lived in societies that differed greatly in terms of social stability and the ruling cultural discourses. Poetry, as indeed any other representational and symbolic act, is embedded in historicity and networks of material practices. The entities designated as literature and history, text and context, are not autonomous and self-contained but porous and interactive.

Poetry, like all other cultural practices, operates within the field of power relations that produced them. Hence, we can legitimately say that a text is itself a part of the context that is believed to facilitate our understanding of the text. The contexts, social, political, and cultural, in which Kalidasa's and Du Fu's poetry were produced were so different from each other that it is hardly surprising that their poetry contrasts so sharply in terms of epistemology and aesthetics.

While Kalidasa sought to present his poetic selfhood as one located outside history, Du Fu's poetic self was clearly inside history, grappling with its manifold imperatives. Kalidasa, in keeping with the dictates of his sensiblity, tries to eroticize Nature, while Du Fu, in large measure, socializes it. If the projected self of Kalidasa is a transpersonal one, Du Fu, with his clear Confucian leanings, presents us with a social self. Kalidasa's nature poetry is not framed by a moral consciousness, while Du Fu's writings clearly bear the imprint of a moral imagination. The self-certainty and self-possession that characterize Kalidasa's work contrast sharply with the self-doubts, at times even self-mockery, that animate Du Fu's writings. Kalidasa's poetry reaches toward romantic fantasies; Du Fu's poetry seeks to promote social engagement. In the case of Kalidasa's descriptions of Man and Nature, it is the element of wonder that animates them; in Du Fu's poems it is the search for order—and an agonized one at that—that undergirds them. Kalidasa tends toward abstraction and distantiation from the specificities of Nature, while Du Fu prefers concreteness and closeness to Nature. What these differences between the poetic selfhoods of Kalidasa and Du Fu signify is the fact that each in his poetry has constructed a complex image of himself that is connected to a plurality of social and cultural forces. This fact becomes evident when we compare passages of poetry from Kalidasa and Du Fu that deal with the identical topic—rain. This is how Kalidasa describes rain.

> Hurling thunderbolts that crash down to strike terror
> bending bows strung with lightning-streaks, letting loose
> fierce sharp-shooting showers—cruel arrows fine-honed—
> clouds, relentless, wound the hearts of men far from home
>
> The Earth, covered by tender shoots of grass
> brilliant as emeralds shivering into points of light
> by up-springing kandali leaf-buds and ladybirds,
> dazzles like a woman decked in gems, green and red.

A bevy of peacocks that sound ever-delightful,
eagerly watching out for this festive moment,
caught up in a flurry of billing and fondling,
now begin to dance, gorgeous plumage spread out wide.[23]

Let us compare this description of rain with the following by Du Fu.

Jiang rains, as ever no fixed hour:
A clear sky suddenly strews its strands.
The waning fall strained things colder,
And now, today passing clouds delay.
I mount my horse, return before I'd left!
I watch the gulls, sitting without stir . . .
A high casement facing Powerful Flow,
As soaking sights still my study drapes.

By the look of things, the year's about done;
From this world's edge, I'm still unreturned.
A tartar wind calls with whispering sighs;
A wintry rain falls in softened showers.
With many ails, I've long forced down my food;
My withered form has just gotten new clothes.
In perilous time, I'm aware of wilting death:
From old friends, even short letters are few.

On southern rain, stone moss battens;
From the capital, tidings are delayed.
Alps in winter: a black brute bellows;
Jiang at evening: a white gull famished.
The goddess' floral hairpin falls;
The mermaid's weaving shuttle mourns.
Close-weft cares that won't disentangle,
All day long stream in silken strands.[24]

In these passages of poetry is inscribed the value characteristic of each of the poets that we described earlier, giving to their poetry their distinctive flavor and constructing a complex image of each of them.

What a contrastive study of the nature poetry of Kalidasa and Du Fu brings to light is the interplay between the empirical selves and idealized normative selves of the two poets. The complex image of the self emerges from this idealized self and is a product of the culturally sanctioned discursive resources available to the poet. The idealized normative self enables the poets to give order and significance to their experiences of Nature in terms of favored epistemologies, rhetorical strategies, image repertoires, narrativities, and signifying economies. In other words, the image of the poet that emerges from his writings is a product of the poet engaging the available corpus of culturally grounded discursive resources. The construction of this idealized image, then, entails ontological and epistemic choices and the concomitant effort to impose a sense of unity and coherence on the textualized experience. It is indeed through this projected image that the poet acquires the sense of authority that is required to persuade the reader. The relationship between Man and Nature is indeed complex and multifaceted, and the self-image of the poet both shapes and is shaped by that relationship.

So far we have been discussing the ways in which poetry serves to construct a complex image of the author. In this effort, it is very important to bear in mind the fact that language is by no means a transparent instrument that serves to project a pre-given entity. It is indeed language that is at the bottom of the constructional project. Hence the materiality of language as well as the constitutive role it plays in self-making has to be borne in mind. When Kalidasa, through his poetry, seeks to project an idealized poetic self, we need to examine the complex ways in which his language—denotations, connotations, juxtapositions, tropes, figuralities—enables, disenables, expands, enlarges, or subverts that effort. In linguistic communication, there is always a surplus of meaning that cannot be fully contained by the manipulations of the author, and hence can challenge and contradict the intentions of the author.

This fact is evident in Kalidasa's poetry as well. Although in his poetry we see his desire to present his poetic selfhood as one that is transhistorical and transpersonal, his language and the rhetorical devices he employs at times stand in the way of this effort. For example, the poem is addressed to his lover, and this has the effect of bringing it to a more mundane level.

> The sun blazing fiercely,
> the moon longed for eagerly,
> deep waters inviting
> to plunge in continually,
> days drawn to a close in quiet beauty,

the tide of desire running low:
scorching Summer is not here, my love.

Sprays of full-blown mango blossoms—his sharp arrows
honey-bees in rows—the humming bowstring;
Warrior-Spring set to break the hearts
of Love's devotees, is now approaching, my love.[25]

The effect of the poem being addressed to his lover is to position the reader in a more mundane setting and tends to undercut the poet's project of creating supramundane reality. Similarly, his dominant image that informs the "The Cycle of Seasons" is the human body. Nature is given a human body; it is the somatic aspects of men and women that are underlined in the poem. Bodily union is the informing topos of the poem. What this emphasis on the human body does is to once again undermine the transpersonality that the poet is seeking to achieve. Moreover, the cultural norms, linguistic resources, poetic conventions, repertoires of imagery, and discursive resources that Kalidasa invariably draws upon serve to pinpoint the constructedness of his poetic effort. All such manifestations, as concretized in language, contribute to contradicting the poet's intended objectives. Hence, when discussing the ways in which Kalidasa or Du Fu—or any other poet, for that matter—has attempted to project an idealized poetic self through language, we need to constantly bear in mind the fact that language is not a transparent instrument and that the surpluses of meaning that linguistic communication inevitably engenders serve to, at times, undermine the poet's avowed intentions.

In this essay, then, I have sought to compare and contrast the nature poetry of two of the greatest classical poets in India and China, and to point out certain significant dimensions related to the interconnections among self, image, and poetic communication. In poetic communication it is important for the poet to achieve a sense of poetic authority. This enables the poet to win the confidence of the readers and lead them in his preferred direction. In the above analysis of Kalidasa's and Du Fu's poetry dealing with nature, I sought to focus on the interplay between the biologically determined and historically constituted empirical self and culturally sanctioned normative self as a way of gaining access to the deeper recesses of their poetry and the sense of poetic authority that powers the poetry. The empirical self focuses attention on the historical and social specificities; the normative self calls attention to the cultural values and epistemologies within which the poets operate. And the complex image that emerges as a result of the intersection and intertwining of the empirical and normative selves, I hope, serves to illuminate an important aspect of self as image in relation to lyric poetry.

Notes

1. Chandra Rajan, *Kalidasa: The Loom of Time* (New Delhi: Penguin Books, 1990), 105.

2. Ibid., 110.

3. Ibid., 116.

4. Ibid., 126.

5. Barbara Stoller Miller, *The Cloud Messenger* (New York: Columbia University Press, 1988).

6. Ibid., 12.

7. Rajan, *Kalidasa*, 43.

8. Miller, *Cloud Messenger*, 46.

9. Burton Watson, *The Columbia Book of Chinese Poetry* (New York: Columbia University Press, 1984), 224.

10. David McCraw, *Du Fu's Laments from the South* (Honolulu: University of Hawaii Press, 1992), 21.

11. Ibid., 121.

12. Ibid., 49.

13. Stephen Owen, *Poetry of the Early Tang* (New Haven: Yale University Press, 1977), 196.

14. Ibid., 195.

15. Ibid., 43.

16. McCraw, *Du Fu's Laments*, 92.

17. Ibid., 115.

18. Ibid.

19. Ibid., 156.

20. Owen, *Poetry*, 201.

21. Ibid., 208.

22. Vikram Seth, himself a distinguished poet, says, "Du Fu's poetry is informed by deeply suggestive and often sad reflections on society, history, the state and his own disturbed times, all central concerns of Confucianism. But what especially endears him to the Chinese is his wry self-deprecation combined with an intense compassion for oppressed or dispossessed people of every kind in time of poverty, famine and war." *Three Chinese Poets* (Boston: Faber and Faber, 1992), xvi.

23. Rajan, *Kalidasa*, 110.

24. McCraw. *Du Fu's Laments*, 145.

25. Rajan. *Kalidasa*, 105.

$$8$$

Late Colonial and Postcolonial Selves in Hindu and Marathi Poetry

Vinay Dharwadker

At some time between 1930 and 1940, a number of Indian poets, writing in languages like Hindi and Marathi with an acute awareness of contemporary politics in the late colonial period, experienced a general disenchantment with the nationalist freedom movement. Their disenchantment was simultaneously literary, political, and philosophical, and led them to reject the rhetorical, matriotic poetry of the 1920s (in which the country had become Mother India), as well as the elitist politics of the Indian National congress in the 1930s. The Hindi nationalist poets of the years after the First World War, for example, had essentially conceived of the modern Indian self in heroic, reactionary terms as "the brave son of Mother India," a valiant agent of struggle—empowered by his zeal—against domination and suppression by a foreign power. Responding negatively to this rhetoric, the late colonial poets reconceived the literary project of their generation at two basic levels. At the level of literary practice, they developed a broadly modernist poetics centered around free verse, density of thought and expression, skepticism and satire verging on invective against the age, and a rewriting of "the great tradition" in Indian poetry in premodern times. At the level of politics, they generally adopted an adversarial Marxist or socialist position on social and economic issues, insisting on the need to reexamine the "real nature" of Indian society in terms of class interests and exploitative power structures, and to redefine the "nation" from the view-

point of the impoverished, effectively disenfranchised, and ruthlessly ma-
nipulated rural majority of the population.

The generation of late colonial poets began to introduce these ideas
into the Indian literary world in the 1930s, and by the early 1940s their
poetics and politics had begun to constitute a new self that was the antith-
esis of the zealous matriotic soldier. The late colonial self was often skeptical, rationalist, moved by obscure feelings of distaste and revulsion, dis-
tracted by doubt, unable to act quickly or resolutely, and sure only of "the
vast panorama of futility and anarchy that is contemporary history." Fashioned in this way, it ceased to be an agent in or of history. Instead, it
became the location within history of an acute consciousness of history,
and hence turned into the very site of history, the space in which the
historical process itself takes place.

In Hindi and Marathi poetry, there are two major variations on this
concept of the late colonial self. We find the first in the Marathi poetry of
Bal Sitaram Mardhekar (1909–56), whom most Maharashtrian readers regard
as one of the two greatest modern poets in the language (the other being P.
S. Rege). The best example of a Mardhekar poem that represents the self as
the site of history or as a zone of historical consciousness is "The Forest of
Yellow Bamboo Trees" (1950).

The Forest of Yellow Bamboo Trees

The forest of yellow bamboo trees
underlines the sky with its song;
between the lines, the mind grinds up
the promise to live (not now, but tomorrow).

The lemon tree carves in the wind
old neuter futures horned with antlers;
and footprints are printed on that wind,
but they're dead, though new.

Countless crows splotch their lime
on the pylons of the centuries;
and verbs stand guard round the clock,
but though they're alert, they're merely robots.

The polestar that never sets has set,
the Seven Sages have botched their answer;

hail that's not yet frozen falls,
and on the radio, Radha and Krishna.

The poem is obscure because it deals with the twilight hour close to the end of the colonial period, the hour of the transfer of power from one political order to another. At this moment of transition or liminality, the self becomes the zone of consciousness in which the worldly order of things becomes essentially a disorder of things. The world that the self inhabits (and that in turn inhabits the self) is now upside down, its realty turned into a series of surreal images. In this topsy-turvy world, the long-promised national independence arrives in the form of "old neuter futures horned with antlers," and the glorious ancient past becomes a place where "Countless crows splotch their lime / on the pylons of the centuries." The ordinary logic of connections breaks down and deteriorates into irrational disconnections: the same interior/exterior landscape contains a bamboo forest, a lemon tree, an antlered stag, pylons, verbs, robots, hail, radios, songs, and lines of poetry. The self does nothing except to hoard this accumulation of surreally intertextured experiences, turning into a center of decentered historical consciousness.

The second important variation on such a representation of the late colonial Indian self appears late in the career of a poet of the same generation, Gajanan Madhav Muktibodh (1917–64), usually regarded as the most radical and original modern poet in Hindi. Muktibodh was an intense critic of colonialism in the "classical" Marxist mode, was more overtly theoretical than Mardhekar, and attempted to represent the Indian self under British rule as the historical site of colonial subjugation. However, as Muktibodh argued often in his long poems, the self subjugated by colonial power was also the self long exploited and marginalized by the dominant castes and classes in premodern Indian society. As a consequence, this self was a zone of consciousness doubly dispossessed of a substantial identity. In one of his late, shorter poems on the subject, called "The Void" (1960–61), Muktibodh represents the late colonial self as a thing that is still alive but emptied out of all its human qualities, and reduced to a violent, retaliatory animal presence-that-is-an-absence.

The Void

The void inside us
has jaws,
those jaws have carnivorous teeth;
those teeth will chew you up,

those teeth will chew up everyone else.
The dearth inside
is our nature,
habitually angry,
in the dark hollow inside the jaws
there is a pond of blood.
This void is utterly black,
is barbaric, is naked,
disowned, debased,
completely self-absorbed.
I scatter it,
give it away,
with fiery words and deeds.
Those who cross my path
find this void
in the wounds
I inflict on them.
They let it grow,
spread it around,
scatter it and give it away
to others,
raising the children of emptiness.
The void is very durable,
it is fertile.
Everywhere it breeds
saws, daggers, sickles,
breeds carnivorous teeth.
That is why,
wherever you look,
there is dancing, jubilation,
death is now giving birth
to brand new children.
Everywhere
there are oversights
with the teeth of saws,
there are heavily armed mistakes:
the world looks at them
and walks on,
rubbing its hands.

As these examples may suggest, Hindi and Marathi poets like G. M. Muktibodh and B. S. Mardhekar, writing out of their experience close to the end of the colonial period, frequently dramatized the self in its relation to the large-scale history of the subcontinent. In contrast, the poets of the subsequent postcolonial generation, who began to publish their work in the 1950s and 1960s, often explore, analyze, or define the self in smaller-scale contexts. But, contrary to what this statement may suggest, the shift from a late colonial sensibility to a definitely postcolonial poetic sensibility does not involve a complete or drastic break. For instance, the notion of the self as a victim of forces beyond its control and as a site of contestation, erasure, and debilitation continues to preoccupy Hindi and Marathi poets into the 1990s. Such continuities between the two generations, however, are substantially modified by the creation of new, alternative commonplaces about the self and of new strategies of poetic representation.

Among the new orientations that emerged in the early postcolonial decades is the conception of the self as an apolitical presence, structure, or process, that can be evoked lyrically and positively in relation to its various "others" outside the domain of politics and history. In this sort of conception, a Hindi or Marathi poet may place the self either in a relatively private, self-reflexive sphere of existence and experience, or in a more social realm of depoliticized relationships to people, places, situations, and events. This sort of conceptual and thematic change frequently goes hand in hand with a perceptible shift in poetic technique, with freer free verse, with more colloquial diction, and with a more informal overall manner predominating.

Two poems in this style of self-representation should help to exemplify the nature of the partial shift away from the work of earlier poets like Mardhekar and Muktibodh. One is Kedarnath Singh's "Signature" (1960), a comparatively simple poem, and the first poem in the poet's first volume of poetry. It made a memorable break from the Hindi poetry of the late 1950s by inventing a voice, a tone, and a texture that were to become commonplace in the language a decade later.

Signature

The day has begun.
Before its noise
begins,
    on the unseen
    unimprinted

roads
that open up
across the land
    I sign my name.

I enter houses
and homes.
    Quietly I pick up
the featureless things
left lying
here and there
    and set them
      down again
        in a new sequence,
and on a doubt
crouching
in a corner
somewhere
    I sign my name.

I enter the rivers.
I clear away the moss
gathered on their
surfaces,
    I shake up
      their waters,
and somewhere
on the deep
still
riverbeds
    I sign my name.

I enter the seasons.
I separate
the living threads
of hope
and desire
from the bark
of the sad

broken
ocher trees
    and tangle them up
    with the wings
    of every directionless bird
    before it flies away,
and somewhere
on the daily
wagers
of life
    I sign my name.

In this poem, Singh's primary purpose seems to be to keep out as much of the historical and political world as possible, and to make an absolutely fresh beginning by establishing a relationship between a pristine self and the pristine landscape it inhabits. Interestingly enough, Singh's primary figure for that relationship is a signature, the imprinting or inscription of a human name on a landscape that contains no other human presences, as though the self could discover and recover itself only by stamping its presence in writing on the places and things around it. Since signatures constitute the marks by which we record and legitimize our acts of possession, the poem as a whole turns into an act of possessing or repossessing the self through a landscape. This act, however, is also an act of beginning, since the poem brings together, in its text and in its contexts, a surprisingly large number of inaugurations: the beginning of a book, the beginning of a career, the beginning of a new historical period, the beginning of a new style, the beginning of the day, and the beginning of a new relationship to the land.

If Singh's reclamation of an apolitical self around 1960 is other-oriented—the "other" in this instance being a place—the definition of a depoliticized, dehistoricized self in the poetry of Purshottam Shivram Rege (1910–78) is often self-reflexive. As mentioned, Rege, along with B. S. Mardhekar, are now frequently regarded as the best modern poets in Marathi. He began his literary career in the 1930s, and helped to invent the "new poetry" of the late colonial period. But because of his unflinching aestheticism and formalism, he remained outside the circle of social and political poetry that dominated Marathi in the 1940s and 1950s. In the mid-1960s, however, with the emergence of a pluralistic postcolonial world, Rege's long-lasting poetics of emotion, desire, eros, lyricism, lyrical abstraction, myth, and "private" meaning suddenly seemed to be in step with the times again. His "Mirror" (1965) is a good example of a self-reflexive variation on the theme of the self defined as a presence (or a comfortable absence) in a private, apolitical, ahistorical realm.

Mirror

See how the mirror sees everything the other way round,
draws each object here into a perspective of its own,
mixes up left and right without our knowing it,
but then sets down everything before it sensibly again

in one rectangular frame. Its directions are different,
its edges impartial, its textures finespun at close range,
its patterns of light and shadow just as they are,
the faces it makes, mute, apt—behind the opaque wall

of our first incomprehensible encounter with it.
There we suddenly find the faces we don't possess,
their rage, greed, conflict, self-preservation—
and a trembling of lost colors, every now and then.

The last two examples are not meant to suggest that postcolonial Hindi and Marathi poetry, reacting to the intensely political consciousness of the preceding period, lapsed into introspection and introversion. On the contrary, during the 1960s and 1970s, poetry in a language like Marathi rapidly found new political contexts for self-discovery and self-definition, in a literary culture that developed an essentially multilinear approach to the self and its representations. Two lines of poetic exploration within this multilinear trajectory are especially important for my discussion here. One is the line of development that leads to the representations of women's selves in postcolonial India, and the other is the one that leads to avant-garde modes of representing the socially determined contemporary self.

In the case of women's poetry in Marathi, the most important figure is Indira Sant (1914–), who began publishing her work in the late 1930s, at the time when B. S. Mardhekar and P. S. Rege were inventing the new poetry of the late colonial period. For about two decades she wrote mainly emotionally charged personal and love poetry, becoming the most admired lyric poet in Marathi in the 1950s. Around 1960, however, her work began to undergo an internal split, one half continuing the earlier personal-lyric mode and the other half diverging into a powerful social realism focused chiefly on women's feelings, experiences, and life patterns. To a significant extent, Sant invented feminism on her own, probably out of her bitter personal experience as a woman widowed tragically in her twenties in a Hindu society that is often cruel to widows. Most of her feminist poems are in free verse (her love poetry is usually metrical) and deal with the woman's self as wife, mother, sister, and trapped victim. In "Household Fires" (c. 1965), she brings together all these roles in a complex postcolonial middle-class family situation, in which mother and children are caught in a web of tight controls and exhausting chores, and the mother is reduced to a cipher at the center of the web.

Household Fires

The daughter's job: without a murmur
to do the chores piling up around the house
until she leaves for work,
to pay the younger brother's fees,
to buy her sister ribbons,
to get her father's spectacles changed.
To take the others to the movies on holidays,
to keep back a little and hand over the rest
on payday.

The son's job: to get fresh savory snacks
for the whole household to eat;
to bring back the clothes from the washerman,
to clean and put away the bicycle,
to sing out of key while packing his father's lunch
just in the nick of time,
to open the door sulkily
whenever someone comes home from the movies,
to wrinkle his brow
when he puts out his hand for money
and is asked instead, "How much? for what?"

The younger daughter's job:
to savor the joys of shyness,
to shrink back minute by minute.
The younger son's job:

to choke all the while, grow up slowly
in states of wet and dry.
Four children learning in her fold,
her body drained by hardship,
what's left of her,
this mother? A mass of tatters,
five tongues of flame
licking and licking at her on every side,
fanning and fanning the fire in her eyes
till her mind boils over,
gets burnt.

A literary and artistic avant-garde appeared in the Marathi world around 1960, adding one more layer to the many-layered shift that occurred at that time from a late colonial sensibility to a postcolonial sensibility. This avant-garde was styled explicitly on two apparently incommensurate models—the European avant-garde movements in the early twentieth century and the subversive or subaltern literatures and arts within the premodern Indian traditions. The principal figure in this movement has been the bilingual poet Arun Kolatkar (1932–), who writes laconic, surreal verse in Marathi as well as English.

For Kolatkar, both the world and the self are surreal, just as their interdependence and interpenetration are surreal. The surreal postcolonial self possesses the imaginative power to dismantle the logic with which the world organizes itself, but the world—conceived mostly in social rather than political terms—is more invasive than the self, and the self soon turns into its besieged victim. The most articulate representation of the self as a socially besieged victim in recent Indian poetry appears in Kolatkar's "The Life and Times of Mr Nene" (1978), a late comic poem that draws its structure from orally transmitted satiric songs and children's rhymes in Marathi.

The Life and Times of Mr Nene

the midwife tied a knot at my navel and said
lay out the feast lay out the feast
the goldsmith pierced my ears and said
two rupees that'll be two rupees
the nurse inoculated me for smallpox and said
it doesn't hurt it doesn't hurt at all

baban measured my cock with a stick and said
mine's bigger than yours bigger than yours
baban punched me in the back and said
our dads are wrestling our dads are wrestling
baban kicked me in the balls and said
crybaby you're a crybaby

bunny pedalled my feet with her feet and said
let's play cycle let's play cycle
bunny moistened her belly with spittle and said
let's play doctor let's play doctor
bunny pinched me in the belly and said
come under the covers under the covers

a master rapped me on the head and said
how much is eight times thirtythree
a master boxed my ears and said
where's sheffield town where's sheffield town
a master stroked my thigh and said
come to the mango grove the mango grove

the barber twisted my head around and said
don't move saheb please don't move
the tailor measured my chest and said
thirtyone inches just thirtyone inches
the cobbler stuffed my foot in a shoe and said
it'll loosen up it'll loosen up

my son mounted my back and said
horsey horsey horsey horsey
my boss planted his foot in my stomach and said
there's no solution mr nene there's no solution
my wife caught hold of my cock and said
I'll cut it off one day I'll cut it off

a doctor shone his light on my balls and said
hydrocele definitely hydrocele
a doctor pricked my soles with a pin and said
it's leprosy it's leprosy

> a doctor slapped my stomach and said
> an ulcer an ulcer it's an ulcer for sure
>
> a man stepped on my toes and said
> I'm sorry my friend I'm sorry
> a man poked his umbrella in my eye and said
> forgive me brother forgive me
> a man rammed his truck into me and said
> can't you see motherfucker can't you see

For Kolatkar, however, the self is a victim not only because it is invaded and controlled by others in its social world and is unable to resist, but also because its very nature in a world full of objects is to be an object rather than a subject. In "Licked Clean" (1978), another late poem, Kolatkar conflates the object and subject "aspects" of the self at a quasi-metaphysical level by meditating—again in the surreal comic mode—on the relation of the immaterial human self to its death in a material world.

Licked Clean

> one day you'll become a morsel for the crow
> a morsel for the sparrow
> and one for the flapping sheets of paper
>
> the footstool will leap at you like a hyena
> the radio will charge at you like a wildboar
> the shoes will troop out of the closet licking their lips
>
> hangers will pounce on you
> taps will come slithering out of their holes
> clacking clothespins will attack you like locusts
>
> all at once it will be
> dinner time for all of them
> all of them will suddenly want to stop starving themselves
>
> how will you ask them to stop
> in the wink of an eye you'll be gone
> absorbed like sugar into the blood of things

Of the five postcolonial poems I have discussed so far, Kedarnath Singh's "Signature" (Hindi) is the only instance of positive self-fashioning. While P. S. Rege's "Mirror" (Marathi) wavers subtly between a positive and a negative portrayal of the self, Indira Sant's "Household Fires" and Arun Kolatkar's "The Life and Times of Mr Nene" and "Licked Clean" (all Marathi) insist quite strongly on a negative self-fashioning. In this respect, there is an important continuity between the dark portrayal of the self and its political-historical situation in B. S. Mardhekar's late colonial poem, "The Forest of Yellow Bamboo Trees" (also Marathi) and that in Sant's and Kolatkar's postcolonial poems written fifteen or twenty-five years later. This sort of continuity between the two periods is part of a larger pattern of commonalities and dissimilarities, which becomes most clearly visible in the case of political poetry.

In the 1940s and 1950s, the politicized selves that poets like G. M. Mukti-bodh and B. S. Mardhekar articulated in their work (in verse and in prose, including fiction) were almost exclusively agonized, agonistic selves, racked by their internal evacuation and disempowerment under an order of colonial and cultural domination. In the late 1960s and early 1970s, when political poetry surfaced with renewed vigor in Hindi and Marathi (and a dozen other Indian languages), the selves it dramatized were caught in a new form of political anguish. This was not the anguish of a subject trapped at the receiving end of an asymmetric power relation in a colony but that of a supposedly free citizen, invested with individual rights and a place in a modern civil society, living in a new, independent nation intended to function as a democracy.

The postcolonial Hindi and Marathi poets represent this anguished self in several modes, and here I would like to confine myself to three interesting examples. In one type of representation, the anguish of the postcolonial political self is tempered with self-deflating irony and with a recognition of its impotence as a characteristic of the age. One source of such anguish in the postcolonial condition is, of course, the problem of patriotism (or matriotism), the grounds for which have now been permanently displaced from the earlier, energizing context of the nationalist freedom movement. In this situation of displacement, the self has access neither to nationalist heroism nor to late colonial agony, and is reduced by its altered circumstances to a state of postcolonial pathos, and thus becomes a mere caricature of the truly politicized self. "Traitor" (1968), one of the best-known poems in Marathi by Vinda Karandikar (1918–), captures this (and much more that accompanies it) in a particularly striking way.

Traitor

A crazy man who lives in one of Bombay's narrow lanes
Says that even if you pour blood enough to fill the Indian Ocean
On a mound of soil as big as the Himalayas, it won't sprout a fistful of green
    grass.
When the dogs in the neighborhood bark in a dog-fight, he trembles with a
    nameless fear
And goes in to relieve himself. Don't call him crazy, call him a coward.
In the morning he eagerly drinks up the dose of fire offered by the
    newspapers,
And runs his fingers through his children's hair to make amends.
Having read the Bhagavad-Gita he warns himself, "Don't you ever
Touch a weapon." When he opens his umbrella in the street, he remembers
The mushrooming umbrella of a nuclear explosion—an umbrella of dogs
    around him—
And puts his hand on the shoulder of any passer-by to steady himself.
And when he hears the battle songs in khaki uniform, he weeps like a eunuch.
Don't call him a eunuch, call him a traitor.
He chews on the betelnut of his unchanging destiny with his rotten molars,
And mutters even when he's wide awake, "I still want to live,
To see Picasso's dove flying through the cloudless sky."

In a second type of representation characteristic of postcolonial times, the politically powerless self is dramatized with little comic irony and instead is cast in a more tragic mold. The best instances of such a representation are to be found in the work of a politically extreme Hindi poet like Dhoomil (Sudama Pandeya, 1935-75), for whom the agonizing over political choices and the nature of disempowerment in the postcolonial period led to a massive rethinking of the nature of Indian politics—the constitution of the modern nation-state, the state's monopoly on physical force, the institutions of parliamentary democracy and of civil society, the division (and the complicity) between the politics of legislation and the politics of the street, and so on. In his tragically short career, Dhoomil was unable to resolve many of these issues poetically to his own or his readers' satisfaction, but he was at least able to imagine new political selves and new forms of political consciousness that anticipated a great deal of what emerged in the Indian political arena only after his death.

Two of Dhoomil's poems indicate how the powerless political self may be represented in a serious or tragic mode in postcolonial times, in styles that are distinct from those of the late colonial period. One is "Twenty Years After Independence" (1967), which depicts a political landscape deeply marked by violence, raises questions, and ends without waiting for answers.

Twenty Years after Independence

Twenty years later
those eyes have come back to my face
which have shown me the jungle
for the first time:
a solid sea of green
where all the trees have drowned,

where every warning
has overcome the danger it foresaw
and turned into a green eye.

Twenty years later
I ask myself—
how much endurance does it take
to turn into an animal?
And move on in silence
without an answer,
for these days the weather's moods are such
that it's almost dishonest
to go chasing the little leaves
blowing about in the blood.

It's afternoon now,
there are padlocks hanging on every side,
a disaster's written in the language
of the bullets buried in the walls
and the shoes scattered in the street,
a cow has slopped its dung
on the map of India
flapping in the wind.

But this isn't the time
to measure a frightened people's shame
or ask the question—
who's the country's greatest misfortune,
the policeman or the saint?

No, this isn't the moment
to go back and put on the shoes
left behind in the street.
Twenty years later and on this afternoon
I pass through the deserted lanes
like a thief
and ask myself—
is freedom only the name
of three tired colors
dragged by a single wheel
or does it have some special significance?

And I walk on in silence
without an answer.

The other poem is "The City, Evening, and an Old Man: Me" (1971), which
provides some answers to the questions raised in the previous poem, but provides them with an atmosphere of serious (rather than comic) irony, stopping
short of the kind of self-mockery and humor we find in Vinda Karadikar's
"Traitor," which I quoted above.

The City, Evening, and an Old Man: Me

I've taken the last drag
and stubbed out my cigarette in the ashtray,
and now I'm a respectable man
with all the trappings of civility.

When I'm on vacation
I don't hate anyone.
I don't have any protest march to join.
I've drunk all the liquor
in the bottle marked

FOR DEFENCE SERVICES ONLY
and thrown it away in the bathroom.
That's the sum total of my life.
(Like every good citizen
I draw the curtains across my windows
the moment I hear the air-raid siren.
These days it isn't the light outside
but the light inside that's dangerous.)

I haven't done a thing to deserve
a statue whose unveiling
would make the wise men of this city
waste a whole busy day.
I've been sitting in a corner on my dinner plate
and leading a very ordinary life.

What I inherited were citizenship
in the neighborhood of a jail
and gentlemanliness
in front of a slaughter-house.
I've tied them both to my own convenience
and taken them two steps forward.
The municipal government has taught me
to stay on the left side of the road.
(To succeed in life you don't need
to read Dale Carnegie's book
but to understand traffic signs.)

Other than petty lies
I don't know the weight of a gun.
On the face of the traffic policeman
doing his drill in the square
I've always seen the map of democracy.

And now I don't have a single worry,
I don't have to do a thing.
I've reached the stage in life
when files begin to close.
I'm sitting in my own chair on the verandah

without a qualm.
The sun's setting on the toe of my shoe.
A bugle's blowing in the distance.
This is the time when the soldiers come back
and the possessed city
is slowly turning its madness
into windowpanes and lights.

In the foregoing discussion I have consciously resisted the temptation to develop a single, overarching narrative that will contain the "story" of the modern Indian self and its representations in late colonial and postcolonial poetry in languages like Hindi and Marathi. As a consequence, I have also stopped short of theorizing systematically about the "nature" of the Indian self or of Indian subjectivity in the twentieth century, and of relating any such speculation to contemporary theories of self and subjectivity developed in Europe and the United States. My reason, of course, is that the Indian case is far too large and complex to be exhausted in a single paper of this kind, and since even the primary texts are largely inaccessible to readers here, it is practically impossible to deal with the more general and theoretical issues without first spending a lot of time preparing the grounds for such a discussion. In this context, I hope that my inevitably schematic and highly selective survey of the work of eight poets writing in two different traditions in two different historical periods has at least furnished the kind of material with which we can begin exploring the larger historical and philosophical issues; and that my translations and brief comments on the poems have at least indicated how rich the Indian material is, and how complicated its shape is with regard to the self and its poetic representation.

Notes

1. For a general introduction to twentieth-century Indian poetry in fifteen major languages, see Vinay Dharwadker and A. K. Ramanujan, ed., *The Oxford Anthology of Modern Indian Poetry* (Delhi: Oxford University Press, 1994). The Afterword to the anthology, "Modern Indian Poetry and its Contexts," pp. 185–206, offers a more comprehensive critical account of the historical, literary, and social circumstances surrounding recent Indian poetry. The "Select Notes on Poets and Translators" at the end of the anthology provide basic biographical and bibliographical information on the following poets discussed later in this essay: B. S. Mardhekar, G. M. Muktibodh,

Kedarnath Singh, P. S. Rege, Indira Sant, Arun Kolatkar, Vinda Karandikar, and Dhoomil. For other material on the poets and some of the poems discussed below, see Vinay Dharwadker, "Twenty-nine Modern Indian Poems," *TriQuarterly* 77 (Winter 1989/90), pp. 119–227. All the translations of Hindu and Marathi poems presented here are my own.

2. "The Forest of Yellow Bamboo Trees" is a translation of *"Ban bambooche pivlya gate,"* in B. S. Mardhekar, *Mardhekaranchi Kavita* (Bombay: Mauj Prakashan, 1959, rpt. 1982), p. 74.

3. "The Void" is a rendering of *"Shunya"* in Nemichandra Jain, ed., *Muktibodh Rachnavali*, vol. 2 (New Delhi: Rajkamal Prakashan, 1980), pp. 236–38.

4. The original of "Signature" is *"Hastakshar"* in Kedarnath Singh, *Abhi Bilkul Abhi*, 2d ed. (Hapur: Sambhavana Prakshan, 1980), pp. 11–12.

5. "Mirror" is a translation of *"Arsa kasa sgla ulta pahato"* in P. S. Rege, *Dusra Pakshi* (Bombay: Mauj Prakashan, 1966), p. 19.

6. "Household Fires" is based on *"Jvalanchya ya pancha jibha"* in R. A. Tendulkar, ed., *Mirinmayi: Indira Sant Yanchi Nivadak Kavita* (Pune: Suvichar Prakashan Mandal, 1981), pp. 102–3.

7. "The Life and Times of Mr Nene" and "Licked Clean" are my renderings of *"Charitra"* and *"Chatta-matta,"* respectively, in Arun Kolatkar, *Arun Kolatkarchya Kavita* (Bombay: Pras Prakashan, 1978), pp. 78–80, 124.

8. "Traitor" is a translation of *"Himalayaevdhya matichya dhigavar"* in Vinda Karandikar, *Jatak* (Bombay: Popular Prakashan, 1968; rpt. 1983), p. 50.

9. "Twenty Years After Independence" and "The City, Evening, and an Old Man: Me" are renderings of *"Bees saal baad"* and *"Shahar, sham aur ek budha: main"* in Dhoomil, *Sansad se Sadak Tak* (Delhi: Rajkamal Prakashan, 1972), pp. 11–12, 79–81.

9

Communal Self and Cultural Imagery
The Katha *Performance Tradition in South India*

Gayathri Rajapur Kassebaum

Introduction

The focus of the present volume is on the idea of self as image in three different Asian cultures. This idea can be usefully examined at two different levels of artistic perception. First, the idea can be explored in terms of the individual, the person, and the emphasis here is on the complex relationship between the individual and image. Second, it can be explored at the level of a group, a community, and here the stress will be on the collective image a community has of itself and how this is articulated symbolically. My essay deals with the second of these levels. In this essay I discuss *Katha,* a form of performance, distinctive of certain groups and regions, that brings together music, poetry, drama, and narration in an integrated and mutually nurturing manner while presenting a complex communal image of the region, in this case Karnataka, south India. The idea of communal self-understanding and self-representation is central to this performance. This chapter is taken from a larger study I have just completed.

In 1981, in Bangalore, I saw a young man at a bus stand carrying an unusual stringed instrument that looked like a small *vina* with its head carved as a hooded cobra. I walked up to him and asked whether he would play his instrument for me. In spite of his surprise and suspicion of my question, he offered that he traditionally performed *kathas* in the Telugu language and that

presently he was on his way to a "gig" in the town of Kanakapura, but he would return next day. He and his wife would come and perform on the following Monday evening, and their fee would be sixty rupees. He politely asked me to give him an advance of six rupees for a short performance later. I gave him my address and the advance, explaining how to get to my house. I thought to myself that the worst thing could happen would be the loss of six rupees if he didn't show up. The performer kept his appointment and performed a (partial) *katha* until midnight.

The sheer accident of meeting this performer started my study of *katha* traditions. Luckily, Anjanappa is the best performer of this genre of any that I have met, although he has not as yet received any award or recognition from the government as some other folk musicians have. My curiosity about the snake-hooded small *vina* led me to discover *burra katha* performance. Later, different performance traditions of story narratives from different communities, in different parts of Karnataka, came to my attention. Finally, I realized that these variations were several types of a single *katha* genre. *Katha* eventually became the central subject of my scholarly inquiry.[1]

Story and Narratives

"[T]he spell of story has always exercised a special potency in the oral-based tradition and Indians have characteristically sought expression of central and collective meanings through narrative design"(Kakar *Intimate Reflections,* 1). This statement of Kakar is further heightened when narration is produced through the medium of music. *Katha* is a musical performance which tells a story. The performer is the narrator/singer of the stories. "The stories they tell are worked and reworked into the stories of their own lives. For stretches of time a person may be living on the intersection of several stories, his own as well as those of heroes and gods." (ibid., 2) The *katha* performances are the stories of the performers, other individuals as well as their communities, their beliefs, gods, heroes, and goddesses, presented as an art form through music, to the accompaniment of instruments and often dance.

The stories performed are the autobiography of communities, hidden in their *katha* performance. "[E]thnographies are guided by an implicit narrative structure, by a story we tell about the peoples we study" (Bruner, "Introduction," 139). Franz Boas maintains that "oral genres are a people's autobiographical ethnography." (Coplan "Ethnomusicology," 47).

In my studies, I focus on both the stories of the performers and the stories (texts) they sing. "[T]he stories we tell ourselves, in narrative mode, stance, and voice are far from unified" (Neuman "Epilogue," 272). Although referring to the heterogeneous nature of scholarship that exists in the field of ethnomusicology, Daniel Neuman's statement is applicable to the *katha* performance of Karnataka. The stories performed in the six types of *katha* presented in the study are not unified. They are differentiated by gender, instruments, deities, tunes, dialects, language, *jatis* (castes), and communities.

Katha and Other Disciplines

One of the important features of ethnomusicology is its interdisciplinary nature; it encompasses many fields, ranging from humanities to physical science. "[E]thnomusicology is a field whose fundamental nature results from its association with several disciplines which have nourished it." (Nettl "Introduction," xv). *Katha,* although a unified performance genre, lends itself to many interpretations from several disciplines of social science and humanities because of its complexity. The few important published works on *katha* performance are in the field of folklore studies. For specialists on religion, the themes and symbols represented as metaphors in the stories communicate the religious beliefs of the community of *katha* performers and their audience. Alms seeking *(unca vritti),* which is part of the tradition, is a celebrated fact, especially in the religious music studies of India.[2] Anthropologists take interest in *katha* performers and their social organization. Almost all *katha* performing groups are associated with distinct sects, having elaborate initiation rituals, totemic practices, dedications, pledges of children to sects, and purity rules. Finally, for musicologists, *katha* is a fascinating subject in part because various kinds of musical instruments are indispensable for *katha* performance. In fact, particular *katha* types and performing communities are often identified by the name of the instrument used for accompaniment.

Another musically important feature of *katha* is that both Karnatic and Hindustani tune families are used in *katha* performances. Additionally, different varieties of leader/follower singing patterns are sung, chanted, and spoken while narrating a story.

The actual performance involves a small ensemble consisting of singers and instrument players. Often the *guru* and *sisya* (teacher and students) perform together. Intense training is essential, and only a competent practitioner can become a performer and eventually a teacher. Some of the *katha* performances include dance. Thus, *katha* performance, in the context of ethnomusicology, has many aspects that are informed by related disciplines.

Katha, a Living Oral Tradition

Although there is a growing interest in regional studies of South India in the discipline of ethnomusicology, virtually no studies have been conducted relating to the sociomusical practices of regional music of Karnataka. My first objective is to describe and define *katha*, that is, to state its distinctive properties and to differentiate it from other related genres such as *tatva* and *sampradaya*, as well as to include it under a general set of defining ideas. This requires that we examine the local variations of *katha*, compare performances in Kannada and Telugu languages, and study *kathas* performed in south Mysore and north and west Karnataka.

My second objective is to account for the social reproduction of *katha* as a continuous art form in a region that has undergone great social change in recent decades. Urbanization and the growth of mass media have profoundly affected performers of *katha* and their patterns of music making. In this changing environment, *katha* musical tradition persists, although not always in unmodified forms. In this study, I provide an ethnographic description of present-day *katha* performers and their performance practices that are closely tied with local religious sect affiliations and distinct social practices. In the process, I also report the tendencies of performers who ideologically resist the two dominant factors of urbanization and sanskritization, yet subconsciously assimilate some features of both as an adaptive strategy. They do so by a process of "communalization" of their musical performances in a changing urban environment.

Communities and Their Religion

Katha performers originate from the villages, even if many now live in urban areas. Some people of rural origins can enter closed sects honoring local folk deities because of their hereditary connection to them. The tradition, however, allows those with no hereditary connection to enter if they are performers. So many interested in joining the religious lineage of dedication ceremonies to local deities become performers and thus gain membership to the sect. The dual, contradictory functions of closed and open (hereditary and nonhereditary) entry to the *katha* performing art, sanctioned by religious practices of this region, permit the *katha* performing art to flourish from the past to the present.

There are many sects that perform *katha*. I have found six types. Most of the *katha* performers are musical specialists and itinerant alms seekers. A performing group usually consists of a teacher and three to four disciples who sing stories to the accompaniment of the instrument that serves as the icon of the sect. They often perform the stories of their sect as well as secular stories to a rural/urban audience of sect and nonsect members. They are revered, often being thought of as representatives of the local gods and goddesses, and they serve the local community in the capacity of religious specialists. *Katha* performers employ melodic formulas with repetition, imitation, and reduction techniques, as well as use chant and dramatic speech while narrating a story.

As mentioned, the communal basis for *katha* performance is defined by religious practices embedded in the Karnataka regional folk tradition. These practices include initiation or the pledging of adults of both sexes, and also the dedication of infants at birth to local deities. The description of these deities from the sung narrative texts of the *katha* performances and from interviews with the performers reveals that local gods combine animistic and human qualities and are endowed with "good" and "bad" magic power. *Katha* performers, while enacting stories through their performances, communicate symbols of personal and communal identities. The performance rests on *jati* (caste) attributes and the personal credibility of the individual performers.

The *katha* provides religiously based guides on how to deal with recurrent concerns in the lives of the people comprising the supporting audiences. The life concerns range from status and caste concerns, untouchability, and good and bad luck, to hell and heaven, love, lust, hate, and adventure; all are portrayed in the *katha* performances. In particular, the vulnerability of women in marriages, the stigma of childless status *(banje)* and widowhood, and complex family conflicts involving mother-in-law and daughter-in-laws or sister-in-laws and generally adverse relationships are emphasized in the stories. Thus, it is a very earthy representation of people's lives and their beliefs.

The descriptive account and analysis of types of *katha* from six different communities of Karnataka reveals that there are common features that bind the genre of *katha* together. However, although *katha* as a genre is unified, there are variations in each *katha* type as shown in the chart of the six *katha* traditions.

Comparative Chart of Six *Katha* Traditions

1 *Kamsale*	2 *Tambure*	3 *Caudike*	4 *Jogi*	5 *Burra*	6 *Shani Mahatma*
Location					
South Mysore	South Mysore	South & North Karnataka	South & West Karnataka	South East Karnataka & Bangalore city	South Karnataka & Bangalore city
Language					
Kannada	Kannada	Kannada Telugu	Kannada	Telugu	Kannada
Gender					
male	male	female, male, transvestite	male	husband & wife	male
Medium					
song, story, & dance	song & story	song, story, & dance	song, story, & dance	song, story, & dance	song & story
Identified with					
instrument	instrument	instrument	sect & instrument	instrument's sound	planet
Name and gender of the deity					
male Madesha	male Manteswamy & Siddappaji	female Ellamma	male Kalabhairava	male Siva	male Shani Mahatma
Traditional Occupation					
alms seeking	alms seeking	alms seeking	alms seeking	alms seeking	performing
Membership					
initiation	initiation	initiation	initiation	hereditary	talent
Authorized Performers					
hereditary & recruited individuals	hereditary & recruited	hereditary & recruited	hereditary members only	hereditary members only	hereditary & talented
Performance Context *(akam, puram)*					
domestic & public	domestic & public	domestic & public	domestic & public	domestic & public	domestic &public
Traditional *Jati* (caste) Affikuatuibs					
shepherds & other castes of tribal origin	*holeya & madiga* (untouchable) castes	*holeya & madiga &* other lower	*jogi* associated with performing	*Jangama* associated with performing	*Gouda* & other peasant communities
Dravidian, Pan Indian, or Mixed Myths					
Dravidian connected w/ male	Dravidian connected w/ male	Dravidian/Pan-Indian Hindu legends connected w/ female	Dravidian and Pan Indian connected with epic *Mahabharata*	Pan Indian goddess Saraswvati & Siva	Pan Indian powerful deity of Hindus
Symbolic Animals					
Snake & tiger	Snake, scorpion, elephants, & tigers	Snake & termites	Snake, frog, & fish	snake	Swan & snake
Symbolic Plants and Products					
bamboo banana fruit & flowers	*bhangi/* leaves	*Neem* tree arce nut & palm trees ficus tree tumeric powder	pawn arace nut & coconut	pawn arce nut & coconut	Sesame oil blue flowers
Name of the *Katha*					
Satyavante Sankamma	Mydala Rama	Ellamma	Rajahamsa/ Paradamsa	Nalla Tanga Devi	Rajavikrama

All six types have an obvious common feature: they narrate a story, either historical or sect -oriented depending on the context of the performance. The stories portray life's joys and sorrows familiar to an audience of hard-working, low-income men and women, yet the stories are always connected to religious mythology. A common theme brought out in all the six stories is the status of *banje,* those barren wives and childless husbands, their stigma in society, and the attempts made to alter their status. Infertility is a mundane problem, but the theme is treated in *katha* in passages that connect testing mortals with the intervention of gods, so it becomes a kind of human problem overcome by religious devotion, a problem that can be solved by being a devout worshipper.

It is interesting to note that a seven-hooded snake appears in all story narratives as a symbolic creature associated with gods, whereas the cow is usually the animal representative of religious purity in Hindu ritual and thought. The snake is a reptile of the hill and the forest, not a familiar village member.[3] The tiger, whether female or male, appears as the vehicle of one god (Madesha) and, like the snake, is a fertility symbol, an unusual feature found in Karnataka.

These stories commonly depict a harsher, less orthodox social life. The principal gods are bachelors or are independent (nonconsort) feminine goddesses. Stories revolve around domestic violence, the problems of wives, the concerns of a schoolboy without any powerful patron, or the piety of a toddy tapper. Prostitutes have speaking parts; brothels are humorously mistaken for temples; the value of daughters is argued; mothers-in-law are criticized; and the untouchability of unclean work is repudiated.

Many of the stories are set in simple houses, huts, or other ordinary settings, not battlefields or chariot races. Most of the *katha* communities are poor, some extremely poor, except for some patrons of *Shani Mahatma,* who are of a higher social status and are economically secure. With the exception of *Shani Mahatma katha,* all of the other five types (*kamsale, tamb-ure/nilagaru, caudike, jogi,* and *burra*) are sanctioned alms seekers from the poor, and serve their community as representatives of their deity.

The deities worshipped and the stories narrated are Dravidian in origin, although some are mixed with pan-Indian Hindu gods and goddesses, notably Siva and Saturn. For example, in the tradition of *kamsale* and *tamb-ure/nilagaru,* the deities Madesha, Manteswamy, and Siddappaji are the local Dravidian god/heroes found only in local village areas of south Karnataka. The deity Ellamma of *caudike* appears in the Hindu legends *(puranas),* and the *jogi* story is linked with the ancient Hindu epic *Mahabharata,* yet both stories are centered on regional and local beliefs. These particular stories are only appreciated in this region. Thus the origins of *katha* are combination of pan-Indian and Dravidian gods, but are mainly regional.

There are, however, also many differences within the *katha* genre. The sources of the names vary. Some *katha* performance traditions are identified with the instruments or the way in which sounds are produced. Others are identified with a sect. Some do not have *katha* in their common name, while others are suffixed with the word *katha* and the title of the story.

The language varies in different *katha* genres: five of the six types *(kamsale, tambure/nillagaru, caudike, jogi,* and *Shani Mahatma)* are performed in Kannada, and *burra* is performed in Telugu. The Kannada used in *kamsale,* and *tambure/nilagaru* is a local dialect of Mysore, Mandya, and some parts of Kanakapura *taluk* (sub division) of Bangalore district. The language used in the *caudike* performance of south Karnataka is spoken in parts of Bangalore district with some Telugu phrases and song forms used with the Kannada. The dialect of Kannada used in *Shani Mahatma* is a combination of urban colloquial Kannada mixed with the formal language used in drama. *Caudike* of north Karnataka and *jogi* employ a dialect of Kannada spoken in the northern areas in which the vocabulary is different from Mysore Kannada because of the influence of Marathi. *Burra* uses the Telugu dialect understood by the migrant (Adi Karnataka and Adi Dravidian) Telugu communities.

The geographical location of performers varies. Two *(kamsale* and *tambure/nilagaru)* are exclusively from the southern districts of Karnataka, but *caudike* traditions are found in both the southern and northern regions of Karnataka. *Jogis* are found in the southwest and adjacent districts of Karnataka, although they are originally natives of a village (Hangal) of north Karnataka. *Burra katha* is found in the southeastern part of Karnataka, and the performers live in and render their services to the migrant communities on the outskirts of the Bangalore metropolis. *Shani Mahatma katha* is found in the southern part of Karnataka, from which performers had migrated to the city of Bangalore. (See the map of the six *katha* traditions and their locations).

The gender of the performers varies in the six types of *katha. Kamsale, tambur/nilagaru, kinnari jogi,* and *Shani Mahatma* types are performed only by males. *Caudike* in south Karnataka is only played by males, but in north Karnataka, no gender distinctions are made, and males, females, transvestites, and eunuchs perform *caudike pada.* In *burra katha,* husbands and wives are the principal performers, and their cooperation is essential to the performance.

The performance mode also varies. In four *katha* types *(kamsale, caudike,*

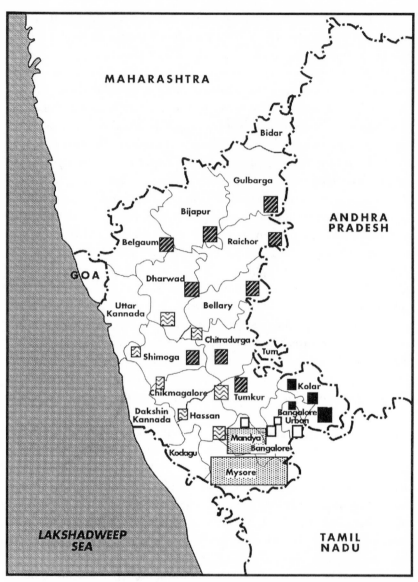

Kamsale/Tambure
Caudike
Jogi
Burra
Shani

Distribution of the six *Katha* performing communities

jogi, and *burra),* dance becomes an integral part of the story narration. As for the other two, *(tambure/nillagaru* and *Shani Mahatma),* dance is not necessarily a part of the performance.

There is variation in the gods and goddesses that are worshipped. Both *kamsale* and *tambure/nilagaru* performers are devotees of the local, bachelor hero/god figures Madesha and Manteswamy/Siddappaji, respectively. Both *jogi* and *burra katha* performers worship Siva, although the *jogis* worship Kalabhairava, a fierce personification of Siva. In contrast, *caudike* performers worship the nonconsort goddess Ellamma. Finally, a planet, Saturn, a popular god, is the source of *Shani Mahatma* performance.

For the *kamsale, tambure/nilagaru, caudike,* and *jogi* traditions, performers must be initiated into the sect, whereas for *burra* and *Shani Mahatma,* initiation is not essential. The *jogi, burra,* and *caudike kathas* of south Karnataka authorize only hereditary performers. For *Shani Mahatma,* although there are a few hereditary performers found among the priests of the temple, talent and competence are the main criteria for becoming a performer. In the religious traditions of *kamsale, tambure/nilagaru,* and *caudike* of north Karnataka, the practice of recruiting new members to the sect is very common. In addition, the hereditary system is alive, and thus, both open and closed systems operate simultaneously.

Performers' caste *(jati)* associations for all six traditions are within the fourth ranked caste hierarchy of Hindus. They include *goudas* and *kurubas* (farmers and shepherds) and *holeya* and *madiga* or Adi Dravidian and Adi Karnataka. Traditionally, *jogis* and *jangama (burra)* performers are mendicants, as their customary caste *(jati)* occupation previously depended on some form of the *jajmani* system.[4]

The six traditions have different symbolic markers: bamboo, banana, *neem,* ficus, coconut trees, *pan* and *bhangi* leaves and turmeric and vermilion powder are represented as sacred plants and objects. In addition, the alms bag and the way it is held signify different sects of performers. Other material objects, such as bamboo or wooden staves, represent totems of magical powers and serve as symbols for each sect. Most importantly, the musical instruments identify each type of *katha.*

Theoretical Considerations

The performance analysis of the six types of *katha* tradition in Karnataka reveals that it is neither a story (as in a book) nor a verbal narration (as in discourse mode), although it incorporates both in the performance.[5] What then, is the nature of *katha* as performed in Karnataka? As I stated in the introduction, it is a complex genre of story narrative in which performers bring drama into their performances using tunes, songs, chants, and dramatic speech to portray characters in the story. The stories are regional, expressing the belief system, myths, and legends of the communities. Some do not have any connections with the Hindu epics and legends, and some are linked to the Hindu legends *(puranas),* but with local interpretations. Although mythological, they represent human sentiments of attraction, love, lust, poverty, and jealousy, and depict happy as well as tragic events of life. The gods and goddesses are endowed with human qualities combined with magical and supernatural powers.

The introduction also stated that social organization is imbedded in the *katha* genre. In *katha,* music becomes a major mode of communication to impart religious, moral, ethical concepts, and messages layered in the form of story narratives as symbolic representations of the community. Blacking's statement concerning the Venda musical culture of Africa is relevant to the discussion of the regional music traditions of Karnataka, although it needs qualified comment, for "music can never be a thing in itself. . . . [A]ll music is folk music, in the sense that music cannot be transmitted or have meaning without association between people." (Blacking, *How Musical is Man?* x)

The musical culture of India is complex in the sense that both classical and regional music have coexisted for a long time. In Indian studies, the term "folk" has often connoted music performed by peasant communities and other groups often subaltern ones. In contrast, classical performing groups include higher castes, although not always, as documented in Yoshitaka Terada's study of the Nagasvaram performing tradition of south India. (Terada: "Multiple Interpretations")

The term "folk music" sometimes means simple songs that ordinary people sing to ease their work or to accompany home-related tasks like rocking the baby or working in the fields. Clearly, this would not accurately describe *katha* performers. They are initiated and apprenticed, must learn long texts, and must coordinate several musical elements in their ensemble. *Katha* is skilled work, taught and learned by people who derive their living from it.

As Ramanujan has said, in India there exists a happy combination of written tradition as well as an oral tradition, feeding off of each other; they do not necessarily correspond to a classical folk dichotomy.[6] The foundation for both classical and regional music is oral, although often one may draw resources from the other. Although treatises concerning music have been written in Sanskrit, Persian, and Urdu, most musicians derive their musical knowledge from their gurus or hereditary family members, as pointed out in Neuman's classic study of music and musicians of the Hindustani tradition. (See Neuman, *Life of Music in North India:* 1980) Discourses on music concerning classical traditions have a long history. This fact has been proudly acknowledged by musicians and patrons of Indian classical music. However, when it concerns performing practices, *katha* performers as well as classical musicians draw their sources from their gurus, who may be nonliterate but possess a wealth of local cultural and religious knowledge.

Music performance in *katha* transmits this knowledge to the nonliterate audience with religious authority. It is folk music because it expresses the oral tradition of a defined community that has few resources for propagating its culture, which is not viewed as high art. But *katha* musicians do possess a higher status because music making is associated with the divine, leading both performer and the listener to a higher plane of consciousness. Many of the stories in *katha* depict gods disguised as alms-seeking mendicants. The lives and roles of the performers merge deliberately with the voice of the religious tradition. The performer's life, as well as the performance, is an expression of this group tradition.

This religious authority is earned with a "rite of passage" through a "ritual process," a theoretical framework offered by Van Gennep and modified and illuminated by Victor Turner and Frasca. All rites of passage or transitions are marked by three phases—separation (being kept apart from the community), liminality (suspended status), and finally reaggregation (or reincorporation) to the larger society . (See Gennep *Rites of Passage,* Turner *The Ritual Process* and Frasca *Theater of Mchebhereta*)

Turner's ideas and studies are centered on *communitas,* a Latin word that denotes community. According to Turner, the *communitas* is the opposite of structure, which is organized in terms of caste, class, or rank hierarchies. *Communitas* is characterized by "anti-structure" and is a homogeneous, unstructured community of equal individuals who are in a "limbo of statuslessness." Furthermore, Turner believes that in this dialectic of structure and antistructure, society renews itself and is able to continue without dissolution caused by disruptive tensions. *Communitas* provides a necessary liminal period of "release" from structure and, more importantly, defines it by providing its polar opposite, antistructure. The existence of this dialectic periodically redefines society and renews it. (Gennep *Rites of Passage,* Frasca *Theater of Mchebhereta:* 167-68, Turner *Ritual Process:* 94-97)

Katha performers go through these three stages of separation, liminality, and reaggregation in their initiation ceremonies with the help of the guru (who is usually higher in caste and social status) before they gain religious authority to impart knowledge to their communities. Furthermore, examined on a macro level, alms seeking is a form of antistructure that has a double-edged status in the structured community and the *communitas.* However, alms seekers as *katha* performers have religious power over their community; thus, they are privileged in their religious status, if not economically or socially. They are feared because of their association with the powers and even the personifications of disguised gods. At the same time, alms seeking as a profession is despised by the community at large, because it deviates from the structure of the society. The dialectic between structure and antistructure is clearly demonstrated in the *katha* performing communities of Karnataka.

Marga and Desi Interactions

The *katha* genre as a musical story narrative abides by the definition of music expressed in the Indian theoretical works of the classical period. In this definition, music (sangita) includes song (gita), instrument (vadya), and dance (nrtya).[7] *Katha* as a genre consists of *gita* song types that exhibit three elements—pitch *(svara),* rhythm *(tala),* and text *(pada).* The collection of pitches used differs in each type of *katha.* When generalized, only four to five pitches are used in songs and two or three pitches in chants.[8] With these two elements (songs and chants) story narration continues within the rhythmic framework. In addition, prose summary in narration play a very important role. Thus, the meaning of text *(pada)* in the context of *katha* performance not only means song and chant but also prose.

Vadya (instrument) is essential for each type of *katha* and, in fact, the instrument provides the identity for most types of *katha* The third component, *nrtya,* dance, is an integral part of most of the *katha* types. Thus *katha* genre incorporates the concepts of *gita, vadya,* and *nritya. Katha* is performed in small ensembles with a minimum of three persons (teacher and disciples) in which the leader assumes all the characters in the story as opposed to the theater or drama, in which each individual plays one character. Several song genres are incorporated, along with film tunes, in the performance. *Katha* performance is a lengthy one in which a long story needs to be narrated.

In *katha* performance, narration is carried out by three to four individuals in the leader and follower model of interaction, with solo songs and chorus responses that employ reduction, repetition, and alternation techniques that are unique to the Karnataka *katha* performing traditions.

Although the performance models differ for each type of *katha* within the large framework of leader/follower singing patterns, analysis reveals that the overall form consists of three large sections—the beginning, the middle, and the ending section. This form is also seen in the classical performing tradition model of *alap, jor,* and *gat* of Hindustani instrumental music tradition, whose equivalent is expressed in the Karnatic classical music of *alapana, pallavi,* and *kalpana svara* or the *alapana, kriti,* and *kalpana svara* model.[9]

Katha genres incorporate song forms from both the classical and regional folk song traditions. The regional folk songs *(tatva, sampradaya, kalajnana)* are usually sung in the strophic forms. *Gi gi pada* and *kirtana* are types of song form consisting of *pallavi* (beginning section of a song) and *anupallavi* (as second section of a song) with many stanzas.

One of the modes found in all *katha* performance is the *Suddha Todi,* an auspicious raga found in the Hindustani music tradition called *Bhairavi.* The mode used in Karnatik music is called "Sindhu Bhairavi," popularly believed to be borrowed from the north Indian. It is interesting that the regional music genre of Karnataka has preserved this raga, which might have once been used in the Karnatic performing tradition as a varied form of a present day *Todi* raga. These musical features of the *katha* traditions emphasize the common musical and textual features embracing *marga,* classical music principles, while preserving their *desi* quality.

The song forms and narrative singing, when analyzed, produce a reduction pattern resembling the classical text formation employed by the classical eighteenth-century composer Muttuswamy Dikshitar. A similar structure of text reduction with repetition used to highlight the meaning was discovered during the process of analyzing *katha* musical performance. Thus, there are broader relationships or at least similarities between the classical and folk traditions.

As the text analysis reveals, *katha* performers have adopted the post-vedic Hindu gods and sing benedictory songs in addition to singing songs to their sect hero/gods and goddesses. The *katha* performers and their community and audience neither follow nor accept Brahmanic ritual practices and have greater beliefs in their sect's gods, goddesses and the guru as broadly embracing the *virasaiva* religious principles. However, over the years they have incorporated songs of Hindu deities. Perhaps a form of "sanskritization" has taken place in the musical culture of Karnataka.

Ramanujan mentions two renderings of the same tale in the Tamil poetic tradition: *akam* (domestic) and *puram* (public) renderings and performances. *Katha* genre is sometimes part of a domestic rendering *(akam)* in life cycle or temple rituals, and, at other times, the same story is performed as a public performance *(puram)* as entertainment, despite its religious base. Thus a *katha* narrative might be used in two versions (domestic and public), each rendering different functions.

Urbanization and Change

During the past decade and a half, the state of Karnataka has grown in population, urbanization, and industrialization, and that has affected the small towns and villages. The mass media of television and radio have brought information to the villages. Employment, or even the promise of it, in the changing economy and the expansion of a public transportation system have stimulated migration to urban areas. Both have affected the village way of life, which is assimilating secular practices.

The communities here consist of "Scheduled Castes." They react and adapt differently to social change. The descriptive account and analysis of *katha* depicts the lower status and economic problems of both performers and their audiences. These problems weigh upon them and to some extent, press them into their own community networks and cultural practices. "Scheduled Castes" create parallel institutions, break away from mainstream traditions or never join them. These small communities may adapt or absorb certain elements from the dominant community, especially in democratic, contemporary and urban India, but essentially, they maintain distinct social practices, with which the identity of the community is strongly associated.

Those performers who move away from the countryside may absorb certain urban ways of life but keep their ruralness and practice local traditions (ritual practices of worshipping local deities, *bhangi* consumption, *tadi* offerings to the goddess, dedication of children to the deity). The meaning of these survival techniques and community concerns are produced and reproduced in long *katha* performances. These traditions are complete religious traditions, sometimes linking with and sometimes diverging from other Hindu traditions. Such immigration from the village is a process of "ruralization" of the cities.

The word "communalization" is used to mean the opposite of sanskritization. It implies both a community (a place and a collection of people living in that place) and communion, meaning to join together, to affirm membership in some symbolic order, to share beliefs and actively take part in rituals.

In the *katha* study, the counter processes of "communalization" and "ruralization" are expressed in regional art *(katha)* even in the big city. The performers are working, in opposition to the two dominant forces of urbanization and sanskritization, to preserve and reproduce the essentials of the little communities in this environment, contributing to and expressing their tradition through musical performances in the cities as well as the villages.

In the past, the village provided economic and spiritual stimulus for the *katha* performers. Even though performers have moved to the city, they have maintained their traditional life patterns. Although *katha* performers retain their performing practices and continue to be alms seekers, their traditional occupation is changing along with their patrons; both are in transition. The alms-seeking life pattern is now kept to a minimum as a religious act, and the performers have taken to farm labor and work in factories, while others have formed performing groups in which performers can offer services. Although initiations to the sects continue, the youngsters attend village schools and divide their time between learning school subjects and honing their performing skills. Thus, a full-time apprentice learning process is replaced with secular training. This might bring a different kind of performance in the near future.

Institutions such as Janapada Academy and folk music promoters have introduced the performers to television and radio and have recognized a few *katha* performers as artists. This has made some performers gain a different identity for themselves in society. Although most *katha* performers of Karnataka are not recognized, awareness is growing and the performers are altering their performance to suit public presentations. However, "[m]usic once ceremonial becomes entertainment but its sound has been substantially maintained" (Nettl *Western Impact:* 163) The process is now occurring in Karnataka.

The hill temples of the gods and goddesses previously had the limited function of recruiting members for the sect and offering initiation ceremonies through *lingayat* priests. Recently, these centers have become popular pilgrimage destinations, offering tourist accommodations and hostels for people to attend annual fairs and festivals. These enlarged institutions run schools for many children residing in the hill area as a service of the temple. The temples also have added certain Brahmanic worship patterns to gain prestige and power.

> [It] is a truism that once we have mechanical modes of reproduction in the arts, exemplified in records, films, cassettes, and books, the "folk" world of production, performance, and reception is somehow dramatically transformed. (Appadurai et al, *Gender, Genre, and Power:* 472)

Although, the authenticity of *katha* performance is maintained at present, what transformation *katha* performance will take in the near future is yet to be seen.

In this study, I have provided an ethnographical account of *katha* that reveals a religious system and social practices of Scheduled Castes as expressed through performances. These local *(desi)* musical communities sing about life ideals and struggles, but the characters and ideas in the stories are connected with a broader range of ideas and mythologies of the great *(marga)* traditions of India.

Katha traditions, although alive, are not immediately accessible. Fieldwork has become essential for this study for two reasons: first, the social marginality of the sects or migrant communities who are the patrons of *katha* are not easily traceable. Only through a network of performers is the tradition accessible. Secondly, because of the oral tradition, *katha* performers preserve and disseminate the local culture through their musical performances. Fieldwork has become essential to capture this oral tradition that is otherwise unavailable through any other sources.

In this study, I have attempted to show a type of local *desi* musical tradition *(katha)* and its complexities. Since performers are the conveyers of this regional *katha* art form, I have tried to focus my attention on them. I tried to present their ideas as they were expressed and enacted in the changing environment of the cities, villages, and towns of Karnataka and to enhance the understanding of the music of the little communities of Karnataka, south India. I will end with a quote from the late A. K. Ramanujan.

> As spider emerges (from itself) by (spinning) threads [out of its own body] . . . so too from this self do all the life-breaths, all the worlds, all the gods, and all contingent beings rise up in all directions. (Ramanujan *Speaking of Siva:* 41)

Katha performance is a an act of spinning stories with musical tunes and in the process of this spinning, performers' social organization, their heroes, gods, and goddesses are revealed through their bodies (dance) and life breaths (songs), thus quietly perpetuating the art of *katha* performance in Karnataka for centuries.

The *katha* performance traditions discussed here, being so rich, complex, and multifaceted, can be profitably examined from different perspectives and vantage points. This essay suggests some of these perspectives. *Katha* are a symbolic articulation of the autobiography of the community. Seen in this light, the idea of self as an image on a communal basis is central to the intent of this performance tradition.

Notes

1. After an exploration of several techniques to integrate the data, at a difficult juncture I almost gave up on it. Finally, it came together after taking several experimental paths that temporarily derailed the whole process. I consider my whole affair with the snake-hooded *vina* a decade ago as a lucky accident, without which this study would not have been possible to accomplish.

2. Prolific Karnatic music composers from Purandara Dasa of the fourteenth century to Tyagaraja of eighteenth century lived simple lives, following the Hindu ideals of alms seeking and being devotee *(bhaktas)* of a particular deity. At present, many organized devotional singing groups *(bhajana mandali)* follow this practice on certain days of the year to continue the tradition.

3. In woman-centered tales, the snake is a benign figure. He is often a transformed brother, a grateful helper, a father figure, . . . the best of lovers who gives the woman everything—child, husband, even a reputation for chastity. On the other hand, in many male-centered tales, the snakes are rivals whom the hero kills or who try to kill the hero (Ramanujan "Toward a Counter-System," 51).

4. In a traditional social order, now replaced by the market economy in India, there was a nonmoney form of exchange called *jajmani,* relations between "a food-producing family and the families that supply them with goods and services." (Mandelbaum *Society in India,* vol. 1: 161). *Jajmani* relations were obligations of lower server castes to provide articles or services to a higher caste patron, in return for diffuse supports at various times of the year.

5. Comparing the *katha* genre of Karnataka with the folk theater of *Tirukutu* of Tamilnadu as described and defined by Fraska, *katai* in that context means a written story in performance. *Kuttu,* is not written. The element of drama is associated with enactments and stylized makeup combined with song forms, narratives, and dramatic prose. In *kuttu,* the dramatic part is emphasized and it exists only in performance. (Fraska *Theater of Mchebhereta* 4–6)

6. "[F]olk and classical transmissions of a single story [sound or elements] parallel each other in time, and any one version may draw from each other or both. As in language, [in music,] the relation of written to oral variants is a complex, many-phased interlacing." (Ramanujan "Two Readings of Kenneda Folklore," 5)

7. Lewis Rowell elegantly charts and describes the three divisions and subdivisions of the concept *gita, vadya,* and *nrtya* in his historical and theoretical study of Indian music. (Rowell *Music* 9–16)

8. The word "chant" is used in this study to mean that two to three pitches are used in narrating a story, then immediately switched to song mode, which uses more than five pitches.

9. *Alap* is a nonmetrical improvisation on raga. In the *Jor* section slow pulse is introduced and *gat* (a composed section with meter) is played employing improvised melodic variations in Hindustani instrumental music concerts. The performers play these three sections as one unit. In Karnatic music tradition, *alapana* (a nonmetric) section is performed first, a *kriti* (composed piece) is sung or played next, and finally there is *kalpana svara* (improvising on pitch syllables) to a section of *kriti*.

Works Cited

Appadurai, Arjun, Frank J. Korom, and Margaret A. Mills, eds. In *Gender, Genre, and Power in South Asian Expressive Traditions,* Philadelphia: University of Pennsylvania Press, 1991.

Blacking, John. *How Musical is Man?* Seattle: University of Washington Press, 1974.

Bruner, Edward M. "Ethnography." In *The Anthropology of Experience,* edited by Victor W. Turner and Edward Bruner, 139–55. Urbana: University of Illinois Press, 1986.

———. "Introduction: Experience and Its Expressions." In *The Anthropology of Experience,* edited by Victor W. Turner and Edward Bruner, 1–30. Urbana: University of Illinois Press, 1986.

Coplan, David M. "Ethnomusicology and the Meaning of Tradition." In *Ethnomusicology and Modern Music History,* edited by Stephen Blum, Philip Bohlman, and Daniel Neuman, 35–48. Urbana: University of Illinois Press, 1991.

Frasca, Richard Armando. *The Theater of Mahabharata: Terukkuttu Performances in South India.* Honolulu: University of Hawaii Press, 1990.

Gennep, Van Arnold. *The Rites of Passage.* Translated by Monika B. Vizedom and Gabrielle L. Caffee. Chicago: University of Chicago Press, 1960. [Originally published in 1909.]

Kakar, Sudhir. *Intimate Relations: Exploring Indian Sexuality.* New Delhi: Penguin Books, 1990.

Mandelbaum, David. *Society in India.* Vols 1 and 2. Berkeley: University of California Press, 1970.

Nettl, Bruno. Introduction to *Comparative Musicology and Anthropology of Music: Essays on the History of Ethnomusicology,* edited by Bruno Nettl and Philip Bohlman, xi-xvii. Chicago: University of Chicago Press, 1991.

————. *The Western Impact on World Music: Change, Adaptation and Survival.* New York: Schirmer Books, 1985.

Neuman, Daniel M. "Epilogue: Paradigms and Stories." In *Ethnomusicology and Modern Music History,* edited by Stephen Blum, Philip Bohlman, and Daniel Neuman, 268-77. Urbana: University of Illinois Press, 1991.

————. *The Life of Music in North India: The Organization of Artistic Tradition.* Detroit: Wayne State University Press, 1980.

Ramanujan, A. K. "Toward a Counter-System: Women's Tales." In *Gender, Genre, and Power in South Asian Expressive Traditions,* edited by Arjun Appadurai and Frank J. Korom, 3-29. Philadelphia: University of Pennsylvania Press, 1991.

————. "Two Realms of Kannada Folklore." In *Another Harmony: New Essays on the Folklore of India,* Stuart H Blackburn and A. K. Ramanujan, 131-64. Berkeley: University of California Press, 1986.

————. *Speaking of Siva.* Harmondsworth, England: Penguin Books, 1973.

Rowell, Lewis. *Music and Musical Thought in Early India.* Chicago: University of Chicago Press, 1992.

Terada, Yoshitaka. "Multiple Interpretations of a Charismatic Individual: The Case of the Great *Nagasvaram* Musician, T. N. Rajaratnam Pillai." Ph.D. diss., University of Washington, 1992.

Turner, Victor. *The Ritual Process: Structure and Anti-Structure.* Ithaca: Cornell University Press, 1967.

————— *10* —————

Carving a Self: Feminist Consciousness, the Family, and the Socialization Process
A Study of Ashapurna Devi's Trilogy

Shivani Banerjee Chakravorty

This paper is a study of three novels by a contemporary Indian woman writer, Ashapurna Devi (b. 1909). It attempts to understand the historical, social, and political processes that define femininity in nineteenth- and early-twentieth-century Bengal. The objective is to trace the development of the feminist[1] consciousness as it evolves through a latent conflict between the self, the family, and the socialization process. It is extremely important to accept women's literature as the chief source of social history from the women's perspective. Mainstream social history has tended to be a history of power struggles carried out predominantly by men. Women have been reduced to cultural constructs with no contribution of their own. In literature—the site of this ideological construction—women have been seen merely as objects of discourse. Women writers have been marginalized into secondary positions and their writings undervalued, distorted, or simply rendered invisible. However, it is in their own writings that their own negotiations with patriarchy and the construction of gender can be seen as having a life of its own. In the documentation of their day-to-day existence their anxieties, struggles, and resolutions become a palpable actuality.

The trilogy[2] under study traces a century of women's lives in colonial and early postcolonial Bengal. The author, Ashapurna Devi, a woman with no formal education, is one of the major women writers in contemporary India; her writing has had popular appeal as well as won critical acclaim. The focus of this trilogy is on the changing sociopolitical situation of women's roles in upper-middle class Bengali society, the impact of these changes in women's lives, and women's own participation in these changes. In the background is an omnipotent patriarchal power structure that, even while moving from tradition towards modernity, refuses to accept change in women's status or to see the individual woman's need for change and growth as a human being in her own right.

As a response to the elaborate code of socialization imposed on women, the dominant mood of all three novels is "rebellion." Each reflects a different stage in women's rebellion. The struggle is against the institutionalized construction of women's inferior status through the denial of education, equal rights, access to the outside world, and of all opportunities of fulfilling latent potentialities—all disguised under the myth of ideal Hindu womanhood, whose most prized vocations are that of devoted wife and sacrificing mother. According to the author, the novels are her "tribute to those pioneer women, who, from within the confines of the women's sphere, struggled to bring about the first assurance of freedom and equality. It is also a depiction of that aspect of social reality which has always been neglected and undervalued—the day-to-day existence of women's lives. This may not transmit the same romance and excitement as that of the outer world, but it is actually here that the roots of social change lie" (foreword to *Prothom Protisruti*).[3]

Much of the narrative centers around an era when women's issues played a significant role in the politics of the nation—first in the social reform movements in the nineteenth century, then in the nationalist movement in early twentieth century, and then in independent India. Ironically, in all national discourse, Indian women were seen as synonymous with the upper-caste Hindu women. In the novels under study too, the point of view of this trilogy is essentially Hindu upper caste and upper and middle class. Exclusion of all other religious communities and marginalized groups should not be seen as the author's limitation, as her writing assumes a life of its own mainly because she writes about the world most familiar to her—the day-to-day existence of such women confined to their domestic sphere. The most interesting factor about the narrative is how little the ideological battles taking place in the real world touch the lives of the objects of the debates—at least overtly. Change enters the private sphere much later and much more insidiously than it does in the public sphere. The battles taken on by the women themselves within the domestic sphere seem small by comparison with the national controversies over women's lives. However, these "little battles" are the ones that eventually contribute to bring about change.

The Pioneer: Satyabati

The first book of the trilogy, *Prothom Protisruti* (The first assurance) is one of the finest studies of women's rebellion of all time. Set in that crucial period in Indian history—the mid-nineteenth century—when the whole nation was focused on women's issues, the novel traces the life of a woman from early childhood to middle age. It is a life of constant battle for gender justice, gender equality in all spheres, and opportunities for a more self-fulfilling life for women. A lone woman's struggles against patriarchal double standards, social repression, and injustice in women's lives in nineteenth-century middle-class Bengali society.[4]

In the world outside the fictional world of *Prothom Protisruti*, the Woman Question dominated much of the social reform movements—the abolition of *satidaha*, or the self immolation of widows on the husband's funeral pyre; child marriage; *kulin*, or upper caste polygyny; female infanticide; the sanctioning of widow-remarriage; the raising of the age of consent; the introduction of women's education. The social reformers were arguing that Hindu upper-caste women were a threatened group and needed to be rescued from regressive customs before the nation could move towards progress and modernization. For them women became the symbol of a barbaric civilization. On the other hand, the upholders of cultural nationalism saw women (again upper-caste and upper-class Hindu women were considered normative for all Indian women) as repositories of Indian tradition and culture and authentic Hindu values. They were guardians of chastity and of the honor of the country. The colonial state wooed both groups according to their own convenience; supporting the former was in tune with their "civilizing goals" but at the same time they did not want to alienate the latter too much by interfering in "native rituals." All the ensuing legislative reforms were made with great reluctance and under tremendous pressure. They attempted to mark a compromise between both points of view by interpreting *brahminic* injunctions from the *shastras* to support their decisions.

However, the national debates or the legislative changes had little impact on the lives of the average middle-class Bengali woman, particularly in the rural areas. They remained confined to their "ideal vocation." Satyabati, the protagonist of the novel, is such a woman. At the start of the novel she is an eight-year-old girl in an upper-middle-class joint family in rural Bengal. It is a patrilocal and patrilineal family in which women enter the household as brides. Daughters are given away in marriage as early as possible. Women's role in this setup is to oversee the smooth running of the household in terms of the men's comfort, the training of younger women to proper womanhood, and the facilitation of the male mode of descent by producing sons. A woman has no access to education; no share in property; no power of decision-making except in household matters; no direct participation in religion, except the obligation to observe rituals pertaining to the welfare of husbands and sons; and no access to the world outside the realms of domesticity. The role of the family is to socialize her into internalizing the belief that her existence is rooted in marriage and motherhood and that her fulfillment lies in a strict adherence to her duties to her in-laws and husband. Her worth is measured by her capacity to produce male heirs.

Satyabati is the only daughter of an idealistic patriarch. Her father is a philanthropist who has the courage to follow his principles. However, he too follows the prevalent custom of marrying a daughter off before puberty as part of one's religious duty. Despite all the arguments against child marriage, high-caste Hindu girls continued to be married before the age of ten, often to men much older than they. The optimum age of marriage for girls was eight, the age when *gouridaan,* the gift of the virgin daughter, could be performed to guarantee salvation for the father. Women were property, and their virginity was necessarily bound to family honor. The objective of early marriage, was, like the earlier practice of *satidaha,* the prevalent custom of *kulin* polygyny, and the oppression of widows was to ensure the maintenance of family honor and purity of lineage through the controlling of female sexuality within the family fold. So, in order to facilitate her father's attaining salvation through *gouridaan,* Satyabati is married off at the age of eight.

Consequently, she enjoys the relative freedom of her parental home for a very short time. Since early marriage was the norm, little girls had to be conditioned to accept their fate and to be trained to perform their future duties effectively. This training program began very early, and older women took on the role of teachers of duties and transmitters of values. Satyabati is surrounded by women, grandmothers, aunts, cousins, and sisters-in-law, whose joint function is to drill into her the dos and don'ts of women's lives. She is told that her mission in life is to be a "good daughter-in-law," a "good wife" and a "good mother"; and she has to devote all her time to training herself for this future. The first part of the training program consists of chanting hymns to God and performing a number of rites to propitiate the deities so that they will bless her with a good husband and kind in-laws. These rites—*bratas*—are socioreligious observances that were an integral part of the Hindu girls' upbringing. They were used to socialize young girls to traditional feminine roles by teaching them a sense of self-discipline, self-sacrifice, and patience—qualities necessary to cope with the inevitable travails of a woman's life. Next, the woman has to remain indoors and perfect the crafts of domesticity, which included cooking; knowledge of religious rituals; taking care of children, the sick and the aged; domestic crafts like stitching; drawing *alpana* (designs on the floor made on auspicious occasions); and so forth. And finally, she must inculcate the values of submissiveness, servitude, and dependence. Only by perfecting all these can she be worthy of her onerous task of creating an ideal family and redeeming the nation.

The entire process of this kind of socialization is aimed at making very young girls internalize the concept of dependency and inferiority. This crippling of the natural development of a human being is legitimized by Hindu tradition and culture. "Motherhood," the most authentically biological experience that differentiates man and woman, is made the central fact of female existence and used as an alibi to exclude women from power, authority, and decision making. In colonial Bengal, motherhood assumes extreme significance as a cultural myth of strength and power. In actuality, motherhood is just another form of women's powerlessness, with its necessary virtues of self-denial, suffering, and sacrifice, all of which are glorified in an ideological realm. Women's predominance in the domestic sphere is extolled as compensation for her exclusion from everything else. The docile and self-denying woman is seen as the repository of authentic Hindu values, the agent of social stability, and through a unique capacity of servitude, endurance, and self-discipline, she can maintain harmony in the family and thereby the state and the nation. Ironically, women are conditioned to internalize this myth so deeply that they eventually become the agents for its propagation.

The women in Satyabati's family collectively train her for the future, but her obsession for justice and truth gets in the way of a smooth socializing into "true Hindu womanhood." She questions, reasons, argues and dares to criticize her father. The source of horror, anger, and admiration to the women who have all had to internalize the code of silence, endurance, and acceptance, she is threatened with dire consequences; that of future rejection by her in-laws, a great tragedy for a woman. But she pays no heed to these threats, and at the age of eight begins her war against gender injustice.

Her major grudge is against women's enforced illiteracy. She sees the roots of women's deprivation in the denial of education. Around the 1840s schooling for girls was gaining acceptability among a few urban, westernized families. The public debates on women's education were getting vociferous. The social reformers saw the necessity of women's education not only as a way of emancipating women from oppression but also as a way of training women to become ideal partners for the new bourgeois gentlemen. They argued that education would render women more efficient as wives and mothers. The cultural nationalists feared the disruption of traditional family and declared women's education sacrilegious. A small number of girls schools were established in urban areas, and some women from upper-class urban families received what was known as *zenana* education, or education at home. However, upper-middle-class Hindu families, especially in rural areas, remained untouched by these controversies or the ensuing changes. Here, it was still considered a sin for females to touch books, a rule that, if defied could lead to dire consequences, like the inducement of widowhood. Satyabati is told that God has ordained that education is one of the "higher pursuits" reserved for the naturally superior sex, while the "baser activities of cooking, child-bearing and child-rearing" are meant for women. She refuses to accept this. "God cannot be so prejudiced, this has got to be a creation of man's distorted interpretation of the holy texts," she says. And in any case, "the deity of learning, Saraswati, is female" (*Prothom Protisruti*, 157–61). She has a clear perception that "gender" is a patriarchal construction and not a natural phenomenon. Women are not born inferior to men; they are conditioned into thinking of themselves as such. She is determined to learn to read and write, and teaches herself by observing her male cousins. She even tries to compose verse, much to the horror of her mother and other women in the family. Fortunately, her father supports her desire to be educated and teaches her to read and write. While he admires her courage and determination and her questioning mind, he can't help regretting that she is not a male and all her potential will eventually be submerged in domestic drudgery. He can do nothing to change her "fate," he has "sealed" it himself by his "holy act of *gouridaan*."

So, Satyabati has to go through the traumatic experience of cutting off all her ties and loyalties with her parental family and entering her new home as a bride at the age of ten. Her early training has been thorough, and she has internalized traditional values enough to assume her role of daughter-in-law and perform all her duties without complaints. Yet she does not hesitate to speak out, question, and even take action whenever she sees injustice or dishonesty, as when she discovers her father-in-law's womanizing and its tacit acceptance by the family, as per the code that moral lapses in men may be condoned. She will nurse him in his illness, but she will not perform one of her daily duties, that of touching his feet as a mark of respect. Her strength of character makes her an object of fear and her in-laws dare not send her back to her father's home. She also gets some kind of support from her husband. A nervous weak man, he tries to assert himself in an effort to retrieve his male ego, but is too much in awe of her to override her decisions and lets himself be led by her, secretly wishing that he had a more "normal" wife. Satya cannot love or respect him as her equal, but is conditioned to believe in the irreversibility of a Hindu marriage. So she serves him faithfully and takes care of his home and family, performing her "duty" till it comes in the way of her pursuit of truth or her sense of social responsibility.

Satyabati has read enough to be aware of the world beyond the four walls of her home. She sees the values enshrined in village life as retrograde. The city of Calcutta becomes to her a symbol of futurity and change. She wants to bring up her sons in this progressive new world. Like a traditional Indian woman, she too wants to live her life vicariously through her children. But her dreams are not of their success/prosperity, but of their emergence as liberated, idealistic men, who would respect women as equals and have the courage to fight all kinds of social injustice. She convinces her husband to move to Calcutta. It was a common occurrence at the time for men to move to cities seeking higher education and better jobs. But it was considered selfish, undutiful, and shameless for women to abandon in-laws and follow husbands. Satyabati remains blind and deaf to criticism and moves to Calcutta.

The move from the village to the city, from the joint to the nuclear family, brings about the first sense of liberty. Satyabati has the autonomy to run her home and bring up the children the way she wants to. Her husband's mild protests are not enough to deter her and she takes on one iconoclastic project after another, one of which is learning English. Women were not supposed to be educated, and to learn English, a non-Hindu language, was a mortal sin for a Hindu woman. Of course, Hindu men were allowed to learn English; they were too superior to be tainted by anything. Satyabati also becomes aware of the social reform movements that were shaking the structures of traditional Hindu society at the time. Ignoring her husband's protests, she attends the meetings of *Brahmo Samaj,* a reformist progressive community, and is motivated to actively join in the crusade for the improvement of the Indian women's status. As she had realized intuitively as a child, she now traces the deprivation of Hindu women to the ancient scriptures that deny them the basic civilizing factor—education, the lack of which reduces women to the level of beasts. Her mission in life is to contribute to the elimination of this deprivation, and she begins to teach housewives to read and write, so that they can use their leisure constructively, as well as gain a sense of self-esteem. She becomes the Bengali configuration of the twentieth-century middle-class Western feminist, using education and consciousness raising as the first step to fight gender discrimination.

Her sons have failed her. They have grown up resembling their father—conservative and prejudiced. At this point she hears of a ten-year-old girl brutally murdered by her husband and mother-in-law for the "crime" of refusing the adult husband's sexual advances (a real-life incident fictionalized by the author). This was the time that the country was holding heated debates on the issues of child marriages and the "age of consent," which was officially fixed at "ten years" in 1860. Obviously the debates between social reformers, the orientalists, the cultural nationalists and the colonial state were chiefly at the rhetorical level, as thousands of little girls continued to be married off to much older men. Satyabati is infuriated by the murder as well as by the apathetic grief of the girl's family, who are partly responsible for her fate. She vows to save her daughter Subarnalata and thousands of girls like her from similar tragedies. For her, her daughter becomes a symbol of the girl child who must be saved; a symbol of the girl child's potentialities that must be nurtured; and a symbol of the new woman who will get opportunities she and other women never had. To her, child marriage seems a symbol of the end of a woman's life even before she has had a chance to live. She makes her husband promise that he will not let Subarnalata be married till she is sixteen (*Prothom Protisruti,* 589–92).

Soon after, in Satyabati's absence, the six-year-old Subarna is married off by her father at his mother's insistence. All Satyabati's dreams turn to ashes in the "holy matrimonial fire." She cannot condone this betrayal and leaves her husband, home, and family, forever. The novel ends with her decision to spend the rest of her life seeking the answer to her questions on the institutionalized inferior status of women, on their helplessness in terms of their "inevitable fate," and on the validity of child-marriage. She wants to spend her last days searching for answers to these questions in the scriptures, creating awareness of the systematic oppression of women and infusing in women the strength to face oppression through knowledge and self-esteem (*Prothom Protisruti,* 650–56).

Satyabati is the prototype of the earliest feminists in India. She wages a single-handed war against gender discrimination and strives to achieve autonomy and self-respect. She has realized that women's inferiority and weakness are myths created by men through a systematic denial of education and equal rights, and interiorized by women. If women muster up enough determination and courage, and if they have access to education, they can demand gender justice and get it. She is an exceptional woman living in a world where most women live their lives following the code of "true womanhood," suffer-. ing all kinds of indignities and oppression in silence, sometimes turning oppressors themselves. Satyabati is more than a fictional character. In her, the author creates a symbol of women who must have existed. Such women, while remaining within the domestic sphere, resisted the pressures of socialization and forced their way out of the ideological grids and actively struggled to change their predetermined roles in the family and in society. It is unnamed women like Satyabati who set out to search for answers and were the first to carve out a self for themselves rather than conform to the demands of traditional femininity. These were the women who eventually showed the light of emancipation to future generations of women.

Transition: *Subarnalata*

Ashapurna Devi continues her attack on a social system that oppresses women by imposing on them a regressive value system as a reaction to social change. She writes in the foreword to the second novel, *Subarnalata* (1967), that it is the depiction of a moment of history that has just passed. Subarnalata, the woman, is symbolic of the pain of an individual bound by the fetters of this age struggling to free itself. The two novels are connected not only in fictional terms but also in terms of history, political changes, and social values and their impact on women's lives.

Set against a background of the Nationalist Movement in early-twentieth-century India, the novel is a bleak depiction of a social system desperately resisting change. The setting is the city of Calcutta, the center of political activity at the time. The social reform movements have been subsumed by the Nationalist Movement and a new ideological existence has been constructed for women. Earlier, the social reformers had wanted to improve the condition of women in order to improve the image of their society as well as enrich their own lives. Now the nationalists felt the need for mass participation in their movement, and in order to facilitate women's new duty to the nation, apart from their role of wives and mothers, a new ideological existence was constructed for women. The parameters of domesticity were extended to the public sphere as patriotism was infused with religion. A new deity was added to the Hindu pantheon—"Motherland," demanding sacrifice from all her children. Gandhi naturalized the feminine virtues of servitude and sacrifice in his Nationalist discourse, and was able to mobilize women in the public sphere without upsetting domestic boundaries. Women's new function, in the Nationalist movement, was an extension of their "natural duties"; their roles remained essentially supportive. Now they had to revitalize and energize their men to overcome the colonial powers with passive resistance (the Gandhian version of a feminized form of rebellion), and rescue the newly reconstructed icon for the nation, *Bharat Mata* or Mother India, from the evil clutches of the invaders. This version of cultural nationalism gave women a redefined image of strength and responsibility, an agency of purification and rejuvenation. This was actually an offshoot of the earlier image of Hindu women as the repository of traditional Hindu values, of being morally superior, combined with the educated, progressive image of femininity of reformist discourse. The new woman was, at a symbolic and ideological level, patient and long-suffering in keeping with the now indigenized Victorian ideals of domestic virtues, but, at the same time, she was self-confident and autonomous.

However, in the average middle-class Hindu family, the traditional patriarchal family structure continued to be glorified. The gendered hierarchy of family roles was enforced with greater rigidity as a reaction to the fear that with women's emergence from the domestic sphere, the basic social structure would be disrupted. What we see in *Subarnalata* is an extreme form of such a reaction. The family here plays a diabolic role and becomes an active agent of repression as it forcibly curbs defiance and resists change to maintain its power structures.

Subarnalata has inherited her mother's spirit of rebellion. She has entered her marital home at the age of nine, bearing the stigma of her mother's desertion—the ultimate weapon used to humiliate her. Her new family is ruled not by a man but by an iron-willed matriarch, the widowed mother-in-law. After years of struggling to bring up eight children by herself, this woman has turned dictator. The family can be the only source of women's power. Tradition bestows age and the mothering of male children with a modicum of power that is so fragile that it requires fierce protection and subterfuge, and the need to create discord between family members to prevent insurgency. Daughters-in-law become pawns in this power game, as they are the biggest threats to this mythical power. The young wives do not have even this mythical power. They spend their days in the kitchen serving their mothers-in-law, and their nights in the bedrooms serving their husbands. Marriage does not mean security, as women are constantly threatened with desertion—if they fail to satisfy all expectations, if they incur displeasure of the men, if they defy rules, if they fail to produce sons. Education, political empowerment, economic rights, and employment opportunities are sacrilegious words. The Nationalist Movement that is becoming more vociferous in its demands for women's participation is painted as a monster threatening to destroy the stability of the system. They are not allowed out of the house on their own. They cannot speak unless spoken to, and even then, they can speak to elders and males only through intermediaries. They have to endure all indignities silently. All dissenting voices are silenced, with brute force if necessary.

Subarnalata, like her mother, questions and argues against the severe restrictions on a woman's freedom and double standards that define a man's and a woman's role. From the day she enters this home, she yearns to transcend the narrowness of her existence. Initially, she tries to make the most of her fate. Appalled by the unhygienic environment in which women have to live, cook, eat, give birth, and bring up children, she wants to improve the conditions by making the house aesthetically pleasing, clean, and healthy. Next, she hopes to infuse in the family members a desire for knowledge, culture, literature, and an awareness of the exciting world outside. At the age of fourteen, she believes that she can accomplish this and change her life, but every attempt she makes to bring about change is thwarted with deceit, humiliation, or violence.

Subarnalata's relationship with her husband is a very important aspect of the novel. Her early education has imbibed in her a love for reading and her reading has brought about an awareness of the possibility of mutual trust, respect, understanding, and companionship between husband and wife—the kind of ideal companionate marriage that was the subject of reformist discourse on women's education. But her husband is possessive, suspicious, and completely insensitive to her needs. He sees her desire for knowledge and yearning for the world outside as the stubborn defiance of his family code of appropriate behavior for wives. To restrain her "insane" whims, he uses false promises, violent abuse, physical torture, and emotional blackmail. Subarnalata grows to despise him but is bound by social norms and her commitment to her many children to continue to live with him. She compares him to a "python, which wraps its cold body around his victim, and soon its caress begins to feel like shackles of iron cutting into the flesh. This embrace crushes the insides of the victim while keeping the external appearance intact" (*Subarnalata,* 124). The metaphor captures poignantly her relationship with her husband, with the family, and with society. All three collaborate to crush an independent spirit, yet force the body to live on.

Yet Subarnalata continues to seek outlets. Whenever she hears of anyone traveling, she is wistful. She is drawn to anyone who is different, who is broadminded, who shares her ideals. On each occasion she is accused of harboring adulterous desires. She smuggles in books and lives vicariously in the fictional worlds. This avenue is also closed to her as books are blamed for her "unnatural whims." She is told repeatedly that a woman's virtue lies in ignorance, in keeping with the current rationale against women's education that knowledge will make women aggressive and unwomanly. On occasion, she is even sent to her father's home as punishment. But all her father and brother can offer her are age-old notions of a Hindu woman's true sanctuary being her husband's home, and she has to return to her prison. Since she can find neither support nor understanding from anyone, she becomes increasingly frustrated. She seeks escape in suicide, but her attempts fail, and even death fails to be a viable alternative to her.

The Swadeshi Movement (the movement against foreign goods) appeals to her ideals and she gets emotionally involved with the nationalistic fervor intensifying in the outside world, glimpses of which are all she has access to. Hearing of thousands of people courting arrest and police torture by burning all imported goods and textiles, she feels that the men in her home have deliberately blinded themselves to these changes. She is incited to action by the housemaid, who points out how the poorer classes have also been engulfed in this wave of patriotism. Identifying women's freedom with political freedom, she sets aflame all the new imported clothes bought for the family. The men are terrified of angering their colonial masters and punish her violently. She still persists in pursuing her ardor for the nationalist movement by reading secretly. She reads of women like Swarnakumari Devi, Sarojini Naidu, Kamini Roy, Jnadananini Devi, and many others who have been able to move out of traditional realms, who are socially, politically, or culturally active. But she is told that it is only women from families who have abandoned their religion and have turned *Brahmo* or Christian who have rejected their duties and moved into the public sphere. If respectable Hindu women like her walked out of their homes, the entire social structure would disintegrate, the morality of the nation would lay in ruins. (*Subarnalata*, 322–23). She is ashamed that the unlettered maid is far more liberated than she is. The privileges of class confines her to an airless closed space, whereas the deprived lower-class woman has the mobility to enter a world of ideas and action far beyond her reach. In this novel the author introduces a number of such "free" women—the maid-servants, the saree sellers, etc. Such subaltern voices provide the only link between the inner courtyards and the outside world, bringing with them news of the sweeping changes taking place in the world outside and rendering the stagnation of the world within even more claustrophobic to those yearning to reach out.[5]

Eventually, Subarnalata does move out of the joint family to a home of her own. She can now run her home independently, her husband is prosperous, the children have grown up, and even her tyrannical mother-in-law is pathetically dependent on her. She is the object of other women's envy. Yet she is far from content. Her attempts to teach her children values of humanism and respect for women have failed. The joint family's socialization process has been far more effective that her own efforts. Her sons are mirror images of their father and uncles: narrow-minded, petty, and full of self-importance. They too have no love or respect for her. Having seen her aggression criticized by one and all, they have grown up despising her and thinking of all women as inferior, unintelligent creatures who have to be confined to the kitchen and bedroom. The ugliness in their values is a living reminder of the failure of her life.

Around this time, Subarnalata is informed of the death of her parents, and is given a letter from her mother in which Satyabati explains her desertion of the family. Her attempts to find answers, in the *shastras,* to her questions on women's subordination have failed and she has realized that the male sages who have interpreted these scriptures can never give unbiased answers. Women have to fight for their rights and claim these as their own, and not expect men to support a cause that threatens their own power base.

Satyabati's last days have been spent in a small school she founded to educate young women and create awareness of their equality. She hopes that change is inevitable and sees it related to the nation's imminent independence (*Subarnalata*, 371–76). Here, as in the first novel, Satyabati validates the feminist consciousness in thought and action. She has a sense of social responsibility and thinks of women collectively. She has had the courage to break out of the traditional bonds of marriage and motherhood and actively work for women's emancipation. She sees education as a means of financial and emotional self-sufficiency, and thinks in terms of a future when women, through their own participation, will succeed in bringing about change and emerge as individuals in their own right.

Compared to Satyabati, Subarnalata appears to be a victim of oppression. The daughter of a woman who left her husband for one single act of betrayal continues to live with a man who betrays her repeatedly. Her failure is partly due to the fact that she lives in a far more hostile and oppressive environment, and partly because, even before she is grown up, she is burdened with a long procession of children whom she cannot abandon. She is socially and biologically trapped, and the more she struggles, the tighter the trap becomes. Her mother's letter helps her find a channel for her inner anguish—writing. Handing over the reins of the household to her daughters-in-law, she begins writing an autobiography. Women's writing in the nineteenth and twentieth century Bengal very often took the form of autobiography. It was as if writing was a cathartic experience, in which women could pour out all their pains, fears, and joys, express their innermost feelings, and share their thoughts, ideas, experiences. Writing gave them an outlet for their latent creativity and suppressed potentialities. Through writing they attempted to appropriate and negotiate with patriarchal demands on them. For Subarnalata too writing takes on this role and gives her a sense of complete fulfillment. She dreams of attaining immortality through her writing and her family's understanding and appreciation of her struggles. Unfortunately, her book turns out to be a badly printed pamphlet—a caricature of her dreams. Her insensitive husband and sons taunt and ridicule her, goading her to the limits of her endurance, and she sets her cherished dreams on fire. As she watches her creation turn to ashes, her struggles end. She loses interest in life, in her children, and even in the fierce Nationalist Movement impelling India towards the much longed for independence. She wills herself to die, lying on her once yearned-for balcony, in the arms of a husband she has never loved, surrounded by children who are strangers to her. Ironically, the pomp and ceremony of her funeral rites exhibit to the world a show of the love and respect denied her in life.

However, Subarnalata's spirit has found a descendant—her youngest daughter Bakul. Bakul has been a secret witness to Subarnalata's burning her books, and the experience has changed her feelings for her mother from indifference to curiosity to sympathy. Yet she is too shy to reach out to her mother in her last days. And Subarnalata is too broken by her many failures to notice the undemanding Bakul. The only thing she has done for Bakul is insist that she be educated. Surprisingly, this has been grudgingly sanctioned by the males in keeping with the current trend of increasing the number of upper-middle-class Bengali girls going to school. After her mother's death, Bakul vows to search for those destroyed manuscripts and illuminate to the world the painful history of an oppressed life. The novel is, in a way, the result of this vow, and Bakul becomes, as seen in the final novel of the trilogy, the author's alter ego.

Subarnalata is the story of transition and resistance to change. *Prothom Protisruti* expressed hope; *Subarnalata* expresses frustration. The society is far more restrictive as a reaction to the turmoil outside. As desperate measures to mend the cracks in its bastions, the custodians of society unleash brutal forces and manipulate words to maintain the familial power structure. Here the family becomes a frightening social construct that has the sanction to maim the individual to keep its "stability" intact. Subarnalata, the symbol of the individual, of human endeavor to carve out an autonomous self, is eventually destroyed because she refuses to give in to the pressures to conform. She is like a caged bird that flutters its wings, trying to free itself, and gradually loses energy. In this social order, there is no room for women who don't follow the beaten track of submissiveness. She can only hope for a future when men and society will realize a woman's true worth and admit their mistake in denying her rightful status as an equal human being (*Subarnalata*, 305–06).

Liberty/Equality? *Bakul-katha*

Bakul-Katha (the story of Bakul, 1974) depicts an age when women are apparently free to make their own choices. Set in the mid-twentieth century, the setting is an India that has been independent for some years. The Indian Constitution has guaranteed the complete "equality" of all citizens, irrespective of caste, religion, ethnicity, class, or gender. With increasing urbanization, greater mobility, and exposure to Western culture, the middle-class joint family system has disintegrated. Traditional values are being increasingly questioned. Education among the upper-class urban women has become the norm. Access to greater opportunities and the desire to exploit these opportunities, even at the risk of conflicts with existing traditional institutions has increased. Consequently, a large number of women are becoming more and more visible in public life.

However, such changes do not always represent the emergence of positive attitudes towards women outside the domestic sphere in Indian society. The basic social structure depicted in the novel is still patriarchal, and women are still governed by traditional role-expectations. They do have the freedom to choose, but marriage and motherhood are still the cherished goals, and making one choice necessarily precludes other choices. Although they have come a long way since Satyabati was told that it was sin for a girl to touch a book, women still remain victims of patriarchy as much as their predecessors were; only the modes of oppression are different. It is a complex world for women. Governmental programs, constitutional rights, social movements, and women's voluntary organizations have taken up women's issues as the reformers and the nationalists did earlier, and have achieved a lot more than rhetoric and paper tigers. However, the required attitudinal changes are slow to come about. The pervasive socialization process continues, and aided by popular media, stereotypical women's roles are perpetuated. Sacrifice, servitude, and self-denial are still glorified, and independence, defiance, aggression are still censured.[6]

These norms define the world of *Bakul-katha*. The author has said, in an interview, that her concern is not the political and historical world but the emotional tensions created by social change in the individual and the family. Dealing with contemporary times, when a dispassionate, objective stand is not always possible for the author or the reader, *Bakul-katha* becomes the most complex and problematic book of the trilogy. *Prothom Protisruti* was an idealistic vision of the past and *Subarnalata* contains the memories of the anguish of an immediate past. *Bakul-katha* deals with an ethos when old values are losing their meaning, and new ones have not yet taken roots. The author seems somewhat confused at what she sees.

Consequently, the novel is more a series of questions posed by the author than a structured narrative. There are constant cross-references to the past. The approach is analytical. For this the author has chosen an objective narrator as her center of consciousness. Anamika Devi becomes the author's stand-in, a famous woman writer weaving fictional webs out of the raw material of social reality. The pseudonym *Anamika* (anonymous) has been chosen by the character Bakul as an identity through which she can articulate her own pains, and her observation of the conflict between the old and the new. Her perspective is kaleidoscopic. Unlike the previous novel, *Bakul-katha* has a number of protagonists whose lives coalesce and meander. The purpose of this multiple narrative is comparative. Lives of several women are depicted simultaneously, just as past and present are juxtaposed to illuminate one another. Rebellion is still the leitmotif, but in a much more diffuse form than that of the earlier novels.

In the forefront are Parul and Bakul, Subarnalata's daughters. Both have personally experienced the old order being replaced by the new and have not been able to find a niche for themselves in either. They can see the drawbacks of both systems and have sympathies for both. They view the same thing from two points of view—the poet in isolation, the novelist from the periphery of social life. And both come up with similar questions.

Parul, was deprived of education and married off young. Her husband gives her wealth and the freedom from an oppressive older generation, but his love is demanding and restrictive. He suspects that she has a secret lover, because she writes romantic poetry. To maintain domestic peace, she devotes herself to playing "good wife and mother," with her secret diary as the only outlet for her latent creativity. In the narrative timeframe, Parul is an aging widow. Unlike the conventional Hindu widow, she is not dependent, financially or emotionally, on her sons. She shuns the "normal" activities of widowhood—religious rituals, pilgrimages, domestic chores, gossip. Fortunate to be economically independent, she can chose to live life on her own terms. Her choice is to live alone, silently observing the ebb and flow of the river, as of life, and occasionally communicating with Bakul through letters. Her observations parallel Bakul's, as she thinks about women of the past—her grandmother, mother, mother-in-law, aunts, and cousins, all victims of the patriarchal family structure in varying degrees. The present confuses her, with its shifting values, new morals, and an unimagined freedom for women. Despite this freedom, she finds that women are still victims. Education and economic independence have still not earned them respect as autonomous individuals. Whose fault is it? Parul asks. Society's, for not granting women their rightful worth, or women's, for not using their freedom the right way? And what is the right way?

Bakul, as a character in the narrative, has spent her childhood and adolescence in the constrictive environment of the traditional joint family, with its iron clamps of authority. She is prevented from marrying the "boy-next-door" partly because of difference in caste and partly because of her daring to make an independent choice. The patriarchal family is determined not to let go of its inherited power over its "inferior" members. Thwarted love and family neglect become for Bakul the catalyst to social critique. She feels for humanity at large but has learnt from her mother's experience that emotion, excitement, and expectations lead to self-destruction. As a personal defense mechanism, she detaches herself from society. She is content to live on the fringes of family life, observing, assimilating and recreating. She remembers with pain her mother's craving for the outside world. As she looks around her, she sees that women born to this freedom have no idea of the suffering of their ancestors. They have not known the anguish of being denied access to the world outside the home, and therefore do not value their freedom.

These are women who remain the eternal victims, sometimes out of their own choice. One such woman is her nephew's daughter, Krishna, who becomes the victim of a destructive ultramodernism. Ironically, Krishna is pushed into a permissive lifestyle by her mother, who considers "progress" and "upward mobility" synonymous. The traditional codes of female chastity and submissiveness have become obsolete as Krishna moves with ease from the career of a stewardess to that of a cabaret dancer. But the moral code does exist, and after she undergoes a secret abortion she eventually commits suicide. Deviants have to be punished, and there is no way she can return to "respectable" family life. Through her the author critiques the indiscipline of modernization, where misguided women are still as much victims of sexual exploitation as their ancestors were.

Namita is another victim. A deserted wife, she has lived the major part of her youth as the model Hindu woman—submissive, docile, chaste, silently slaving in her benefactors' home. Anamika Devi senses anger and resentment lurking beneath her conformity, and their meeting motivates Namita to revolt. She breaks all barriers of convention, but finds no doors opening for her. Without a "man" to "protect" her, without a "family" to "support" her, without financial backing or educational qualifications, she is compelled to sell her body. She eventually achieves independence and fame as an actress, but her new personality is a glittering facade. She too commits suicide. Her death leaves Anamika Devi questioning the worth of fame and independence without a base of emotional security. And in middle-class Bengali society, security still comes from traditional sources: family, marriage, motherhood. Why do independent women have to face tragedy, loneliness, and despair if they move away from the beaten track?

Rekha, Parul's daughter-in-law, is another product of the changing social process. She is, initially, a traditional homemaker, married to an ambitious executive. He wants her to be a companion in his social activities, an asset to his career, a foil to his progressive image. He makes her shed her traditional garb and put on that of a socialite. He wants her to dance to his tune just as his forefathers did; it is only the tune that is new. The consequences are increasing incompatibility, as Rekha refuses to be a puppet for too long. They divorce, and Rekha opts for self-respect in a lowly ill-paid job rather than living under her husband's wing. This situation poses the question of what is really important in a woman's life—love and security, or self-respect and independence? And why are the two irreconcilable? Satyabati and Subarnalata had questioned the bondage of matrimony. To Parul and Bakul, the trauma of divorce and its painful impact on the children bring up the question of the validity of the "modern" option for women—divorce, an ugly word in Ashapurna Devi's fictional world.

There seems to be an ambivalence in the narrative here. The author seems to be advocating an adherence to the same values of traditional femininity she had critiqued so harshly earlier. Here there is also a nostalgia for the disintegrating joint family system and the breakdown of familial values which in the earlier novels had attacked for as stifling women's needs and potentialities. There is also an inherent critique of modernization and its impact on the family and on women. In fact, the author counteracts her feminist posturing of the earlier novels by corroborating all the stereotypical women's roles churned out by popular media, glorifying sacrifice, self-denial, and endurance through images of the "good wife," the "bad mother," the "promiscuous young girl," and so on. However, these ambivalences do not necessarily tarnish what she says in the earlier novels. I see them as the author's reaction to an age of rapid social changes somewhat confusing to one who belongs neither to the old era nor to the new one.

Even in *Bakul-katha,* not all women are victims. There is, for instance, Shompa. She has inherited her grandmother Subarnalata's and great-grandmother's spirit of rebellion. She can fight for what she wants and actually achieve it. She is educated, which gives her the courage to defy the authority of her parents and the capacity to be economically independent. She takes joy in shocking society by refusing to conform to its rules. However, her goal is also marriage. The difference is that she refuses to submit to a marriage arranged by her family; she wants to marry someone of her own choice. In keeping with her spirit of defiance of norms, she chooses as her spouse an unattractive, uneducated, lower-caste young laborer, inverting all the rules for the "eligible husband" among middle-class Hindus in Bengal. The alliance creates a furor in the family, but Shompa refuses to give in to social pressure, emotional ties, or adverse circumstances. She has an unceremonious wedding and finds a job to support her now invalid husband. She is ultimately reconciled to her family but refuses to be dependent on them. She lives on her own terms and is content. Of course, this pairing is also somewhat problematic, as the author seems to be appropriating and reconstructing working-class concepts in terms of middle-class morality. She does not really attempt to understand the issue of class as a determining factor in the relationship, which remains that of a mistress and her servant. Shompa makes all the decisions; her husband is not given a voice at all. Her power lies in her upper-class status, and at the end of the narrative her husband is incapacitated, both literally and figuratively.

However, here the issue is not class differences between Shompa and her chosen man, but her determination to set goals for herself and go ahead and achieve them. In her Parul and Bakul see the true descendant of their mother and grandmother. In a way, Shompa moves one step further than they did and demonstrates the possibility of achievement the new freedom has given women. It does not matter what the goal is; if the woman is determined enough, she can achieve it. This is exactly what Satyabati was trying to prove all her life, and what Subarnalata lived and died to vindicate. Society has changed at least in the options now available to women through education and economic independence. The novel ends with an Anamika Devi/Ashapurna Devi observation. Like everything else, social norms and individual freedom are relative concepts. Time manipulates life, and something yearned for in one lifetime can become a liability in the next. Part of society will change, part of it will remain static. But what is really eternal and transcends time and space is human will power and the refusal to bow to external pressures (*Bakul-katha*, 440–41).

Conclusion

Each of these novels is complete in itself, but taken together, they complement one another, even the problematic *Bakul-katha*. Each is one stage in the process of search for the roots of gender injustice and an active in the efforts to bring about change in the official formation of women's inferiority.

They also question the validity of this change in terms of the actuality of contemporary women's lives and pose a question as to why, even after a century of struggle, women have to begin yet another search for that elusive gender justice.

What Ashapurna Devi writes in her foreword to *Subarnalata* can be applied to each novel. Each is a reflection of an ethos that is passing. And each is bound together by one thought. This is the expression of anger at a system that will not heed the passage of time, that will not accept new values, and that will not perceive the human need for growth. The author criticizes the patriarchal family for constructing gender hierarchy and denying women basic human rights. She has seen women's weaknesses created by this process and internalized by women through centuries of usage. Her protagonists become symbolic of her protest against this process. Her feminist posture is that women have to learn to fight for their rights without depending on anyone. A strict adherence to traditional roles is not the only source of women's self-fulfillment. It is more important to be self-respecting, to stand up for one's principles and actively participate in the removal of women's institutionalized inferiority. Her protagonists challenge the validity of social criteria of female fulfillment and concentrate on fighting for gender justice, hoping for an eventual emergence from the prison of custom.

Ashapurna Devi depicts the society she knows best—the Bengali, Hindu middle class. However, the novels transcend the region and religion, as she traces the roots of women's second-class citizenship to a denial of education, a conditioning to low self-worth, and a constructed dependency on men. While she demands gender justice and criticizes whatever is an obstacle to achieving it, she also respects values of love, honor, respect for others, and purity of body and spirit, provided they are equally treasured by men and women. She criticizes the distortion of eternal human values with as much gusto as she fights against women's oppression. She feels that human beings are not essentially evil, their outward distortions are created by pressures of their environment. Her own strength is in her empathy and compassion. As a writer, she feels it is her duty to reach out for a paradise of understanding even while challenging the validity of the social criterion for happiness. A liberal feminist, with certain contradictions inherent in her liberalism, her battle is as much against mindless change as it is for change. The enemy is a power-hungry social system that ignores the needs of the individual and makes women pawns in its game of maintaining its power structure.

Notes

1. I have used the term "feminist" from the perspective of liberal feminism that Ashapurna Devi espouses. It is an ideology rooted in privilege and a sense of identification with the dominant culture, and assumes that women like men, have natural and inherent rights as individuals, and given equal opportunity, education, and legal rights will be equal to men. It does not take into consideration the issues of class, ethnicity, religion, or any factors leading to marginalization other than gender. Ashapurna Devi' s feminism is an awareness of an autonomous identity beyond the realms of traditional femininity; a capacity to fight gender injustice and patriarchal double standards; a willingness to actively wrench equality in all spheres; and the willingness to think beyond the personal to the collective and work towards change and futurity—qualities embodied in the characterization of Satyabati in *Prothom Protisruti*. However, in her vast body of literature, Ashapurna Devi reveals certain contradictions and ambivalences of attitudes. While in the novel she is an ardent admirer of the values of liberal feminism, in several other places, as well as in an interview I took of her in 1991, she is highly critical of what she calls a false Westernization among modern Indian feminists, who have moved away from traditional values of love and respect for others.

2. The trilogy consists of the three novels: *Prothom Protisruti, Subarnalata,* and *Bakul-Katha.* Ashapurna Devi has written countless other novels and short stories besides these. She started writing at the age of fourteen and continued to write through marriage, motherhood, and widowhood, writing in moments of freedom from her domestic duties. She continues to write even now, and her writing is enormously popular in Bengal. Some of her work has been translated into other Indian languages, and she has won countless awards for writing. Her most prestigious award was the Jnanpith award for *Prothom Protisruti* (1965).

3. All translations from the original texts quoted in the paper are my own.

4. When I interviewed Ashapurna Devi in 1991, she said that as a child growing up in a conservative home, she used to observe the restrictions and double standards that bound women. She herself could not articulate her protest at that time. When she eventually found a voice in her pen, she went back in time in an attempt to retrace her personal history. She created Satyabati, the main character of *Prothom Protisruti,* as a symbol of her critique of patriarchal double standards.

5. Such women are present in *Prothom Protisruti* also, as messengers and social commentators. Although these women are underprivileged, they have an advantage over their more privileged sisters. They have mobility in the public sphere. They also have freedom from restrictive patriarchal codes, the integral part of middle-class ideology that makes its entry with upward mobility. Through an in-depth study of Ashapurna Devi's writing, I have come to the conclusion that Ashapurna Devi's

perspective of the lower stratas of society is limited to the services they render to the upper classes. Consequently, her understanding of them and their need is from above, and they remain functional characters in most of her writing.

6. I will not touch on the crucial issues of increasing unemployment, inflation, the population boom, poverty, and ethnic, religious and caste conflicts of contemporary India, as they are outside the purview of this paper. That is not to deny the extreme significance of these issues, especially in terms of women' s status in India. But as I mentioned earlier, Ashapurna Devi does not incorporate any of these issues in her novels, which tend to view the Hindu upper-middle-class family as more or less as the norm. This novel is set in the 1960s, before women's issues emerged as an integral component of a new policy. Ashapurna Devi's India of *Bakul-katha* still has one foot firmly in the past.

A Selected Bibliography

Anurupa Devi. *Sahitye Nari.* Calcutta: Calcutta University, 1949.

Ashapurna Devi. *Bakul-Katha.* Calcutta: Mitra & Ghosh, 1974.

———. *Prothom Protisruti. Calcutta: Mitra & Ghosh, 1965.*

———. *Subarnalata.* Calcutta: Mitra & Ghosh, 1967.

Bagchi, Jasodhara. "Socializing the Girl Child in Colonial Bengal." *Economic and Political Weekly,* 9 October 1993, 2214-19.

———. "Representing Nationalism: The Ideology of Motherhood in Colonial Bengal." *Economic and Political Review of Women's Studies Weekly,* 20-29 October 1990, WS 65-71.

———. "Naribadi Protibhangite Adhunik Bangla Kathasahitye Du-Charti Katha." In *Bharat Itihase Nari,* edited by Ratnabali Chattopadhyay and Goutom Niyogi. Calcutta: K.P. Bagchi & Co., 1989, 119-28.

Banerjee, Himani. "Fashioning a Self: Educational Proposals for and by Women in Popular Magazines in Colonial Benegal." *Economic and Political Weekly: Review of Women's Studies,* 26, no. 431 (26 October 1991): WS 50-62.

Bhattacharya, Malini. *"Meyeder Itihas o Sahitya Sakhhya." Bharat Itihase Nari,* edited by Ratnabali Chattopadhyay and Goutom Niyogi. Calcutta: K.P. Bagchi & Co., 1989, 110-18.

Borthwick, Meredith. *The Changing Role of Women in Bengal, 1849-1905.* Princeton: Princeton University Press, 1984.

Chakravorty, Usha. *Conditions of Bengali Women around the Second Half of the Nineteenth Century.* Calcutta: Bardhan Press, 1963.

Chatterjee, Partha. "The Nationalist Resolution of the Women's Question." In *Recasting Women: Essays in Colonial History,* edited by Kumkum Sangari and Sudesh Vaid, 233-68. New Delhi: Kali for Women, 1989.

Desai, Neera, and Maithreyi Krishnaraj, eds. *Women and Society in India.* 1987. Delhi: Ajanta Publications, 1990.

Dutt, Romesh Chunder. *Cultural Heritage of Bengal.* Calcutta: Punthi Pustak, 1962.

Fruzetti, Lina M. *The Gift of a Virgin: Women, Marriage and Ritual in a Bengali Society.* Delhi: Oxford University Press, 1990.

Guha, Shibani Pal. *Bangla Upanyashe Nari Charitrer Bibartan.* Calcutta: Delight Books, 1969.

Jayawardene, Kumari. *Feminism and Nationalism in the Third World.* New Delhi: Kali for Women, 1986.

Jyotirmoyee Devi. *Chirantan Nari Jigyasa: Sekaler Smriti.* Calcutta: Ananya Prakashan, 1988.

Karlekar, Malvika. *Voices from Within: Early Personal Narratives of Bengali Women.* Delhi: Oxford University Press, 1991.

Kaushik, Susheela, ed. *Women's Oppressions: Patterns and Perspectives.* Delhi: Shakti Books, 1985.

Krishnaraj, Maithreyi, and Karuna Chanana, eds. *Gender and the Household Domain: Social and Cultural Dimensions.* New Delhi: Sage Publications, 1898.

Liddle, Joanna, and Rama Joshi. *Daughters of Independence: Gender, Caste and Class in India.* New Delhi: Kali for Women, 1986.

Mahindra, Indira. *The Rebellious Home-makers.* Bombay: SNDT Women's University, 1980.

Mani, Lata. "Whatever Happened to the Vedic Dasi? Orientalism, Nationalism and a Script for the Past." In *Recasting Women: Essays in Colonial History,* edited by Kumkum Sangari and Sudesh Vaid. New Delhi: Kali for Women, 1989, 28–67.

Miller, Barbara. *The Endangered Sex.* Ithaca: Cornell University Press, 1981.

Mukherjee, Meenakshi. *Realism and Reality: The Novel and Society in India.* Delhi: Oxford University Press, 1985.

Mukherjee, S. N. "Raja Rammohan Roy and the Debate on the State of Women in Bengal." In *Women in India and Nepal,* edited by Michael Allen and S. N. Mukherjee. New Delhi: Sterling Publishers, 1990, 155–70.

Murshid, Ghulam. *Reluctant Debutant: Response of Bengali Women to Modernization, 1849–1905.* Rajshahi: Sahitya Samsad Rajshahi University, 1983.

Ray, Bharati. "Beyond the Domestic/Public Dichotomy: Women's History in Bengal, 1905–1947." In *Modern Bengal: A Socio-economic Survey,* edited by S. P. Sen and N. R. Ray. Calcutta, 1985.

Roy, Monisha. *Bengali Women.* Chicago: University of Chicago Press, 1972.

Sangari, Kumkum and Sudesh Vaid, eds. *Women and Culture.* Bombay: SNDT Women's University, 1989.

———. "Introduction." In *Recasting Women: Essays in Colonial History,* edited by Kumkum Sangari and Sudesh Vaid. New Delhi: Kali for Women, 1989, 1–27.

Sarkar, Sumeet. "The Women's Question in Nineteenth-Century Bengal." In *Women and Culture,* edited by Kumkum Sangari and Sudesh Vaid. Bombay: SNDT Women's University, 1989, 157-72.

Sarkar, Tanika. "Nationalist Iconography: Image of Women in Nineteenth-Century Bengali Literature." *Economic and Political Weekly,* 21 November 1987, 2011-15.

Tharu, Susie. "Women's Writings in India." *Journal of Art and Ideas,* nos. 20-21 (March 1991) 49-66.

Tharu, Susia, and K. Lalitha, eds. *Women Writing in India,* volume 2: *The Twentieth Century.* New York: The Feminist Press, 1993.

———. *Women Writing in India,* volume 1: *600 B.C. to the Early Twentieth Century.* New York: The Feminist Press, 1991.

11

Satyajit Ray's Secret Guide to Exquisite Murders
Creativity, Social Criticism, and the Partitioning of the Self

Ashis Nandy

I

Many years ago, in the 1940s and 1950s at Calcutta, I read some of the science fiction of H. G. Wells (1866–1946). I had then just crossed the boundaries of childhood. On reading Wells, I remember being especially impressed by *The Time Machine* (1895), *The Island of Doctor Moreau* (1896), *The Invisible Man* (1897), and *The War of the Worlds* (1898). The last two novels I read in Bengali, my English being still somewhat uncertain.

While all four novels intrigued me, two did something more; they jolted me out of conventionality. They made me aware that everyone in the world did not look at science the way my schoolteachers and parents did, or said they did. The criticism of science in *The Invisible Man* and *The Island of Doctor Moreau* was so direct and impassioned that it could not be ignored even by a teenager being constantly exposed to the then-new slogans about scientific rationality, being vended systematically by India's brand new, youthful prime minister.

It was therefore a surprise when, more than a decade later, I began to read Wells on history and society. For I discovered that there was not a whiff of the criticism of modern science that I had confronted in my teens in his novels; there were criticisms only of the social relations of modern science. When Wells wrote on the political sociology of science self-consciously, as for instance

305

in his *Outline of History* (1920), he was prim, predictable, and just like some of my teachers and relatives. This was disappointing at the time but also consoling in strange ways, for his criticisms of science *had* shaken me.

Everyone tries to forget one's childhood heroes. Mine were going out of fashion right before my eyes during my adolescence. Wells, like George Bernard Shaw, Bertrand Russell and Aldous Huxley, was yielding place to the new heroes of the times. Before long, I was keeping the company of others. I had nearly forgotten the two Wells until, many years later, I discovered that one of the other heroes of my teens, Arthur Conan Doyle, was a practicing spiritualist and theosophist. Here was a major writer of crime fiction—whose hero Sherlock Holmes had done so much to sell the ideas of induction, empiricism, and value-neutral, dispassionate, rational knowledge to us in our teens—and he turned out to be, in his other incarnation, a direct negation of all the right values.[1]

I was to remember both Wells and Conan Doyle yet again when, two decades later, I read some of Salman Rushdie's nonfiction soon after reading his *Midnight's Children* and *Shame*.[2] When I read *Midnight's Children*, I had not even heard of Rushdie. Parts of the novel, therefore, came to me as a revelation. Few had written about the Indian middle-class consciousness of our times with such sensitivity. The middle classes Saratchandra Chattopadhyay (1878–1938) wrote about with such deep understanding were no longer there, and few had sensed the new potpourri of multicultural life of the middle-class Indian of the 1960s and 1970s. Before Rushdie, even fewer had tried to capture the interplay among the popular, the folk, and the nascent pan-Indian mass culture in urban India, creating new contradictions and absurdities for millions. Only a handful of writers have matched the insight with which Rushdie speaks in *Midnight's Children* of elements of the new popular culture in urban India, such as Bombay films and professional wrestling bouts, entering the interstices of the middle-class worldview. Rushdie's novel recognizes the inner dynamics of India's upper-middle-brow metropolitanism better than almost anyone else's—the fragments of self derived from the parochial, the local, and the cosmopolitan; the peculiar, shallow mix of East and West that defines many Western-educated Indians; a cauldron of emotions bubbling with the profound, the comic, and the trivial in startling amalgamation.

Rushdie's formal social and political comments are a direct negation of these sensitivities. They have all the "right" values in a predictable social democratic format, but, on the whole, what he has to say in his nonfiction is cliché-ridden and pathetically dependent on categories derived from the popular Anglo-Saxon philosophy of the interwar years. Rushdie's social and political comments are terribly like what Jawaharlal Nehru might have said about the public realm today if he were recalled in a séance by an enterprising medium. And when Rushdie writes on public issues in nonfictional form, he seems even to lack Nehru's grandfatherly charm. He speaks in a tone that may be very comforting to the aging left but that is not even good radical chic, being at least thirty years out of date.[3]

Nothing reveals the insensitivity of the self-declared political sociologist Rushdie, compared to the novelist Rushdie, better than his article on Mohandas Karamchand Gandhi, written soon after Richard Attenborough's block-buster *Gandhi* was released and had captured the imagination of filmgoers, if not of film critics.[4] Rushdie's essay is ostensibly on the film, but it also tells a lot about his understanding of the subject of the film. Rushdie's Gandhi is a slippery partisan of things medieval—a shrewd, if not slimy, politician who could be forgotten but for his tremendous capacity to mobilize public sentiments for irrational, primordial causes. Implicitly, it is a Gandhi who was responsible for the partition of India on religious grounds, a better-edited version of that spokesman for Muslim atavism, Mohammed Ali Jinnah (1876–1948). Rushdie's Gandhi is not even the ultimate social base of the bicultural, alienated Nehru but the political equal of the future prime minister of India, debating crucial issues with the young, modernist social reformer and hero of India's middle classes.

Not being a Gandhian, Rushdie's criticism of Gandhi did not disturb me. What did disturb me was my discovery of Rushdie as the last serious disciple of the late Professor Harold Lasky and Rajani Palme Dutt, and the shocked recognition that this lost child of the 1930s was behind the creation of *Midnight's Children*. Later, it was to help me understand better the reaction of the Islamic world to his *Satanic Verses*, but the discovery, when I first made it, was disheartening, to say the least.

After reading Rushdie, I was back to the curious case of H. G. Wells and the vague awareness it had spawned in me years ago—about the ability of the highly creative to partition their selves, disconcertingly but effectively. Effectively, because by now I had begun to suspect that this partitioning was something Wells and Rushdie had to do to protect their creative insights— their painfully dredged-out, less accessible self—from being destroyed by their "normal," "sane," rational self. It was as if they sensed that their conventionalities would overwhelm their deeper but vulnerable insights into the changing nature of the human predicament, unless they took care to defend that conventionality morally in another sphere of life, a sphere in which "pure cognition" and "rationality" dominated.

Perhaps psychoanalysis tells only part of the story. The conditions under which human passions get less contaminated by interests than does human cognition have remained an under-studied aspect of personality theory. As a result, the pathologies of irrationality today are more vividly recognized than the pathologies of rationality and intellect. Perhaps the trend began not with Sigmund Freud but with the crystallization of the culture of Galilean Europe—with Francis Bacon himself. After all, over the last three hundred years, only a few thinkers such as William Blake, John Ruskin, Joseph Conrad, Hannah Arendt, and Herbert Marcuse have paid some attention in the Western world to the pathology of rationality, though it has continued to be a major concern of many non-Western thinkers, Gandhi being the most conspicuous recent example. The great minds of Europe after the Enlightenment—from Giovanni Vico to Karl Marx to Sigmund Freud—have all been more keen to unravel the pathologies of human irrationality.

Both Wells and Rushdie, professed champions of Western modernity and the Enlightenment, demonstrate in their own ways the perils of this intellectual imbalance. To make my point in a more roundabout way (after all, that is what scholarship is all about) I shall now discuss the same process in more detail in the case of a highly creative, contemporary Indian filmmaker, Satyajit Ray.

II

Satyajit Ray was born into a well-known family of litterateurs and social reformers in 1921. It was originally a Kayastha family that had probably come from Bihar to settle at Nadia in western Bengal in medieval times. Since the sixteenth century, the Rays also had an East Bengali connection through their landed estates in Mymensingh, now in Bangladesh. They had acquired the surname Ray (originally Rai, a Mughal title) when an ancestor held office under the Mughals. Previously, they had been known as Deos and then Debs. Unlike a majority of Bengali Kayasthas who are Shāktos, the Rays were Vaisnavas.[5]

By the time Satyajit was born, the Rays were already an important presence in Calcutta's social and intellectual life. Satyajit's grandfather, Upendrakishore Raychowdhury (1863–1915), had renounced orthodox Hinduism and embraced Brahmoism early in his life, as an act of social defiance and a statement of commitment to social reform. He had joined the Sadharan Brahmo Samaj, the most radical of the Brahmo sects, and married into a well-known family of Brahmo social reformers. Upendrakishore's father-in-law, Dwarkanath Ganguli, was one of the founders of Sadharan Brahmo Samaj, and Dwarkanath's wife and Upendrakishore's stepmother-in-law, Kadambini Ganguli, was the first woman graduate in the British Empire, South Asia's first modern woman doctor, and a delegate to the fifth session of the Indian National Congress. Despite these connections, however, Upendrakishore managed, in life as well as in death, to avoid being typed as an abrasive activist. He was primarily known as a famous writer of children's literature, a printer, and a publisher.

Upendrakishore's eldest son and Satyajit's father, Sukumar Ray (1887–1923), has been described by many as India's greatest writer of children's stories and verses in modern times. He began to publish from the age of nine, specializing in writing nonsense verse. Apart from Gijubhai of Gujarat, one cannot think of another major Indian writer during the past hundred years whose fame has depended so entirely on writing for children. Sukumar was also a talented printing technologist, illustrator, actor, and the editor of Bengal's finest children's magazine, *Sandesh,* which had been founded by Upendrakishore.[6]

There were other eminent persons in the family, too. Sukumar's cousin, Leela Majumdar, was a gifted humorist and writer of children's fiction; so was Sukhalata Rao, Sukumar's elder sister. Upendrakishore's brother Sharadaranjan pioneered the game of cricket in eastern India; another brother, Kuladaranjan, was a recognized artist. Kuladaranjan and his younger brother Pramadaranjan translated into Bengali popular English science fiction and crime thrillers for children.

On the whole, the family had a special relationship with children's literature, art, and theater—having written and published for children for so long, it turned that specialization into a family tradition. Each member of the family had to support the weight of the tradition and, simultaneously, affirm his or her own distinctive style of creativity. This balance was in turn influenced by the ideological tilt of the family; by the time Satyajit was born, the family culture had become, through the Brahmo connection with late Victorian culture, aggressively rationalist, antihedonistic, and, despite their nationalism, Anglophile. The Rays were proud of their British connection, of the fact that many of them were trained in England, and that they played the civilizing role demanded of them by the modern institutions introduced by the Raj into the country.[7]

The problem of harmonizing these diverse strains was, however, complicated for young Satyajit by Sukumar's tragic death at the age of thirty-six, when his only child was less than two years old. Sukumar died of *kālājvar*, literally black fever. At that time it was a fatal disease that, like tuberculosis in Victorian England, had acquired a special meaning for some sections of the Bengalis. *Kālājvar* carried the contradictory associations of pastoral life and the new threats to it, the growing chasm between city and village, and the lurking fear of the abandoned countryside, taken over by the darker forces of nature and thus no longer hospitable or nurtural, as well as associations of fatalism, melancholia, and self-destruction. When set off against Sukumar's robust humor and zest for life, the disease must have had a strange, ominous, tragic presence. Its impact was certainly magnified by the family's awareness that Sukumar's impending death would also mean the end of the family's publishing business and lead to their financial decline. They were not wrong; the business folded up soon after Sukumar died, and the family's fortunes fell sharply.

A joint family protects its children from the full impact of such bereavement. In Satyajit's case, for instance, there were his uncles and cousins to cushion the loss of his father.[8] It is likely that for Satyajit his father survived in memory mainly as a mythic, larger-than-life figure, serving both as a prototype of charismatic but distant male authority and as a figure that was vaguely vulnerable and fragile. The theme of a childlike, gifted adult, in whom loneliness masquerading as search for privacy was combined with obsessive preoccupation with creative work, would later on be an important one for his son both in his life and his work.[9]

Satyajit naturally grew up close to his young widowed mother, Suprava, an impressive, firm, self-disciplined woman and a good singer. She constituted not only his first and immediate model of care and adulthood but also of power and resilient authority. Indeed, one critic has hinted that she was for her only son an authoritative symbol of purity and expiation through widowhood that was to recur in his works in two different guises—as a nurtural mother who invests in her son her all (as in *Aparajito*) and as a seductive, eroticized presence, fighting against and finally yielding to the demands of her "lost" conjugal self (as in *Aranyer Din Rātri*).[10] In addition, Suprava might have become an immediate, "real" authority for her young son and even have been for him a sturdier, more tenacious, nuanced, and acceptable target of ambivalence. He may have been spared the sharper edges of oedipal tussles in a crypto-Victorian family in the tropics, but not the problems of authority common in a culture with a marked substratum of matriarchy. Many years afterwards, he remarked:

> In my movies I have brought in a certain detachment in the women. I like to think of women as lonely, unattached and self-absorbed. I can understand the power and the beauty of women easily. I think women have more power of mind.[11]

But that power of mind was not isolated from feelings:

> . . . many among the women around us keep us alive emotionally. . . . the qualities in women that I admire most are intelligence, grace and sophistication. Much of the beauty of women is captured in their patience and tolerance. . . . In some areas, men are much more fragile than women. In those areas only women can protect men.[12]

In sum, one guesses that the family culture and mythologies underpinning it were to shape Satyajit's life and work through four dominant themes. First, the Ray family encompassed and summarized within itself the cataclysmic changes that had taken place in the social world of the Bengalis over the previous 150 years. Marie Seton and Chidananda Dasgupta have summarized these changes and shown how the Rays represented as well as responded to the changes and turned them into distinctive strains—and sources of creativity—within the family.[13] Indeed, the very fact that the family had arrived at a large frame of reference, within which could be located these representations and responses, brought the family traditions close to being a worldview that could not be easily defied but within which there was some scope for dissent.

Secondly, since the end of the nineteenth century the family had consistently been in the forefront of social change in Bengal and faced the consequences of it. The emphasis on humor and children's literature, and the self-confident style most of them cultivated, often obscured the fact that they were part of a small minority and perhaps even felt isolated and beleaguered. When Seton speaks of the combination of "sensitivity" and "imperviousness" in Satyajit the filmmaker, one is tempted to relate it to the experience of the Rays over the previous hundred years, to the peculiar mix of respect, love, social distance, and defiance with which the family had learned to live.[14]

Also, it was a dissenting family, and in that dissent the ideology of modernity had played a major part. The ideology justified their nonconformism

and gave meaning to their "odd," occasionally "eccentric," experimental ca-
reers. The Rays had reason to be grateful for the process of Westernization
in Indian society and to post-Renaissance Europe for the distinctive style of
creativity they evolved.

Third, their Brahmo faith—a quasi-puritanical protest against the hedo-
nism of the babus of greater Calcutta, in turn triggered by the disorienting
and violent entry of the colonial political economy into eastern India—gave a
sharp edge to moral issues, especially those that involved sexual norms and the
channeling of violence in society. In a culture that was traditionally not greatly
inhibited in the matter of heterosexual relationships, this quasi-puritanical
strain was paradoxically not an indicator of conformity but of dissent.

As part of this attempt to reinstate a moral universe, emphasis on the
public role of women and on the problems of women was something more
than a matter of ideology for the Rays; the emphasis represented an unself-
conscious, probably latent, attempt to rediscover one's relationship with a
culture that included an identifiable substratum of matriarchy and with a
society that, in facing the alienation and anomie produced by the colonial
intrusion, had begun to wreak vengeance on women, seeing in them symbols
of continuity with a capricious maternal principle in the cosmos that had
begun to falter and sometimes failed altogether.[15]

Finally, as a result of this configuration of cultural and psychological
strains, there persisted in the Rays an inner tension between unfettered imagination and disciplined rationality, perhaps even a tendency to live on two
planes, which they could not fully reconcile. The imaginativeness was primarily
reserved for what they wrote, drew, and fantasized for the children; the rationality for organized intervention in society and for defining their social responsibility in an adult world in which children, too, were a part of one's trust.

III

*Because you believe in the indivisibility of life, you seem
to me to be the most Indian of all film directors.*

—Ranjan Bandopadhyay to Satyajit Ray

Against these details of Ray's background and early life, I shall now attempt a
capsuled reading of his creativity and the "controlled split" and divisibility of
self the creativity presupposes, hoping that my reading will also have some-

thing to say about the relationship between popular culture and high or classical culture in South Asia.

Satyajit Ray lived simultaneously in the East and the West and operated at two levels. As a filmmaker, which is what Ray at his best was, he was a classicist; his style was classical, even though heavily influenced by post-World War II neorealism. In the context of the Apu trilogy, Dasgupta defines this classicism as follows:

> The depth of feeling which Ray creates . . . , all his fragile and ineffable evocations of beauty and mortality, are contained firmly within the story framework and expressed with the utmost economy. . . .
>
> Ray's own stories are even more tightly constructed, to the point of being over-structured.[16]

As a person, however, Ray lived in the prewar, bicultural world of Rabindranath Tagore that had a touch of Edwardian England. "Ray's classicism like so much else in his outlook is derived from Tagore," for "it was in Tagore that the restless reformism of the 'Bengal Renaissance,' of the East and West, had found its equilibrium."[17] The ideological basis of that equilibrium was, to a significant extent, constituted by the values of the Enlightenment—scientific rationality, uncritical acceptance of the theory of progress, and secularism being the most conspicuous among them—and aspects of Indian high culture. Among the latter were certain readings of Vedānta and the Upanisads, once aggressively pushed by the Brahmo Samaj in Bengal and the Prarthana Samaj in West India. These readings were monistic—many would say monotheistic—and puritanical in scope and rationalist in orientation. To this mix of West and East, some of the nineteenth-century social reformers of India, including Ray's Brahmo forebears, gave respectability.

The "Tagorean synthesis," as Dasgupta names it, had, however, its own strengths and weaknesses.

> At its best, . . . it resulted in the emergence of noble images of character; at its worst, it was hypocritical, a little puritan, a little afraid of Freud. It was never suited to the depiction of life in the raw.[18]

The passions that drove the Bengali social reformers of the last century have long since subsided, but they do survive as an intellectual and cultural underside of modern consciousness in Bengal. Understandably, in this world, neither the mass culture of the post–World War II West nor Indian folk or popular culture has any say. An exception is made for some elements of Bengali nonclassical culture, but that is probably an accidental by-product of personal socialization in most instances.

As part of the same cultural-psychological baggage, Ray was not satisfied with being a mere film director. He saw himself as a Renaissance man in the tradition of the great Calcuttans of the last century, and his movies are witness to this self-definition. Like Charles Chaplin and Orson Wells he was more than a director. He usually wrote the scripts and the music for his films, and at least one cameraman, Subrata Mitra, left his unit on the grounds that Ray only technically hired cameramen for his films, for he was primarily his own cameraman. Ray also wrote the stories for four of his films.

Apart from the cinema, Ray had a number of other interests—he was a famous art designer and editor of a highly respected children's magazine. He was best known, however, as a writer of immensely successful crime thrillers and science fiction. He did try to maintain a distinction between the two genres, but there are clear continuities. Much of his science fiction veers around crime, and violence remains the central concern of both genres. During the last two decades of his life, Ray published nearly thirty books of popular fiction, two of which he also turned into successful films.[19]

Though his popular fiction was apparently meant for children, Bengalis of all ages adored Ray's thrillers and science fiction and eagerly waited for the next adventures of the young private detective Pradosh C. Mitter, alias Feluda (the anglicization of the surname is Ray's) and Professor Trilokeshvar Shanku (some of whose Western friends affectionately call him Shanks), a researcher-inventor who looks like Professor Calculus of the Tin Tin series and lives alone in a small town near Calcutta, while keeping in touch with the best scientific minds in the world.

For those acquainted with late-nineteenth-century thrillers and science fiction, Feluda is the more predictable of the two characters. He is a young professional detective who works in tandem with his teenage cousin, Tapesh. Unlike Dr. Watson in the Sherlock Holmes stories, Tapesh is bright and observant; nonetheless, he acts as a foil to Felu because of his Watson-like inability to fathom the master's analyses and game plans. His pet name, "Topse," reminds the Bengali reader of *topse* fish, known for its perplexed and blank look. There is a third person in the team, the famous thriller-writer Lalmohan Ganguli, better known by his pen name Jatayu, who provides comic relief of the Dr. Watson variety. However, it is not Jatayu but young

Topse who narrates the Feluda stories, often making snide asides on Jatayu's style of narration in his highly popular crime thrillers. The events usually take place within India, though one story has been set in Kathmandu and another in England.

Professor Shanku's diaries, which were accidentally recovered from a crater left by the eccentric professor when he took off in a homemade space rocket, are the basis for the Shanku stories. Shanku is a peculiar familiar-but-strange surname. It is usually a shortened form of Shankara in Bengal but unknown as a surname. The name gives Ray's hero a regionless and casteless identity, somewhat in the manner of the conventional hero of popular Bombay commercial films, who is rarely given a surname. The diary was written in a magic notebook that was fireproof, elastic, and chameleon-like in its ability to change color. Each Shanku story is a long extract from the diary. Prima facie, Shanku is a more original character than Felu, for he resurrects a romantic model of the creative scientist who has nothing to do with the practicing research scientists of today. He is a lonely researcher who works in a laboratory in his own home in Giridi, a small, insignificant town on the Bengal-Bihar border that has for decades served as summer resort for Bengali babus. His loneliness is mitigated by his cat, Newton, his very human robot with a very Bengali name, Vidhushekhar, and his devoted servant Prahlād, who is courageous but foolish, given to the kind of "simple faith" that prompts him to read the *Ramayana* while traveling on a space rocket. Shanku is a physicist, but he conveys the impression of being a gifted amateur in a number of other sciences also. His discoveries and inventions span a wide range of disciplines—from archeology to chemistry, from weapons research to biology, and from computer science to botany. He even builds an interplanetary rocket in his backyard and discovers a drug, miracurall, which miraculously cures all illnesses except the common cold (though in one story it cures colds, too). As one would expect, Shanku loves to work alone.[20] However, his work and inventions bring him in touch with a wide variety of people from all over the world. So, unlike Feluda's adventures, Shanku's take place in different continents.

For the psychologically minded reader, both genres deal with all-male worlds, though the "homoerotic" impulses in them are differently patterned. In the crime stories, by making the elderly novelist a comic figure and the assistant a cousin, Ray leaves little scope for explicitly sexual spoofs of the kind that have dogged the Sherlock Holmes stories in recent decades. In his science fiction, the homoeroticism has been given a Hegelian master-slave dimension. It is playfully done, but there is in it just the hint of sadomasochistic content that is, in turn, legitimized by a conventional theory of progress and Baconian scientific rationality. Thus, there are instances in the stories of Shanku harassing Prahlād by means of some newly invented drug or contraption, not in spite but in fun.

The Bengali middle classes may respect the filmmaker Satyajit Ray, but they love the popular fiction writer Ray. The writer Ray reminds them of his father, Bengal's most loved humorist and writer of nonsense verse, and his grandfather, Bengal's most popular writer of fairy tales in this century.

In response to the respect and the love, Ray has partitioned his self into two neat compartments. Into one he fits his "classical" ventures—the feature films he has made over the last three decades. Into the other he fits his popular, lowbrow ventures—his thrillers and tales of mystery, adventure, and violence.

The first category has a number of identifiable features. The most prominent of them is the centrality given to women and his use of women as windows to some of the core social problems of his society and his times. This place given to women's issues is not unique to Ray. From Rammohun Ray (1772-1833), who made the cause of women central to his platform of social reform in the first decades of the nineteenth century, to Gandhi, who saw the role of women as vital to his movement for winning political freedom for India and for expanding the sector of freedom for all humanity, nearly all great thinkers and social reformers have consciously viewed womanhood as the arena where the moral consciousness of the Indic civilization has to be recontextualized in response to the new social forces emerging on the Indian scene.[21]

This is equally true of the creative writers who have influenced Bengali social life. From Bankimchandra Chattopadhyay (1838-94) to Rabindranath Tagore and Saratchandra Chattopadhyay (1876-1938), the great Bengali writers have been consistently concerned with the problems of women and used them to mirror the crises of society in general. (I deliberately avoid using here the examples of women reformers and writers, lest their attempts to make the problems of women central to the society look interest-based and sectoral.)

In Ray's case, however, both these strands of awareness have been further underscored by the experiences of his family. No wonder he saw himself as heir to the nineteenth-century Bengali "Renaissance" and, though some scholars now find the term inadequate and misleading in the context of Bengal, the term and its progressivist implications did not lose their shine for Ray. For he lived intellectually and morally in the prewar world of Tagore.[22] To Ray, the continuity between the problems of women and the crisis of the Indian society seems obvious and in evitable. And women constitute a formidable maternal as well as conjugal presence in his important films. Even in movies where there are few women characters—for instance *Parash Pathar, Jalsaghar* and *Goopi Gyne Bagha Byne*—the issues of gender and potency enter the scene indirectly and constitute a salient theme.[23]

In Ray's world femininity is not merely an important principle; it is given added power by telescoping into all situations of conjugality a clear touch of maternity. Here Ray is in the company of the great mythmakers of late-nineteenth and early-twentieth-century Bengal, perhaps in that of the great Indian mythmakers of all times.

The second major feature of Ray's movies is exclusion of the sentimental and dramatic. Ray loved to tell a story in his films; he does not provide a political or philosophical text. He considered movies that do away with a proper story line self-indulgent. On the other hand, he would take great care not to overload his films with events, to have too dense a plot, or to assume too partisan a tone. One critic repeatedly speaks of Ray's *parimitibodh,* sense of restraint, and considers this restraint part of Ray's personality.[24] Another has gone so far as to say:

> Ray is not naturally drawn towards contradictions in mental make-up. . . . The grace in Ray's films often comes from the way he approaches confrontations, averts actions, decisions, events. Where he tries to be direct, the result is often ineffective or jarring.[25]

Even *Charulata* and *Ghare-Baire,* movies that stick close to the novels on which they are based, de-dramatize their originals to some extent.[26]

The fear of being melodramatic or maudlin that dogs many contemporary creative writers in Bengal is partly a reaction to the somewhat maudlin world of Saratchandra Chattopadhyay, who dominated Indian middle-class consciousness in the interwar years. Ray is no Ernest Hemingway or Bertolt Brecht, to give two random examples of Western authors who made tough-minded detachment their hallmark; but even when he deals with a subject as cataclysmic as the Bengal famine of the early 1940s, he makes a special effort not to be emotionally too involved with his subject. As a result, when *Ashani Sanket* was released, some of his critics accused him of producing a pretty picture postcard on a subject as grim as famine.[27] They have interpreted his somewhat detached gaze as an indicator of inadequate social commitment.

Partly, however, this *parimitibodh* and "distance" come from the fact that Ray usually avoided dealing with subjects with which he was directly acquainted.[28] By underplaying the stress and anomie of urban India, by concentrating on rural India about which he knew little, Ray has paradoxically acquired a comprehensive, dispassionate view of the gamut of macroscopic changes to which his family had been an important witness. He saw it whole, Dasgupta says, because he saw it from a distance.[29] There are obvious deep, unresolved passions behind his restraint; as a result, the demands made on him for direct, impassioned social commitment only cramped his style. He was never able to match the creativity of his first decade as a director, when his cinematic voice was soft and his commitments understated.

Third, despite his emphasis on femininity, Ray's films are characterized by a low-key, almost hesitant, treatment of sex. As a recent assessment puts it,

> In nearly every film where a frank treatment might have been appropriate, a natural barrier to intimacy has existed. In *The Goddess* it was Doyamoyee's reluctance, in *Charulata* Amal's, in *Kapurush* Amitava's, in *Days and Nights in the Forest* Sanjoy's (although intercourse between Hari and the tribal girl is suggested), in *The Chess Players* Mirza's, and in *Pikoo* the mother's (though seminakedness is shown because the film was being made for French television).[30]

This avoidance of sexuality is matched by an avoidance of overt conflict.

> In *Charulata,* intensity of love is expressed without the lovers even holding hands; there is a rather impulsive, rather brotherly, embrace, but it contributes only a minor note in the tension created between the two. The fascinating scene of the memory game in *Aranyer Din Ratri,* together with the walks, the interplay and repetition of themes, creates a musical statement in which the seduction scenes are only the fortissimos, not raucous even in violence.[31]

Dasgupta recognizes in the context of *Apur Sansar* that Ray's ambition, given his anti-hedonistic Brahmo heritage, is nothing less than to redress the overemphasis on conjugality at the expense of maternity and to reemphasize love in its all-embracing sense:

> Apu and Aparna's love for each other is only another aspect of Sarvajaya's love for her children or theirs for their aunt or father—a comprehensive all-pervasive, non-sexual love which has seldom been celebrated in the cinema with such purity.

The first time Ray showed a couple kissing in his films was in *Ghare-Baire,* made in the mid-1980s; even when he made an avowedly adventure film such as *Abhijan,* he took care to avoid showing extreme violence.[33] Many have attributed this restraint to his Brahmo puritanical upbringing; others have seen in it a compromise with conventionality and an inability to "let go." Ray himself is clear on the subject:

> People do not seem to bother about what you say as long as you say it in a sufficiently oblique and unconventional manner—and the normal-looking film is at a discount. . . . I don't imply that all the new European film makers are without talent, but I do seriously doubt if they could continue to make a living without the very liberal exploitation of sex that their code seems to permit.[34]

Certainly, in Ray's world sex enters stealthily and fearfully, whether he is dealing with conjugality directly or with eroticized maternity (as in *Charulata*). Similarly with violence. It enters Ray's world as something that is sinister by virtue of what it implies or what it can be, rather than by what it is. Often the violence is not physical but involves injuries to a person's or a group's dignity, self-definition, or way of life. For instance, *Abhijan, Pratidwandi,* and *Seemabaddha,* particularly the first two, offer ample scope for disturbing, if not spectacular, violence.[35] The temptation is consciously avoided. Even in the two movies Ray has made out of his own crime thrillers, overt violence is minimal.

To begin with, this restraint may have been Ray's attempt to mark off his work from the Indian and Western commercial films and create a specific audience for his kind of cinema. He pioneered art films in India; he did not have a ready audience, at least for his early works. Some of these features extend into Ray's fiction. But there are important distinctions in the way they appear in their low- or middle-brow incarnations, primarily designed to amuse children.

First, Ray's popular fiction is set in a nearly all-male world. If Ray's cinema tends to shrink from the details of man-woman relations,[36] the tendency is given yet fuller play in his fiction. Women enter this world rarely and as subordinate presences, much as they do in classical Victorian thrillers such as Arther Conan Doyle and G. K. Chesterton's works. The deeper relationships, whether of love or hate, are invariably between men. Not only is the device of pairing the sleuth with a somewhat obtuse imperfect man of science imported from Victorian England for the Feluda stories, but even Ray's science fiction introduces a similar doubling: Professor Shanku has an innocent, loyal servant on whom he tries out his ideas. Occasionally, Shanku goes farther than Holmes; the scientist literally tests out on his servant Prahlād some of his new inventions. To make this inoffensive, there are the "mitigating" aspects of the relationship—Shanku's paternal concern for the welfare and "upliftment" of Prahlād, Prahlād's poor intelligence and "distorted" awareness of the world (which places him in an intermediate category between his master, representing scientific rationality and professional expertise, and the "things" his master has mastered), and the load of the inferior culture Prahlād carries by virtue of being embedded in the local and parochial. Together they ensure that his subjecthood is complete and Ray has no self-doubt about it.

Second, Ray's popular fiction places much emphasis on scientific rationality which is identified entirely with Baconian inductionism and empiricism. The stories usually posit a clear cut division between the cognitive, on the one hand, and the affective and normative, on the other, and here again Ray's direct inspiration is the Victorian crime thriller. The underlying assumption in both cases is that objective reality lies hidden behind manifest reality, and the detective, using superior techniques and unencumbered scientific rationality—that is, by disjuncting cognition from affect—tears the mask off false innocence. The detective, thus, not merely reveals the objective reality underneath but ensures that authentic, informed innocence reasserts itself socially. As I have discussed the psychological profile of such thrillers in more detail elsewhere, I shall leave the issue at that.[37]

Third, Ray's detective stories and science fiction are two forms of adventure story. But his idea of adventure has a geographical content. Many of his stories assume that while crime is universal both in theory and practice, science is universal mainly in theory, less in practice. The criminals in Ray's stories of detection are home-brewed; in his science fiction, they are usually whites with German names or what the South Africans once used to identify as honorary whites.[38]

The reasoning seems to be as follows. To do "great science," as the moderns define it, one has constantly to rub shoulders with Western scientists, for creative science is primarily a Western pursuit. Naturally, Shanku's status in the world of science can only be established through his jet-setting participation in the "global" community of first-class scientists, a community that is predominantly white. Shanku's Indianisms, his home in a small town (not too far from a metropolis, though), his family traditions (his father was a well known *āyurvedā* and his great-grandfather a *sānnyāsin* who renounced the world at the tender age of sixteen), he and his occasional khadga-clad associate

Nakurbabu's openness to things such as telepathy and clairvoyance, and the contradiction between his self-image as a pure scientist and his actual life lived out as a brilliant practicing technologist and inventor—they are all hitched to this global hierarchy of scientists. (If, however, the hierarchy is accepted, its obverse, too, has to be stipulated: the great scientific frauds and the great scientist-psychopaths, like the great creative scientists and the great scientist-savants, also come mainly from the West.)

Fourth, many elements of the commercial Bengali and Hindi movie, the exclusion of which negatively define Ray's concept of good cinema, are introduced in his popular fiction. Not only do magical elements return in the guise of superscience to play an important part in his science fiction, but so does the element of predictability in his crime stories. One knows for instance that Shanku as well as Felu will negotiate all crises in style and emerge intact. It is the content of the style and the events through which the style unfolds that are less than predictable for readers. And to ensure this unpredictability, there is an emphasis on dramatic events—and an avoidance of details—that would be unthinkable to the filmmaker Ray. In this respect, the popular writings of Ray fit in with the dominant frame of popular cinema in India.[39] Within that frame, the search of both the popular filmmaker and the viewer is not for the entirely unpredictable, the original, or the unique, but for a new configuration of the familiar, updated in terms of contemporary experience and therefore found novel.[40]

In this configuration, there is hardly any semblance of the patient, leisurely—some would say labored—development of character and setting one finds in Ray's serious movies. As in popular Bombay films, the narratives in Ray's popular fiction are built almost wholly around a structure of fast-moving events. The characters are revealed, to the extent they are revealed, through the drama of the events.

Fifth, one suspects that Ray's identification with his scientist-hero and detective-hero is at least partly powered by his self-image as a Renaissance man, straddling the disjunctive cultures of the humanities and science to defy the likes of C. P. Snow. The identification is located in a self-definition on which three generations of Rays and modern Bengalis have worked diligently for nearly a century. It also seems to be powered at the personality level by a certain insecure narcissism of a once highly protected child who has been the carrier of his mother's hopes, ambitions, and feelings of insecurity, and who has internalized the image of a male authority that is overwhelming as well as vulnerable.

The result is again an even distribution of certain qualities between Ray's films and his popular fiction. There are in his films reflections of what appear to be conspicuous forms of anxiety-binding strategies—enormously detailed technical work and workmanship and a search for complete dominance or control over the entire technical process of filmmaking. In popular fiction, however, his commitment to the worldview of science is romanticized. Especially in his science fiction, the events on which he builds his stories often reveal an openness to experiences (such as paranormality and extrasensory perceptions of various kinds) that might be taboo to the other Ray. Ideologically, he may be more closed in his popular works; methodologically, he is much less encumbered. Even a casual reader quickly finds out that Ray is not a perfectionist in his popular writings: he is less careful about his workmanship and his imagination is less controlled.

Finally, there is a distinctive quality of violence in Ray's popular works. It is immediate, concrete, and personalized. It is often physical, though carefully sanitized. This difference can be traced to the different ways Ray treats evil in the two genres. In his films, the source of evil is usually diffused and not easily identifiable (a feature Ray fails to maintain in his lesser films) and the carriers of evil do not stray beyond the reach of humanity and morality. They are driven by uncontrollable forces and motivations. As in many traditional Indian epics, Ray gives his audience a choice between reading his "villains" as villains and reading them as figures twisted by life.

The focus and concreteness of evil in Ray's lesser work come from characters which are guided—as in the works of Conan Doyle and other Victorian writers of crime thrillers—by a scientific rationality that is untouched by any moral approach to life; the villains are only villains; they are openly guided by amoral passions and self-serving greed, backed by a value-neutral science. The clash is usually between two kinds of reason—the self-interest-backed psychopathic reason of the criminal and the socially acceptable, normative reason of the sleuth. (Actually, the criminal expertise of the sleuth is also amoral; only the sleuth as a person is governed by conventional social morality.)

All three features make Ray the producer of popular fiction complementary to Ray the filmmaker. And in this respect, he is not unique. All the persons we have mentioned in this essay show a similar interarticulation among their partitioned selves. Thus, the Wells of science fiction is not conceivable without the Wells of *The Outline of History* (which is, of course, a history of Western civilization, even though it is written in the innocent belief that it is a global history that does full justice to the non-Western world). The Conan Doyle of the Sherlock Holmes stories neatly complements Conan Doyle the theosophist; and the Rushdie of *Midnight's Children* is possible only because there is the other Rushdie, the brainchild of the easy theories of progress of the 1930s.

Is this complementarity a matter of an ex post facto search for order, the artificial imposition of a deterministic theory of aesthetics on these authors? Possibly not. Psychologically, the Ray of the Apu trilogy, *Devi* (1960), and *Ghare-Baire* seems to have been made possible by Ray the tame, uncritical believer in the emancipatory and educative role of Enlightenment values. In this respect, the complementarity is not merely aesthetic; it is personological. By writing for children and by upholding the conventional Victorian norms as the embodiment of Enlightenment values—thus intervening in child rearing and education to inculcate, institutionalize, and perpetuate these values—Ray does appear to make peace with his social conscience. He can then be more daringly "free associative" and give controlled expression to his less socialized, less tamed, less "educated," more intuitive self in his serious cinematic work. It is Ray's way of making peace with himself and using the integrative capacities at the disposal of his self.[41]

Such a mode of partitioning, one suspects, comes more easily to the South Asian, traditionally accustomed to live in many cultures and, in fact, in many worlds. This alternative is available of course to creative writers in the modern West, but they have to search more self-consciously for internal consistency in their work. Perhaps that is why, in Wells' case, the more well-thought-out cognitive ventures are conventional and conformist, whereas in someone like Ray, the more serious and carefully thought-out ventures are more imaginative and less constrained by values derived from the dominant culture. Wells is more conventional in history, Ray in fiction, which, for him, is a "freer" medium than cinema.

Note that Rushdie, too, driven by his internalization of the West, tries in his nonfiction to be allegiant to Enlightenment values, to win through such conformity the freedom to be more careless about these values in serious fiction. In the West, you can be playful only in fiction, not in science, not even in scientized social analysis. When Rushdie self-consciously tries his hand at serious social analysis through playful fiction, as in *Satanic Verses*, it ends in disaster.[42] He loses almost entirely the targets of his reform, who feel humiliated and provoked by his style of social analysis and intervention.[43]

One may also note that in Wells' serious novels, such as *Ann Veronica* and *Tono-Bungay,* the political and social ideology of the author intrudes to shape the narrative more perceptibly than it does in Ray's work. Wells is more influenced by his ideas of scientific history and rationality in serious literature; Ray, perhaps despite himself, in popular fiction. It is a minor paradox that both do better at social analysis when they cease to be self-consciously social-scientific and socially relevant.

Some of these comments apply to another tormented, internally split writer, Rudyard Kipling. He, too, came close to partitioning his self in his works in the manner we have described, but he could not do so successfully, despite being part Indian. He failed to keep at a distance his highly conventional, imperial values when writing even his more creative, intellectually daring novels. As Edmund Wilson points out, it comes as something of a shock that in *Kim,* which comes close to being one of the great novels of our times and one of the most sensitive ever written about India—Bernard Cohn calls it the best fictional ethnography of India—the hero, after all his encounters with the mysteries of nature and human nature and after all his encounters with an alternative worldview and an alternative vision of human potentialities (represented in the novel by the kaleidoscope of India's cultural diversity and by the haunting figure of the Lama, respectively), ultimately decides to become a servant of the colonial administration.[44]

The two Satyajit Rays are not in watertight compartments. There is an occasional leak. He made charming films based on two of his own thrillers, and once wrote a script for a science fiction movie, *The Alien,* on which two Hollywood blockbusters, *E. T.* and *Close Encounters of the Third Kind,* were reportedly based.[45] Likewise, some of the early Professor Shanku stories, such as the charmingly gothic "Professor Shanku o Robu," do have a latent critique of science built into them.[46] However, here I am not talking of such self-conscious bridges but of the subtler communication and "division of labor" between the two selves. Thus, what we have identified as an understatement of violence in Ray's cinema often becomes a form of sanitized violence in his popular fiction. Professor Shanku's discovery, the anihilin gun, is a weapon that not only kills immediately but does so cleanly, smokelessly, and soundlessly. It vaporizes its target, leaving no messy blood-drenched body or injured victim to be taken care of.

However, the leak is usually in the other direction. The identification with the ordinary person confronting life incompetently but nobly—as in *Aparajito, Apur Sansar, Mahanagar, Abhijan,* or even *Parash Pathar*—does enter the world of the other Ray.[47] It even acquires a touch of romantic grandeur in a story such as "Bankubābur Bandhu," cast in the mold of science fiction, about a harassed schoolteacher who is the constant butt of the crude humor of a village landlord and his cronies. The teacher acquires a new sense of dignity and self-confidence when he accidentally encounters and befriends extraterrestrial beings in the village woods. Technology here puts one in touch with things larger than oneself and with an awareness that positivist knowledge knows nothing about.[48]

Notwithstanding such leaks or exchanges, there are reasonably clear principles by which the selves are separated. We have already hinted at the presence of three of the principles. First, the alternate self is primarily a pedagogic self. (Though, the public stereotype about the selves is exactly the reverse — the filmmaker Ray is seen as being serious, the popular writer Ray as fun.) It may be true that "in Ray's stories there is no crude attempt to provide a moral,"[49] but the Brahmo concept of what is good for children informs much of Ray's crime thrillers and science fiction indirectly. Ray's aunt, Sukhalata Rao, another gifted writer of children's literature, once started a brief controversy in Bengal by arguing that ghost stories should not be written, for they were bad for the character — read moral development — of children.[50] Others may not have taken Sukhalata's advice seriously, but her nephew has, for though Ray *has* written ghost stories and often brilliantly, his popular fiction always has a series of unstated morals and has been guided by an implicit concept of "healthy pastime" or "healthy fun," parallels to which can only be found in some writings on cricket produced in Victorian England and in Lord Baden-Powell's concept of the Boy Scout movement.

Second, the alternate Ray is distinguished by a masculine concern — the term is not entirely appropriate — with the world of machines, power, intrusive or invasive curiosity, and competition for priorities and dominance, combined with an often astonishing insensitivity to nature, including human nature. As if Ray's concern in his popular fiction was nothing more than telling a story in which his hero would solve a proper criminal puzzle. All subtleties of characterization are seen as diverting from a good, strong narrative line. The androgynous sensitivities of Ray, so evident in cinema, seem to give way to a romanticized, two-dimensional, materialistic, phallocentric world where puzzle solving and a certain toughness predominate. I use the word "romanticized" advisedly, for the element of romance does not run counter to the materialism and the tough, positivist view of the world. Rather, Ray works with a romantic vision of materialism and positivism with which mostly non-Western ideologues of scientific rationality feel comfortable and which was first popularized in India in the nineteenth century by the babus of Calcutta. There is a perfect and innocent continuity between Father Eugène Lafont's physics classes at St. Xavier's College, Mahendralal Sarkar's science movement in fin-de-siècle Calcutta, and the dreary enthusiasm for modern science shown by many like Ray in postindependence India, blissfully unaware of the altered social relations of science in the country.

Third, readers may have noticed that, in the partitioning of the self, the values and concepts associated with the European Enlightenment have a special role to play. Among these values are scientific rationality; the idea of dispassionate, impersonal, falsifiable knowledge, obtainable through a scientific method strictly defined by positivist criteria; the idea of expertise, represented by the experimental scientist and the private detective-as-a-professional-criminologist; and a wholly instrumental concept of knowledge that allows one to see true knowledge as value-neutral, usable either for good or for evil. Ray's crime thrillers and science fiction pay homage to these values.

Ray's message in cinema is profoundly different. We have already described it. It is that message which makes his films, to borrow an expression from Ronald Laing, an experience of experience.

IV

A creative person can be at times a sounder critic of himself than his critics are. There are at least three stories by Ray, all formally classifiable as science fiction, that try to capture the tragedy of the creative person in a conformist society. In all three, but particularly in "Aryashekharer Janma o Mrtyu," Ray depicts how the creative are forced to opt for survival at the cost of creativity because, in the environment in which they live, the extranormal is no different from the abnormal and both are repressed by the society to protect and restore the domain of normality.[51] All three stories carry the latent message that creativity is often destroyed because the creative fail or refuse to internalize the social need to repress the strange and the mysterious in them. For instance, in "Āryashekharer Janma o Mrtyu," the saddest and most direct of the three, the hero, a child prodigy in mathematics, first loses his genius and then dies because he is uncompromising in his scientific curiosity and recklessly confronts his staid, unimaginative father with his socially daring "scientific theory." When dying, in pain and perhaps with an awareness of the futility of it all, it is only his mother that he remembers.

That is about all I can say. We have no direct clue as to whether Ray saw himself as a survivor who had made realistic compromises, or as an uncompromising rebel who nurtured a latent fear of being destroyed by his surroundings, or, more likely, as one who had in him elements of both. Ray's stories, usually pitched in a low key, do not seem to address themselves to other questions that dog the steps of psychologists researching creativity: In what way do the ego-defenses of a creative person operate? In what kind of work can the creative "let go"? Where does he or she tighten the reins of imagination?

No clear answers to these questions emerge from Ray's life story, either. The only additional comment I can make on the subject sounds, therefore, so näively Freudian to my own ears that I shall have to ask the reader to take it as entirely tentative for the moment.

Creativity—to the extent that it involves the interplay of the conscious and unconscious, the regressive and the ego-integrative, the rational and non-rational or irrational—must at some point encounter the creative person's own moral self. Behind this clinical platitude lies the fact that over the last three hundred years the structure of morality in the dominant culture of the world has gradually come to include a number of Baconian values: a specific form of rationality, a specific concept of knowledge, and a specific set of methods to live by that rationality and to generate that knowledge. In the dominant global culture today, these, too, are part of our socialized—one may say, oversocialized—self and an aspect of the demands of the modern superego. Who does not know that while all selves are equal, some selves are more equal than others.

As a consequence, it appears that creativity has begun to demand from the creative person both defiance of conventional morality and also some conspicuous conformity to an aspect of conventional morality that is not overtly conventional. To meet this demand, the creative person creates a kind of shadow self that is perfectly compatible with the dominant social ideals and one's oversocialized self, but wears successfully the garb of unconvention-ality. This shadow self allows freer play to one's undersocialized self, having greater access to the primitive, the nonrational, and the intuitive.

The partitioning of the self we have seen in Ray and others is, it seems to me, part of this larger dynamic. It allows greater play to the internalized aspects of social processes that would otherwise have been irreconcilable. Some manage to do this partitioning painlessly, others painfully; some do it with self-conscious finesse, others clumsily and unself-consciously. But in each case, they pose a challenge to the students of creativity to crack the code of this shadowy self and decipher the writer's language of communication with the other self as a crucial component of the creative process.

This issue of communication often becomes part of a larger politics of cultures, too. The reader may have noticed that, in the case of Wells and Rushdie, their imaginal products are less encumbered by the authors' prim theories of life; with Ray, it is the lighter works that are more encumbered. Is this accidental? What about the fact that in all three cases, time and the changing concepts of social knowledge have shown that their concepts of reliable, valid, scientific social knowledge were less reliable and valid than they might have thought? Does not the very fact that these two questions can be asked today have something to tell us about the changing landscape of the intellectual world?

I shall leave the reader with these questions, in the belief that all questions cannot—and need not—be answered by those who raise them.

Notes

1. See a discussion of this issue in Ashis Nandy, *The Tao of Cricket: On Games of Destiny and the Destiny of Games* (New Delhi: Viking and Penguin, 1989).

2. Salman Rushdie, *Midnight's Children* (London: Pan, 1982); and *Shame* (Calcutta: Rupa, 1982).

3. Though Rushdie is Bombay-born, in his adult life he may have been in closer touch with Pakistan. And his social and political näiveté may have something to do with the Pakistani connection. For I have noticed this touching, unqualified Nehruism in many Pakistani intellectuals. I suspect that certain social or cultural processes were short-circuited in Pakistan by the country's obtuse military rulers and what was a natural and necessary phase in Indian politics has become an unfulfilled dream in Pakistan. Perhaps, Pakistanis need Nehru more today than Indians do. I say this not in empathy with the unthinking though understandable anti-Nehru posturing of many Indian intellectuals, but in the belief that Nehru's humane, "progressivist" concept of the public realm once had an important role to play in Indian politics but has been, alas, badly mauled by time and almost entirely co-opted by India's ruling elite.

4. Salman Rushdie, "Gandhi: How and Why the British are Continuing to Distort our History," *Telegraph*, 5 June 1983.

5. On the psychological correlates of Shākto and Vaisnava cults, see a brief discussion in Ashis Nandy, *Alternative Sciences: Creativity and Authenticity in Two Indian Scientists* (New Delhi: Allied, 1980; Reprinted in 1993 by Oxford University Press), p. 2.

6. The most elegant and charming invocation of Sukumar Ray as a person is in Leela Majumdar, *Sukumar Ray* (Calcutta: Mitra o Ghose, 1969).

7. The ideological bias was reflected in Ray's youthful apathy and perhaps contempt for Indian cinema, music, and painting. Till his college days his tastes were completely Western. His sojourn at Shantiniketan, where he went on his mother's insistence, reluctantly leaving his beloved Calcutta, changed his attitude radically. Partha Basu, "Garpārātheke Shantiniketan," *Anandalok*, 9 May 1992, 16–21, esp. 21.

8. Basu, "Garpārātheke Shantiniketan," 17.

9. Aparna Sen, "Purono Ālāp," *Sananda* 6, no. 21 (15 May 1992): 63–67; esp. pp. 63–64.

10. Ranjan Bandopadhyay, *Visaya Satyajit* (Calcutta: Navana, 1988), 39. Bandopadhyay reads the second image differently. He sees in it Ray's inability to discover in his widowed characters the stern, sanitized standards set by his own mother. Satyajit Ray, *Aparajita* (Calcutta: Epic Films, 1956), Story: Bibhutibhushan Bandopadhyay; and *Aranyer Din Rātri* (Calcutta: Nepal and Ashim Datta, 1970), Story: Sunil Gangopadhyay.

11. Ibid., 32.

12. Ranjan Bandpadhyay, "Satyajiter Chabir *Nārīrā*," *Anandalok*, 9 May 1992, 92–95; see 93, 95.

13. Marie Seton, *Portrait of a Director: Satyajit Ray* (London: Dennis Dobson, 1971), chaps. 2–3; Chidananda Dasgupta, *The Cinema of Satyajit Ray* (New Delhi: Vikas, 1980), 1–14.

14. Seton, *Portrait*, p. 64.

15. For a brief discussion of this process, see Ashis Nandy, "Sati: A Nineteenth-Century Tale of Women, Violence and Protest," in *At the Edge of Psychology: Essays in Politics and Culture* (New Delhi: Oxford University Press, 1980), 1–31.

16. Dasgupta, *The Cinema*, 65–66.

17. Ibid., 68.

18. Ibid., 69.

19. Ray's popular fiction also includes some brilliant stories that cannot be classified as science fiction or tales of detection. I have not taken them into account in this essay except tangentially.

20. These personal details of Sanku are scattered in a number of stories, most prominently in Satyajit Ray, 'Byomyātrir Diary,' *Professor Sanku* (Calcutta, n. d.), 9–38.

21. This issue is discussed in some detail in my "Women Versus Womanliness: An Essay in Cultural and Political Psychology," in *At the Edge of Psychology*, 32–46.

22. Even Ray's favorite actor, Soumitra Chatterji, who often played the hero in his films, looks remarkably like young Tagore. Dasgupta, *The Cinema*, 71.

23. Satyajit Ray, *Parash Pathar* (Calcutta: L. B. Films International, 1957), Story: Parasuram; *Jalsaghar* (Calcutta: Satyajit Ray Productions, 1958), Story: Tarashankar Bandopadhyay; and *Goopi Gyne Bagha Byne* (Calcutta: Purnima Pictures, 1969), Story: Upendrakishore Raychaudhuri.

24. Bandopadhyay, *Visaya Satyajit*, 13.

25. Dasgupta, *The Cinema*, 70, 80-81.

26. Satyajit Ray, *Charulata* (Calcutta: R. D. Bansal, 1964), Story: Rabindranath Tagore; and *Ghare Baire* (Calcutta: NFDC, 1984), Story: Rabindranath Tagore.

27. Satyajit Ray, *Ashani Sanket* (Calcutta: Sarbani Bhattacharya, 1973), Story: Bibhutibhushan Bandopadhyay.

28. Bandopadhyay, *Visaya Satyajit*, 19.

29. Dasgupta, *The Cinema*, 43-44.

30. Andrew Robinson, "Ray's View of the World," Telegraph, 3 December 1989, 6-9.

31. Dasgupta, *The Cinema*, 81.

32. Ibid., 22. Satyajit Ray, *Apur Sansar* (Calcutta: Satyajit Ray Productions, 1959), Story: Bibhutibhushan Bandopadhyay.

33. Satyajit Ray, *Abhijan* (Calcutta: Abhijatrik, 1962), Story: Tarashankar Bandopadhyay.

34. Satyajit Ray, quoted in ibid., 67.

35. Satyajit Ray, *Pratidwandi* (Calcutta: Nepal and Ashim Datta, 1970), Story: Sunil Gangopadhyay; and *Seemabaddha* (Calcutta: Bharat Samsher Rana, 1971), Story: Sunil Gangopadhyay.

36. Bandopadhyay, *Visaya Satyajit*, 25. Ray, it seems, once confided to writer Sunil Gangopadhyay that he was not comfortable in creating women characters. Gangopadhyay guesses that could be the reason why Ray liked to write for children and not for adults. Memorial meeting on Satyajit Ray, organized by the Sahitya Academy at the India International Centre, New Delhi, 15 May 1992.

37. Nandy, *The Tao of Cricket*.

38. Of the twenty-one villains in the Shanku stories, only two are Indian. Most of the villains are immoral scientists misusing their scientific talent. See the excellent "guide" to these stories in Anish Deb, "Professor Shanku," *Anandamela*, Satyajit Ray special no. 13 May 1992, 15-31.

39. Ray himself has contrasted the enormous "respect given to detail" in traditional Indian art with the "poverty of detail" in Indian cinema. According to him, all great artworks except the abstract ones are set apart by their emphasis on details. Satyajit Ray, "Detail Samparke Du'car Katha," *Visaya Calaccitra* (Calcutta: Ananda Publishers, 1976), 26-29.

40. Ibid.

41. On ego strength as a crucial personality factor in the highly creative, see for instance, Frank Barron, "The Psychology of Creativity," in *New Directions in Psychology II* (New York: Holt, Rinehart and Winston, 1965), 1-134.

42. Salman Rushdie, *Satanic Verses* (New York: Viking, 1988).

43. See, for instance, an impressive analysis of the responses to *Satanic Verses* among the Muslims in B. C. Parekh, "Between Holy Text and Moral Void," *New Statesman,* 24 March 1989, 29-33.

44. Edmund Wilson, "The Kipling that Nobody Read," in Andrew Rutherford, ed., *Kipling's Mind and Art* (Stanford, Calif.: Stanford University Press, 1964), 17-69.

45. Amrit Rai, "Satyajit Ray: A Rare Creative Genius," paper presented at the Memorial Meeting on Satyajit Ray, 15 May 1992, mimeo. Rai's unwitting source was writer Arther C. Clarke, who wanted Ray to sue the producers of the two Hollywood films.

The main attraction of Ray's script for the Hollywood filmmakers might have been its positive attitude to the unknown, the strange, and the otherworldly. For Hollywood, the alien has traditionally been an evil and hostile presence, a source of fear. For it, the prototypical science fiction movie is *The War of the Worlds*. For Ray, the stranger is a source of self-enriching and self-expanding experience.

This belief colors not merely Ray's science fiction but of his fantasy life in general. His last film *Agantuk* (Calcutta: NFDC, 1991, Story: Satyajit Ray) can be read as a moving effort by its maker to reaffirm this faith. In it, Ray defies the conventions of his own thought and his self definition as a chosen carrier of the European Enlightenment in India even more dramatically than he usually does in his more ambitious movies. The defiance comes through a painful process of self-transcendence and self-negation; he has to set up a formidable antiself in the form of a truant anthropologist who rejects all progressivist definitions of civilization and gracefully lives out his faith.

46. Satyajit Ray, "Professor Shanku o Robu," in Professor Shankur Kandakarkhan (Calcutta: Ananda, 1970), 1-18.

47. Satyajit Ray, *Mahanagar* (Calcutta: R. D. Bansal, 1963), Story: Narendranath Mira.

48. Satyajit Ray, "Bankubābur Bandhu," *Ek Dozen Gappa* (Calcutta: Ananda Publishers, 1970), 17-28. For a fascinating discussion of the theme of lower-middle-class, humble persons living a life of imagination or in touch with things larger than themselves, see Sen, "Purono Ālāp," 63-4.

49. Bandopadhyay, *Visaya Satyajit,* 52.

50. Buddhadeb Bose, "Bhuter Bhaya" (1932), in *Racan samgraha* (Calcutta: Granthalay, 1982), 5: 466-72.

51. Bandopadhyay, *Visaya Satyajit,* 53-54; Satyajit Ray, "Āryashekharer Janma o Mrtyu," in *Tin Rakam* (Calcutta: Kathamala, n.d.), 9-24. See also "Professor Sanku o Khokā," in *Professor Sanku* (Calcutta: Newscript, 1987), 169-90.

Part Four

Self as Image in Japanese Theory and Practice

INTRODUCTION

Thomas P. Kasulis

A basic principle to bear in mind when analyzing a culture's images of self is that the understanding of those images may evolve in history. This is a major lesson we learn from Arthur Thornhill's essay opening this section. Thornhill deftly distinguishes the fundamental aesthetic underlying the poetry of three different eras of Japanese culture. In particular, he takes up the issue of the relation between poetry and Buddhism, warning us that this relation may vary with the particular cultural milieu of a given period. One striking consequence of his historical analysis is that the haiku of Bashō—often considered the epitome of the Zen Buddhist aesthetic—can be as readily interpreted in terms of Neo-Confucian as Buddhist values. Thornhill strengthens his argument for the Neo-Confucianist influence by explaining how Neo-Confucian ideas were often more au courant than Zen in the literary circles of Bashō's time.

The theme of what is Zen in the "Zen arts" is also central to my own essay, which follows Thornhill's. I claim that the intimate connection between Zen Buddhism and the traditional Japanese arts is often more a presupposition than a fact supported by the internal, historical evidence. The evidence suggests rather that the elaborate idea of the "Zen arts" is more an invention of twentieth-century Japanese cultural criticism than a venerable theory influential on the supposed Zen artists themselves. Zen Buddhism does, however, have within its tradition an understanding of creativity that can be applied to the arts (or to any other human activity). My essay analyzes that philosophy of creativity, showing its basic assumptions and its relation to an idea of self as that which is capable of creative expression.

Just as images of the person can vary historically, they may also vary individually. To help us get a better fix on this issue, Nobuko Ochner's essay performs a intriguing literary triangulation. Taking a traditional story from the Chinese Confucian historical chronicle, *Shih chi,* two modern Japanese novelists recast the narrative to suit their own understanding of the person. Hence, we have the same story in three different forms: one representing ancient China, and two emerging from different viewpoints in modern Japan. Ochner argues that Tanizaki Jun'ichirō's version emphasized the self as structured by one's response to the outer world, the allurement of the senses and one's response to it. Nakajima Atsushi, on the other hand, emphasized the constitution of the self from within, the recognition of the self-cultivation that is developed through, and expressed by, the appropriate forms of human conduct. Interestingly, Tanizaki and Nakajima focus on different characters in their respective retelling of the classical story. It is as if their images of self are intrinsically so different that they gravitated toward different characters who could best represent their own concerns.

Lucy Lower's essay studies the mode of self-understanding in three modern novels: Natsume Sōseki's *Kokoro,* Tanizaki Jun'ichirō's *Bridge of Dreams,* and Ōe Kenzaburō's *Silent Cry.* In each case the novel has the form of a first-person narrative, but in telling their own story, the narrators find personal meaning through the reenactment of others' lives as somehow inseparable from their own. In a complex cyclical dynamic that Lower sensitively analyzes, each narrator's own story is refracted through the events in the lives of others with whom the narrator is intimately related either through personal affection or family history. In each case, in looking into themselves the narrators find images—realistic or transformed—of others. It is as if the narrator's own identity in each case represents a recurrent paradigm, but the paradigm is no universal archetype. As Lower points out, it is instead highly particular; it applies only to the others in one's own nexus. Furthermore, Lower explains how the dynamics of the paradigm differ in each case. In *Kokoro* it sets up parallels or "analogs" across lives. In *Bridge of Dreams* people seem to be reincarnated into the personalities of those to whom they were related (the "avatar"). In *The Silent Cry* the characters play out set ritualistic roles ("figures") so that the "same" event is reenacted over the span of a century. These ways of imaging the self are reminiscent of the *migawari* (surrogate) phenomenon discussed by the anthropologist Takie Lebra in a previous volume in this series: *Self as Person in Asian Theory and Practice.*

Willa Tanabe's essay on Japanese Buddhist art focuses on the problematics of the Buddhist theory of self. On one hand, the technical, traditional doctrine is that the person is impermanent and insubstantial, literally "lacking self [or ego]" (*muga* in Japanese). Yet, as Tanabe points out, there is also in the tradition from ancient times a contrasting theory about continuity of self across lifetimes and into afterworlds. Sometimes there has even been the suggestion of an underlying, eternal buddha-nature. Tanabe shows that this ambiguity in theory runs throughout the praxis of representation in ritual Buddhist art as well. The essay opens with examples of Buddhist art that didactically portray the inevitable decay of the body. In contrast, the essay ends with a discussion of how some Buddhist sects have used mummification, the preservation of the flesh after death, as a sign of eternal enlightenment. Tanabe's conclusion is that, from the standpoint of both theory and of artistic praxis, the Buddhist image of self is either much more complex and ambiguous that we usually assume or, more likely, is not a monolithic theory at all. Rather, there is a variety of images for different purposes in different contexts. Perhaps even "self" is an image subject to the expediency of *hōben,* taking its form according to the needs of the particular audience.

In the concluding essay of this section of the book, Mara Miller draws on the rich tradition of Japanese literature and art to undermine some persistent misperceptions about the Japanese image of self. She marshals convincing evidence to argue that although the self is constituted within a social context, this does not mean that the Japanese necessarily lack introspection, self-examination, or a sense of individual accomplishment. Using both historical and philosophical arguments, Miller reveals the flaw in assuming that the relative lack of individualism in traditional Japanese culture leads to a lack of self-esteem or individuality. Although the importance of self is fundamentally defined within a social nexus, the self-image is nonetheless significantly controlled by the individual. In contrast to our modern Western tendency to formulate our self-understanding in terms of subject and object, the traditional Japanese tendency, Miller maintains, is to understand the self in terms of an intersubjectivity. In this way the social context dominates without necessarily replacing individuality. To take a paradigmatic case, Miller explains how such intersubjectivity is portrayed in the erotic wood block art of the Tokugawa period. Her claim is that unlike most Western erotic art, Japanese eroticism does not reify the woman as the object of the male gaze. Instead, the Japanese tradition sees the woman as a co-agent in an intersubjective encounter.

As we survey the richness of the examples in this set of six essays, it may be difficult to make any generalizations. Yet, I will hazard one common underlying motif. We can begin with Miller's point about intersubjectivity. If we think of the difference between the subject-object model and the intersubjective model, we may note that the former is formulated as an external relation and the latter as an internal relation. The difference can be depicted as follows.

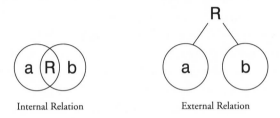

Internal Relation   External Relation

FIGURE 1

In an internal relation the two relatents *A* and *B* overlap and are parts of each other. If *B* ceases to exist, *A* loses part of itself. In an external relation, however, *A* and *B* exist independently and are brought into relationship by an external bond, *R*. If *B* ceases to exist, *A* keeps its integrity as *A*.

The analyses in these essays suggest that in the Japanese context internal relations tend to dominate over external ones. This helps explain how the Buddhist doctrine of "no-self" or "no-ego" (*anātman* in Sanskrit; *muga* in Japanese) is theoretically maintained within a social context in which, as some of the essays note, introspection and even an aesthetic self-absorption often dominate. If I am internally rather than externally related to my aesthetic community, the natural world, and other people past and present (including ancestors, teachers, intimates of any kind), then when I look inward into myself *(A)*, I find also part of the relatents with which I am in internal relations *(B, C, D, . . .)*. It is not exactly that *B, C,* and *D* define me, but rather part of their self-definition is part of my self-definition. I am not an "integer" (literally, an "untouchable" whole) but a nexus of partially overlapping intimate relations. I define my relatents to the same extent they define me. This is the logic of *kokoro*.

In contrast, modern Western cultures tend to place more emphasis on external relations in their models for self-understanding. Hence, when we encounter a culture that emphasizes internal relations, we tend to see the relatents as encroaching on the integrity of the self. A profound misunderstanding can occur. Namely, we may think that, because the self is not isolatable from what is around it, the self is somehow undeveloped. The external relatents, we suspect, have consumed the self. So we often hear the Japanese described as having "social" or "collective" rather than "individual" selves. We may mistakenly think that the "true self" is being repressed or oppressed in Japan by the external social order. In other words, we tend to think that the "social order" has an integrity and separate wholeness that has squelched the integrity and separate wholeness of the individual.

If we carefully think through the paradigm of internal relations, however, we can discover the mistake in such an assumption. From the Japanese standpoint, the society or the natural world, like the individual, does not have integrity or separate wholeness. The outer world is as much "encroached upon" by the individual as vice versa. This is particularly notable in the discussion of the "aesthetic community" discussed in some of the papers. The community is as much shaped by the individual as the individual is shaped by the community. Yet, it is not a dialectical power relation between the two, as we might expect in a modern Western model. Rather, each is an inseparable part of the other. Without the other, each would lose part of itself. In this regard, the mummified Buddhist masters discussed in Tanabe's essay, for example, are as much an expression of the individual in the community as the community in the individual. Similarly, to put relics inside a sculpture is a natural, physicalized expression of the internal relation that already exists. The sculpture would not be fully what it is without those relics, nor would the relics be fully what they are without the sculpture.

We may also note in passing how easily we can be fooled by the language commonly used in talking about Japanese culture. We often characterize the Japanese aesthetics of the garden, for example, as one of naturalness, of letting the natural object be itself. Yet, anyone who has ever had the least exposure to such Japanese arts as gardening, flower arranging, or bonsai is acutely aware of how much human effort—bending, pruning, twisting—is involved in this supposed "naturalness." In fact, when we discover this, we may even feel talk of "naturalness" is somehow hypocritical. If we recall the model of internal relationship, however, we remember that the artist is part of nature. That is, to have something be "natural" does not imply that we should not "encroach" on nature. That would be the rhetoric of external relations. If we pose the issue in the rhetoric of internal relations, however, we find ourselves saying something like: "If it were not for the artist, nature would lose part of itself." That may sound mystical to us, but in the context of using internal relationship as a model, the formerly mystical language becomes straightforwardly descriptive.

Another difficult term is *muga,* often mentioned in the papers and translated as "no-self." The *ga* (in Sanskrit, *ātman*) is, however, "self" in only a very specific sense. It refers to the self as something that exists in and of itself, without internal relationships to other people and things. It is an individual essence or soul that has its own meaning and integrity without relation to anything else. Its relations can only be external. In this highly technical sense of "self," it is hardly surprising that Japanese Buddhists would deny its reality. Yet, in no respect does the term deny the reality of the person or even of individuality.

This discussion, if correct in its analysis, exemplifies how much we can learn through the careful study of self-as-image in another cultural context. As is so often the case in comparative cultural studies, when we gain insight into the other we simultaneously learn about ourselves. In understanding the importance of internal relations to the Japanese, we better see how our own assumptions about external relations influence the ways we view ourselves in our culture. Perhaps we could say that from the standpoint of intercultural studies, cultures are internally rather than externally related: to see the other is to see a part of ourselves.

12

"Impersonality" in Bashō
Neo-Confucianism and Japanese Poetry

Arthur H. Thornhill III

A fundamental irony of the discourse of the self in Japan is that, beginning with the importation of Buddhism in the sixth century, it is based not on a doctrine of self, but rather of no-self. In its original Indian context, Buddhism unequivocally denies the existence of the atman, the individual self that reincarnates. In the rival religious traditions, the atman is a divine essence, the eternal soul of the individual human being. Early Buddhism endeavors to prove that the self is an illusion created by the ideating consciousness; once the nature of this process is fully grasped, the realization of no-self results in blissful release from the endless cycle of birth and death.

However, when Buddhism was exported to the cultures of East Asia, this doctrine of no-self *(anatman)* was not truly embraced. There are many explanations for this. To some, it implicitly denied the eternal life of ancestral spirits, important guardians and symbols of the continuity of the family/clan. And other aspects of the Buddhist religion—its impressive pantheon, associated technologies, and promises of what appeared to be a kind of salvation—overshadowed the subtlety of the *anatman* doctrine, which, along with such later Mahayana notions as the teaching of emptiness, seemed too negative, too pessimistic. But perhaps most important of all in the Japanese case was the simple fact that there was no developed notion of self that could be negated. The power of the *anatman* doctrine is proportional to the entrenchment of that which it overturns.

In fact, in the case of Japan, it could be argued that Buddhism *provided* the first explicit notion of self—at least, in the sense of a soul possessed by every individual. As the Pure Land faith permeated first the nobility in the Heian period (794-1185), and then gradually entered the consciousness of the lower classes in the Kamakura period (1185-1333), the possibility of personal salvation was entertained by large segments of the population for the first time. Prior to this stage, the spirits *(tama, tamashii)* enshrined by the priests of the indigenous religion were limited to those of powerful leaders or feared entities from the outside *(hitogami),* or ancestral spirits which gradually merged into one *(ujigami).* Most explicitly, the Buddhist cosmology of the Six Paths of transmigration provided a clear chart of the spiritual progress of the soul. Properly speaking, the four higher realms of bodhisattvas and buddhas are beyond the bonds of karma, and thus represent the realization of no-self, but in the popular imagination these were often perceived as mere heavenly existences, within the same continuum of rebirth.

Thus it is only in the medieval era that the stage is set for a widespread assimilation of the *anatman* doctrine. Once the classical Buddhist cosmology is in place, the emphasis shifts to internal experience, as embodied in the "single practices" of the Zen and Pure Land movements. Furthermore, the social and political upheaval of the Gempei War (1180-85) helped spread belief in the pessimistic *mappō* ("Latter Age of the Law") doctrine, as impermanence and annihilation were experienced firsthand.

The examination of "secular" literature would seem to provide at least one gauge of the acceptance and understanding of the Buddhist tenets outlined above. For example, in the first major anthology of Japanese poetry, the *Manyōshū* (ca. 759), Buddhistic themes—most notably, the notion of impermanence—appear with some frequency. However, these are mostly generic laments at human mortality or aesthetic appreciations of the mutability of nature. One senses that the Buddhism of the *Manyōshū* is less a reflection of the state religion of the Nara period (710-84) than a literary fad imported directly from the continent by Yamanoe no Okura and others. For example:

Yo no naka o	To what shall I compare
nani ni tatoemu	the way of the world?
asaborake	White waves trailing
kōgiyuku fune no	a boat rowed away
ato no shiranami	at dawn.[1]

(Priest Mansei)

The poetry of the *Kokinshū*—the first imperially commissioned anthology of *waka,* compiled in 905—marks the true beginning of the courtly literary tradition. One notable feature is its remarkable level of subjectivity, of self-absorption. The courtiers of the Heian period (794–1185) discovered the power of reasoning, of casting the world in their own terms through the logic of poetry. Sometimes the result is detached bemusement, as in the style of "elegant confusion"—mock surprise at the inability to distinguish clouds from distant cherry blossoms, or moonlight from snow cover in one's garden. Sometimes it is one of unrestrained emotion, as in the "passionate confusion" of such great lovers as Ariwara no Narihira and Ono no Komachi. But when the *Kokinshū* poets look for analogies in the outer world, their fundamental preconceptions never come into question. If the workings of nature correlate with their feelings, they are delighted; if not, they are upset. They seldom have the urge to listen quietly to nature itself. In a sense, this intense subjectivity reflects a self-confidence in the stable social and political order of the era. As in the case of the Buddhist notion of *anatman,* this heightened sense of self is a prerequisite for its negation.

With the poetry of Izumi Shikibu in the early eleventh century, we find the first mature Buddhist dialectic in *waka,* one that encompasses both suffering and its cessation. This is the age of *The Tale of Genji,* when the path of Buddhist renunciation becomes an attractive remedy for either personal or political misfortune. Izumi's most famous poem reads:

Kuraki yori	From Darkness
kuraki michi ni zo	into the Path of Darkness
irinubeki	must I enter.
haruka ni terase	Shine upon me from afar,
yama no ha no tsuki	o moon above the mountain crest.[2]

Here the darkness imagery, symbolic of the deluded mind of attachment, is derived from the *Lotus Sutra,* and the moon symbolizes Shōkū Shōnin, a famous priest residing in a mountain temple to the west to whom Izumi turned for spiritual guidance.

In another of her poems, the motif of self-annihilation is clearly based on a Buddhist conception:

Itoedomo	Weary am I
kienu mi zo uki	of this flesh that will not melt,

urayamashi	loathe it as I may.
kaze no mae naru	And enviable is the lamp flame
yoi no tomoshibi	flickering in the evening breeze.[3]

Yet there is still a tone of self-obsessed impatience, as the passionate attachment of love transforms into a desperate reaching out for spiritual solace.

The medieval era ushers in a new style of poetry, represented by the *Shinkokinshū* of 1205, which seeks to achieve a new balance between the inner world of the poet and his surroundings. This is achieved first by the detached contemplation of the natural world, a process explicitly represented in the poems. At the same time, *Shinkokinshū* poetry exhibits what has been called "descriptive symbolism,"[4] whereby individual images and motifs imply specific human situations, due to their accumulated associations within the poetic tradition. Thus, the scent of orange blossoms recalls the past, a trailing cloud at dawn represents a departing lover, and a hazy moon is indifferent to the troubles of those below. The metaphorical connections forged in the *Kokinshū* period have been internalized into the poetic landscape, and these human responses well up in the poet who contemplates the external world.

Most prominently, the tonal darkness of medieval Buddhism surfaces in the celebrated aesthetic of *yūgen* ("mystery and depth"). A famous example would be Fujiwara Teika's

Miwataseba	As I look out,
hana mo momiji mo	neither blossoms nor scarlet leaves
nakarikeri	do I see:
ura no tomaya no	along the bay, thatched huts
aki no yūgure	in the autumn twilight.[5]

On one level, this poem is the expression of an aesthetic preference for subdued beauty, for the dark melancholy of late autumn over the more obvious beauty of cherry blossoms and brilliant maple leaves. But, as William LaFleur has demonstrated,[6] it actually contains two successive stages of negation. The reader's attention moves first from the clarity of scarlet leaves and pink blossoms into the obscurity of the distant huts along the shore; and as that scene too vanishes in the encroaching darkness, both obvious and subtle beauty are experienced as equally impermanent, and thus nondual.

In general, the effect of *yūgen* in medieval *waka* depends upon a dialectic of clarity and obscurity within the mind of the observer. The obscurity beckons, drawing the subject not only into a mood of melancholy but into a yearning for a realm beyond clearly differentiated form. The observing self subsequently merges with formlessness, both achieving a union of inner and outer worlds, and—through the symbolism of darkness, originally derived from the Taoist tradition—the realization of no-self. In the poetic treatises of the age, notably those of Kamo no Chōmei and Fujiwara Shunzei, the Buddhist foundations of this aesthetic—particularly, the Tendai meditation practice of *shikan* ("cessation and contemplation")[7]—are clearly evident.

Of all the major medieval poets, the linked-verse *(renga)* master Shinkei (1406-74) is the most insistent in equating the training of the artist with the ascetic practice of Buddhism. For example, he consistently emphasizes that conformity to the orthodox rules of *renga* composition is the key to the successful training of the beginning and intermediate poet. These rules are likened to the *vinaya,* the Buddhist monastic regulations. However, just as Mind is the foundation from which all phenomenal existences arise, so the mind/heart *(kokoro)* of the poet is the origin, the essence of a poem. Therefore, once a master has developed the requisite purity of *kokoro* to produce poetry of deep feeling and inner grace, he may occasionally violate the externally imposed rules.

Correspondingly, Shinkei's verse embodies a new configuration of inner and outer, of self and other. In part due to the brevity of the individual links in *renga*—14 or 17 syllables—many of Shinkei's verses are purely descriptive, providing no direct representation of the observer on the scene. Yet one also senses his impatience with the careful balance of *Shinkokinshū* poetry. We can see this clearly in an important passage from *Sasamegoto,* Shinkei's major treatise on *renga* theory, which contains an allusion to the following poem by Saigyō (1118-90):

Mireba ke ni	As I look, strangely,
kokoro mo sore ni	my mind goes out
nari zo yuku	to become one with the scene:
kareno no susuki	miscanthus grass on a withered field,
ariake no tsuki	under the dawn moon.[8]

Here, as with our previous *Shinkokinshū* example, the observing poet's mind/heart fuses with the scene before his eyes. However, in his discussion, Shinkei mentions only the final two lines:

Long ago, when someone asked one of the poetic sages, "What disciplines should one observe in practicing the way of poetry?", he is said to have replied, "Miscanthus grass on a withered field, under the dawn moon." This means, "Focus your mind upon what is not said, and awaken to the cool, sad nature of things *(hie, sabitaru kata o satorishire)*." The elegance of poets who have entered the realm of accomplishment has these qualities. Thus, to the line "Miscanthus grass on a withered field," he adds only "The dawn moon." Could those who do not observe this practice accomplish such a verse?

This . . . is an exhortation to concentrate on the gentle charm *(en)* and tranquility produced by atmosphere and suggestion. It means that those who aspire to enter the way of poetry must endeavor to make gentle charm the basis of their art. Gentle charm is not necessarily dependent upon a verse's configuration, or the use of gentle or flowery words. It appears in a verse which comes from the heart of a man whose inner spirit is pure, whose human passions are weak, who is deeply moved by all things, realizing that every one will vanish without a trace—a man who has not forgotten human feeling, and in his benevolence toward others shows little concern for his own life. Verses of poets whose sentiments are [merely] ornate *(kokoro no kazaritaru tomogara)* sound false to the ears of the sincere person *(makoto no hito)*, despite their gentle configuration and diction. . . .[9]

On one level, Shinkei's omission of Saigyō's first three lines, which describe the penetration of the poet's mind into the scene, represents a distaste for obvious representation of the human presence. In this sense, his verse is more subtle and more exclusively descriptive. At the same time, the meaning changes: in the couplet, the harmonization is not between inner and outer, but between the two images of withered grass and the moon—between the common and the sublime. This fusion of elements of the landscape becomes an objective correlative for a process whereby the inner grace of the master poet brings to life his humble poetic materials.

In the above passage from *Sasamegoto,* the diminished attachment and compassion of the ideal poet are clearly Buddhist-derived ideals. Indeed, Shinkei is best known for his aesthetics of *hie* (coldness) and *yase* (slenderness), embodied in the hibernal landscape and emblematic of mental clarity and freedom from desire. At the same time, we must remember Shinkei's fundamental identity as a poet. His point is not that artistic activity is inherently spiritual, but rather that self-cultivation is necessary for the highest levels of artistic attainment.[10]

An example of Shinkei's linking style:

Waga kokoro	To whom shall I speak
tare ni kataran	my heart,
aki no sora	under the autumn sky?

(Shinkei:)	
Ogi ni yūkaze	The evening wind speaks to the reeds,
kumo ni karigane	the geese to the clouds.[11]

The language of this verse is entirely traditional. The reeds and the geese are associated with autumn, continuing the setting provided by the previous verse. Yet the linking technique is startling in its originality. The persona of the previous link desires to share her feelings with a lover, but Shinkei's response implies that, by contemplating the autumn landscape before her eyes, she will find the intimacy she desires in the caress of the wind and the call of the geese. Human agency vanishes, as the act of intimate communication has been sublimated into components of the natural landscape. At the same time, her unspeakable sadness is correlated with the ineffable beauty and emotion of the natural scene.

We can say two things about Shinkei's new attitude. On the one hand, he prefers the oblique expression of "distant linking" *(soku)*, whereby the poet makes unconventional, difficult connections between verses. Often, the "distant link" is entirely descriptive, mingling with the human emotion of the situation that precedes it. Yet his poetry presents not merely a scene we can observe and empathize with. Rather, the qualities of the landscape and the human heart are interpenetrating; a component of the landscape itself becomes the observing, feeling subject. At the same time, this is still "symbolic" poetry; the imagery communicates the human emotions dictated by convention. Burdened by the tradition, *waka* and classical *renga* can never break away into the realm of pure description.

The poetry of Matsuo Bashō (1644-94) represents both a continuation of Shinkei's style, and a major departure from it. Bashō explicitly traces his poetic lineage to Saigyō, and to Shinkei's disciple Sōgi. At least in part, Bashō singles out these two as travelers. Saigyō is the prototypical poet-priest who journeyed on pilgrimage to such sites as Mt. Kōya and Yoshino. He is a traditional pilgrim, in the sense that he visits holy places; and of course wandering itself is an ascetic practice. Sōgi is a transitional figure: while his poetry is clearly of the same tradition, his persona (largely at odds with his actual life style) is that of the recluse poet who spends lonely nights in his leaky hut, savoring the poetry of past and composing his own verses. Sōgi's travels are motivated by a desire to visit the celebrated sites of natural beauty throughout Japan, the inspiration for his poetic ancestors. Bashō's travels emulate both of these great poet-wanderers.

At the same time, Bashō's poetry is a radical break with the past. He is a *haikai* poet; practically speaking, this means he is free to use unconventional, "inelegant" diction not found in the classical anthologies of *waka*— thus, crows and snails, as well as the moon and cherry blossoms. But he departs from the earlier *haikai* tradition as well, abandoning both the tired wit of the Teimon poets who poke gentle fun at courtly attitudes, and the fashionable urban poetry of the Danrin school. Bashō's new style combines the common (although not unrestricted) diction of the recent past with the attitude of high seriousness found in Saigyō and Sōgi.

One frequent explanation given for this new tone, especially by Western observers, is that Bashō is a "Zen poet." Certainly, Bashō is known to have studied Zen in Edo with the monk Butchō. But in what sense might his poetry be "Zen"?

First of all, we must realize that Bashō is not a religious poet in the true sense. The most cursory glance at genuine Zen poetry, such as that of Ikkyū Sōjun or Musō Soseki, reveals the consistent inclusion of an explicit enlightenment motif—usually accompanied by appropriately paradoxical language. The speaker of the poems is identifiably a religious aspirant. This manifest religious urge is simply not found in most of Bashō's poetry.

What people see as "Zen" in Bashō seems to be twofold. First, many of his most famous poems contain the rustic imagery of Chinese Ch'an poetry and painting: crows, woodcutters, and the like. These are emblems both of an ascetic lifestyle, and of the hidden wisdom that exists beyond the world of learned doctrinal study. But even more important is the atmosphere of spontaneity in Bashō's verses. The sudden insight into the beauty of the humble and the plain, the unpremeditated moment of rapt awareness—these seem to resemble Zen accounts of realizing one's Buddha Nature while chopping bamboo or eating shrimp. Yet, it must be noted that unrestricted poetic expression is not permitted in the Bashō school. His style of linked-verse is, in its own way, just as confining as classical *renga,* with countless rules of linking, acceptable imagery, limits on repetition and interval, etc. For the reader, the literary allusions are numerous and often even more difficult than those of Shinkei, for example. And even the *hokku*—the independent seven-teen-syllable form now popularly called *haiku*—has the technical require-ments of seasonal and "cutting" words. Furthermore, we know from historical evidence that Bashō was a very deliberate artist who often revised his verses several times. Still, he does manage to create an *illusion* of spontaneity.

Among Western critics, the most eloquent proponent of Bashō as Zen poet is Robert Aitken, whose study *A Zen Wave: Bashō's Haiku and Zen* is full of rich insights. In order to get a flavor of his readings, we need look no farther than this most famous of all Japanese poems:

Furuike ya   Old pond—

kawazu tobikomu   a frog jumps in,

mizu no oto   the sound of water.[12]

As with Shinkei, many of Bashō's verses are composed of two elements, fused through a dynamic process of perception. These are traditionally de-scribed as (1) an eternal, unchanging background, and (2) a transitory ele-ment.[13] Here, the background is the old pond, utterly still; the frog of course provides the transitory excitement. The key to the poem is the third line, where the merging of the two elements is represented in the phrase *mizu no oto*. Note that Bashō does not say "kerplop"—this is not onomatopoeia, although Japanese has such expressions in abundance. "Sound of water" is conceptual, and even somewhat paradoxical: the stuff of absolute stillness has come alive, as the eternal and the transitory meet for one instant. Aitken equates the old pond with the deep clarity of mind that results from extensive *zazen* experience, and the moment of impact with a nudge into *satori:* the whole world is filled with one sound, and then drops away.[14] Another, more philosophical Buddhist reading might detect the presence of *riji muge,* the Kegon doctrine of the inseparability of principle (emptiness, the absolute) and phenomena, originally represented by a water-and-waves analogy.[15]

My own view of the poem is more subdued. It depicts a gentle experience widely shared, mildly humorous, a fond memory from childhood. To equate the poem with a transcendent Zen experience seems to violate its spirit. Yet at the same time, it seems necessary to account for the philosophical dimen-sion. An alternative reading might see its dialectic of motion and stillness[16] not from the perspective of Buddhism, but rather as an embodiment of the bipolar, mutual interaction of yin and yang,[17] as presented in the Confucian (and Taoist) tradition. The static tranquility of the old pond is the apex of the yin principle; at that point the gentle splash of the frog occurs, the first manifestation of yang. The effect, then, depends upon an organic relation between two natural elements, rather than a thunderous transformation of consciousness.

It is important at this juncture to consider the status of Chinese thought in Bashō's time. Certainly, yin-yang thought is found in the traditional "Chinese learning" of the Heian period, based on the orthodox canon of Confucian and Taoist classics. However, yin-yang studies were revitalized in Japan through the importation of the writings of the Sung Neo-Confucianists, whose reexamination of the *I Ching* ("Book of Changes") provides an extensive discourse on the permutations of yin and yang within the flux of human and natural events. And of course the functioning of *ch'i*, ("vital energy," "material force"), a fundamental component in the thought of the seminal figure of Neo-Confucianism, Chu Hsi (1130–1200), is consistently expounded in terms of its particularistic forms of yin/yang and the five phases. In the Muromachi period, Neo-Confucian writings were transmitted largely through Zen temples, which had become the new centers of Chinese learning. Therefore, in his contact with Zen clerics, Bashō was inevitably exposed to Neo-Confucian thought as well. For example, his interest in the hexagrams of the *I Ching* through the auspices of the Zen priest Daiten of Enkaku-ji in Kamakura is documented.[18]

Another famous poem of Bashō, composed six years before the "old pond" verse, reads:

> Kareeda ni   On a withered branch,
> tomaritaru ya karasu no a crow has perched:
> aki no kure   an autumn evening.[19]

Aitken sees this as excessively quietistic, lacking the dynamism of the previous verse.[20] But from the point of view of yin/yang relation, the poem is easily appreciated as more than a tranquil picture. The static background is the withered branch of late autumn; this yin quality is enhanced by its lack of vital energy. By comparison, the black crow is the active component, the energy of flight still present in the perfect tense of the verb *tomaritaru*. The darkness of the crow's presence extends outward, as the yin of night expands slowly. Thus the microcosm of the crow coming to rest is reflected in the larger natural process of nightfall, and even beyond in the "close of autumn"—another meaning for the final line, *aki no kure*.

As we have seen, the solemnity of an autumn evening is not an unusual theme in *waka*. But this poem explicitly rejects the traditional human associations of the setting—the lover or hermit looking out into the deep autumn sky, feeling "the sadness of things." This meaning is not possible, due to the presence of the *haikai* element, the inelegant crow. Nor is there the kind of transformative perception, the merging of the observing self with emptiness, that we find in Teika's *yūgen*. The interaction is entirely between two descriptive images, fused in a third.

Another example:

Horohoro to   Softly, softly,
yamabuki chiru ka   yellow mountain roses fall—
taki no oto   the sound of the rapids.[21]

Rather than overwhelming the delicacy of the blossoms, the forceful roar of the water enhances their tranquility, even as their flutter is more difficult to "hear." Once again, the two elements are in a yin/yang relationship, devoid of any specific symbolized emotion. Bashō's poetry is at once sensuous—delighting in the texture and rhythms of nature, freshly observed—and restrained, revealing the inner moral aspect of things. Natural phenomena are not mere representative objects of consciousness, to be transcended; they speak for themselves in their own particularity.

In Bashō's descriptive poetry—and, to be sure, not all of his verses are such—the symbolic expression of human feeling has been cleansed. The sensitive interactions of nature are portrayed not in the emotional, human intimacy of Shinkei, but in organic intimacy. For both men, the mind/heart of the ideal poet is pure, but their visions of purity differ significantly. Shinkei's ideals of *hie* and *yase* are emblematic of the Buddhist aspirant's retreat from human passion, from the entanglement of human relationships. In contrast, for Bashō the purity of the mind/heart is a mirror, reflecting things as they are.

Makoto Ueda has described this as a quality of "impersonality" in Bashō's poetry. He cites a famous passage from the *Sanzōshi*, recorded by Bashō's disciple Dohō:

> The Master said, "Learn about a pine tree from a pine tree, and about a bamboo plant from a bamboo plant." What he meant was that the poet should detach his mind from his own selfish ideas *(shi'i)* . . . "Learn" means to enter into the object, perceive its delicate life, and feel its feeling *(sono bi no arawarete jōkanzuru)*,

whereupon a poem forms itself. Even a poem that lucidly describes an object cannot attain a true poetic sentiment unless it contains the feelings that spontaneously emerge out of the object. In such a poem the object and the poet's self *(mono to ga)* would remain forever separate; the poem would not attain sincerity *(makoto)* of feeling, for it would be composed of the poet's selfish ideas.[22]

Ueda's term "impersonality" seems entirely appropriate. Yet in his subsequent analysis, he is led astray by what he takes to be a *Buddhist* attitude in Bashō's art. Since the medieval discourse on artistic praxis is dominated by Buddhist metaphors of spiritual progress, Ueda assumes that Bashō was engaged in a religious quest for enlightenment, for detachment from human feeling; yet his poetry kept drawing him back to the "world of things."[23]

This incongruity can be resolved by a careful reading of the above passage. In my view, the language suggests not a Buddhist, but a Neo-Confucian conception of poetic composition. In particular, the expression "selfish ideas" *(shi'i)* points to Chu Hsi's conception of self-cultivation. The ontological foundation of the universe—Heavenly Principle, or the Great Ultimate—is fundamentally good, but when the activity of knowing gives rise to the duality of good and evil, the impurity within man's individual allotment of material force *(ch'i)* distracts him from his true Nature, which is principle *(li)*. The impure, clouded *ch'i* is that which makes man private, or "selfish," alienated from the public, moral good. For Bashō, to be impersonal is not to be unfeeling, but rather impartial. If there is a discernible gap between the self and "things," the poet's private emotions intrude. Instead, the emotion of the poem should emerge from the subtle feeling that things themselves exude. Clearly this cannot be a Buddhist conception; Buddhists will neither admit the substantiality of things, nor that feelings are anything more than projections of a deluded mind, the result of karmic residue. Above all, this passage recalls the Neo-Confucian practice of the "observation of things" *(ko-wu)*, in order to discover principle within them.

Finally, it should be noted that the ideal of sincerity, or *makoto*—the opposite of "selfish ideas" in the above passage—is none other than a native Japanese reading for *ch'eng*, the central ideal of *The Doctrine of the Mean*, the Confucian classic resurrected by Chu Hsi as one of his Four Books. *Makoto* is frequently evoked by Bashō to denote the unchanging, eternal spirit *(fueki)* of *haikai*.[24]

One of the most explicit references to Neo-Confucian thought in Bashō's poetry is the headnote to a *hokku* dated 1686: "All things have their own accomplishment." Its probable source is a couplet by the Neo-Confucian pioneer Ch'eng Hao (1032–85): "When all things are quietly contemplated, each has its own accomplishment." The verse illustrates:

Hana ni asobu	Do not eat the horsefly
abu na kurai so	frolicking in the blossoms,
tomosuzume	o fellow sparrows![25]

This poem juxtaposes a lowly horsefly perched on a flower with a small group of sparrows flitting through the branches. Although the birds are intent upon securing sustenance, the observing poet's tranquil mind projects a human sense of restraint, urging them to "live and let live." At first glance this poem may appear to employ the familiar personification technique of *Kokinshū*-era verse, as the poet begs an element of nature to comply with his wishes (e.g., blossoms not to fall from the branches). But here the concern is not the self-centered gratification of the observer, but rather compassion for the natural realm, an appreciation of the larger scheme of interrelation. In the Neo-Confucian orientation invoked through Bashō's stated topic, each element of the universe has its own function, identity, and value, and the sparrows, as an emanation of the poet's inner morality, are urged to realize their own nature by demonstrating restraint, by recognizing that they share with another living being the common act of "frolicking in the blossoms."

There are many other indications of a Confucian orientation in Bashō's stated views on poetry. Most prominently, he writes at the opening of his travel diary *Oi no kobumi*:

Saigyō in *waka*, Sōgi in linked-verse, Sesshū in painting, Rikyū in tea ceremony—there is a single thread[26] running through their art. In the elegant art of *haikai* as well, we follow the permutations of nature, befriending the four seasons. Nothing we see is but a flower, none of our thoughts are but of the moon. When the image before our eyes is not of a flower, we are equivalent to savages; when our hearts are not filled with flowers, we belong to the realm of animals. We must abandon barbarism and depart from the beastly by following the permutations of nature, by returning to nature.[27]

In the context of Bashō's own poetry, this is clearly *not* an injunction to write only of cherry blossoms and moonlight; that is precisely the traditional style that *haikai* rejects. Rather, the refined mind/heart finds within itself only goodness, only the purity and beauty *symbolized* by these images. This mind is attained by "following the permutations of nature." The term used here is *zōka*,[28] the "created transformations" of material force. Thus, the requisite purity is attained by observing the subtle metamorphosis of vitality—the interactions of yin/yang and the five phases—within nature. Similarly, in the *Sanzōshi* Dohō records, "The master said, 'The changing cycles of Ch'ien and K'un are the seed of elegance in *haikai*,'"[29] referring to the major yang and yin principles of the *I Ching* embodied in the first two hexagrams, "The Creative" and "The Receptive."

I do not wish to dismiss all traces of Zen within Bashō's poetry—he himself wore Buddhist robes (although largely as the emblem of a literary man), and his poems and journeys are full of Buddhist images. A small percentage of his poems can indeed be identified as Zen in both theme and expression, embracing a kind of Mādhyamika-derived nondualism.[30] Furthermore, Bashō's aesthetics, and the spiritual attitudes embodied in his art, undeniably embody Buddhist values. Yet I would argue that Bashō did not conceive his literary praxis in fundamentally Buddhist terms. Buddhism is only part of his literary heritage, a heritage also replete with Chinese poetry and prose. And the literary life, based on the model of the Chinese gentleman-scholar, is at heart Confucian. During the Buddhist-dominated medieval age, we sense an uneasiness, as the soteriological value of the arts is hotly debated; poets go to extraordinary lengths to justify their avocation. But Bashō never expresses the need to give up his attachment to poetry. His few moments of self-doubt are occasioned by imagined inadequacies as an artist.[31]

In the "impersonality" of Bashō, the discourse of the self in Japanese poetry takes a new turn. The merging of subject and object found in *Shinkokinshū* poetry is ultimately a reflection of Mahāyāna nonduality: not to distinguish between good and evil, self and other, form and emptiness, delusion and enlightenment. This mode of thought is at the heart of such medieval literary monuments as *setsuwa* tale literature, Nō drama, and the poetry of the Zen master Ikkyū. In the Tokugawa period, dualism returns with a vengeance, in the form of an insistence on purity. In this sense, we can see Shinkei's emphasis on the primacy of *kokoro* in poetry, on the "sincere person," as an ominous first step. And in turning his gaze to the outer world of "things," Bashō exacts a high price, requiring an inner mind/heart of utter purity. In the process, the psychological transformations that routinely occur in medieval art—from delusion to enlightenment, from sinner to saint—are no longer possible.

Under Tokugawa rule, profound changes have taken place in the cultural sphere; none is more important than the emergence of a Neo-Confucian orthodoxy. Yet to judge by the tenor of the times, the humanitarian, egalitarian spirit of Neo-Confucianism seems largely lacking. Within the popular imagination, at least, there is an unbridgeable gap between the austere requirements of duty and obligation *(giri),* and emotionalism *(ninjō).* This dilemma, which denies internal personal growth (except through death, as in the double-suicide dramas of Chikamatsu Monzaemon), leads to an extreme reaction against Confucianism—the Nativist *(kokugaku)* movement of the eighteenth century. But within Bashō, and other poets of his school, perhaps we can find the true transmission of Neo-Confucian values.

Notes

1. *Manyōshū* 351.

2. *Seishū* 150, 834. Translated by Edwin A. Cranston.

3. *Zokushū* 976. Translated by Edwin A. Cranston.

4. As discussed in Robert H. Brower and Earl Miner, *Japanese Court Poetry* (Stanford: Stanford University Press, 1961), 30-31, 469-70.

5. *Shinkokinshū* 363.

6. William R. LaFleur, *The Karma of Words* (Berkeley: University of California Press, 1983), 101-3.

7. For a discussion of *skikan* and Shunzei, see Brower and Miner, *Japanese Court Poetry,* 257.

8. The poem appears in *Saigyō Hōshi kashū.* See Ichiji Tetsuo et al., ed., *Rengaron shū, nōgakuron shū, hairon shū* (Tokyo: Shōgakkan, 1973), 124, n. 7.

9. Ichiji, et al., *Rengaron shū,* 124-6.

10. This distinction is discussed in Tu Wei-ming, "The Idea of the Human in Mencian Thought: An Approach to Chinese Aesthetics," in Susan Bush and Christian Murck, eds., *Theories of the Arts in China* (Princeton: Princeton University Press, 1983), 57.

11. *Shinsen Tsukabashū* 706. There is a pivot-word in the first line: the first syllable of *yūkaze* ("evening wind") also means "to speak." An alternate translation would be "In the reeds, the evening wind, / in the clouds, wild geese."

12. Imoto Nō'ichi et al., ed., *Matsuo Bashō shū* (Tokyo: Shōgakkan, 1972), *hokku* 142 (pp. 102-3).

13. Some modern commentators use the terms *fueki* ("the unchanging") and *ryūkō* ("the flowing") to denote these principles. However, Bashō originally used *fueki* to describe the enduring spirit of classic poetry, and *ryūkō* to denote the changing fashions of poetic style.

14. Robert Aitken, *A Zen Wave: Bashō's Haiku and Zen* (New York: Weatherhill, 1978), 25–29.

15. The "four views of the Dharmadhātu" are inspired by the water-and-waves analogy in the *Awakenmg of Faith*.

16. Ironically, the "motion and stillness" terminology so prominent in Neo-Confucian thought derives from the tradition of Hua-yen Buddhism. See Imai Usaburō, *Sōdai ekigaku no kenkyū* (Tokyo: Meiji shoten, 1958), 437–43.

17. Of course the relationship between the absolute and relative aspects of existence is sometimes represented as a yin-yang bipolarity in Chinese Buddhism. However, I prefer to read this poem as the interaction between yin and yang elements within the material dimension of *ch'i*, rather than as the symbolic representation of a metaphysical process.

18. See Yamamoto Yuiitsu, *Bashō no shisō* (Osaka: Izumi sensho, 1986), 16.

19. Imoto et al., *Matsuo Bashō shū, hokku* 48 (p. 61).

20. Aitken, *A Zen Wave*, 29.

21. Imoto et al., *Matsuo Bashō shū, hokku* 214 (p. 136).

22. Ichiji, et al., *Rengaron shū*, 547; translation modified from Makoto Ueda, *Literary and Art Theories in Japan* (Cleveland: Case Western Reserve, 1967), 157–58.

23. Ueda, *Literary and Art Theories*, 171–72.

24. The origins in Chinese thought of many of the terms presented here are discussed in Hori Masato, "Bashō to Chūgoku shiso," in Nakamura Yukihiko, ed., *Bashō no hon* vol. 1: *Sakka no kiban* (Tokyo: Kadokawa shoten, 1970), 232–68.

25. Imoto et al., *Matsuo Bashō shū, hokku* 155 (p. 108).

26. An allusion to *Analects* 4:15, where Confucius states that "one thread" runs through his teachings.

27. Imoto et al., *Matsuo Bashō shū*, 311–12.

28. Although this expression can be found in early Taoist texts such as *Lieh Tzu* and *Chuang Tzu*, Nieda Tadashi argues that Bashō's usage is more likely influenced by its meaning in the *I Ching*, as explicated by the Sung Neo-Confucianists. Nieda Tadashi, *Bashō ni eikyō shita kanshibun* (Tokyo: Kyōiku shuppan, 1972), 196.

29. Ichiji et al., *Rengaron shū*, 551.

30. For example, see discussion in Aitken, *A Zen Wave*, 101–5.

31. See the opening of *Oi no kobumi*, Imoto et al., *Matsuo Bashō shū*, 311.

13

Zen and Artistry

Thomas P. Kasulis

In thinking about the traditional Japanese arts, we often associate them with Zen Buddhism. In the parlance of the nonspecialist, the terms "Japanese" and "Zen" may even be interchangeable. A Japanese garden is a Zen garden; a Japanese teahouse is a Zen teahouse; Japanese archery is Zen archery. This identification seems to assume that where there is art, there is Zen. It has led to the plethora of books having the phrase "Zen in the Art of . . . " in their titles. Some authors of such Western books actually know very little of Zen — having imbibed a bit of Suzuki and sat with some Zen Buddhists for a week or two — but their expertise in the arts qualifies them to talk about Zen. At least, so they think. In fact, in one rather popular book in this genre the author uses quotes from the Zen masters to show how his art has an affinity to the Zen tradition. He also informs us that he has changed the translation of some of the masters' passages "based on my own insight." Knowledge of Japanese or Chinese, it seems, is not necessary. If you are good enough at your art, such pedantic skills are superfluous to the understanding of Zen.

The relationship sometimes seems to go in the opposite direction as well: Where there is Zen, there is art. We have come to expect our Zen masters to be master artists as well. When we hear of a Zen master, we wonder which of the arts is his or her specialty: tea ceremony? flower arrangement? painting? poetry? archery? We cannot even imagine that there might somewhere be a great Zen master who has bad handwriting.

I am not mocking the idea that there is an affinity between Zen and the arts. There is indeed an affinity and a legitimate one. Yet, it is the precise nature of that affinity that demands scrutiny. This paper will attempt to set at least the basic context within which that scrutiny may occur.

First, we should note the title of this paper is "Zen and Artistry," not "Zen and the Arts." Our focus, then, is not on the artistic products of the Zen tradition but on the manner in which they are produced. We are interested in what Zen might say about what makes a person a great artist, rather than what characteristics are found in the artwork itself. The strong emphasis on the way of artistry over the work of art is common in East Asian aesthetic treatises, often in contrast with Western aesthetics in this respect.

Furthermore, in choosing to focus on Zen artistry rather than Zen arts, we avoid certain difficulties. For one, we do not have to deal with the ambiguities in the term "Zen art" and its related Japanese terms such as *zenga*.[1] What makes a work of art a Zen artwork? Sometimes it seems helpful to think of Zen art as art produced by Zen monks and priests. Sometimes it is more useful, however, to think of such artworks as fitting a certain style. In still other contexts it seems more appropriate to use the term as a communal designation, indicating the artwork was produced in a monastery for some spiritual purpose. If we focus instead on what makes an act of artistic creation a Zen experience, we not only avoid these taxonomic issues but we also become capable of penetrating the philosophical anthropology, the theory of person, at the heart of Zen Buddhism.

A further advantage in our focus on Zen artistry is that it presents a context within which one could then look at multiple artistic forms of expression. A poem, an inkwash painting, a flower arrangement, a tea ceremony, and an archery performance are obviously different kinds of artistic products. In inquiring into their relation to Zen, we will find it more useful to examine their creative source than their end result. This paper will suggest that the Zen aspect of Zen art is primarily in the mode of creation rather than the style of the final product. What forms of concrete expression might take the form of Zen art is, therefore, an open question. If swordsmanship can be a Zen form of art, why not baseball batting as well? Professional baseball teams in Japan have frequently arranged for a Zen master to hold a retreat for their players. They hope to improve their concentration and, consequently, their performance.

Of course, this does not imply that the end result of the creative expression is irrelevant. If there is a certain psychophysical state characteristic of Zen creativity, it would not be surprising that such a state show itself in the final product. To the extent that that state is distinctive to Zen, there may well be something distinctive in the artwork produced as well. Still, the point is that in analyzing what Martin Heidegger called the "origin of the work of art,"[2] we can have a clearer idea of what the various Zen arts have in common or at least what family resemblances they may share.

The paper will have three parts. First, we will briefly consider the way the Zen tradition developed, going back to its Chinese roots in Chan Buddhism. Our discussion will focus on the way self-expression developed as an integral part of the tradition. Second, we will turn to the Japanese cultural context of spiritual expression, trying to locate the Zen tradition within it. Thanks mainly to D. T. Suzuki's highly influential book, *Zen and Japanese Culture*,[3] we often think of Zen Buddhism as being the single most important force in the development of various cultural and artistic traditions in Japan. The Japanese translation of Suzuki's book has also been influential on the popular level in the Japanese view of their own culture. Yet, surely the relationship cannot have been unilateral. Zen Buddhism must have been a product of Japanese culture as well as a creative force of change within it. Part 2 of this paper will explore some general Japanese spiritual and aesthetic themes influential in Zen and preserved or enhanced by it. Finally, part 3 will outline a theory of Zen creativity and its relation to personal expression. In this discussion we will be able to see how the Chan tradition inherited from China merged with traditionally Japanese themes into a theory of the person essential to the Zen understanding of artistic expression.

From Zen Mind to Zen Expression: The Chan Buddhist Background

Chan Buddhism was the precursor to the Japanese Zen tradition ("Zen" is the Japanese pronunciation for the Chinese character "Chan"). Tradition states Chan began with the arrival of Bodhidharma in China during the early sixth century. Most major developments within Chan occurred between that time and the ninth century. For our purposes, the critical theme to examine is Chan's evolution from an idealistic system emphasizing the purity of mind to one focused increasingly on the expression of enlightenment through action. To make our point succinctly and without resort to technical detail, let us consider two well-known traditional Zen stories, one reflecting the beginning and one the end of the era with which we are concerned.

It is significant to note how tradition characterizes the new Buddhist practice Bodhidharma brought from India to China. On arrival, Bodhidharma supposedly set himself up in the Shaolin Temple, plunked himself on a mat, and gazed at the wall for nine years. He barely spoke to anyone, and when he did, the message was mainly about how he wanted to be left alone. He desired no disciples, and only accepted Huike after he lopped off his arm and presented it to Bodhidharma as a sign of his earnestness.

For purposes of contrast, let us compare it with another famous story from a later chapter in Chan history. One day, the ninth-century Master Linji was lecturing to his disciples on the "true person without status."

> "In this clump of raw flesh [the body] there is a true person without status continually entering and exiting your sense organs. Those of you who have not yet authenticated this fact, look! Look!"
>
> Then a monk came forward and asked, "What is this person without status?"
>
> Coming down from his seat, grabbing the monk, Linji shouted, "Speak! Speak!"
>
> The monk deliberated.
>
> Releasing him, Linji said, "The true person without status—what a dried-up shit-stick he is. " He then returned to his chamber.[4]

Let us now compare these two stories in light of themes having a bearing on monasticism, mind, action, and expression. First, we note that the monasticism of Bodhidharma is eremitic rather than cenobitic, that is, it is solitary rather than communal. It is not simply that Bodhidharma had no disciples because he was new to China. He seemed not to want disciples. For him, Zen was a solitary way of life. Of course, Huike's action started a new tradition, the beginning of the master-disciple relationship in Chan. From that point on, the dynamic between master and student would be crucial to Chan training.

As the story shows, by the time of Linji, the Chan context of training was clearly communal. The master was lecturing to an assembly of his students. Still, we may note the crucial part of the story is still dyadic, the direct confrontation between master and disciple. The community had by then become the context for training, but the most important dynamic remained the personal encounter with the master on a one-to-one basis.

Second, let us consider the treatment of mind in the two stories. Although we do not know exactly what Bodhidharma's "wall-gazing" technique amounted to, the terminology of early Chan texts has a markedly idealistic tone. Chan meditation was understood to be primarily a yogic practice for purifying the mind. Even in a text as late as *The Platform Sūtra of the Sixth Patriarch* (early eighth century),[5] there is much talk of the mind and mental states. Some of the language is reminiscent of Indian Buddhist traditions related to the *Laṅkāvatāra Sūtra*[6] and Yogācara philosophy.

This is not to say that early Chan was simply an offshoot of Indian idealism. It discarded much of the Yogācara emphasis on stages of deepening realization and emphasized total enlightenment in the here and now. Furthermore, it eliminated the notion of intermediary practices of increasing complexity and profundity. Chan practice, as suggested even by Bodhidharma's enigmatic wall-gazing, seemed to be a pure introspection with the goal of emptying the mind of distraction and needless conceptualization. This led to the notion of no-thought (as in Huineng's *Platform Sūtra*) and the related term, no-mind.

The earlier terminology of "no-thought" had mainly apophatic nuances. It denoted a cutting off of the delusory thoughts and ideas defiling the mirrorlike, reflective quality of the pure mind. This has parallels with a yogic goal of penetrating the delusory levels of conceptualization to realizing what the *Laṅkāvatāra Sūtra* called the "womb" of enlightenment, the *tathāgata-garbha*.

Originally, there was probably little difference between the notions of no-thought and no-mind. As the latter term became the more common of the two, however, it assumed some more positive nuances as well. The "no" (in Chinese, *wu;* in Japanese, *mu*) of "no-mind" began to suggest not merely the negative obliteration of thought but also the ground of all things. In this respect, it was undoubtedly under the influence of the Daoist use of the term to designate the creative "nonbeing" at the basis of everything, both positive and negative. In short, whereas no-thought suggested not doing something— not entertaining delusory thoughts and feelings—no-mind eventually suggested something active. For this reason, Huineng's disciple, Nan'yang Huizhong, related the no-mind state to the "functional mind" (in Chinese, *yongxin,* in Japanese, *yōshin*).[7] It is significant, therefore, that the traditional stories portray Bodhidharma's insight in terms of nine years of quiet sitting, whereas Linji's in terms of his lecturing, grabbing people, shouting, and demanding responses from others. This brings us to the third theme in our comparison between the two Chan stories: the notion of action.

In both stories, we have a master's responding to the action of a disciple, the dynamism for which the Zen literature is so famous. There is an important difference in the role of action between the two stories, however. In the older story, Huike cut off his own arm as a sign of his seriousness in undertaking the Zen way of life. His was a gesture of commitment. In the later story, however, Linji demands an act not of commitment but of realization. Linji calls on his student to manifest the true person without status. The student is being challenged to show his enlightenment, not his desire for enlightenment.

The difference is crucial in the development of a major strand of the Zen tradition. Enlightenment came to be no longer the state of having a pure mind but an enactment or expression of that true mind. Action was not the prerequisite to enlightenment but its manifestation.

Given this perspective on the meaning of enlightenment, the master can test the depth of students' realization by their ability to express, in Linji's terms, the "true person without status." Enlightenment is an act, or at least, a capacity to act in a certain way, not a state. This led to an important shift in the understanding of the relation between Chan and self-expression. This is our fourth theme of comparison in the two stories.

Chan places an emphasis on the transmission of the truth from master to disciple. This transmission involves not the mastery of a set of teachings but a way of mastering the self. In returning to the nonbeing of no-mind, the Chan student finds the emptiness out of which all personal activity emerges. Hence, the master tests to see if the student is really responding to the moment as it is in itself or whether the student is filtering the experience of that moment through a set of preconceived, and not necessarily appropriate, categories. The dynamic of the encounter with the master is to create a context in which previous experience and previous ways of thinking do not apply. If the student can make an appropriate response, that is a sign of liberation from the fixed categories that can limit the direct experience of the world.

In this way, Chan put an emphasis on the student's capacity to express that no-mind. From early in the tradition, the modes of expression could be of two forms. First, one might give a spontaneous response to the situation created by the master right then and there. This is what Linji was demanding in our story, for example. Second, one could display a creative product of that same no-mind. In the *Platform Sūtra,* for example, the master chose his successor by asking his students to write a poem to show their level of insight. In this way, artistic expression became a possible vehicle for enacting enlightenment.

One important point to note in this development of traditional Chan is that artistic expression was not a form of practice to help one achieve enlightenment. Being an artist could not make one enlightened. Only the traditional activities of meditation, kōan practice, and the self-imposed discipline of the monastic life could trigger that enlightenment. Rather, artistry was one—and only one—of a list of ways in which one might manifest one's insight to be authenticated by the master.

Let us turn now more explicitly to the Japanese, the Zen instead of the Chan, context. In part 2 of this paper we will consider some of the Japanese cultural context in which Zen art developed and flourished.

Japanese Culture and Its Influence on Zen Buddhism

We have already noted the significance of Suzuki's 1959 book, *Zen and Japanese Culture,* and its account of Zen's impact on the development of traditional Japanese arts. In fact, the original title of the 1938 version of the book was more revealing of its actual theme: *Zen Buddhism and Its Influence on Japanese Culture.* Most of what Suzuki said was insightful and not controversial. His sin, if any, was one of omission, not commission. In particular, his account did not suggest any of the spiritual and aesthetic context of Japan preceding the introduction of Zen. Zen did not enter Japan until the thirteenth century. Suzuki did not indicate how the five or six hundred years of earlier Japanese culture might have developed a nurturing milieu in which the Zen aesthetic could flourish, enabling it to become eventually so dominant in many of the arts. This is no place for a detailed analysis of such a complex topic, but three aesthetic motifs will help prepare us for our philosophical account of Zen and artistic expression in part 3. These three motifs are simplicity, the spirituality of the ordinary, and genuineness of heart.

Simplicity is often stressed as a major characteristic in Zen art. Indeed, it is. Yet, the Japanese admiration for simplicity had Shintō roots in the culture long before the introduction of Zen Buddhism. The indigenous religious tradition, which we might call proto-Shintō, had virtually no artistic representation in its religious practices. There were, for example, no painted or sculpted images of its religious personages, the *kami.* The Shintō shrines were simple in line, minimalist in decorative woodwork, and generally unpainted. The priests and priestesses of the tradition typically wore plain white sacred robes. All these patterns continue as a major aesthetic motif in Shintō today.

It was Buddhism that brought artistic representation and bold colors to the Japanese religious experience in the sixth, seventh, and eighth centuries.

When we compare the ritual robes of a Shintō priest with a Zen priest today, we note that the Zen priest wears a gold embroidered mantle, whereas the Shintō priest retains the plain white robe. We could even say that the indigenous, Shintō aesthetic was of utmost naturalness and plainness, whereas a competing aesthetic of color and decoration was introduced from the mainland Buddhists by the eighth century. Hence, there was an aesthetic spectrum from the native minimalism to the elegance imported from high Tang culture.

Of course, in comparison with other forms of Japanese Buddhism such as the esoteric or Pure Land traditions, Zen chose the Shintō, rather than Chinese, end of the spectrum. This is not to deny that there is a distinctive Zen aesthetic—even the Chan tradition in China had a tendency toward simplicity rather than elaborate decoration. The point I want to stress, however, is precisely one that has not been stressed by the Zen aestheticians best known to the West, such as Suzuki and Hisamatsu Shin'ichi.[8] That is, in preferring simplicity, the Japanese Zen tradition was also affirming something anciently Japanese. Even in admiring the rustic simplicity, the *wabi* and *sabi*, of a Zen master's tea bowl, we should see not only the minimalist style of Chan and Zen but also the minimalist style of prehistoric, late Neolithic Yayoi pottery, for example.

A second widely recognized theme in Zen aesthetics is the celebration of the ordinary, the everyday, and the natural, even the seemingly trivial or ugly. Again, this trend has roots in pre-Zen Japan. Let us consider the topic from two standpoints: the value-orientation of ancient Shintō in relation to nature and the philosophical contribution of esoteric Buddhism in the early Heian period.

The indigenous or proto-Shintō religion valued the sacred presence *(kami)* of any awe-inspiring object in the natural world—the sun, an especially striking mountain such as Fuji, an uncanny rock formation, an exotic tree. In the ancient myths recorded in *Kojiki* even the inanimate rocks and streams were capable of speech, and their constant bickering caused one of the deities to strike them dumb. In the earliest official collection of ancient poems and songs, *Man'yōshū*, we find a resonance and interactive quality between the objects of the natural world and human emotions. For example, one poem by Yamanoue no Okura, "Elegy for a Dead Wife," depicts the fog of Mount Ōnu as rising in response to the grief felt by the bereaved husband. All this suggests not merely a respect for the natural world but a sense of continuity with it. There is no sharp bifurcation between the human and nonhuman, the animate and inanimate.

Furthermore, it is significant that for Shintō even today, the spiritual power resides in the thing itself as a thing. Mount Fuji is sacred in a way different from, say, Mount Sinai or Mount Olympus. Sinai is sacred because of the holy events that happened there. Olympus is sacred because it is the residence of the gods. In the case of Fuji, however, nothing special happened there to give it religious meaning and no gods inhabit the mountain. Rather, Mount Fuji itself, as a mountain deserving our awe, is *kami*.

I once asked a Zen master about how one decides where to put the stones in a rock garden. He replied that the "gardener helps the rock be where it belongs and wants to be." To a twentieth-century listener, that answer might seem strange—how can one help a rock? In his answer, however, the Zen master was true not only to his Zen tradition but to the sensitivities of the ancient Japanese as well.

If the proto-Shintō tradition maintained an affective resonance between humanity and the natural world, the esoteric Buddhism of the early ninth century intensified that view by giving it a philosophical framework.[9] The focal doctrine from esotericism was *hosshin seppō,* a theory so influential that the noted Buddhist scholar, Tamaki Kōshirō has labeled it the "fundamental idea" in Japanese Buddhism.[10]

The trenchant phrase *hosshin seppō* literally means "the Buddha-as-embodying-everything (the *dharmakāya* or *hosshin*) expounds *(setsu)* the truth *(dharma* or *hō)*." The theory is that each thing in the universe reveals the truth of the Buddha's enlightenment. The world is literally telling us something through the manifestation of each phenomenon. This notion represents a spiritualization of all things. Later in both the esoteric and exoteric traditions, this same principle was articulated as the claim that all things, even inanimate ones, manifest Buddha Nature.[11] In the Zen tradition, Dōgen (1200–1253), for example, said that the mountains and waters were themselves sacred texts.[12]

We should note an important aspect in the evolution of the *hosshin seppō* notion from its roots in ancient esotericism to its flowering in the late medieval Zen arts. By its very nature, esotericism assumes a multidimensional reality. What appears is only the macrophysical manifestation of microphysical resonances and cosmic forces. For Kūkai (774–835), the founder of Japanese Shingon Buddhism and the most articulate and systematic of the esoteric philosophers, all phenomena are the "written characters" *(monji)* in the cosmic Buddha's text. Hence, on one level things are what they are, but on another level, they are expressive symbols of something else.[13] For

Zen, however, the layered view of reality collapses and the everyday, as the everyday, is imbued with spiritual significance. Things are not symbols to be spiritually interpreted, but rather, they manifest their spiritual significance directly in their "being as they are" (*immo,* sometimes translated "suchness").

Obviously, the *hosshin seppō* doctrine asserted an axiological equality for all things. Since each phenomenon is an exposition of the enlightened truth, nothing is trivial or devoid of the most profound significance. As this idea became deeply embedded in virtually all traditions of Japanese Buddhism, the distinction between the ordinary and the spiritual tended to collapse. Clearly, this tradition lent philosophical support to elevating the preparation of tea or flower arranging or the simple painting of a sparrow on a tree branch to the highest level of spiritual significance. In this respect, the Zen aesthetic was again a continuity rather than a divergence from ancient Japanese principles.

As our third theme in discussing how ancient Japanese culture might have influenced the flourishing of Zen, let us consider the idea of the "genuine heart" (*makoto no kokoro* or *magokoro*). The term had its exposition in the ancient theories of poetry first developed in the Heian period (turn of the ninth through the late twelfth centuries). The fullest development of the term, however, did not occur until the eighteenth century. At that time the Native Learning *(kokugaku)* theorists, often with impressive philological sophistication, tried to articulate the view of language found in the ancient tradition of verse written in Japanese (as opposed to Chinese, which was equally popular among the ancient Japanese aristocracy).

The key term in their interpretation is *kokoro,* a native Japanese word roughly equivalent to the German word *Geist* or Greek *psyche.* That is, the term encompasses the English notions of "mind" (the seat of thought), "heart" (the seat of emotions), and "spirit" (the quality of life, meaning, and value). Significant to our study is the fact that *kokoro* is not just a human characteristic. For the ancient Japanese, things have *kokoro* (*mono no kokoro*), as do "events" or "words" *(koto no kokoro).* Hence, in giving this native word a Chinese character, the Japanese used either *shin* (the "mind" of "no-mind") or *i* ("intention" or "meaning").

Within these terms and characters, we can glimpse an aesthetic and spiritual metaphysics. In the poetic context, if the poet has a genuine heart *(makoto no kokoro),* the event *(koto)* expresses its *kokoro* as the poet's words (also *koto*). In this way, the *kokoro* of things *(mono no kokoro)* and the *kokoro* of the poet *(makoto no kokoro)* express themselves through each other. The "word-event" *(koto)* sprouts its "leaves" (*kotoba,* "word-event" + "leaves," the ordinary Japanese word for "words" or "language.")[14]

The significance of this early understanding of creativity clearly underlies the traditional aesthetic that Zen Buddhism eventually preserves and enhances. An irony, however, is the emergence of a new traditional Japanese poetic term (used by Fujiwara Teika in the thirteenth century, for example): *ushin.* The term literally means "having *kokoro,*" or "being mindful," but when written in characters, it is visually the opposite of *mushin,* "no-mind." Both terms exclude bringing one's own ego-centered presuppositions to the experience of reality. They advocate letting the experienced phenomena express themselves naturally through one's creative expression. Hence, despite their graphic appearance when written, they are virtually synonymous. Only context can indicate when the terms *ushin* and *mushin* are being used as positive or negative aesthetic terms.

Perhaps the most important point to make about the influence of this earlier tradition on Japanese Zen is that it becomes a vehicle for strengthening the importance of the affective component of creativity. Indian Buddhism generally strove for the elimination of all emotions. Emotions, it was said, are the attempts of the ego to attach itself to things that are ultimately impermanent. That very attachment is the cause for human suffering and must be eradicated. Hence, the enlightened mind is one of equanimity and perfect tranquility. Only a philosopher the caliber of Arthur Schopenhauer could generate an aesthetic out of such austerity. In a significant sense, therefore, there is no distinctively Buddhist aesthetic in India.

The East Asian Buddhist tradition, of course, is different. In China, the Chan tradition especially became known for its impact on the arts. As we saw, masters like Linji called on their disciples to manifest their enlightenment through their whole selves. In grabbing his student by the throat, he was hardly looking for equanimity or tranquility. He was instead demanding a response that would show the courage and spontaneous energy he associated with the true person without status. Hence, emotions revealing uncertainty, lack of conviction, and needless rumination were chastised, but those revealing the egoless confidence of conviction and creativity were admired.

My impression is that the Japanese Zen tradition took this trend a step further. From the ancient Japanese theory of poetics, one could argue that the state of aesthetic sensitivity yields no emotion arising from the ego. Emotion is in the *kokoro,* something personal yet also something objectively there in the things themselves. Hence, genuine emotions are not ego-centered.

The Japanese aesthetic of the cherry blossoms serves as a good example. Presumably, an Indian Buddhist would say that one should feel no emotion at seeing the petals blow away in the wind. The blossoms can be appreciated for their beauty as they bloom, but having no attachment to such ephemeral things, an enlightened person should feel no regret or sadness at seeing them perish. All things come into being and expire. Nothing is permanent. From the Japanese standpoint, however, the pathos of the passing away of something beautiful is objective, not merely the expression of a human caprice fueled by the desire for permanence. As the Heian period term *mono no aware* suggests, the "sadness" or "poignancy" *(aware)* is of the "thing" *(mono)*. It is not a projection of the ego. In fact, only a "heartless person" *(kokoro naki hito)*, a person without *ushin* who is caught up in his or her own world, would be so out-of-touch with such phenomena as to be untouched by them.

In this way, the Japanese Buddhist tradition developed a tendency to evaluate the emotion not on what it was, but how it arose, and how it was experienced. It is not surprising in this light that the Japanese Zen tradition could produce poet-monks like Ikkyū who could write poetry about his amorous experiences.[15] The genuineness of the emotion, not the species of emotion, was critical in his Zen aesthetic. Such a phenomenon would be quite foreign not only to Indian Buddhism but even to Chinese Chan. This again shows the impact of Japanese culture on the development of Zen.

Japanese Zen and Artistic Self-Expression

With our discussion of Chinese Chan and the spiritual-aesthetic dimensions of ancient Japanese culture as background, we can now sketch our portrait of the Zen person as artist. To understand Zen artistry, we must come to grips with Zen anthropology. As we have seen, for the Zen tradition, artistic expression only has value as Zen art if it is a self-expression of the Zen artist's enlightenment. So, we must turn to the Zen view of personhood, enlightenment, and self-expression. This is, of course, a broad topic, but we can use the materials already covered to present a brief account.[16]

Training in a Japanese Zen monastery is designed in various ways to take the students out of the contexts through which they have previously learned to understand themselves and the world. Entry into the monastery severs the web of familial and social ties normally so important to the definition of self in Japanese society. Furthermore, the master challenges the student to understand the world not through thinking but through without-thinking. Through objectless meditation, students learn to soften the outlines of their cognitively structured gestalts of reality. The attempt is to see the world anew, as if for the first time.

There are various techniques a master may use to help the student do this, and each tradition and each individual master may have a particular trademark. A common motif, however, is the master's continuously challenging the student with the unexpected. As long as the student reacts as if surprised, then the master (and eventually the student) knows the unexpected was indeed unexpected. Yet, for the student to experience something as unexpected, there must have been expectations. Where there are expectations, experience is being prepackaged. The what-is is being experienced as what one expects it to be, rather than as what it is.

This approach to enlightenment is basically apophatic. It denies the value of ordinary mental constructs and undermines them. But, we may ask (as the Zen tradition itself had to ask eventually), how do we prevent the abandonment of thought from becoming a reckless abandon? How do we know the questioning of rigidity will not degenerate into wanton antinomianism? When does no-mind become mere mindlessness? How can the quest for emptiness not degenerate into mere nihility or nihilism?[17] This leads us to look for the positive aspect of enlightenment.

By freeing disciples from the rigid constructs inherited from their pasts, the master demands that the no-mind become a functional mind. Detachment is the prerequisite, not replacement, for involvement. Zen has a metaphysical conviction that when things are experienced fully with the heart and mind emptied of prejudice and egoism, they will convey their own appropriateness. Things have their own *kokoro*. At the same time, the Zen person has his or her own *kokoro* as well. In the resonance between the two, expression takes place.

In an attempt to be more philosophically precise, we can state the point in this way. The raw "given," as most Western phenomenologists would agree, is meaningless. (In the first volume of *Ideas*, Husserl calls it the "indeterminable X.") It is not that the given is nothing, only that, as just the given, it is "empty" of meaning. Zen suggests that meaning is a construction out of that emptiness *(mu)*. Yet, (in contrast with some deconstructionists) Zen maintains that meaning is not an arbitrary construction. It arises out of the contextualizing of the rawly given. The context itself takes form in the interplay between the possibilities within the experiencer and within the givenness.

As Dōgen said in his fascicle *Genjōkōan,* when we convey ourselves to things, that is delusion. When we let things convey themselves to us, that is enlightenment or, to use his preferred term, "authentication." This does not mean that the self does nothing. Without the self, there can be no formation of context. Expression demands not merely the *kokoro* of things but also the *kokoro* of persons. Yet, we cannot simply bring our contexts to the experience of the world. If we do, we will experience only what we expect. There will be no creative expression. We must let the things come to us, and in our openness to them, allow the context to take form. To consider this theory in a different way, let us examine one more traditional Zen story.

The master held up his staff and demanded a response to his question, "What is this?" He glowered at them and tied the knot of the double bind. "If you say a staff, you are attached to words. If you say not-a-staff, you are attached to nothingness. So, without saying it is a staff or not-a-staff, what is it?" A disciple jumped up, grabbed the staff and whacked the master with it. The master smiled.

As Ludwig Wittgenstein said, "the meaning is the use." The master had snatched away the normal contexts giving the staff meaning. The given stood there in its raw nakedness, shaking in the master's fist, an indeterminable X vibrating in the void. The student accepted it for what it was and found himself in a context in which that X and he himself would find their self-expression together. He did not have the power to simply stipulate a meaning for the stick. If that were true, he could, like Moses standing before Pharaoh, have made the staff into a snake.

Yet, the stick itself, because of the master's theft of the expected contexts, also had no intrinsic meaning. The meaning arose in the action that made the stick a stick and the disciple a Buddha. As the gardener helps the rock be where it wants to be and belongs, the disciple had made an expression where both he and the stick belonged.

Such is the basic principle of Zen artistry. Whatever the eventual artwork might be—a rock garden, a painting, a poem, a tea ceremony, a movement of the sword—without that element of artistry, it may be Japanese, and it may be art, but it cannot be Zen.

Notes

1. As a technical term for Zen painting, the word *zenga* seems to be primarily a modern (post-1868) convention of cultural historians. This suggests that most producers of "Zen art" in history did not explicitly consider themselves to be "Zen artists."

2. See his essay, "The Origin of the Work of Art" in Martin Heidegger, *Basic Writings* (New York: Harper & Row, 1977).

3. Suzuki, D. T. *Zen and Japanese Culture.* (Princeton: Princeton University Press, 1959).

4. Translated from the Chinese text found in: Akizuki Ryōmin's *Rinzairoku* series: *Zen no goroku.* (Tokyo: Chikuma shobō, 1972), 10: 19. For an English translation of the whole work, see Ruth F. Sasaki's *The Record of Lin-chi* (Kyoto: Institute for Zen Studies, 1975), 3.

5. For an English translation of this central text in the Chan tradition, see Philip B. Yampolsky's *Platform Sūtra of the Six Patriarch* (New York: Columbia University Press, 1967).

6. For an English translation, see Daisetz Teitaro Suzuki's *Laṅkāvatāra Sūtra* (London: Routledge and Sons, 1932).

7. For a discussion of this functional mind, see Daisetsu Teitaro Suzuki, *The Zen Doctrine of No-mind* (London: Rider, 1959), 75.

8. Shinichi Hisamatsu, *Zen and the Fine Arts* (New York: Kodansha International, 1982).

9. For more details on how Kūkai's esoteric philosophy gave a foundation to many assumptions in the indigenous spiritual tradition, see my "Kūkai (774-835): Philosophizing in the Archaic," in Frank E. Reynolds and David Tracy, eds., *Myth and Philosophy* (Albany: State University of New York Press, 1990), 131-50.

10. See Tamaki's essay "On the Fundamental Idea Underlying Japanese Buddhism," *Philosophical Studies of Japan* 11 (1975): 17-39.

11. For a good discussion of the poet-monk Saigyō's view of nature as exemplifying this tradition, see William R. LaFleur's "Saigyō and the Buddhist Value of Nature," *History of Religions* 13, no. 2 (Nov. 1973): 93-128 and 13, no. 3 (Feb. 1973): 227-48.

12. This was expressed by the phrase *sansuikyō,* the "mountains and waters sūtras," in the *Shōbōgenzō* fascicle by that name.

13. See my "Truth-Words: Kūkai's Theory of Interpretation," in Donald Lopez, ed., *Buddhist Hermeneutics* (Honolulu: University of Hawaii Press, 1988).

14. This traditional Japanese understanding of poetic language is the background for Martin Heidegger's "Conversation with a Japanese" in his work *On the Way to Language.*

15. For a study of Ikkyū, see James H. Sanford's *Zen Man Ikkyū* (Chico, Calif.: Scholars Press, 1981).

16. For a fuller account. see T. P. Kasulis, *Zen Action/Zen Person* (Honolulu: University Hawaii Press, 1981).

17. For a philosophically sophisticated and insightful examination of this issue for Buddhism, see Nishitani Keiji's *Religion and Nothingness* (Berkeley: University of California Press, 1982).

14

Perceptions of Self in Modern Japanese Literature
Two Adaptations of Classical Chinese Historiography

Nobuko Miyama Ochner

Using perceptions of self as a means of inquiry seems to be premised on the assumption that one's sense of "self" is shaped by different forces, both external and internal, and that by looking at the effects of these forces we can find the nature of these forces. As a starting point of my inquiry, I take a position such as the one espoused by A. Irving Hallowell in *Culture and Experience* (1967) that the concept of self differs according to the specific society and culture: "[T]he individual's self-image and his interpretation of his own experience cannot be divorced from the concept of the self that is characteristic of his society."[1]

It is an acceptable enough position. Yet it immediately raises a question, particularly in the case of a relatively complex society such as modern Japan, as to how one might conceive of what is characteristic of that society. The terms "culture" and "society" are used in an almost interchangeable manner by Hallowell, when he states that the nature of the self is a "culturally identifiable variable."[2] Perhaps the term "culture" refers to the overall attributes of a society. A classic definition of culture is that of Edward Burnett Tylor, in his *Primitive Culture* (1871), that "Culture . . . is that complex whole which includes knowledge, belief, art, morals, law, custom, and any other capabilities and habits acquired by man as a member of society." It further defines culture as "behaviour peculiar to *Homo sapiens,* together with material objects used as an integral part of this behaviour; specifically, culture consists of language, ideas, beliefs, customs, codes, institutions, tools, techniques, works of art, rituals, ceremonies, and so on." Clearly, culture is a manner in which society exhibits its uniqueness.

If the nature of the self is, as Hallowell puts it, a "culturally identifiable variable," then by examining the self-perception of someone in a particular culture, we may learn about some aspects of the characteristics of that culture. This approach, however, has inherent problems. For example, a question may be asked: how much is one bound by one's culture? What about the case of someone who moves from one cultural sphere to another, as in the case of immigrants? [A comparative study of Japanese and Korean immigrants to the United States, conducted by George A. De Vos, Curtis A. Vaughn, and Dorothy M. Holly (1989), addresses this question. Cultural embeddedness of self-perception is also the central topic in Alan Roland, "Selves in Motion: An Indian Japanese Comparison" (1989).[3]] Which culture forms his or her perception of self? If we have the sustained sense of self regardless of the culture surrounding us, then something at our core of self must resist straightforward influence from the outside. Clearly, individual differences need to be considered. At any rate, how much of our sense of self is culturally variable is a difficult question to answer, especially if we deal in generalities.

Despite such reservations, I believe that it is worthwhile to investigate specific cases of self-perception as given in the depiction of individual characters in works of literature; for in the specific cases narrated in stories or novels, internal and external forces that shape the self may be viewed somewhat more distinctly.

Before proceeding further, my choice of the two particular narratives should be explained briefly. It would seem that an examination of perceptions of self in modern Japanese literature may be conducted more profitably among the works of *shishōsetsu*, the so-called I-novel, or personal narratives, rather than among the works of *rekishi shōsetsu* (historical fiction),[4] since *shishōsetsu* treats the author's personal life almost exclusively, with only a thin disguise such as the use of a fictitious name. Therefore, my choice of the two fictional narratives, "Kirin" (Kylin, 1910) by Tanizaki Jun'ichirō (1886–1965) and *Deshi* (The disciple, 1943) by Nakajima Atsushi (1909–42), is not intended to be a standard procedure for such an undertaking as this. Nevertheless, since the two works "Kirin" and *Deshi* derived their basic material from the same source—namely, the classical Chinese historiography *Shih chi* (Historical records, ca. 91 B.C.) by Ssu-ma Ch'ien (145-ca. 90 B.C.)—it seemed that comparison of their treatment might shed light, in a limited way, on the ways in which the two modern Japanese writers found the significance of the historical anecdote and expressed their understanding of it based partly on their perception of the characters' "self." It is hoped that a limited comparison between the account in the *Shih chi* and the two narratives will clarify the points of differences, which may be attributed partly to culture and partly to individual writers' views of human nature.

The project at hand is a difficult one, because one of the most complex issues in Japanese literature is the role China's literary tradition played in its development.[5] Literally beginning with its script, Japan has been continually borrowing and adapting Chinese writings, especially the classics, including Confucian texts, for more than a millennium. Confucian thought was taught as a part of the basic curriculum at Japanese educational institutions, serving as "the common denominator of education in premodern East Asia."[6] Therefore, trying to separate Chinese elements from purely Japanese elements in a literary adaptation of Chinese historiography is almost an impossible task. It is particularly problematic when concepts of culture are involved. In the case of modern Japanese literature, the question of literary borrowing is further complicated by the continual infusion of Western ideas and literary forms since about the mid-nineteenth century, when Japan ended its nearly two and a half centuries of seclusion policy. Nonetheless, it is encouraging for my present undertaking to note that Wm. Theodore deBary, adding to the above remark on the common Confucian heritage of East Asia, states that "Culturally speaking, this might not keep the diverse peoples of East Asia from each having a different sense of self. . . ."[7] Moreover, Nakane Chie asserts that, despite Japanese willingness to accept change and the apparent superficial change in modern Japan, such a change "has not the slightest effect on the firm persistence of the basic nature and core of personal relations and group dynamics."[8] In other words, certain aspects of Japanese perception of self, as a member of society and a part of the network of personal relations, may be regarded as relatively constant despite overt change. With these views in mind, we may proceed to examine how two modern Japanese writers used classical Chinese historiography in their works.

Historiography and *shōsetsu* in Japanese tradition, and also in East Asian tradition, complement each other. *Shōsetsu,* a term adopted by the pioneer of modern Japanese literary criticism, Tsubouchi Shōyō (1859–1935), to translate the English term "novel," is the Japanese reading of the Chinese term *hsiao shuo* (its literal meaning is "small talk"). In the Confucian view, *hsiao shuo,* or fictional narrative, was generally disparaged as frivolous pursuit, whereas historiography (and poetry) was esteemed as a repository of past wisdom.[9] Official historiography was called *cheng shih* (Japanese: *seishi*) in contradistinction to *pai shih* (Japanese: *haishi*), which were fictitious histories or unofficial histories comprising stories and gossip current among the common people. The *pai shih* gave rise to fictional narratives *(hsiao shuo)*. Therefore, historical writings and fictional narratives are, in a sense, related to one another at their roots. Rather than simply being a representation of past reality, historical fiction often depicts a parallel story of what might have been or what is left unexpressed in historiography.

Tanizaki Jun'ichirō's short story "Kirin" and Nakajima Atsushi's novella *Deshi* both depict the ancient Chinese sage Confucius (551–479 B.C.) but in vastly different ways. Besides deriving their material from Chinese historical writings, most notably the *Shih chi,* the two writers also used the Confucian *Lun yü* (The analects), and *Ch'un ch'iu Tso-shih chuan* (Spring and autumn annals with Commentary by Master Tso; often referred to as the Tso Commentary, ca. fifth century B.C.). Thus, the same historical background, the lifetime of Confucius, forms the time setting in "Kirin" and *Deshi*. In addition, the two stories may be considered somewhat similar in their approach, since the great historical figure Confucius, while being an important character, is not treated as the protagonist upon whom the reader focuses. Instead, Confucius is viewed primarily from the outside.

The short story "Kirin" was first published in the December 1910 issue of the coterie journal *Shinshichō* (New currents of thought), when Tanizaki was twenty-four years old. It was the heyday of naturalism in Japanese literature. This European-inspired literary movement, represented particularly by the works of Emile Zola and the Goncourt brothers, had been introduced to Japan about 1900 and quickly gained popularity in the years following the Russo-Japanese War of 1904–05. Reacting against the romanticism of the 1890s and aiming to move from fancy to reality, Japanese naturalist writers emphasized the frank description of a slice of life, which was often the thinly disguised personal life of the author, rather than the working out of scientific determinism in a large canvas of a society, as in European models. Tanizaki rebelled against the drab ordinariness of such an approach to literature, preferring instead the exotic, the unusual, and the aesthetic. He found the kind of exotic setting he sought in the accounts of the past, either in Japan of the Edo Period (1600–1868), as in "Shisei" (Tattoo, 1910), or in China of the Spring and Autumn Period (770–403 B.C.) as in "Kirin." Although "Kirin" did not attract as much attention as the explicitly sadomasochistic short story "Shisei," which had appeared two months earlier in the same journal, it is nonetheless a seminal work, because its central theme of the overwhelming power of sensual beauty that a domineering woman wielded over a weak man is one of the most prominent recurrent themes in Tanizaki's fiction. Indeed, this theme is repeated even in his last novel, *Fūten rōjin nikki* (Diary of a mad old man, 1962), more than half a century later.

The novella *Deshi* (The disciple) by Nakajima Atsushi was completed in June 1942, when Nakajima was thirty-three years old, and published posthumously in the February 1943 issue of the major literary magazine *Chūō kōron,* just one year after Nakajima's literary début with publication of two short stories titled "Sangetsu ki" (translated as "Tiger-Poet" by Ivan Morris) and "Mojika" (The curse of graphs). Nakajima's fictionalized biography of Robert Louis Stevenson in Samoa, *Hikari to kaze to yume* (Light, wind, and dreams), published in May 1942, had been nominated for the prestigious Akutagawa Prize. The publication of *Deshi* occurred between the first two installments of Tanizaki's novel *Sasameyuki* (The Makioka sisters, 1943–48), in the January and March issues of *Chūō kōron*. By then Tanizaki had achieved the status of a major novelist; therefore, the publication of Nakajima's *Deshi* between the two installments of a novel by Tanizaki indicates the high regard in which the editors of *Chūō kōron* held Nakajima's novella. *Deshi* treated the evolving relationship of Confucius's disciple Tzu-lu to his master over the period of some forty years. The segment that shares the same anecdote as "Kirin," however, is short, occurring close to the midpoint of the novella.

The Chinese historiography *Shih chi* gives the account of discourteous treatment of Confucius by Duke Ling and his consort Nan-tzu in the state of Wei, which occurred during the fourteen-year wandering of Confucius and his followers (*shih-chia* 17, *K'ung Tzu shih-chia* 23). It does so in a characteristically concise manner:

> There was a consort of Duke Ling named Nan-tzu, who sent a message to Confucius: "Those gentlemen of the realm who wish to have friendly association with the master of this state would always meet his consort. She wishes that you meet her."
>
> Although Confucius declined, in the end he was obliged to pay a visit to Nan-tzu. She was behind a thin hanging curtain. Confucius entered the gate, faced north, and performed the formal obeisance. The consort returned a bow. The jewels on her sash jingled. After he left the palace, Confucius said, "At first I declined to meet the lady, but I was obliged to go in for an audience and bow to her." Tzu-lu was not pleased with Confucius's meeting Nan-tzu. Confucius

vowed, saying, "If I have done anything to be blamed for, Heaven would abandon me. Heaven would abandon me."

They had lived in Wei for a little over a month, when Duke Ling went riding in a carriage with his consort, accompanied by the eunuch Yung Ch'ü. On that occasion, they had Confucius ride in a carriage behind them. The party drove around the city. Confucius said, "I am yet to see one who likes virtue as much as he likes women." And, hating Duke Ling, he left Wei and went to Ts'ao.[10]

Such is the bare-bones structure of the anecdote, which is developed by Tanizaki and Nakajima into very different stories.

Since Confucian teaching regarded *hsiao shuo,* or fictional narratives, as frivolous and history (and poetry) as serious and elevated, using material from historiography in a fictional narrative was a way of adding seriousness, weight, and respectability to fictional narratives. Many premodern Chinese stories begin as if they were chronicles, with the specific historical time setting and geographical location stated. This is a technique employed by Tanizaki at the opening of "Kirin." Following a quotation from *The Analects* (18, 5) of a song attributed to Chieh Yü, the madman of Ch'u, warning of the danger of political involvement, the narrative proper of "Kirin" begins simply: "It was the year 493 B.C. in the Western Calendar."[11] "Kirin" comprises eleven short scenes that are almost cinematic in their effect. This effect may be attributable to Tanizaki's abundant use of dialogue. Tanizaki had originally conceived of "Kirin" as a play, and this fact seems to explain why he assigns direct speech not only to the three main characters but also to minor characters.

The first significant scene is the philosophical dialogue with a Taoist sage, whom Confucius's group encounters on their way to the capital of Wei.[12] As noted by the critic Ōshima Maki, their exchange on the relativity of happiness, life, and death is reminiscent of an early scene of Anatole France's novel *Thaïs* (1889), in which the devout monk Paphnutius exchanges religio-philosophical thoughts with an old ascetic.[13] Both Tanizaki's Taoist and France's ascetic claim that they are happy because they have no attachments. Anatole France's works, especially *Thaïs, Balthazar* (1889), and *The Crime of Sylvestre Bonnard* (1881) were introduced to Japan at about this time, and Tanizaki himself counts France among his favorite Western authors.[14] Therefore, we may assume that a parallel exists between a scene from *Thaïs* and one from "Kirin."

Tanizaki then describes the capital city of Wei, starkly contrasting the exhausted and hungry commoners and the sumptuous and resplendent palace of the duke. The duke is weak-willed and ineffectual, being controlled by his beautiful and evil consort Nan-tzu. Tanizaki portrays the duke as a well-meaning ruler in that, when he reviews the domain from the observation platform, he wonders why the countryside is barren. This scene recalls a *chōka* (long poem) from the eighth-century anthology of Japanese poetry, the *Man'yōshū* (Collection of myriad leaves, ca. 759), on the topic of the ruler surveying the land from the hilltop *(kunimi)*.[15] The duke invites Confucius to stay in Wei, so that Confucius may advise him on the way to regulate and enrich the state and control the entire realm. However, in keeping with the Confucian tradition, Tanizaki describes Confucius as telling the duke that, if he truly wishes to acquire the virtue *(te;* in Japanese, *toku)* of the ruler, he must overcome his own private desires—in other words, to practice self- discipline and self-cultivation. This is the principal means of improving oneself and also a requisite of good rulers.[16]

Following Confucius's advice, the duke rectifies his conduct by staying away from Nan-tzu and paying attention to the work of governing. As a result, when he surveys his land again, Duke Ling is rewarded by the pleasing sight of his people prospering and praising his virtue. Duke Ling believes that he can become a new person, one who is in possession of self and who can discipline himself to follow the moral precepts of Confucius. He confidently tells Nan-tzu that, instead of worshipping her beauty as man worships a deity, henceforth he will love her as a husband loves his wife. Nan-tzu is angered by her loss of control over her husband. She decides to reassert her power over him. She mocks him, saying that he is not so strong as he thinks, and she declares that she will win him back from under the influence of Confucius and even tempt the sage by her charms. Despite his resolute words, Duke Ling's eyes already express his attraction to her. In this short story, Duke Ling plays an important, though largely passive, role, since he is the object of the psychological tug-of-war between Confucius and Nan-tzu. In the portrayal of Duke Ling, we see an example of Tanizaki's view of the self as being pulled between lofty moral aspirations and the human desire for sensuous beauty.

Thus, with a scheme in mind, Nan-tzu summons Confucius to an audience with her. Unlike the brief account of the *Shih chi,* Tanizaki's version of this confrontation between Nan-tzu and Confucius comprises the heart of the story. It is Nan-tzu who takes the lead in this scene. First, Nan-tzu points out her resemblance to the beautiful and cruel women from previous ages, asking Confucius to tell her if there had been a woman more beautiful than she since the beginning of history. Tanizaki describes her gorgeous appearance, comparing her to the bright sun. Confucius denies any knowledge of beautiful people. Next, Nan-tzu mentions the unusual and strange objects that she owns, adding, however, that she has seen neither the kylin (a Chinese unicorn) that is said to appear when great sages are born nor the seven apertures that are believed to exist on the chest of a sage. She would like to see those apertures on Confucius's chest. To this request, Confucius replies sternly that he knows no unusual or strange things, merely what ordinary people have to know.

Then, Nan-tzu tries to tempt Confucius by appealing to his senses. In succession, she has servants bring seven kinds each of rare incense, wondrous liquor, and unusual morsels of meat. The use of specific details—color, scent, shape, places of origin—creates the characteristically Tanizakian richness of texture. Obviously, Tanizaki is concerned here exclusively with sensory pleasures. Throughout this temptation scene, Confucius's expression becomes increasingly dark and stern. Yet, Nan-tzu declares with a smile that his face is becoming brighter and more beautiful. This ironic statement may be interpreted as suggesting that Confucius and Nan-tzu stand at the polar opposites and what is perceived as "bad" by Confucius is perceived as "good" by Nan-tzu. It may also be regarded as Nan-tzu's deliberate decision to ignore Confucius's reaction and assert herself.

The crowning touch of Nan-tzu's strategy clearly illustrates Tanizaki's so-called diabolism and aestheticism in his early career. Nan-tzu shows Confucius a courtyard full of mutilated prisoners: some are branded, pilloried, or chained, and some have had their noses and feet severed. They are cruelly punished by Nan-tzu mainly for having offended her, for instance, by attracting the duke's amorous attention. As Nan-tzu delightedly looks on the scene, she is described as being "as beautiful as a poet and as solemn as a philosopher" (p. 26). Tanizaki does not describe Confucius's reaction to this scene at all, thereby producing the effect that the sage is powerless to change Nan-tzu.

This figure of Nan-tzu is also reminiscent of Salomé in the play by Oscar Wilde (1854–1900): the two female characters share the same will for dominance. Salomé demands that the prophet Jokanaan be beheaded, because he has spurned her advances three times.[17] Wilde's play *Salomé* (1891) was just introduced to Japan through translation (1907–9) by Mori Ōgai (1862–1922), and Tanizaki in his early career is known to have been influenced by Wilde.[18]

In the next scene, Tanizaki returns to the *Shih chi* account, in which Confucius is made to ride through the city behind the duke and Nan-tzu, in a public display of his demeaned status. Tanizaki adds the onlookers' comments that the virtue of the sage is apparently unable to check Nan-tzu's tyranny and that her arrogant face has never looked more beautiful. To emphasize the victory of Nan-tzu, Tanizaki describes in the subsequent scene how the duke returns to Nan-tzu's embrace; that is, he is under the dominance of her sensual beauty and powerful will, despite his hatred of her evil nature. Confucius and his disciples leave Wei the morning after his public humiliation.

Thus, Duke Ling's perception of his self as that of a wise and morally upright ruler suffers a crushing blow. He realizes that he is weak after all, that he cannot resist, let alone overcome, Nan-tzu's attraction to his senses. Despite the moral education by Confucius, and the duke's temporary success in self-discipline, in the end the weak-willed ruler succumbs to the urging of the flesh, a base part of his nature.

Tanizaki's portrayal of Confucius is thus one-sided. He obviously wished to emphasize the triumph of beauty over virtue in the tug of war over the all too human Duke Ling. In the process, the character of Nan-tzu, the prototypical Tanizaki femme fatale, emerges more forcefully than the virtuous Confucius. It is a natural result of Tanizaki's artistic predilection. His use of Chinese historiography is thus essentially to provide the exotic background for his tale illustrating the tenets of his own aestheticism. In a rather simple, schematic manner, Tanizaki's story illuminates the external forces influencing the shaping of Duke Ling's "self" as well as the internal condition of his own nature that decides the final choice.

In contrast to the rather free adaptation Tanizaki made of the *Shih chi* anecdote, Nakajima's *Deshi,* notwithstanding its somewhat episodic structure, closely follows the individual episodes of the Chinese account and focuses on the evolving human relationship of the disciple Tzu-lu to his teacher Confucius. Nakajima was familiar with Confucian classics and Chinese historiography, since he grew up in a family steeped in classical Chinese studies, and in his adaptation Nakajima generally shows a strong respect for the text. The novella depicts how Tzu-lu changes from an impetuous young man who loves fighting and who scorns learning to a true Confucian "gentleman" *(chün tzu;* in Japanese, *kunshi)*[19] as a result of his meeting Confucius.

In describing the relationship of the disciple to the master, Nakajima projects some of his own thoughts onto Tzu-lu. An example of such a projection may be seen in Tzu-lu's admiration for Confucius. What impresses Tzu-lu about Confucius is the well-roundedness of his personality; all of his faculties are well-developed and in perfect balance with one another. This admiration for well-roundedness is connected to Nakajima's admiration for Goethe—a theme that recurs in other works by Nakajima. Tzu-lu's complete admiration of his master sometimes makes him rely totally on Confucius's judgment. Nakajima compares Tzu-lu's relationship of spiritual dependence on Confucius to a child's dependence on his mother.[20] We may regard this relationship of dependence (or *amae*) as a Japanese element,[21] since there is no such mention in the *Shih chi* account. Despite his dependence, Tzu-lu does not allow even his mentor to alter his ethical sense, the pure and simple feeling that accompanies all things good. Accordingly, he selects only those teachings of Confucius that strengthen it. This ethical sense lies at the core of Tzu-lu's being, or self, and regulates all his basic moral choices.

Historically, it is true that Tzu-lu was the most devoted disciple of Confucius, following his master regardless of the changes of fortune, until near the end of some forty years of their association. Nakajima calls such an attitude in Tzu-lu "*botsu rigai sei*" (disinterestedness), a quality so rare that most people in China regard it as incomprehensible foolishness; however, Confucius has discerned the superior virtue of this disinterestedness. This may be regarded as an example of Nakajima projecting his value system onto both Tzu-lu and Confucius, for, according to D. C. Lau, in the Confucian view, "being moral has nothing to do with self-interest" and "there is no relationship whatsoever between them, either positive or negative."[22]

One of Tzu-lu's ideas that change under the influence of his master is his instinctive dislike of form. At first Tzu-lu scorns even outward expressions of filial piety as being hypocritical. However, when his zither playing is criticized for its expression of spiritual roughness, he realizes that form is an expression of content, or spirit. Even though Tzu-lu is unable to change his music through fasting and contemplation, he has made an important discovery. Another change that occurs in Tzu-lu concerns his anger at the indifference of heaven that permits injustice. Through his association with Confucius, Tzu lu comes to understand his teacher's role as the model for the world to emulate for all posterity. With such a view of one's own position in history, a view of a self that simultaneously exists within time and transcends time, Confucius is able to endure and rise above the present injustices meted out to him. Nakajima adds that, because of his extremely simple affection for his master, Tzu-lu alone among the many disciples comprehends Confucius's historical role and sense of mission. Before Tzu-lu gains such an understanding, however, many vicissitudes befall Confucius's group during their fourteen-year journey. The anecdote involving the duke of Wei and his consort Nan-tzu is among those unpleasant events.

Unlike Tanizaki, who particularized the episode with so many sensuous details, Nakajima chose to narrate the event concisely in a manner closer to the account in the *Shih chi.* One of the conspicuous differences between Nakajima's style in this section and Tanizaki's style is the complete absence of independent dialogue in the former. Nakajima incorporates what would otherwise be a dialogue into the narration. The effect such a style produces is one of narratorial distance. The characters and events narrated in such a manner do not have the sense of nearness to the reader. We surmise that this distancing is intentional, for there are other sections of the novella, though not many, that contain direct speech. Perhaps for this reason, the effect of reading *Deshi* is sometimes compared to viewing a mural.[23]

Nakajima uses a three-part structure to narrate the short episode that comprises chapter 9 of the sixteen-chapter novella. The first part tells of Duke Ling's weakness, his consort Nan-tzu's licentiousness and willfulness, and Nan-tzu's summons to Confucius for an audience, followed by a brief description of their meeting. In contrast to Tanizaki's elaborate description in "Kirin," of Nan-tzu's beauty and her wiles, Nakajima closely follows the *Shih chi* account, virtually citing from it: "Since there was no other way, Confucius paid a visit to her. Nan-tzu, seated behind a thin hanging curtain, received him. It is written that when Nan-tzu returned a bow in response to Confucius, who had faced north and performed the formal deep obeisance, the jewels on her sash jingled."[24] Such is the extent of Nakajima's description of Nan-Tzu in this scene. Clearly, Nakajima is not interested in depicting Nan-tzu's beauty. Nakajima's Nan-tzu does not even try to charm Confucius. As for Duke Ling, his role is even more limited in *Deshi;* he appears only in the scene of the carriage ride. Instead of elaborate description, Nakajima essentially follows the Chinese account in giving the reactions of Tzu-lu and Confucius to this audience with Nan-tzu; however, he amplifies the thoughts and emotions of Tzu-lu. Tzu-lu is displeased with this meeting, not because he thinks that Confucius may be deceived by Nan-tzu's charm but because the thought of his morally pure master bowing to a wanton woman is intolerable to him. Confucius observes with mixed feelings how the child in Tzu-lu persists side by side with his mature practical ability as an administrator. Thus, we see that Nakajima emphasizes and amplifies the internal reactions of the two men instead of Nan-tzu's external action.

Interestingly, Nakajima elaborates the scene of Confucius being made to ride behind the duke and Nan Tzu; whereas Tanizaki's account is closer to the *Shih chi* in its brevity. Nakajima sets up the scene in such a way that a silent but open confrontation takes place in public. Duke Ling invites Confucius to ride with him through the capital of Wei and discuss various matters; when the duke and Confucius go to the carriage, they find Nan-tzu already seated where Confucius was supposed to sit. Angry that she is left out by her husband, she has deliberately defied the duke's authority. Unable to tell Nan-tzu that she is not wanted, the embarrassed Duke Ling silently points to the second, shabby carriage. Waiting along the street, Tzu-lu sees this public humiliation of Confucius and attempts to strike the offenders; however, he is held back by two of his fellow disciples.

The closing part of this chapter in *Deshi,* consisting of two brief sentences, is stylistically similar to both the *Shih chi* passage and Tanizaki's rendition. The difference is that in the *Shih chi* it is stated that Confucius hated Duke Ling; however, neither Tanizaki nor Nakajima make any references to Confucius's hatred. It seems that, to modern Japanese writers' sensibilities, great sages such as Confucius should not be described as harboring an extreme, negative emotion. Such concurrences of views notwithstanding, the overall differences of treatment of the *Shih chi* material in "Kirin" and *Deshi* are considerable. The chief reason for such differences lies in the authors' apparent intent. While the primary focus of Tanizaki's "Kirin" is on the vivid description of the beautiful and wicked Nan-tzu with her scheming and domineering ways, in Nakajima's *Deshi* the Nan-tzu episode is simply one of many cases of the ruler's unwillingness to adopt Confucius's political philosophy. Nakajima's primary interest lies in the "education" of Tzu-lu: how the influence of Confucius's teaching interacted with the innate qualities of the disciple.

Nakajima shows a culmination of this gradual evolution and "dialectic" between self and other (in the form of external influences) by describing how Tzu-lu dies. At about age fifty, Tzu-lu is recommended by Confucius to serve the most powerful statesman of Wei, and he proves his administrative abilities. Duke Ling had died nearly a decade earlier. When the powerful statesman dies, however, the complex political situation of Wei finally results in a coup d'état. The ruling duke flees, and Tzu-lu's employer, the young son of the deceased statesman, is held captive by the rebels. Tzu-lu follows the dictates of his ethical sense in remaining loyal to his beleaguered employer, and he dies fighting, almost as a Japanese samurai might. Just before he dies he picks up his Confucian hat that had fallen to the ground, puts it on correctly, and shouts with his last breath, "Look! The true gentleman dies—with his hat on correctly."[25] In the *Shih chi* account, Tzu-lu is described as simply stating that a true gentleman keeps his hat on even in death. Thus, this preoccupation of Tzu-lu with the correct placement of his hat acquires a special significance. This is particularly pointed contrast when juxtaposed with Tzu-lu's appearance at the time of his first meeting with Confucius, because, in a manner befitting his love of fighting, the young Tzu-lu had worn his cap in a "slouching" position. (Nakajima derived this description from *Chuang Tzu,* chapter 30, entitled "Discoursing on Swords."[26]) Since Confucius's teaching made Tzu-lu realize that form is a manifestation of content, Tzu-lu's insistence on wearing his hat correctly signifies that he regards himself a true gentleman in spirit. This is an instance of Nakajima's careful and subtle alteration of details in order to express his view that Tzu-lu's manner of death represents the summary statement of the development of his "self." In a sense, Tzu-lu makes a positive choice to die for the sake of loyalty. By portraying Tzu-lu as choosing to define his life by his action in a world that does not make sense or guarantee justice, Nakajima imparts a "bright" quality to the work, despite its tragic ending.

When Confucius hears the news of the coup d'état in Wei, he predicts that Tzu-lu will die. When he learns that his prediction has proved true, Confucius stands still for some time and then tears stream down his cheeks. When he finds that Tzu-lu's corpse had been subjected to the humiliation of preservation by salt, Confucius has all salted food in the household discarded and will not allow any salted meat on the table thereafter. Nakajima thus describes Confucius's reaction to Tzu-lu's death in accordance with the account in the historical writings, simply giving observable facts, without delving into the mind of the sage. Paradoxically, by stating facts only, the restrained narrative heightens the drama of human emotions.

Nakajima uses Chinese historiography, as well as many passages from *The Analects,* in telling the story of Tzu-lu's life; in the process, a composite image of Confucius as a great philosopher and human being also emerges. Nonetheless, the focus of attention is not on Confucius but on Tzu-lu as he develops and changes.

What can be said about perception of self in *Deshi?* According to Nakajima's view, the part of Tzu-lu's self that remains constant is his ethical sense, or sense of righteousness. (It appears to be analogous to the Chinese concept of the nature of *i-li,* rightness and principle, even though the Japanese reading of the same compound, *giri,* signifies a very different matter.) It is what gives him a simple sense of pleasure when he encounters good. Takie Sugiyama Lebra, in her comparative study titled "Compensative Justice and Moral Investment among Japanese, Chinese, and Koreans," finds that "Japanese tend to seek compensation for moral or immoral action in the inner state of feeling."[27] In this respect, when Nakajima interprets Tzu-lu's "core of being," or an aspect of self, as an ethical sense that is similar to a feeling of pleasure accompanying all things good, he may be showing an influence of Japanese culture.

The manner in which Tzu-lu displays the concrete manifestation of his ethical sense is his steadfast loyalty to his employer in time of danger. Even though loyalty (Chinese: *chung*) was one of the virtues espoused by the Confucian school of thought, it was not the most important. By emphasizing Tzu-lu's loyalty, Nakajima's work appeals to Japanese readers, since loyalty is one of the most fundamental characteristics of valued human relationship in Japanese society. In her study of Japanese social organization, Nakane Chie describes Japanese society as a vertically ordered one, and she states that in such a vertical personal relationship between self and other (superiors or subordinates), "Protection is repaid with dependence, affection with loyalty."[28] In the case of Tzu-lu, his loyalty to his employer seems rather misplaced, since there is no indication either in the *Shih chi* or in *Deshi* that Tzu-lu had any emotional ties with the son of the deceased statesman of Wei. It is rather the loyalty to the specific relationship of lord and retainer. However, precisely because there is no significant emotional tie, Tzu-lu's action illustrates his disinterestedness, an ability to view situations without regard to personal advantage or disadvantage. In such a perspective, self and others are on an equal footing. Nakajima expressed his admiration for Tzu-lu who, in Nakajima's view, possessed this quality. If, as D. C. Lau has explained, being moral has nothing to do with self-interest, then this conception of Tzu-lu's disinterestedness as a rare virtue is not a traditional Confucian view but an expression of Nakajima's own value system. The Japanese tendency to admire the courage and nobility of those who sacrifice themselves to a cause, a tendency to admire the disadvantaged heroes *(hōgan biiki)*, may be operating here as well. In any event, the strength of Tzu-lu's conviction and his integrity as depicted in the novella are still capable of deeply moving the reader today.

The part of Tzu-lu's self that changes is, as discussed above, his attitude toward form. Nakajima describes how Tzu-lu at first dislikes "form," including the study of rites (Chinese: *li*) and outward expressions of filial piety. However, when his zither playing is criticized for its roughness, expressing the spiritual roughness of the player, Tzu-lu begins to realize the inseparable connection between form and spirit. Tzu-lu eventually accepts Confucius's belief that "true attitudes must find public expression in observable, appropriate forms."[29] Form authenticates the inner quality or feelings. In this respect, Tzu-lu's natural inclination has been changed through nurture—his education.

Tzu-lu's manner of death thus signifies that, to a certain extent, he has cultivated himself and now regards himself as a true gentleman *(chun tzu)*. It also signifies that for all his self-cultivation and education—learning of the golden mean, the importance of moderation, and the fact that even the act of dying for a just cause must have a proper time and place to be regarded as true courage—all such teachings of Confucius were of no avail when they conflicted with the dictates of Tzu-lu's inner self. Tzu-lu followed his nature in choosing to die fighting.

In spite of many differences in treatment and emphases, concepts of self in Tanizaki's "Kirin" and Nakajima's *Deshi* have a point of similarity. Duke Ling in "Kirin" is a weak-willed sensualist who succumbs to his nature despite higher moral aspirations. Tzu-lu, on the other hand, is a strong-willed, morally upright, loyal scholar-administrator who follows the dictates of his innate ethical sense in choosing to die for the sake of loyalty. The two modern Japanese writers' perceptions of man's self are similar in that, in the final reckoning, the nature of the characters has more power than their nurture in directing their courses of action.

Since the characters and the original anecdote are derived from the classical Chinese historiography, it is difficult to state clearly to what extent the influence of Japanese culture is at work in shaping the perception of self in these two modern adaptations. However, it is surely significant that Tanizaki and Nakajima selected these specific characters to portray in their works. Perhaps they found affinity for or an interest in these characters, who, despite opposing influences, followed their natural predilections. Following the flow of nature is certainly one of the characteristics of the Japanese.

Notes

This article is an expanded, revised, and refocused study of the two literary works treated earlier in my article titled "History and Fiction: Portrayals of Confucius by Tanizaki Jun'ichirō and Nakajima Atsushi," in Jean Toyama and Nobuko Ochner, eds., *Literary Relations East and West: Selected Essays,* Literary Studies East and West, vol. 4 (Honolulu: College of Languages, Linguistics and Literature, University of Hawaii at Manoa, and the East-West Center, 1990), 68-79.

1. A. Irving Hallowell, *Culture and Experience* (New York: Schocken Books, 1967), 76.

2. Ibid.

3. George A. De Vos, Curtis A. Vaughn, and Dorothy M. Holly, "Cultural Continuities: The Relationship Between Social Status, Family Interaction and Achievement Motivation," unpublished MS dated 7 August 1989; Alan Roland, "Selves in Motion: An Indian-Japanese Comparison," a paper presented at the "Conference on Perceptions of Self: China, India and Japan," held at the East-West Center, Honolulu, Hawaii, 14-18 August 1989.

4. The term "fiction" is used here in a conventional sense, i.e., as the narrative literature of basically imaginative variety. It is intended to be a rough English equivalent of the term *shōsetsu* (an inclusive term for short stories and novels), even though, strictly speaking, the two terms are not interchangeable, because a *shōsetsu* may be almost completely factual.

5. This Sino-Japanese literary relationship is treated extensively in David Pollack, *The Fracture of Meaning: Japan's Synthesis of China from the Eighth through the Eighteenth Centuries* (Princeton: Princeton University Press, 1986).

6. Wm. Theodore deBary, *East Asian Civilizations: A Dialogue in Five Stages* (Cambridge: Harvard University Press, 1988), 62.

7. Ibid., 63.

8. Chie Nakane, *Japanese Society* (Berkeley and Los Angeles: University of California Press, 1970), 148.

9. deBary, *East Asian Civilizations* 94; D. C. Lau, Introduction to *The Analects (Lun yü),* trans. D. C. Lau (Hong Kong: The Chinese University Press, 1979), xl.

10. Shiba Sen (Ssu-ma Ch'ien), *Shiki (Shih chi,* Historical records), *seika (shih-chia,* hereditary houses) 17. 23; rendition of *shih-chia* as "hereditary houses" follows the practice of Burton Watson in *Ssu-ma Ch'ien: Grand Historian of China* (New York: Columbia University Press, 1958), 104. However, unless otherwise noted, the English translations of quoted passages, including this one, are mine.

11. Tanizaki Jun'ichirō, "Kirin," in *Tanizaki Jun'ichirō zenshū,* vol. 1 (Tokyo: Chūō Kōron-sha, 1957), 15. All subsequent references to "Kirin" will be from this edition.

12. The writer Akutagawa Ryūnosuke (1892-1927) admired the beginning section of "Kirin" for its 'higher' kind of interest and elevated tone; quoted in Makoto Ueda, *Modern Japanese Writers and the Nature of Literature* (Stanford, Calif.: Stanford University Press, 1976), 138-39. Akutagawa does not explain what he means by 'higher' kind of interest, but it seems to be philosophical and moral.

13. Tanizaki, "Kirin," 16-17; Anatole France, *Thaïs,* trans. Basia Gulati (Chicago: University of Chicago Press, 1976), 38-44; Ōshima Maki, "Tanizaki Jun'ichirō no

debyu to Anatōru Furansu: 'Kirin' o meguru shomondai" (Tanizaki Jun'ichirō's début and Anatole France: Questions concerning "Kirin"), in Nihon Bungaku Kenkyū Shiryō Kankōkai, ed., *Tanizaki Jun'ichirō* (Tokyo: Yūseidō, 1973), 164–68.

14. See, for instance, "Taidan Shiga Naoya, Tanizaki Jun'ichirō" (Dialogue between Shiga Naoya and Tanizaki Jun'ichirō), 16 October 1947, reprinted in Kōno Toshirō and Chiba Shunji, eds., *Shiryō: Tanizaki Jun'ichirō* (Tanizaki Jun'ichirō: Sourcebook) (Tokyo: Ōfūsha, 1980), 209–10.

15. This *chōka* by Emperor Jomei (reigned 630–41) is also a poem of praise in the hope of propitiating the deities of the land and of assuring good harvest. *Kunimi* (survey of the realm) was a part of agricultural rites. The poem is as follows:

> Countless are the mountains in Yamato,
> But perfect is the heavenly hill of Kagu;
> When I climb it and survey my realm,
> Over the wide plain the smoke-wreaths rise and rise,
> Over the wide lake the gulls are on the wing;
> A beautiful land it is, the Land of Yamato!

> (MYS 1. 2)

It is from the Nippon Gakujutsu Shinkōkai, trans., *The Manyōshū* (New York: Columbia University Press, 1965), 3.

16. Such a view is expressed throughout *The Analects*; see, for instance, 1.5, 2.3, etc.; deBary, *East Asian Civilizations,* 56, 71. Ethical self-scrutiny is regarded as a part of the quality of *jen,* in Benjamin I. Schwartz, *The World of Thought in Ancient China* (Cambridge: Harvard University Press, 1985), 74–75.

17. Oscar Wilde, *Salomé: A Tragedy in One Act* (Boston: Bruce Humphries, 1907), 11–14, 33–35.

18. See, for instance, Takada Mizuho, *Nihon kindai sakka no biishiki* (Modern Japanese writers and their sense of beauty) (Tokyo: Meiji Shoin, 1987), 142-47. Later Tanizaki, however, turned away from Wilde's view of art and life; cf. Saeki Shōichi, *Monogatari geijutsu ron* (Storytelling as an art form) (Tokyo: Kōdansha, 1979), 112-15.

19. The term *chün tzu* has been translated variously. I follow the rendition by D. C. Lau in his translation of *The Analects*. James Legge uses the term "superior man" or "scholar" in *The Chinese Classics,* vol. 1 (Hong Kong: Hong Kong University Press, 1960), 141, 150, and passim; Schwartz and deBary render it as "noble man"; David L. Hall and Roger T. Ames choose "exemplary person" in *Thinking Through Confucius* (Albany: State University of New York Press, 1987), 176-92 and passim; Tu Weiming renders it as "nobleman or profound person" in "Embodying the Universe: A Note on Confucian Self-realization," *The World & I,* August 1989, 482.

20. This spiritual relationship of dependence on Tzu-lu's part is also noted by Hirakawa Sukehiro, in *Chūsei no shiki: Dante to sono shūhen* (The four seasons in the medieval period: Dante and his circle) (Tokyo: Kawade Shobō Shinsha, 1981), 205.

21. The concept of *amae,* or dependence, is regarded as central to the Japanese personality and human relationship in Doi Takeo, *Amae no kōzō* (The anatomy of dependence) (Tokyo: Kōbundō, 1971), especially 80-83.

22. Lau, *The Analects,* xvii.

23. See, for instance, Hikami Hidehiro, "Kaisetsu" (commentary), in Nakamura Mitsuo et al., eds., *Nakajima Atsushi kenkyū* (Studies on Nakajima Atsushi) (Tokyo: Chikuma Shobō, 1978), 193.

24. Nakajima Atsushi, *Nakajima Atsushi zenshū* (Collected works of Nakajima Atsushi) (Tokyo: Chikuma Shobō, 1976), 1:483.

25. Ibid., 499.

26. Burton Watson, trans., *The Complete Works of Chuang Tzu* (New York: Columbia University Press, 1968), 343. Nakajima's use of *Chuang Tzu* in the description of Tzu-lu was noted in Sasaki Mitsuru, *Nakajima Atsushi no bungaku* (The literature of Nakajima Atsushi), rev. ed. (Tokyo: Ōfūsha, 1976), 313.

27. Takie Sugiyama Lebra, "Compensative Justice and Moral Investment among Japanese, Chinese, and Koreans," in Takie Sugiyama Lebra and William P. Lebra, eds., *Japanese Culture and Behavior,* rev. ed. (Honolulu: University of Hawaii Press, 1986), 58.

28. Nakane, *Japanese Society,* 64.

29. Schwartz, *The World of Thought in Ancient China,* 85.

Works Cited

deBary, Wm. Theodore. *East Asian Civilizations: A Dialogue in Five Stages.* Cambridge: Harvard University Press, 1988.

De Vos, George A., Curtis Vaughn, and Dorothy M. Holly. "Cultural Continuities: The Relationship Between Social Status, Family Interaction and Achievement Motivation." Unpublished MS dated 7 August 1989. Presented at the "Conference on Perceptions of Self: China, India and Japan," East-West Center, 14–18 August 1989.

Doi Takeo. *Amae no kōzō.* (The anatomy of dependence) Tokyo: Kōbundō, 1971.

France, Anatole. *Thaïs.* Translated by Basia Gulati. Chicago: The University of Chicago Press, 1976.

Hall, David L., and Roger T. Ames. *Thinking Through Confucius.* Albany: State University of New York Press, 1987.

Hallowell, A. Irving. *Culture and Experience.* New York: Schocken Books, 1967.

Hikami Hidehiro. "Kaisetsu" (commentary). In *Nakajima Atsushi kenkyū.* (Studies on

Nakajima Atsushi). Edited by Nakamura Mitsuo et al. Tokyo: Chikuma Shobo, 1978.

Hirakawa Sukehiro. *Chūsei no shiki: Dante to sono shūhen* (The four seasons in the medieval period: Dante and his circle). Tokyo: Kawade Shobō Shinsha, 1981.

Kōno Toshirō, and Chiba Shunji, eds. *Shiryō: Tanizaki Jun'ichirō.* (Tanizaki Jun'ichirō: Sourcebook) Tokyo: Ōfūsha, 1980.

Lau, D. C., trans. *The Analects (Lun yü).* Hong Kong: The Chinese University Press, 1979.

Lebra, Takie Sugiyama. "Compensative Justice and Moral Investment among Japanese, Chinese, and Koreans." In *Japanese Culture and Behavior,* rev. ed., edited by Takie Sugiyama Lebra and William P. Lebra. Honolulu: University of Hawaii Press, 1986.

Legge, James. *The Chinese Classics.* Hong Kong: Hong Kong University Press, 1960.

Nakajima Atsushi. *Nakajima Atsushi zenshū* (Collected works of Nakajima Atsushi). Tokyo: Chikuma Shobō, 1976.

Nakane Chie. *Japanese Society.* Berkeley: University of California Press, 1970.

Nippon Gakujutsu Shinkōkai, trans. *The Manyōshū* (Collection of myriad leaves). New York: Columbia University Press, 1965.

Ōshima Maki. "Tanizaki Jun'ichirō no debyu to Anatōru Furansu: 'Kirin' o meguru shomondai" (Tanizaki Jun'ichirō's début and Anatole France: Questions concerning "Kirin"). In *Tanizaki Jun'ichirō,* edited by Nihon Bungaku Kenkyū Shiryō Kankōkai. Tokyo: Yūseidō, 1973.

Pollack, David. *The Fracture of Meaning: Japan's Synthesis of China from the Eighth through the Eighteenth Centuries.* Princeton: Princeton University Press, 1986.

Roland, Alan. "Selves in Motion: An Indian-Japanese Comparison." Paper presented at the "Conference on Perceptions of Self: China, India and Japan," East-West Center, 14–18 August 1989.

Saeki Shōichi. *Monogatari geijutsu ron* (Storytelling as an art form). Tokyo: Kōdansha, 1979.

Sasaki Mitsuru. *Nakajima Atsushi no bungaku* (The literature of Nakajima Atsushi). Rev. ed. Tokyo: Ōfūsha, 1976.

Schwartz, Benjamin I. *The World of Thought in Ancient China.* Cambridge: Harvard University Press, 1985.

Shiba Sen (Ssu-ma Ch'ien). *Shiki (Shih chi:* Historical records). Edited by Yoshida Kenkō. Shinshaku kanbun taikei, vol. 87. Tokyo: Meiji Shoin, 1982.

Takada Mizuho. *Nihon kindai sakka no biishiki* (Modern Japanese writers and their sense of beauty). Tokyo: Meiji Shoin, 1987.

Tanizaki Jun'ichirō. *Tanizaki Jun'ichirō zenshū.* (Collected Works of Tanizaki Jun'ichirō). Tokyo: Chūō Kōron-sha, 1957.

Tu Wei-ming. "Embodying the Universe: A Note on Confucian Self-realization." *The World & I,* August 1989, 475–85.

Ueda Makoto. *Modern Japanese Writers and the Nature of Literature.* Stanford, Calif.: Stanford University Press, 1976.

Watson, Burton. *The Complete Works of Chuang Tzu.* New York: Columbia University Press, 1968.

————. *Ssu-ma Ch'ien: Grand Historian of China.* New York: Columbia University Press, 1958.

Wilde, Oscar. *Salomé: A Tragedy in One Act.* Boston: Bruce Humphries, 1907.

15

Analogue, Figure, Avatar
Explorations of the Self in Modern Japanese Fiction

Lucy Lower

When first considering literary expressions of the concept of the self, I was drawn to characterization as an obvious nexus. I had been interested for some time in what I saw as a certain tendency or pattern of portrayal. It is a pattern not necessarily found in all works of modern Japanese literature, nor even consistently in works by those authors I will be discussing. Nor do I suggest that it is the most salient in relation to the concept of self in Japanese literature. It provided me, however, with a point of entry into the field, and pondering it has suggested in turn thoughts on characteristic narrative strategies and on the dense subjectivity so often remarked upon in modem Japanese literature.

The pattern that had struck me was a kind of cyclical repetition of person and predicament, person-in-predicament, perceived usually by the narrator or central consciousness of the story,[1] in which the fulfillment of the cycle constitutes the narrator's path to self-realization or self-knowledge, and (thus) constitutes as well what resolution there might be to the story. The cycle is set in motion by the narrator's sense of connection with another character, or as it might be between two "others," a connection that may be characterized by identification, by hostility, or simply by inevitability, fate. Whatever its nature, the connection is frequently unexplained and indeed inexplicable, yet (or therefore) compelling. Taking the case of the narrator's sense of his[2] own connection, he begins to overlap or overlay the object of his fixation, in some cases becoming this "other," taking on the other's character or role, or situating himself in the same constellation of relationships. In thus losing himself, he expresses or finds his truest self.

Natsume Sōseki's best-known novel, *Kokoro* (1914),[3] follows this paradigm. It is the story of a young student's enthusiastic, indeed puppyish, pursuit of a mysteriously reserved older intellectual and the latter's ultimate revelation of the egoism and betrayal (including self-betrayal), the disillusionment and guilt, that have darkened his life. The cycle of betrayal and despair is traced successively by Sensei's childhood friend K, by Sensei himself, and by the young man so drawn to Sensei.

The structure of the novel is not linear, however. It breaks neatly into two halves, each retrospectively narrated by a different first-person narrator. In the first half of the novel, a now older *watakushi* contrasts his relationship as a young man with Sensei, his reluctant mentor and spiritual father, to his relationship with his biological father. The last half of the novel consists of Sensei's "Testament," his suicide letter addressed to the young man, as he seeks in the events of his own youth the reasons for his fatal choice and, inadvertently perhaps but not incidentally, bequeaths to the young man his own place in the cycle. "I shall be satisfied," Sensei writes, "if, when my heart stops beating, a new life lodges itself in your breast."[4] K's own story is enfolded within this letter.

Sensei draws parallels between himself and K in their intellectual interests and in their youthful moral zeal. Although Sensei's account stresses the differences in their characters, especially the incommunicativeness, eccentricity, and stubbornness both take to be moral rigor, the reader, already familiar with Sensei's behavior, must see these traits as equally exhibited by Sensei. Each has suffered betrayals that place worldly values above moral fastidiousness or spiritual aspirations: Sensei has been cheated by his uncle's mismanagement of his estate and K's inclination toward the religious life has been thwarted by his adoption as an heir to another professional line. K's response is to deceive his adoptive family in turn and persist in pursuing his own interests; Sensei's is to impute base motives to everyone around him. Both young men struggle with their individual scruples but in the end succumb to the charm of the daughter of the widow in whose house they have rooms. Sensei's jealousy prompts him not only to secure secretly a promise of the girl's hand but also to goad K over his own susceptibility, deepening the latter's disillusionment with himself. K's brooding leads ultimately to his suicide, and the note he leaves for Sensei expresses his despair of "ever becoming the firm, resolute person that he had always wanted to be." (McClellan, *Kokoro*, 67)

Through the years, as Sensei broods over the reason for K's suicide, he attributes it first to disappointment in love, later to disappointment over his failure to live up to his ideals, and ultimately to a terrible loneliness—the "loneliness [that] is the price we have to pay for being born in this modern age" (31), the loneliness of egotism, the loneliness he himself seeks to escape. He has the "premonition that [he is] treading the same path as K had done" (240-41) and, like K, he wonders "Why did I wait so long to die?" (230).

There are parallels too between Sensei and the father. These are brought all the more into relief by the young man's insistence on their differences. Though the father seems to be somewhat older, both strongly identify themselves with the Meiji era then ending. By the middle of the novel both know they are soon to die. Each associates his own death with the suicide of General Nogi, Sensei with the particular moral values it represents and—again echoing K—with his imagination of the pain caused by its enforced delay, and the father with a somewhat vaguer, though equally emphatic, sympathy.

The meaning of the contrast the young man is always drawing between the two is his guilty preference for Sensei—for his company, for his teaching, for his approbation. Attracted to Sensei first out of curiosity and a sense that they had met before—a notion the older man summarily dismisses—the young man attaches himself more and more tenaciously in the hope that Sensei will teach him "about life" (68) by relating the tragedy hidden in his own past. Sensei's painful account of his own failure and of his inescapable loneliness—again, encapsulating K's own anguished confession—not only reveals the basis for the darkness of Sensei's world but also prompts the young man eventually to present his own "confession," this novel, to the reader. The understanding he has reached is founded not only on learning of Sensei's experience but implicitly on his reflection on his own failures and betrayals, among them his inability to respond to Sensei's appeal in the latter's moment of crisis and his abandonment of his father on his deathbed in a futile dash to reach Sensei before his suicide. Sensei's explanation of what has finally prompted him to reveal himself might well also be that of the narrator of the first part of the novel, the now-older young man, to the reader:

> My own past, which made me what I am, is a part of human experience. Only
> I can tell it. I do not think that my effort to do so honestly has been entirely
> purposeless. If my story helps you and others to understand even a part of what

we are, I shall be satisfied. . . . I did not write simply to keep my promise to you. More compelling than the promise was the necessity which I felt within me to write this story. (247)

That dislocations in the self mirror larger cultural shifts is explicit in *Kokoro*.[5] In response to the Emperor Meiji's death, Sensei says "I felt as though the spirit of the Meiji era had begun with the Emperor and had ended with him. I was overcome with the feeling that I and the others, who had been brought up in that era, were now left behind to live as anachronisms" (245). To his wife's joking suggestion he responds that he "will commit *junshi* . . . through loyalty to the spirit of the Meiji era" (245). But Sensei's suicide is not really *junshi*. General Nogi, at least the General Nogi of the novel, is truly a man of the old order and thus not, paradoxically, an anachronism. So, for that matter, is the father. To that extent both of their deaths are "natural," have meaning. Sensei believes that his young friend "will not understand clearly why [he is] about to die . . . [that they] belong to different eras, and so [they] think differently" (246). The novel is evidence to the contrary. The sense of loss of what seemed, at least, a coherent moral, social, and cultural framework for the self, and an increasingly troubled response to the elaboration of "modernity" and "enlightenment," particularly in the pressure of the Western ideal of individualism that so preoccupied Sōseki, precipitate Sensei's suicide and define it as pivotally modern.[6]

Of course, a great deal of modern Japanese fiction documents the struggle between traditional and "modern" or Western values and ideas. Tanizaki Jun'ichirō's *Tade kuu mushi* (*Some Prefer Nettles,* 1928) is another well-known example. When Tanizaki wrote his *Yume no ukihashi* (*The Bridge of Dreams*) in 1959, however, he had already come down rather emphatically on the side of tradition. His concern is not, as is Sōseki's, with the moral underpinnings of the self and the burden of individualism. Sublimely sensual writer that he is, his concern is rather with aesthetics, with tastes, with a way of life that was fast disappearing even when he was first drawn to it in the 1920s. The story itself can be read as an allusive variation on the *Tale of Genji,* which Tanizaki had twice translated into modern Japanese. It recalls the *Tale of Genji* in its overall theme of the search for a love who recalls and somehow replaces the mother, and in many of its particulars as well—the title, for example, is taken from the final chapter of Lady Murasaki's work and evokes, as it does there, both the ephemerality of life in this world and a subtly sexual connotation. *Genji* was written without benefit of Freud and the balance of love and transgression somehow comes off differently. The seductive dream Tan-izaki weaves in this story is carefully frayed just enough around the edges to enable us to glimpse a sordidness within.

It is told, in the first person, by one Otokuni Tadasu. His character reveals itself in the slyly meandering opening passage, which very effectively draws the reader into a world quite remote from everyday judgments. He quotes a poem by his mother, and after declaring himself unqualified to do so, goes on to comment on the poem and to delectate over the paper on which it is written and on the obscure style and rare quality of the calligraphy. As this and later passages make amply clear, he is a retiring gentleman of exquisitely cultivated tastes. He describes his life in his childhood home—a compound actually, called Heron's Nest—in a large and secluded garden precisely and lovingly located in northern Kyoto.

The events of the story consist of a series of substitutions for a lost love object. Tadasu's first comments on his mother's poem introduce the fact that he has had two mothers and that his memory tends to confuse them, in part because both were named Chinu. His first mother, devotedly loved by both husband and son, died while the narrator was still so young that his recol-lection of her is indistinct. A few years later the father remarries, assuring his son that he does so because the lady in question

> resembles [your mother] in so many ways. . . . [in] the impression she makes, the way she talks, the way she carries herself, her quiet, easy-going personality, sweet and gentle, and yet deep. . . .[7]

The language of substitution shades into the language of becoming. The new mother is to be seen virtually as an incarnation, a kind of avatar. The father abjures the boy not

> to think of her as your second mother. Think that your mother has been away somewhere for a while and has just come home. Even if I didn't tell you so, you'd soon begin to look at it that way. Your two mothers will become one, with no distinction between them. Your first mother's name was Chinu, and your new mother's name is Chinu too. And in everything she says and does, your new mother will behave the way the first one did. (Hibbett, *Bridge of Dreams*, 366)

She does indeed. But her intimacy with her son evolves gradually over the years from the maternal to the erotic. A child born to this second Chinu when Tadasu is about eighteen is hastily sent to the remote countryside for adoption. Tadasu senses a tacit agreement all around to foster the exclusive intimacy between Chinu and himself. The father's health fails, and on his deathbed he tells his son of his concern for "your poor stepmother" (a term the younger man has heretofore been discouraged from using), and another transmigration is initiated:

> She still has a long life ahead of her, but once I'm gone she'll have only you to rely on. So please take good care of her—give her all your love. Everyone says you resemble me. I think so myself. As you get older you'll look even more like me. If she has you, she'll feel as if I am still alive. I want you to think of taking my place with her as your chief aim in life, as the only kind of happiness you need. (380)

At his dying father's request, Tadasu marries, but his wife, the daughter of an old family retainer, is of conveniently lower social status. The marriage is to be for his mother's sake, so that he will have someone to help take care of her.

This little ménage lives peaceably for a brief period, but Chinu's death, from shock brought on by a centipede bite, throws suspicion on the wife and she is sent away. She is no longer necessary, after all. The story ends with Tadasu's retrieval of Chinu's son from his adoptive home. He says of the boy,

> we have become very close. . . . What makes me happiest is that he looks exactly like Mother. Not only that, he seems to have inherited something of her calm, open, generous temperament. (388)

He is determined to devote his life thenceforth to the boy, his "one link with mother" (388).

Lifting bits like this from the narrative make the unwholesomeness of the relationships rather clearer than it in fact is in this languid and evocative fantasy. But even the protected world of Heron's Nest is occasionally intruded upon by the hostile world outside. The view from without is introduced by Tadasu's faithful nurse Okane, as she seeks to arm him against it. It is she who tells him, when he is still an adolescent, of the second Chinu's background, of the dubious respectability of her first marriage and her experience, however dictated by financial necessity, as a professional entertainer. The image of the mother is thus subtly tarnished by that of the whore. When

Okane warns him of the gossip that is circulating on the eve of his marriage, Tadasu tries to exorcise it with his indignation:

> Of course it was true that my relatives were opposed to my forthcoming marriage, but that wasn't the only reason why they disapproved of us. Mother and I were the objects of the criticism, more than the match with [the gardener's] daughter. To put it bluntly, they believed that we were committing incest. According to them, Okane said, Mother and I began carrying on that way while Father was still alive, and Father himself, once he knew he wouldn't recover, had tolerated it—even encouraged it. Some went so far as to ask whose baby had been smuggled out to Tamba, suggesting that Takeshi was my own child, not my father's. I wondered how on earth these people, who had been avoiding us for years, could have heard anything that would make them spread such wild rumors. (384–85)

It is where Tadasu's artful account begins to unravel that Tanizaki's mastery of the confessional form becomes evident. Tadasu's earlier assurance of his truthfulness and his self-consciously casual justification for writing his story have already carried an odor of disingenuousness.

> [I]f no one ever reads [this], I shall have no regret. I write for the sake of writing, simply because I enjoy looking back at the events of the past and trying to remember them one by one. Of course, all that I record here is true: I do not allow myself the slightest falsehood or distortion. But there are limits even to telling the truth; there is a line one ought not to cross. And so, although I certainly never write anything untrue, neither do I write the whole of the truth. Perhaps I leave part of it unwritten out of consideration for my father, for my mother, for myself . . . If anyone says that not to tell the whole truth is in fact to lie, that is his own interpretation. I shall not venture to deny it. (378–79)

Tanizaki remains "modern" enough to delight in the ironic spin he gives his literary models, and in shocking as well as beguiling the reader. He is also modern enough to give us, in this and several other late works, a shamelessly mendacious narrator, a self whose unreliability and manipulativeness are among his most revealing attributes.

We may read the narrators' crises and the narratives themselves as parallels, or analogues, in *Kokoro,* and the successive "incarnations" of *The Bridge of Dreams* as avatars. The cyclic repetitions of Ōe Kenzaburō's novel *Mannen gannen no futtobooru* (Soccer in the first year of the Mannen era, 1967), translated into English as *The Silent Cry*,[8] suggest rather figures, their mystical equivalence supported by the prominence in the narrative of dreams, both waking and sleeping, the stirrings of myth and the supernatural, and of the experiential potency of reenactment.

The narrator, once again first-person, is Nedokoro Mitsusaburō, a disaffected Tokyo intellectual whose younger brother Takashi, a lapsed student radical, talks him into returning to their childhood home in the wilds of Shikoku to start "a new life," in part through supervising the sale and dismantling of the ancestral storehouse. It is a personal and social regression as well as a geographical one, an attempt at once desperate and diffident to recover a self with which the narrator's present "I" has absolutely "no continuity, no consistency." (Bester, *Silent Cry*, 58) The theme of retreat toward recovery of both a personal and communal self is underscored by the etymology for the surname Nedokoro proffered by a villager explaining the ancient choice of the family's grounds for a ritual spirit dance: the Okinawan *nendokoro*, meaning "the soul's root" (132). Mitsusaburō's rejection of this explanation is an expression of his deliberate alienation from the "communal spirit" that Takashi, by contrast, is cultivating within himself. As the final revelations in the story provide an alternate, or at least a fuller, explanation of the connection between the dance and the Nedokoro grounds, Mitsusaburō takes the first steps toward his own self-reintegration.

Mitsu has acceded to Takashi's plan not so much because he believes it will succeed but because he is demoralized by the birth and subsequent institutionalization of a brain-damaged son and by the grotesque suicide of a friend. Both losses are of himself: he and his friend "had been together in everything . . . were like identical twins." "In appearance even," he makes a point of saying, he was more like his friend than his brother (18). The deformed child is both monster and innocent, and a familiar figure from other fictions of Ōe's. The deformity itself, the growth on the baby's head that is being surgically removed, is "awe-inspiring, a vivid witness to the presence of some grotesque power harbored within yet uncontrollable by the self" (43). The father imagines a similar excrescence growing out of his own head and likens it to "something really vital" whose removal is "equal to the physical amputation of some part of my own body." Indeed, he imagines being presented by the doctor with the lump itself and told, "Here's your baby back" (44).

This, then, is the state of our protagonist as the main body of the novel commences. The narrative interweaves the stories of three "risings," three violent episodes involving members of the Nedokoro family. The structure of the novel is so complex and threaded through with pertinent leitmotifs, and the unfolding of understanding—ours and the narrator's—so incremental, that I cannot do it justice in the brief scope of this paper. Indeed, the summary I will now give tracing the connections among the three risings does violence to the point of the novel, which lies largely in the way the symbolic significance various characters assign to events, the symbolic use they make of them, changes radically not only by new factual revelations but by evolutions in their psychological circumstances as well.

The narrative is constructed around the dialectic produced by the diverging recollections and interpretations of the two brothers. Takashi's versions of events insist upon a highly romanticized criminality and heroic violence, and are suitably grisly. Mitsusaburō, better armed with facts, is the deflater, the debunker; he is intent on portraying Takashi's models—and Takashi himself as he strives to emulate them—as self-serving and cowardly when not merely ineffectual.

The first of the three risings occurred in the year 1860, the *mannen gannen* of the title. The core of the story as we eventually come to know it is this: a group of young men, marginalized by birth order and poverty, had rioted to protest onerous new taxes in particular and in the unsettled spirit of the times in general. The younger brother of Mitsu's and Taka's great-grandfather had trained and led them, even though a target of their attack was the wealthy Nedokoro's own compound. Suppression by the authorities causes the farmers to withdraw the support they had secretly given to the rising, and the young men are brutally executed, abandoned by their leader, the Nedo-koro ancestor, who apparently escapes with the aid of his older brother. The undeniably charismatic great-great-uncle is variously cast as heroic rebel, madman, and duplicitous manipulator; the great-grandfather is cast as his murderer, his coconspirator, and the craven pawn of the clan authorities. In the novel's final pages a secret cellar is discovered beneath the storehouse. It becomes clear to Mitsusaburō—Takashi is already dead—that the leader of the 1860 rising, though he survived the massacre of his fellows, had afterwards, in penance, immured himself there with the connivance of his elder brother, emerging briefly to lead the valley folk again a decade later in a bloodless rising that did secure them some concessions from the new authorities. Both brothers had, in their own ways, kept faith with each other and with the community.

The second significant incident involves the death of their elder brother S just after the end of the war. A group of young men had raided the nearby settlement of Koreans, who had been corvéed during the war to cut timber in the surrounding forest. The object of the raid had been to steal black-market stores, but a Korean had accidentally been killed. A second foray had resulted in—had been in some estimations intended to result in—the reprisal murder of S. S's character and his role in this rising are sharply disputed by the surviving brothers, but as in the case of the 1860 rising, the two views are mediated by other accounts. The priest, S's boyhood friend, explicitly links S's self-sacrifice to the 1860 rising. His interpretation, together with another account by an eyewitness, leads us to see S in the end, like the great-great-uncle, as both marauder and architect of his own punishment.

Mitsusaburō has the facts on his side, but Takashi's images are closer to those that have lodged themselves in the communal consciousness. A school play, witnessed by the brothers during their boyhood, recreates Takashi's fratricidal images of the 1860 rising. It also turns out to foreshadow Mitsusaburō's "betrayal" of Takashi, and in the foreshadowing as well as the event Mitsu himself is very nearly lost. Takashi defends his childish recollection of S's death by pointing out that he has merely conflated his childish memory of the actual event with a vivid reenactment witnessed later, as history was already passing over into local myth.

In the novel's present, the mid-1960s, the local community is again in a somewhat depressed state, its moral and financial vitiation due not to exploitation by the feudal authorities or the wasting of war but to a combination of its own backwardness and the entrepreneurial zeal of a former resident of the Korean settlement, whose supermarket chain has become both company and company store to the valley. It is to him that Takashi proposes to sell the ancient family storehouse. We, like the narrator, know him only in effigy and through hearsay until the closing pages of the novel, when the actual character is revealed in an unexpectedly sympathetic light. It is this Korean, incidentally, who recognizes the existence of the cellar—the great-great-uncle's prison—below the storehouse, and who fully clarifies the ambiguity surrounding the death of S. It is against him, "The Emperor" as he has been nicknamed by the embittered residents of the village, that Takashi has led his uprising.

Takashi's rising consists of a kind of excitation of the valley people by direct reference to the 1860 rising and implicitly to the 1945 incident at the Korean settlement as well. He himself calls it "a riot of the *imagination*," claiming that by taking part, everyone is "going back a century in time and experiencing vicariously the excitement of the 1860 rising" (197). He plays not only on the negative feelings of the local population toward their new capitalist overlord but also on the positive energy of local myth. Taking over leadership of a group of aimless and frustrated young men, he first "trains" them by organizing them into a football team. They are the rioters who will supervise the looting of the supermarket, making sure, as their counterparts had in the earlier disturbances, that all the villagers and farmers take part. (Enforced complicity not only encourages solidarity, but it supplies an excuse should the rebellion fail.) As spiritual support, he resurrects the neglected tradition of the *nembutsu* dance, a ritual in which local history is transformed into myth and shame into glory.

But Takashi's fascination with the 1860 rising, in particular with the role of his great-grandfather's younger brother and with S's death, spring from a personal need as well as an aspiration to community. He is impelled by his fear of violence and death to seek violence and death. He sees the great-great-uncle and S as heroically lawless because he sees himself as a criminal and seeks in their bloody self-sacrifice, as he envisions it, the pattern for his own expiation. His last desperate attempt to pose as a criminal is seen through by his brother and he has no choice but to reveal his true criminality, the terrible truth at which he has periodically darkly hinted. Mitsusaburō has discerned the shadow of that kind of truth, a truth that

> if a man tells it, leaves him no alternative but to be killed by others, or kill himself, or go mad and turn into a monster, . . . [a truth that] once uttered leaves you clutching a bomb with the fuse irretrievably lit. (157)

Such a truth lies behind the unexplained suicide of his friend, with whom Takashi is also alternately linked and contrasted.

This begins to sound like Takashi's story, but it is not really. Bracketing the main body of the novel are two scenes in which Mitsusaburō literally descends into a pit, in the wake of a personal trauma, to confront himself and very nearly to seek his own annihilation. The first instance is linked to his friend's suicide and the last, which closes the book, to Takashi's and to all the meanings that have accumulated around it. Mitsusaburō's reemergence, especially in the latter instance from a night spent in the cellar of the storehouse, represents a kind of rising from the dead.

Mitsusaburō knows that he has no "truth" of his own to tell, and is ambivalent about it. He will be the one to translate the adventures of others, a writer whose truths will be comfortably distanced by the convention of fiction, in Takashi's disparaging formulation. Sitting in his great-great-uncle's "prison," surrounded in a recurrent dream by the specters of all those he has "abandoned" in his skepticism and anomie, he finally makes his peace with the spirits of his brothers and his ancestor. He comes to realize the accuracy of his wife's assessment that "the need to oppose Taka has always made [him] deliberately reject the things that resembled [Taka] in [himself]," and that he is now free to explore what he shares with Takashi and with his great-great-uncle (272). He will take the more adventurous of the two positions he has been offered, and he and his wife, now reconciled, will retrieve their damaged child from his institution.

The ending of the novel, with its reconciliation and existentialist resolve, though uncharacteristic of Japanese novels in general, is characteristic of Ōe. Also uncharacteristic of Japanese novels in general, I might add, is the rather strong sense of closure. Perhaps the karmic debt has been paid and the circle closed by the bloody events of the last chapters.

In a certain sense the lessons Ōe's narrator draws from "the horror" he experiences in his own journey into the heart of darkness parallel those in Conrad's modern classic. In Ōe, however, the recognition of Takashi in himself is also a positive acceptance of the communal and ancestral roots of the self truly recoverable not through a detached intellectual effort at ferreting out the real story, but through the imagination.

These three works, spanning slightly over fifty years of the modern era, are more different, to be sure, than they are similar. They vary significantly, moreover, in their employment of a cyclical pattern, yet I think an argument can be made that such a pattern is common to all three. There are two other elements common to all three works that I want to touch on very briefly because I think they are important to the effect of this cyclical organization. One of these is that the cycle, or the reflection on it, is played out in a state of retreat or withdrawal from ordinary social life. Sensei is a near-recluse. The Edenic Heron's Nest not only allows relationships to take their course but allows the narrator to impose his own version of reality within it. Mitsusaburō does some of his best thinking while sitting in a hole in the ground, and the novel as a whole takes place in the atavistic setting of a remote village, far from his normal habitat, Tokyo. This withdrawal provides a kind of freedom and psychic space for the exploration of the self. Indeed, it locks the self in with itself alone.

The other pertinent element is use of the confessional form. The inter-relations of autobiography, literary confessionalism, and confessional forms comprise a very rich vein in modern Japanese literature, one mined in a number of studies.⁹ I will not attempt to explore those interrelations here except to note that none of the authors I have discussed is associated with the mainstream of confessional writing in Japan, the so-called naturalist writers. But the choice of a confessional *form,* like the situating of the narrative in a condition of retreat, deepens the intensely subjective dimension of the novels. All of the narrators speak in the immediacy of the first person. And all of the novels are also, implicitly or explicitly, about writing, about the impulse to tell, the necessity of telling, the story. The cyclical movement in the narratives likewise enhances the density of their subjectivity. It creates, in its open circularity and repetition, the sense of a kind of karmic ineluctability, something self-fulfilling that the self cannot expect to overcome and so must struggle to comprehend.

The overpowering subjectivity in these novels, ironically, reverses what we would normally consider to be the operation of a cycle, that is, the as-similation of the later manifestation to the original pattern. What is striking in these works—and this is especially evident in Tanizaki and Ōe—is the way in which the self appropriates and distorts the other or others according to its own needs. Symbolic use of the other by the self is hardly unusual either in life or in literature, but the particulars here seem to me at least suggestive if not revealing.

I would like to conclude with a few further thoughts on the relation of pattern and cycle to the exploration of the self in modern Japanese fiction. Pattern implies a degree of abstraction, of stylization. It is delimiting in the sense of establishing a certain "symbolic field" or subfield, and yet in practice, as I have tried to show in these novels, the subject's reading of the pattern is all, or very nearly so. Also, and importantly, the pattern is the highly partic-ularized one of an individual, not of a role or a type. (Although almost anything can be typologized, as witness the subcategories tentatively put for-ward in this paper.) The idea of "pattern" contains within itself the idea of repetition, and I have already alluded to the cyclical concept of reincarnation that "the pattern of the person" suggests.

The cycle as a principle for organizing reality is rooted in many areas of Japanese culture, of course, including not only Buddhism but also nature-based indigenous beliefs. In modern secular society it remains at least vesti-gially, in the sense that such basic patterns of thought often outlive their vital relation to a culture. But I tend to ascribe more permanence, or tenacity, to it; it seems to me a kind of *basso continuo* that is still very much a part of an unvoiced cultural cosmology. It is for this reason it continues to be so effective, and not merely useful as a mechanism for reaching into both the past and the future in order to explore the continuities and disjunctions so central to the concept of the self in modern Japanese fiction.

Notes

1. Since it fits my examples here I will hereafter simply shorten this to "narrator."

2. All of my narrators happen to be male: I have not paused to consider whether or how that might be significant.

3. Perhaps the title itself, which so resists translation, may be read as pointing to the essential something that links and conflates the protagonist of each of the three revolutions of the cycle.

4. *Kokoro,* trans. Edwin McClellan (Chicago: H. Regnery Co.. 1957), 129. Subsequent quotations are from this translation.

5. The anonymity of the main characters, despite their detailed representation as individuals, amplifies their significance as cultural allegory. The names of the wives of Sensei and the father appear in passing, but these serve if anything to diminish the importance of those characters, to place them closer to the level of the extremely minor character Saku-san than to the principals of the "cycle."

6. Alan Wolfe, in his *Suicidal Narrative in Modern Japan: The Case of Dazai Osamu* (Princeton: Princeton University Press, 1990), develops a related interpretation in greater detail.

7. Tanizaki Jun'ichirō, *The Bridge of Dreams,* trans. Howard Hibbett, in Howard Hibbett, ed., *Contemporary Japanese Literature* (Alfred A. Knopf, 1977), 365. Subsequent quotations refer to this translation.

8. Translated by John Bester (Tokyo: Kodansha, 1967). Subsequent quotations are from Bester's translation.

9. Among the more recent and penetrating treatments are Wolfe, cited above, and Edward Fowler's *The Rhetoric of Confession: Shishōsetsu in Early-Twentieth-Century Japanese Fiction* (Berkeley: University of California Press, 1988).

—————————— *16* ——————————

The Persistence of Self as Body and Personality in Japanese Buddhist Art

Willa Jane Tanabe

Normative Ideas and Normative Practices

The philosophically normative view of self in Buddhism is that it is a construct with no substance and no duration. A human being is "an existence depending on a series of causations."[1] In opposition to the pre-Buddhistic Upanishadic belief in an eternal and immortal self (in Sanskrit, *ātman;* in Japanese, *jiga*), early Buddhists insisted that the world and all of existence are characterized by insubstantiality or no self (in Sanskrit, *anātman,* in Japanese, *muga*).

The belief in the absence of a permanent, unchanging self or soul is based on the understanding that what we ordinarily call self merely emerges from the interactions of certain psychophysical elements (in Sanskrit, *skandhas*): the physical body, perceptions, mental conceptions, volitions, and consciousness. All of these components are impermanent, and therefore the sum of the components is also impermanent. Self is a momentary phenomenon without eternality and constancy.

While the concept of no-self is affirmed by most Buddhists, it is nevertheless also true that the reluctance to give up a sense of a consistent and persistent self pervades Buddhism throughout time and across cultures. In ancient India, for example, the Pudgalavādins, or Personalists, argued that even though the self appears to be "a series of momentary . . . [elements] which continuously succeed each other. . . . there remained the relative unity

406

of each series, and its distinction from the others. . . . [the Personalists spoke of the self or person as] an indefinable principle . . . [that] persists through the several lives of a being until he reaches Nirvana."[2] The very ideas of rebirth and karma presuppose, they insisted, that there is a persistent self-identity that continues in some form until the individual achieves nirvana.

The Jātaka Tales, stories of the previous incarnations of the Buddha, vividly express the idea that personal identity is not limited to one lifetime. In a typical *Jātaka* story, the Buddha narrates a moralistic story and at the end reveals that the protagonist and other characters of the story were really himself and his followers in earlier existences. In a tale of sacrifice involving a hare, otter monkey, and jackal, for instance, the Buddha identifies these animals as earlier forms of himself and his three principle disciples: Ānanda, Śāriputta, and Moggallāna. Not only are past lives recalled, but in other Buddhist literature such as sutras, the Buddha foretells future lives. In the ninth chapter of the Lotus Sutra, for example, the Buddha assures Ānanda of future Buddhahood, reveals Ānanda's future name, and describes his future activities. Recollection of previous lives and prophecies of future ones on the part of the Buddha provide models for ordinary people, as we shall see, to try to discover their own past and future identities.

The Personalist view was regarded by many as heretical, but it was undeniably persuasive. Xuan Zang counted 66,000 Personalist monks out of a total 254,000, about 25 percent, in India at the time of his visit in seventh century.[3] Furthermore, the popularity of retaining some sense of self continues today. In discussing modern Sinhalese Buddhist practice Gombrich notes, "Despite the doctrine [of no self] . . . people in fact think of themselves as having a more or less stable and concrete existence. From this it is a short step to conceiving this existence as extending beyond death. . . . [the desire for and rituals to carry out] the transfer of merit to dead relatives show that the . . . [no self] doctrine has not more affective immediacy with regard to the next life than with regard to this, and that belief in personal survival is a fundamental feature of Sinhalese Buddhism in practice."[4]

Persistence of Personality: Japanese Ideas of Rebirth

Like the early Indian Personalists and the modern Sinhalese, Japanese Buddhists pay lip service to the concept of no-self but retain a sense of the self as a particular identity that can maintain recognizable personality traits or even physical characteristics through multiple rebirths. We find evidence of this in literature as well as the visual arts.

Based on *The Jātaka Tales,* a whole genre of Japanese literature deals with stories of the rebirths of men and women of all stations, from aristocrats to farmers, from soldiers to priests. While the main point of these stories is often the assurance of future rebirth into paradise, the subjects of the tales frequently discover their past incarnations as well. In many of the tales, aspects of the individual's personality or physical body are carried over into another life. The tale of the devout Priest Raishin, for example, notes that he had a strange habit of chewing by twisting his mouth to the side. After seven days of prayer for revelations about his past life, he learned that he had formerly been a cow who had once been used to carry a set of scriptures to a temple. By this act he had gained sufficient merit to be reborn into the human world, but not quite enough merit to erase the tendency to chew like a cow.[5] Stories of reincarnations appear not just in collections of folk tales but also in biographies of historical figures. Fujiwara Arikuni (943–1011), for example, believed that he had been the infamous Dainagon Tomo no Yoshio (died ca. 866), the man found guilty of and exiled for a conflagration that destroyed the palace gates and imperiled the lives of those in court. Arikuni concluded this when he saw a portrait of Yoshio and found that their faces were strikingly similar; he further noted that Yoshio had vowed to be reborn with a hereditary title that Arikuni himself held. Another Heian aristocrat, Fujiwara Kintsune (d. 1099), in his capacity as governor of Kawachi province restored a temple that had fallen into disrepair and in the process discovered a box hidden in the altar that contained the testament of a long-dead priest who had vowed to be reborn as a governor and to restore the temple. In examining the written vow of the priest, Kintsune was amazed to discover that the handwriting looked just like his own. This was sufficient evidence for Kintsune to conclude that he had been that priest in his former life.[6] Stories such as these both reflected and stimulated Japanese thinking of the self as a persistent identity of body and personality.

In Japanese Buddhist art, paintings that demand that the viewer confront the insubstantiality of the physical body seem at first glance to affirm the doctrine of no-self. There is one hanging scroll that comes to mind that graphically illustrates the process of decomposition of the body. In a setting that moves from the flowering cherries of spring to the barrenness of winter, the fresh corpse of a beautiful court woman bloats, bursts open, and becomes food for worms, birds, and animals until there is nothing left but a hank of hair and a piece of bone. Certainly the painting seems to echo such senti-ments as expressed in the *Vimalakīrti Sutra* that "the human body is im-permanent; it is neither strong nor durable; it will decay and is therefore unreliable. . . . It is empty, being neither ego nor its object."[7]

On the other hand, however, this painting is part of a set that illustrates the six different realms *(rokudō)* into which one might be reborn. In ascend-ing order they are: hell, hungry ghosts, animal, fighting spirits, human, and heaven.[8] The point therefore is not merely that bodies decay, but that the self is reborn over and over into other worlds full of suffering. The poor court woman illustrated in the human world not only suffers the process of decay here, but, even if she is fortunate enough to be reborn into a heavenly world as a beautiful goddess with a lifespan much longer than those of the human world, she will still eventually decay there as well.

Further, hell is not merely some psychological symbol; it is an actual place of recognizable punishments that we experience with our body. The horrors of hell are put to us not as abstractions but as real, and are fleshed out in great detail. In the Hell of Dissections *(geshin jigoku)*, a painting of the late twelfth century, bodies are cut into pieces, ground up, and eaten. In another set of hell scenes that exist as late copies of an earlier work, the tongues of liars are stretched out and plowed by demons.[9] The Japanese were obsessed with the particulars of the sufferings of the body, and the hell scrolls go on unrelentingly describing bodily pains. For those who think of them as symbolic, such detailed and sometimes fantastic retributions may seem hu-morous; but for those who think of rebirth as the persistence of this body and self, the illustrations can be nothing other than horrifying. The famous tenth-century author, Sei Shōnagon, upon seeing screens with hell paintings recorded in her notebook that "They were terrifying beyond words. . . . I was so frightened that I went and lay down in my room next door where I could hide myself from the screens."[10]

Attitudes have not changed even today. My mother-in law, a devout Buddhist, once was discussing her preferences for a simple, inexpensive fu-neral service. She wanted to be cremated but expressed great concern that the urn containing her ashes be placed within the tomb in an upright position. She had heard of a friend's urn that did not quite fit into the vault space and had to be placed in a tilted position. She was adamant about having the space for an upright urn, for, as she said, "I don't like lying on my side." My husband laughed and remarked, "If you really want to have a simple funeral, why don't we just scatter your ashes at sea?" To which remark she responded very seriously, "But I can't swim!" That may be funny to one who thinks that ashes are just ashes, but to those for whom the self exists, the body—even the ashes of the body—retains the same personality.

Mahāyāna Affirmations of the Self

For the Japanese, the persistence of self came to mean not just a continuation of personal characteristics but also a reinvestment of importance in the physical self. This came about not merely because of the concern with rebirth but also because new, powerful Mahāyāna schools of Buddhism, such as the Tendai, Shingon, and Zen sects, emphasized ideas that seemed to embrace rather than deny this existence and even identified elements of absoluteness or permanence. Tendai Buddhists, for example, argued that "There is no noumenon besides phenomenon; the phenomenon itself is noumenon. . . . The true state of things cannot be seen directly or immediately. We must see it in the phenomena which are ever changing and becoming."[11] In other words, through the mundane world and with this ordinary body we can penetrate the spiritual sphere. Moreover, Tendai stresses the eternality and absoluteness of the Buddha. The sixteenth chapter of the *Lotus Sutra*, perhaps the most important chapter in this most influential of all Buddhist scriptures, is entitled the "Duration of the Life of the Buddha," and in a gatha called "the song of self" (in Japanese, *jiga ge*) the Buddha declares "I am eternal / I showed my extinction to you expediently / Although I have never passed away."[12] While this does not preclude an interpretation along the lines that "The Buddha might be eternal, but [it is] an eternal impermanence consisting of the constant rise and fall of transitory existents,"[13] this is not how most believers understood the chapter. They believed it literally.

Another central Mahāyāna idea is that all living beings have the Buddha nature within themselves and thus the self should not be viewed merely as a source of delusion and decay but rather as pregnant with the seeds of enlightenment. Shingon Buddhists expressed this idea in the phrase *sokushin jōbutsu*, which literally means to achieve Buddhahood in this very body. For Kūkai, the founder of Shingon in Japan, the phrase reflected both his "affirmative attitude toward this phenomenal world as the very realm in which the highest enlightenment is to be attained and his basic belief in man's potential for enlightenment. Indeed, Kūkai held that, even in the lowest level of mind, the highest 'glorious mind, the most secret and sacred' is fully present."[14]

The belief in the possibility of Buddhahood in this world and the mutuality of the spheres of appearance and reality is also found in Zen schools, which exhort believers to examine their own minds and become a Buddha by perceiving their own true nature (in Japanese, *jikishi ninshin kenshō jōbutsu*). This is possible because the mind, in other words, the essential self, is identical with that of the Buddha. The Buddha nature within allows one to achieve enlightenment at any moment and in any situation, even, as recorded in Zen annals, while sitting in the outhouse. While it is true that a few religious leaders such as Dōgen cautioned their followers that the idea of Buddha nature simply meant "the quality of Enlightenment and that it was not some entity or essence within themselves,"[15] the very fact that this warning was necessary indicates how readily people accepted these ideas as arguments for some real essence within themselves. Indeed, it was not merely the untrained who believed the ideas in a literal manner, but the masters as well. Hakuin, the great Zen teacher of the eighteenth century, wrote "All beings are fundamentally Buddhas. . . . This very earth is the lotus-land and this body is Buddha."[16]

Artistic Affirmation of Nonduality

The ideas that the Buddha nature is within us, that the possibility exists of enlightenment, even Buddhahood, in this body, and the affirmation that we can see the absolute and eternal in this conditioned and impermanent existence are all represented in art.

The idea of the nonduality of the absolute and conditional is represented in a variety of works of art, but perhaps the most beautiful is the set of fan-shaped sutras *(semmen kyō)* produced by aristocrats of the twelfth century. Scriptures were frequently copied in order to gain merit for a better rebirth or for benefits in this life. The aristocratic sponsors believed that the more elaborate the ornamentation, the greater the benefits, and therefore often employed expensive gold and silver inks, exquisite frontispiece paintings, and dyed and decorated paper. Usually the paintings accompanying the sutras illustrated the religious text; however, in the case of the *Lotus Sutra,* written on fan-shaped papers, the text is written directly over bold and colorful paintings of a multitude of subjects from aristocratic lovers practicing their calligraphy to commoners at the market or the village well. These genre scenes are as important as the text, although they bear no direct relationship to the content. Instead, the sponsors took the brilliant step of representing the co-existence of the divine as represented by the text and the mundane, as represented by the genre paintings. Absolute and transitory intermingle as we read the holy words while looking at a woman hanging clothes.[17]

In this world, then, the body no longer needs to be denied, but should be used as an instrument through which we can experience enlightenment. Just as the spiritual and mundane are inseparable, the body is inseparable from the essential identity of the individual. It can even provide the tangible proof of one's enlightenment. In the remaining part of the paper I would like to illustrate just how literally these ideas about the body are represented in art and ritual.

Persistence of Body: Ritual Affirmation

The dedicatory inscriptions on numerous extant sutra scrolls attest to the fact that they were frequently copied as acts of merit in order to insure that the sponsor would receive a felicitous rebirth or increased benefits in this life. Just as a more richly ornamented work increased the merit, so too did the actual participation in the work by the sponsor. However, copying a text was time-consuming and not everyone had a skilled calligraphic hand. Thus other ways to participate developed. Of particular interest here are the records that show sponsors sometimes offered their own blood to serve as ink. Fujiwara Yorinaga (d. 1156), for example, copied a sutra in blood, although he had the audacity to ask his friend Fujiwara Atsuto to donate the blood for him.[18] In other cases, when a sutra was copied for the benefit of someone who had died, the sponsors sometimes took locks of hair they had saved from their deceased loved one and had these strands mixed with the plant fibers used to make the paper for the sutra scroll. In these cases, then, the merit of the ritual act of copying was transferred to the dead person through a part of his own body that became a permanent part of the ritual object.

The use of the physical body as an instrument in the realization of enlightenment gains even greater impetus with the Shingon belief in *bonnō sokubodai* (passions are enlightenment). In other words the early Buddhist ideal of impassive detachment was overlaid with an idea that fervor, even physical passions, could be part of the path to enlightenment. According to orthodox Shingon Buddhists, the purest and only passion allowed was the desire for enlightenment, but there are cases where these ideas led to expressions of earthly passions as well. The Tachikawa school, a Shingon heresy that flourished in the late eleventh through thirteenth centuries, combined yin-yang theory with Shingon ideas to develop practices that included eating meat, placing human skulls on temple altars as the main image for religious services, and employing sexual intercourse to achieve enlightenment. A sketch of the secret mandala for this rite was drawn within a text of the Ashikaga period (1334–1568). In the drawing the male reclines prostrate while the female lies supine, with their legs and arms pointed to the eight petaled lotus upon which they lie. Their sexual organs, instruments to enlightenment, are shielded beneath cloth. In orthodox Shingon the supreme Buddha is de-scribed both as evincing the diamond sphere of essence and the womb sphere of phenomena. The inscriptions in this mandala make it clear that the male is conceived as the sacred Buddha world of diamond hardness and the female as the womb world of ordinary realms including hell. Here in graphic form is the literal representation of the nonduality of sacred and profane as well as the idea of passion as enlightenment. Moreover, the Tachikawa believers took the spent semen that was thought to contain the essences of male and female and smeared it onto the skulls of the dead in order to transmit the same benefits of ultimate union and enlightenment to the dead.[19] The Tachi-kawa school was declared heretical by orthodox Buddhists and banned in 1335, but one does not have to turn to heretical sects to see the self as body in Japanese art.

Persistence of Body: Artistic Affirmations and Incorporations as seen in Sculpture

In sculpture, the definition of self as body is very clearly worked out in a variety of ways. With the development of hollowing out cavities *(uchiguri)* in parts of wooden images and the more complex method of making images from joined pieces of wood *(yosegi)* that permitted the complete interior of a statue to be hollow, the resulting concavities were used to hold devotional and other objects. Objects placed inside images of Buddhas, bodhisattvas, patriarchs, and priests include such things as dedicatory scrolls that list the people who were involved in the sponsoring and construction of the image, scriptures and other religious writings, paintings and prints of Buddhist dei-ties, illustrations of sutras, and miniature sculpture of Buddhist deities. The Chinese also placed objects within statues, and one of the most prominent examples of this is an image of Śākyamuni, the historical Buddha, made by craftsmen in southern China in 985 and brought to Japan in 986 by the Japanese priest Chōnen (938–1016). Chōnen had been inspired by an image in China that was purported to be a version of the earliest image of the Buddha, the so-called King Udayana image, and the copy he sponsored, which is now installed at Seiryōji, in turn became the prototype for scores of other versions in Japan. The Seiryōji Śākyamuni is constructed of Chinese cherry, stands 160 cm. tall, and has a rectangular opening, measuring 28 by 14 cm., in the back; it is usually covered by a board carved to match the drapery folds on the rest of the body. Inside the cavity were such things as a bronze mirror, symbol of purity and enlightenment; a silver statue of Amitābha; scriptures; an image of the Bodhisattva of Wisdom, Mañjuśrī; and several round crystal pellets that fit into the ear canals of the statue, a unique feature of this work that Japanese copies sometimes imitated. Most interesting, however, was a set of imitation viscera made of silk. The five viscera *(gozō)*—liver, lungs, heart, kidney and spleen—were donated at the time of construction and were one of the last things put inside the image before it was closed. The organs are shaped and padded to give a realistic rendering of the human organs they represent. Some of these silk replicas are inscribed with the Sanskrit characters of the names of the five wisdom Buddhas, suggesting that these individual parts of the body are identified with specific Buddhas. The custom of installing imitation viscera inside statues continued into the sixteenth century in China and also is found in other Japanese works, such as in the thirteenth-century image of the patriarch Shan Dao (d. 681). Silk replicas of the five viscera and small intestine were discovered during repairs to the statue in 1962.[20] The inclusion of the viscera within deities and patriarchs establishes the corporeal nature of the image and recalls the common practice of the eye-opening ceremony performed whenever a statue was dedicated. The last task, that which transformed the image from mere wood to sacred body, was the painting in of the eyes—symbols not merely of sight and insight but of energy and life.

The importance of the corporeal also cannot be ignored in the sculpting in the thirteenth century of naked, or nearly naked, deities. Worshippers clothed the deities as if they were real people. The physical, though not the sexual, body was stressed. The painted wood image (H. 95.7 cm.) of the goddess of music, Sarasvatī (Benzaiten), at Tsuragaoka Hachiman shrine in Kamakura city, was produced in 1266 and sits nearly naked, but when properly prepared wears the robes of a court woman and holds a real lute. Another example, the statue (H. 96.7 cm.) of the Bodhisattva Kṣitigarba, (Jizō) at Denkōji, was commissioned about 1228 by nuns who also sewed the garments for the statue. The Jizō image also had objects placed within its body. In the thigh was a sandalwood image of the eleven-headed Avalokiteshvara (Juichimen Kannon), in its chest were copies of esoteric scriptures and the *Lotus Sutra*, and behind its eyes was a small statue of the healing Buddha and a glass reliquary.

The placement of actual relics (Skt. *śarīra,* Jp. *shari*), usually fragments of bone or ashes, within Buddhist images marks an even more literal incorporation of body into the symbol of the deity. The first recorded example in Japan occurred in 767, and the earliest extant example in Japanese sculpture was discovered behind the *urna* of a one-thousand-armed Avalokiteshvara at Toji made in 877.[21] In the Kamakura period (1185–1334), a revival of older forms of Buddhism led to renewed emphasis on the historical Buddha and his physical remains. The relics were placed first into a miniature reliquary, which was then placed within the statue. The reliquary was fashioned in the form of a *gorintō* or five-element pagoda. The *gorintō* structure represented the five basic elements that make up the universe with five distinct shapes piled atop one another. The square, globe, triangle, half sphere or lunar form, and the jewel form at the top symbolize respectively earth, water, fire, wind, and space. Such structures were and still are often placed at grave sites and inscribed with the name of the dead. It is appropriate to employ the miniature pagoda form as a reliquary when we recall that the original purpose of pagodas was nothing other than to serve as a burial mound or reliquary. Originally, the complex and monumental pagoda was built to enshrine a relic of the Buddha. As seen at the oldest extant temple in Japan, Hōryūji, the central shaft within the five-story pagoda rests on a stone-capped cavity in which was buried a nest of containers whose innermost jar held a relic of Śākyamuni.

Portraits of priests and other historical figures, in contrast to portrayals of deities, allowed for greater uses of the "physical traces" or relics of the individual. Perhaps the best known example of this is the portrait of the Zen master Ikkyū (1394–1481) at the Shūon-an in Kyoto. The wood statue (H. 83.3 cm.) was produced immediately after Ikkyū's death in 1481 and rendered in a highly realistic manner. Hair, which is believed to be the actual hair of Ikkyū, was implanted on the head, eyebrows, and chin areas. As a Japanese art historian has noted, "the hair was applied not only to represent external appearances, but also to inject the spirit of Ikkyū directly into his portrait."[22] The spirit or self of this famous Zen master, then, is inseparable from the body.

If implanting hair could inject the spirit of a person into a sculpture, how much better if the entire body were placed within the portrait sculpture. The painted wood undressed statue (H. 85.6 cm.) of Nichiren (1222–82) commissioned by two of his disciples in 1288 and now at Hommonji in Tokyo not only is robed in real ecclesiastical garments and holds a real whisk, but also contains the urn of Nichiren's ashes. The idea behind depositing actual remains in a sculpture are the same as those used for implanting real hair: the introduction of the physical body infuses the personality and spirit of an individual into the wood image. The incorporation of physical remains into portrait sculptures crossed sectarian lines; even the portraits of Zen masters, sculpted *chinsō*, sometimes contain the ashes of the subject. One could also perpetuate the spirit of others within oneself. Among the objects placed within the wood statue of the eminent Saidaiji priest Eison, sculpted by Zenshun in 1280, ten years before Eison's death in 1290, were the ashes of his father, his mother, and the relics—fragments of three teeth—of Śākyamuni Buddha. In one image then is the intermingling of the spirits of the priest's physical and spiritual parents.[23]

Persistence of Body: Affirmation in the Flesh

One of the least subtle representations of the idea of the Buddha nature within us is found in the statue of Rāhula, the only son and a disciple of the historical Buddha. The work was produced in Japan in 1663 by a Chinese sculptor, Fan Dao Sheng, who accompanied the famous Chinese priest of the Ōbaku sect, Yin Yuan (1592–1673), to Japan. Fan Dao Sheng captures Rāhula at the moment when he tears apart his flesh only to reveal the gilded Buddha within.[24] The desire to peal away layers of ignorance and become a Buddha in this very body was not only a subject of art but also of serious and strenuous practice. Moreover, it was popularly believed that if a practitioner achieved this goal, there would be some sign manifested in or upon his body. After all Śākyamuni himself had physical signs or marks of his enlightened nature.

There could be no more convincing sign of enlightenment or becoming a Buddha than the immortality or lack of decay of the flesh. Historical records reveal that Kūkai, founder of Shingon and the great monastery on Mount

Kōya, died on the twenty-first day of the third month of 835. And, according to the *Shoku Nihongi,* compiled in 869, he was cremated. By the early tenth century however, the belief arose that he had never died but rather entered perpetual meditation at Oku-no-in on Mt. Kōya to await the advent of the future Buddha, Maitreya, who will appear in this world some five billion six hundred and seventy million years after the historical Buddha, Śākyamuni. In the tenth century, priests reported that they had not only seen his body but that his hair continued to grow and his clothes had grown dirty. This gave rise to rituals still performed today at Oku-no-in in which fresh robes are offered yearly and vegetables are prepared and offered daily.[25]

Fantastic as this legend may be, it gave rise to a group of extraordinary ascetics, the *isse gyōnin* of the Yudono sect of Shugen-dō, itself a subgroup of Shingon.[26] These ascetics believed that the proof of their achievement of Buddhahood would be revealed in the failure of their body to decay in the usual way. In order to prevent their body from becoming putrid after death, they practiced abstention from meat and cereals, eating mostly nuts, grass and bark for periods of one thousand to four thousand days (two and a half years to over ten years). The few ascetics who managed to complete this rigorous period were then ready for the final stage of their meditations. This final stage varied according to the individual. Hommyō-kai Shōnin, after eating bark and grass for eight years, entered a stone chamber in 1683 and died. His body was "immediately made to assume a sitting posture with crossed legs like a Buddha, and dried up with a charcoal fire and incense fumes. After that the corpse was buried again in the underground chamber for about three years. When it was recovered, the corpse had become completely mummified."[27] Chūkai Shōnin, on the other hand, after eating only nuts for one thousand days was buried alive. His body was disinterred three years later and smoked and dried at that time. The dried, mummified bodies of the ascetics were dressed in robes and installed as the main images in temples. The reservation of the flesh proved that these ascetics had become Buddhas. They were called mummified Buddhas, but more precisely they were regarded as *sokushinbutsu,* embodied Buddhas.

The existence of such mummified Buddhas was once doubted until the discovery and scientific examination since 1950 of over eight cases that date from the Tokugawa period (1615-1868). Their discovery recalls similar examples from even earlier times. The Chinese priest Jian Zhen (688-763), better known as Ganjin, reported seeing the mummified body of the sixth patriarch of Zen, Hui Neng. The mummified body of Hui Neng was layered with lacquer-soaked hemp that was molded to the body. There is still a temple in southern China that purports to have the lacquered and mummified remains of the sixth patriarch.[28] It is also said that Ganjin was so impressed with what he had seen that he vowed to become a mummy too, but to the chagrin of his disciples, Ganjin's body immediately began to rot after he died, and they were forced to cremate it.[29]

In this paper I have tried to find examples that qualify the generally accepted idea that for Buddhists there is no self. In addition to the philosophically held idea of no-self, there is not only a persistent sense of self in Japanese Buddhist art, but the self as defined by physical body and individual personality was consistently valued. Moreover, the actual physical body was enshrined, embedded, and embalmed as a ritual art object. The literal quality of Japanese Buddhist practice and art is often overlooked, perhaps in part because of our own need to invest the mysterious East with some special spirituality and in part because of our failure to recognize that there are many kinds of Buddhist ideas and practices and that there is no single view of the self.

Notes

1. Junjirō Takakusu, *The Essentials of Buddhist Philosophy* (Honolulu: University of Hawaii Press, 1956), 23.

2. Edward Conze, Buddhism: *Its Essence and Development* (New York: Harper & Row, 1965), 169.

3. Edward Conze, *Buddhist Thought in India* (Ann Arbor: University of Michigan Press, 1970), 123.

4. Richard F. Gombrich, *Precept and Practice* (Oxford: Clarendon Press, 1971), 73, 243. See also Steven Collins, *Selfless Persons* (Cambridge: Cambridge University Press, 1982), 150.

5. Yoshiko K. Dykstra, trans., *Miraculous Tales of the Lotus Sutra from Ancient Japan* (Osaka: Kansai University of Foreign Studies, 1983), p. 53.

6. Willa Jane Tanabe, *Paintings of the Lotus Sutra* (New York: Weatherhill, 1988), 22-23.

7. Charles Luk, *The Vimalakīrti Nirdeśa Sūtra* (Berkeley: Shambala, 1972), 17-18.

8. The painting is one of fifteen large hanging scrolls, measuring H. 155.5 x W. 68 cm., based on *Ōjō Yōshū (Essentials of Salvation)* by the tenth-century monk Genshin. Excerpts of the text appear in the upper right corner. Originally kept at Ryōsen-in on Mt. Hiei, the set was taken to its present location of Shōju Raigōji

sometime after 1525. The scrolls were repaired in 1313 and were probably painted shortly before this, since their style reveals Song influence and stylistic features consistent with a late-thirteenth- or early-fourteenth-century date.

9. The "Hell of Dissection" is now mounted as a hanging scroll, H. 26.1 x W. 90.3 cm. Originally it was a part of a handscroll known as the Masuda A scroll in the collection of Baron Matsuda, which was unfortunately cut up and dispersed among several collections. See Miyeko Murase, *Emaki: Narrative Scrolls from Japan* (New York, Asia Society, 1983), 54–55. The detail of the punishment for liars is from a late-nineteenth-century copy by Tanaka Yubi of the well-known *Kitano Tenjin Engi* dated 1219 in the collection of the Kitano Tenman-gu in Kyoto. See Toru Shimbō, *Rokudō E* (Tokyo: Mainichi shimbun, 1977), 237–38.

10. Ivan Morris, trans., *The Pillow Book of Sei Shōnagon* (New York: Columbia University, 1967), 1: 70.

11. Takakusu, *Essentials of Buddhist Philosophy,* 135, 137.

12. Senchu Murano trans., *The Lotus Sutra* (Tokyo: Nichiren Shu Headquarters, 1974), 223.

13. Daigan and Alicia Matsunaga, *Foundation of Japanese Buddhism* (Los Angeles: Buddhist Books International, 1976), 2: 249.

14. Yoshito S. Hakeda, *Kūkai: Major Works* (New York: Columbia University Press, 1972), 77–78.

15. Matsunaga and Matsunaga, *Foundation of Japanese Buddhism,* 249–50.

16. Takakusu, *Essentials of Buddhist Philosophy,* 163.

17. The fan-shaped sutras originally formed ten booklets containing the texts of the *Lotus Sutra,* the *Sutra of Innumerable Meanings* and the *Sutra of Meditation on Samantabhadra Bodhisattva.* They are now divided chiefly among the collections of Tokyo National Museum and Shitennoji. Although not all scholars agree, it is generally thought that they were produced at the request of the consort of Emperor Toba and dedicated in 1152 at Shitennoji. For further details see Tanabe, *Paintings,* 75 and Yoshirō Tamura and Bunsaku Kurata, *Hokekyō no Bijutsu* (Tokyo: Kōsei Publishing Co., 1981), 207.

18. Tanabe, *Paintings,* 56.

19. The sketch appears in a work that I am unfamiliar with entitled *Tachikawaryū Daitō On-yō Kompon.* It is reproduced and the Tachikawa rituals are briefly discussed in Shūyū Kanaoka et al., *Mandara no Uchū* (Tokyo: Shueisha, 1988), 162–68.

20. The objects within the Seiryōji Buddha and the Shan Dao image are described and discussed in detail in Bunsaku Kurata, *Zōnai Nōnyūhin, Nihon no Bijutsu* 86 (1973): 19–27.

21. Ibid., 29.

22. Hisashi Mōri, *Japanese Portrait Sculpture* (Tokyo: Kodansha International Ltd. and Shibundo, 1977), 44.

23. The Chinese also incorporated physical remains into portraits, but varied the

technique. The Chinese mixed the ashes of the deceased subject with clay to mold a likeness in which body and image became inseparable. Sherman Lee likens such clay and ash sculptures with fetish and magical functions. See Sherman Lee, *Reflections of Reality in Japanese Art* (Cleveland, Cleveland Museum of Art, 1983), 19.

24. For further discussion of this work see Takeshi Kuno ed., *Nihon Hyaku no Butsuzō* (Tokyo: Nihon Kōtsū Kōsha, 1988), 154.

25. For a summary of the development of the legends surrounding Kūkai, see Kanaoka et al., *Mandera no Vehū*, 128–41.

26. The ensuing brief discussion of mummies is based on Ichiro Hori, "Self-Mummified Buddhas in Japan," *History of Religions* 1, no. 2 (Winter, 1962): 222–42. A more detailed study can be found in Akira Matsumoto, *Nihon no Miira Butsu* (Tokyo: Rokkō Shuppan, 1985).

27. Hori, "Self-Mummified Buddhas," 224.

28. Joseph Needham, *Science and Civilisation in China*, vol. 5, pt. 2 (Cambridge: Cambridge University Press, 1974), 294–304 and fig. 1330.

29. An excellent discussion on the origins and development of portrait sculpture that incorporates the physical body of the subjects is found in Bukkyō Bijutsu Kenkyū Ueno Kinen Zaidan (ed.), *Shōzō Bijutsu no Shomondai: Kōsōzo o Chūshin ni* (Kyoto: Kyoto National Museum, 1973), 2–5. A brief English summary is also included.

Art and the Construction of Self and Subject in Japan

Mara Miller

Evidence afforded by the arts suggests that, contrary to the findings of historians and social scientists to the effect that the Japanese lack a clear sense of self, Japan has a strong tradition of selfhood and subjectivity in something like the modern Western sense—a highly self-conscious and self-reflective self capable of independent moral action and radical individuality.[1] This is surprising, given social scientists' repeated discovery of a Japanese suppression/denial/devaluation of the individual self in favor of what has been appropriately termed a "we-self." The we-self is characterized by strong identification with members of an in-group, flexible and permeable ego-boundaries, de-emphasis of absolute or invariant definitions of self, and lack of concern about self being consistent and self-identical over time, with concomitant context-dependency.[2] Indeed, the very notion of "self" is problematic in the Japanese case, and not only in the context of modern social science. Studies of Japanese texts in religion, history, law, and language uncover a long history of theories of no-self. Such theories function as repeated challenges to the apparent isomorphism between body and self (which is assumed in some Western self-theory) presented by the Buddhist theory of reincarnation, to the insistence in the ideological Confucianism in the Tokugawa period on corporate identity and on the undesirability of individualism, its success in equating individualism with selfishness in the popular mind, and to recent findings by social scientists that group identity takes precedence over personal identity.

Yet, in spite of a large body of theory that denies either the existence or the value of the self, in spite of linguistic structures that problematize and destabilize the "self," and in spite of a wealth of practices which stress group identity at the expense of personal identity, this self is well-attested—in the history of Japanese arts, in the striking artistic contributions of individuals, in the recurrent self-reflective voicing of subjective experience, and in images of the desiring subject.

The difficulties of studying the Japanese self come not only from the complexities of the type(s) of self under examination (and of reconciling conflicting Japanese views such as conflicting Buddhist views of this self, or "no-self"), but also from the limitations and biases of our methodologies and theoretical assumptions. Until recently, Western selfhood theory has been ill-suited to the perception, much less the analysis or appreciation, of Japanese forms of selfhood. Fortunately, a superb critique can be found in Nancy R. Rosenberger's introduction to her edited anthology, *Japanese Sense of Self*. A few earlier studies, which focus on practices as well as linguistic situating of the individual self, also do justice to the strength of Japanese subjectivity and individuality, notably T. P. Kasulis's *Zen Action Zen Person* and Takie Lebra's *Japanese Patterns of Behavior*. (Of course the adequacy of standard Western, and especially *philosophical,* models for the description of even Western selves has also been challenged recently, on many grounds, especially their gender bias and their avoidance of both power issues and the political dimensions of self construction, and their bias in favor of essentialism and stasis.)

The Japanese self differs from the Western paradigm in critical respects: it is constructed intersubjectively, rather than by opposition to an objectified Other, and it is equally feminine and masculine: it does not privilege the male position. The arts not only bear witness to this distinctively Japanese self, they also play an important role in its constitution.[3] Japanese visual art presents us with evidence of the varieties in types and usages of selves and subjects, while literary evidence suggests that practice and appreciation of the arts are integral to the formation of the self/subject and crucial to its successful functioning in the world.[4]

The history of the self, as it has been chronicled and analyzed in the past two decades by philosophers, social scientists, and cultural historians, is a history based on verbal evidence (Elvin, "Between the Earth and Heaven"; Foucault, *Language;* Lienhardt, "Self: Public, Private"; Momigliano, "Marcel Mauss"; Olney, *Metaphors of Self*). Wimal Dissanayake has given an excellent summary of the importance of linguistic analysis to the study of the self in his paper "Understanding the Concept of Self: Some Western Perspectives," in which he points out its crucial role in the theory not only of Foucault but of Jacques Lacan and of psychoanalysis in general.

I strongly concur with Dr. Dissanayake's conclusion that "Questions of language are central to an understanding of self. The formative influence of language on self is inescapable and the linguistic construction of self merits very close analysis" (Dissanayake, "Understanding the Concept of Self"). At the same time, I believe it is now time to challenge the hegemony that theory, even post-modern theory, has accorded to language and to extend the study of the self to include visual, kinesthetic, and other artistic modes of construction, constitution and dissemination.

Knowledge, Self and Subject in the Arts of Classical Japan

There is a long history in Japan both of subjective vision and individuality in literature and art, and of ethical actions taken by individuals that run contrary to social expectations. The arts of the classical Heian period (794–1185) have been *both* the champion of what Roland calls the "private self" (challenging philosophical, legal, and religious dictates and countering the evidence of the social sciences) *and* constitutive of the intersubjective subject, while being themselves intersubjectively constituted.

These classical arts remain highly influential today. While the acute self-consciousness found in the "I-novel" *(watakushi-shosetsu)* of the Meiji (1868–1912) period (documented also in the work of psychiatrist Morita as the *shinkeishitsu*-type personality [Reynolds 1989]), appears closely akin to that of the "alienated intellectual" of modern Western literature appearing at about the same time, the "I-novel" builds on a history of literary self-consciousness dating back to *The Tale of Genji*. Like the eighteenth-century psychological novels believed to have helped secure the foundations of the modern European self, this eleventh-century psychological novel, the world's first, written by (Lady) Murasaki Shikibu (d. 1014?), (plate 1), is fundamentally concerned with issues we take to be definitive or constitutive of the self and personal identity—the emergence of an independent voice, the role of memory, the relations between what we do and who we become, the taking of moral responsibility for one's life, the identity of the person, conflicts between social roles and individual inclinations, and the discrepancies between inner feelings and thoughts and the appearance one makes to others.[5]

Plate 1. Okumura MASANOBU. *Lady Murasaki*. Late 17th c. The James A. Michener Collection, the Honolulu Academy of Arts.

These tensions—between the self as it appears to others and the self as it is known internally, and between the two roles of arts in establishing the subject, as both expressive and constitutive, of *both* the private self and the intersubjective self—are illustrated in the episode called *Shoshi Arai Komachi* ("Washing the Book Komachi") taken from the life of the Heian-period female poet Ono no Komachi (fl. ca. 833–857). As Howard A. Link tells it, "Komachi . . . wash[es] the copy book of her dishonest rival O-Tomo no Kuromuoshi at a poetical competition held at the Imperial Palace. Upon overhearing Komachi recite an ode, the jealous rival copied it into an early manuscript of her own and then accused Komachi of plagiarism. By washing away the fresh ink in which the ode was written, Komachi refuted the accusation."[6] In the eighteenth-century illustration by Torii Kiyomasu (plate 2) Komachi is shown demonstrating her independent voice and her right to sit among them before a group of other poets.[7]

The self formed in the Heian period (784–1184) is intensely self-reflective. In her diary (Bowring, *Murasaki Shikibu*) as well as her novel, Lady Murasaki, like St. Augustine (who is a favorite forefather of the modern self among those who study its history), evinces a fascination with time, a concern over the unreliability of memory, and a keen awareness of the differences between objective knowledge and what the choosing self selects to know. The

Plate 2. Torii KIYOMASU. *The Seven Komachi, no. 1: Shoshi Arai Komachi (Komachi Washing the Book).* Early 1710's. The James A. Michener Collection, the Honolulu Academy of Arts.

Heian self is formed (almost as if to fit Western theory of the self) as a response to the look of the Other, which makes it aware of itself first as an object for the Other's sight, knowledge and judgment. Lady Murasaki, Sei Shonagon, and other diarists record painfully acute awareness of being judged by others in the act of being observed, of being made the object of others' observation. Now, this awareness of the Look of the Other is said, by Sartre and Lacan among others, to be a critical step in the constitution of self-consciousness and the ego. Yet in spite of this thousand-year literary history expressive of the most acute self consciousness and response to the look, the arts in Japan, unlike those in the West, have been conditioned by assumptions of intersubjectivity or co-subjectivity, rather than by an idealization of the autonomous self-identical and self-sufficient Self (the outcome in Sartre's and Lacan's theories), and have consistently posited—indeed assisted in constructing—the Self as Subject in a context of intersubjectivity rather than by opposition to an Object.[8] The philosophical question is how can such different types and theories of Self result from such similar experiences of being the object of the Look and descriptions of the experience?

Examples of Japanese co-subjectivity are numerous. Literature of the Heian period establishes the norm; *The Tale of Genji,* the various poetic diaries, and the *renga* or linked verse that develops later all present poetry which does not aim to stand entirely on its own but rather alludes to previous poems via the use of lines and phrases (Brower and Miner, *Japanese Court Poetry*; Miner, *Japanese Poetic Diaries*). This is done in two ways. First, the poems alluded to may be part of the generally familiar body of literature. Second, as the process is described by Murasaki, new poems are often composed as parts of letters, especially love-letters; in such cases and in *renga,* the poems referred to are poems written by someone the poet knows, someone who shares the same social, literary, and often physical context; they may even be written to (in the case of letters) or for (in the case of *renga*) the poet.

Two implications of this early poetic practice are pertinent to our philosophical question. First, the poet demonstrates his or her participation in the cultural community and contributes to it at the same time. Although writers' abilities are acknowledged to vary greatly, poetry writing is an amateur activity and expected of everyone as part of the (aristocrat's) quotidian routine. The poet, like the poem, takes his or her place within the community and does so by means of the poem, which establishes the poet's identity not as an isolated genius but as a member of a cultural community. Secondly, the works are not meant to stand alone but to be received as part of a dense network of poetic allusion, a body of literature that they expand even as they mine it. The originality desired of the poet is differently emphasized than in the West; it consists of the ways he or she brings new pleasures and meanings to a preexisting poetic core. The new work is not intended to be understood as complete or self-contained but offers itself for further adumbration to subsequent poets. This means that the author relies upon the audience to complete the meaning, as it were, (foreshadowing current reader-response theory and deconstruction); the fact that the audience can do that reassures the poet that his or her meaning is received within a process that is reciprocal. The success of the poetic project convinces the poets/lovers of the validity of their assumptions of being understood, of the soundness of their trust in intersubjectivity, and of their knowledge of the Other. This ability to trust and take for granted our knowledge of the Other, testified to again and again by modern novelists like Ryūnosuke Akutagawa (1892–1927) and Fumiko Enchi (1905–), stands of course in the sharpest contrast with Western premises, which in their extreme form insist that we not only do not usually know the other but we *cannot* know the Other.

If we claim, as I believe we may, that poetry is the paradigmatic form of verbal communication in Japan, in that limited but crucial sense in which one might claim that philosophical argument or scientific discourse has become the paradigmatic form in the West, (that is, that it is not just prevalent but in an important sense normative), then the importance of poetry, in setting up a model that both embodies and validates intersubjectivity and the reliability of our knowledge of the Other, cannot be underestimated. Since in this tradition no poem is ever finally isolate, objective (independent of the subjectivity of the sender and receiver), or context-free, this precludes the adoption of a poem as an object of knowledge, an unchanging absolute or ideal, in the Western sense. Meaning, on this view, is not independent of the knower, not objective; it is intersubjectively constituted and varies with its context.

This has important consequences not just for how we understand the work of art but, since this model serves as the paradigm for the possibilities of knowing, for how we understand the Other as well. It means, among other things, that the Other can be known (a) accurately and with confidence, and (b) not simply as an Object about whom one infers information, but as a Subject, in ways like those by which we know ourselves (when we are not making ourselves into Objects of self-reflection/knowledge), i.e., prereflectively, directly, albeit with gaps.[9] It further implies that knowledge of the

Other and of the art work may alter our knowledge of ourselves—may alter what we are. This implication that knowledge of art will change us runs consistently throughout Japanese history.[10]

The mid-twelfth-century picture scrolls painted to accompany *The Tale of Genji* exemplify yet other ways in which art can be used to teach intersubjectivity. First, the style of painting faces, called *hikime-kagihana*, or "dash for eyes, hook for nose," is extremely sketchy, with no individualization of the face. Although this has been interpreted as typifying the alleged Japanese lack of individualization, a far more astute reading proposed by Akiyama Terukazu suggests that this style permits the viewer to read herself or himself into the situation; it facilitates identification by the viewer with the character, who is presented not as someone with a distinct appearance, as someone else, but as someone whom we are encouraged to inhabit (Akiyama, *Heian Jidai Sezoku-ga no Kenkyu;* Akiyama, *Genji E;* Murase, *Emaki*).[11] Second, the choices of which scenes to illustrate display confidence in the shared knowledge of artist and viewer. Rarely is a climax chosen for illustration; indeed, in a number of cases the scene "illustrated" is not strictly speaking in the story at all. This is the case with the "Suzumushi" ("Bell Cricket") chapter, in which Genji and his friends are summoned from a party to visit the Reizei Emperor, who is supposed to be Genji's half brother (by a previous emperor) but is really Genji's illegitimate son, although no one knows this fact except Genji—and, we presume from the illustration, the Emperor. In the story, the retinue arrives at the palace, the author makes one or two remarks in her own voice about the quality of the poetry that night, and the narrative moves on to a new episode. In the painting, however, the moment of silent confrontation between Genji and the Emperor (who never in their lives acknowledge their relationship openly to anyone) is selected for illustration—perhaps one should say, this moment is invented by the artist. Although there are no actions, nor even any verbal exchange, to depict, this is one of the most poignant moments in the whole *Genji* (painted or literary version), for what is depicted—by means of the tension in the architecture, the empty space in the center of the composition and the column that (from our point of view) stands between the two men and blocks their view—is the compression of their knowledge, their tacit agreement never to speak it, and their mutual awareness of the knowledge of the other and *his* tacit agreement. As Miyeko Murase describes it:

> It is a delicate moment of complicity and cognizance. Reizei, his face in full view, faces Genji, who leans against a pillar and bows his head slightly; neither says

anything explicit as they quietly acknowledge Reizei's awareness of the secret of his birth. Thought by everyone to be the younger son of Genji's father, the former emperor, Reizei is in fact Genji's son, the issue of an illicit affair between the youthful Genji and his father's favorite concubine. In this tightly knit composition with its absence of female figures, the sharply slanting beam that separates the two men appears to emphasize their inability to speak of their kinship. Only the flute music seems to express their unspoken thoughts. The steeply sliding diagonal line of the tatami mats, which seem to carry the two figures out of the picture frame, echo the uncommon nature of the relationship. Yet the disturbing diagonals are counterbalanced with brilliant effect by the vertical lines of the columns, and the courtiers' diaphanous black trains draped over the railings echo the vertical balancing elements. Finally, the sliding movement of the diagonals is caught by the gentle arc created by the figures of the four young courtiers seated on the verandah. . . . That the Genji paintings convey the emotional impact of the story with profound poignancy in spite of their stylized approach is brilliantly demonstrated in this composition. Those diagonal lines that collide with one another or slide precariously out of the picture frame suggest disturbance and agitation. In other paintings a sense of serenity or a feeling of impending doom pervades scenes in which the horizontal lines of wooden beams, curtain frames, or long, uninterrupted borders of tatami mats dominate the composition.[12]

It is a moment of perfect harmony between father and son—and one deserving of the keenest attention, given that Genji's wrongdoing in this affair is a crucial link in his chain of karma (or, from a modern point of view, repetition compulsion) that motivates and unifies much of the narrative. Note that the artist assumes an ability on the part of the reader to supply the emotion and even the anti-events for the scene from his or her own feeling, without reliance on the text. Note too that what is depicted is an example of two people's knowledge of the Other that is perfect, true, and infinitely resonant—as well as unspoken.

A second telling example of intersubjective knowledge, this one from the seventeenth century, is the Moon-Viewing Platform at Katsura Imperial Villa. Katsura constantly alludes to, and in many ways embodies, the refined elegance of the imperial court of *The Tale of Genji*, in which one of the favorite activities is moon-viewing parties. The Moon-Viewing Platform alludes specifically to *The Tale of Genji*, therefore, even as it provides a site for the re-creation of a typical *Tale of Genji* experience. The way it does this, however, is entirely new. As the guests walk along the verandah, they spot a pond at the far end and expect to see the moon reflected in it (which of course will be much more subtle and elegant than looking at the moon itself). The designer, however, confident that he could assume this expectation (complete with its literary allusions) on the part of the guests, has arranged the pond so that the moon *cannot* be reflected in it, its reflection being intercepted by the building. The viewer is caught off guard, surprised and delighted—and can rejoice at the fact of his host understanding him well enough to know his expectations and to take the trouble of providing this unusual fare. A host of other examples could easily be illustrated, from the tea ceremony, presentational theater forms like Kabuki and Bunraku (puppet theater), and gardens.[13]

The deployment of architectural elements—and of gardens and the natural environment as well—to convey the emotional resonance of the characters in a painting, which is so characteristic of Heian painting style and which continues to be used in the Tokugawa Ukiyo-e prints, may be compared to the use of gardens and nature imagery in *Genji* and in classical poetry for the same purpose.[14] The technical practices of both visual and literary art reflect an underlying premise about what we might call the *location* of emotion, namely that emotion is not to be understood as isolated within a discreet individual. This view of emotion as transcending the individual in some important sense differs sharply from the usual Western view and makes criticism in terms of the pathetic fallacy inappropriate. If feeling is understood to be the "property" (in the logical sense) not of the individual but of the situation or of the relation, the epistemological problem of understanding other minds cannot arise, and reliable "communication" between persons *can* be taken for granted[15] (see Kasulis, "Zen and Artistry," in this volume). (Properly speaking, of course, this is no longer a problem of "communication" per se, since communication presupposes independent entities. The common feeling discovered in the Japanese situations is the shared effect of a common cause—the various parties are understood to be sharing a situation.)

The result of such artistic practices, I would argue, is that the arts in Japan have played a crucial role in the construction of a Subject that is conditioned by assumptions of shared knowledge and intersubjectivity rather than, as is the case with the Western subject, opposition to—and domination over—an Other constructed as an object, via acts and representations which objectify and overpower.

Desire and the Representation of the Subject in Ukiyo-e[16]

The woodblock prints of the Ukiyo-e school of the Edo period (1600–1868) illustrate the major claims of this paper: that the Japanese do have a strong tradition of individual selfhood, that selfhood and the subject position are neither the exclusive privilege of men nor modeled on male experience, that this selfhood is intersubjectively constituted and premised upon confidence in knowledge of the other, and that art both illustrates and contributes to the construction of this self. This section presents a preliminary examination of the first three of these claims in the light of Ukiyo-e.[17]

Depictions of the Individual as Self and as Subject

Recent studies of Western art and film (Berger, *Ways of Seeing*, Mulvey, "Visual Pleasure," Nochlin, *Women, Art and Power*, Pollock, *Vision and Preference*) have analyzed the visual codes of representation that objectify women and establish the position of the viewing subject as (exclusively) male.[18] In Linda Nochlin's summary:

> representations of women in art are founded upon and serve to reproduce indisputably accepted assumptions held by society in general, artists in particular, and some artists more than others about men's power over, superiority to, difference from, and necessary control of women, assumptions which are manifested in the visual structures as well as the thematic choices of the pictures in question . . . Assumptions about women's weakness and passivity: her sexual availability for men's needs, her defining domestic and nurturing function; her identity with the realm of nature; her existence as object rather than creator of art; the patent ridiculousness of her attempts to insert herself actively into the realm of history by means of work or engagement in political struggle—all of these notions, themselves premised on an even more general, more all-pervasive certainty about gender difference itself—all of these notions were shared, if not uncontestedly, to a greater or lesser degree by most people of our period, and as such constitute an ongoing subtext underlying almost all individual images involving women.[19]

Similar assumptions were shared by the neo-Confucianist rulers, educators, and intellectual leaders of Edo Japan.[20] For this reason—and because many of the pictures of women are of courtesans, who made their living by giving pleasure to men—most scholars and interpreters of the prints have assumed that the women pictured function primarily or only as objects for male desire. If we read the prints with eyes trained to the assumptions of Western visual structures, this seems true, but once we base our reading on the Japanese social and artistic contexts, the Ukiyo-e prints give quite a different picture.[21]

There are four ways in which Japanese artistic practices differ from the Western with regard to this paradigmatic correspondence between gender and status as subject or object. First, men are depicted not only as Subjects, but as objects. Second, women are depicted not only as objects but, far more commonly, as Subjects. In addition, both are shown in intersubjective relation, that is, in the act of mutual acknowledgement of the subjecthood of the other (with simultaneous acknowledgement of their own subjecthood). Finally, the female gaze is recognized and incorporated; men are expected to be able to identify with a female Subject as well as a male one, and vice versa.[22] This situation may reflect the realities, if not the statistical norms, of real life; it certainly does *not* reflect the contemporary Confucianist ideology expounded by the government.

The middle-class Ukiyo-e audiences craved images of the heroes of their new popular culture: actors of the Kabuki theater and *bijin* (literally "beautiful women") and courtesans of the pleasure quarters. Although the stylization of these images is undeniable, so is a fascination with realism. From this realism emerges a type of portraiture distinctly different from that of the West, in that it is primarily interested neither in physical resemblance nor in the character of the person, but in those aspects of the person which reveal what we might call the "intended" self, the self-fashioned self, the self as it has decided to reveal itself to others.

Precursors of this understanding of the Self are found in the portraits of classical poets (male and female) dating from the Kamakura period on, like the portrait of the female poet which is from a pair of six-fold screens (in the Shin'enkan Collection at the Los Angeles County Museum of Art), on the cover of this volume, by the sixteenth-century Rimpa artist Sakai Hōitsu (1761–1828). There is no interest in the facial features; they convey no information of interest.[23] Individuality resides in the set of the body, in the costume—the elegance of the twelve-layer kimono is crucial—and, significantly, in the words of the poet, written alongside the poet's name in expressive calligraphy. Ukiyo-e portraits of contemporary actual people also capitalize upon this tradition of indicating selfhood as a combination of name, posture

Plate 3. Katsukawa SHUNKO. *The Actor Ichikawa Danjūrō V in His Dressing Room*. 1787–1801. The James A. Michener Collection, the Honolulu Academy of Arts.

Plate 4. Suzuki HARUNOBU. *Sekidera Komachi (Komachi Leaving the Temple).* The James A. Michener Collection, the Honolulu Academy of Arts.

Plate 5. Suzuki HARUNOBU. Untitled. The James A. Michener Collection, the Honolulu Academy of Arts.

or deportment, costume, and one's work.[24] They understand the achieved selfhood of such personages to be a complex comprised of individual identity, public persona, and the person's mood or intention at a particular moment. Individual identity is comprised of identifiable facial features, inscription of the actor's or courtesan's name, etc. Public persona is interpreted both as a function of social role, (indicated by such features as identifying insignia, perhaps the actor's family crest or the name of the courtesan's house, that help to determine for the viewer the social position) and as a set of choices made by the individual as to how to present herself or himself.

Men in Ukiyo-e: Desiring Subjects or Objects of Desire

Men in Ukiyo-e, like their counterparts in Western painting and in film, are shown as Subjects—as independent moral and political agents (often as heroes from history or legend), with all indications of their social status and public persona, and in poses signifying control. When they are actors this may mean either an anonymous, stylized aggressive pose or one of their (male or female) stage roles (Azabu Museum, *Kabuki;* Keyes and Mizushima, *The Theatrical World;* Narazaki, *The Japanese Print,* Stern, *Master Prints of Japan*).[25] Less common is the sort of intimate view captured in plate 3, Katsukawa Shunko's portrait of the famous Kabuki actor Ichikawa Danjuro V in his dressing room.[26] Shunko's depiction shows Danjuro in a private moment before he has adopted his public artistic persona, or rather in the very process of taking it on. He, like the artist, is identified by name on the print, but his face is recognizably his. The individualized face and the signs of professional status (such as wig, make-up, costume) and of his personal tastes (the pipe) indicate, as they would in European or American work, a compound selfhood comprised both of position in the community and a more personal interior sense of self.

Yet even as they establish themselves as subjects, the Kabuki actors, who may play aggressive male heroes or effeminate antiheroes or women, self-consciously set themselves up as *objects* for the scopophilic gaze of the desiring Subject. This double role as object functions both in relation to the other characters within the play (who serve as fictive viewing subjects) and—much to the consternation of the neo-Confucianist government—in relation to the actual viewing subjects in the audience, male and female, who often sought them out as lovers. Not only the prints but the Kabuki plays exploit the theme of the man who is the object of female desire.[27] Prints like Shunko's take this even further to depict men as desirable not merely as Kabuki actors in a sublimating spectacle but in their own right, as potential lovers, either male or female, and for either men or women. In his portrait of Danjuro, Shunko exploits this ambiguous status of the actor as both Subject and object.

Women in Ukiyo-e: The Active Female Subject

The complexities and ambiguities of the male Subject/object are recapitulated in Ukiyo-e portraits of women. Superficially some prints of beautiful women or *bijin* seem to exemplify the woman-as-object model described by Berger,

Plate 6. Suzuki HARUNOBU. Untitled. The James A. Michener Collection, the Honolulu Academy of Arts.

Mulvey, Nochlin and Pollock.[28] In such works the female body, with gentle curves that invite completion by the viewer, is presented as spectacle, an ideal beauty without claims on or by the nonvisual reality, a perfect scopophilic object, passively awaiting the male. (As indicated above, however, this is a partial description of many prints of men as well.) Suzuki Harunobu's demure and fragile beauties seem to represent the type (plates 4, 5, 6, 9). Harunobu, like many other Ukiyo-e artists, virtually invented his own style of female beauty. His is distinguished by the apparent youth, innocence, and daintiness of his subjects, quite different from the mature, majestic, bold styles of wo-men by Kiyonaga and Utamaro (plates 7 and 8).

Plate 7. Torii KIYONAGA. *Gyokuwashi Emio Performing Calligraphy.* c. 1783. The James A.
Michener Collection, the Honolulu Academy of Arts.

姿見七人化粧

Plate 8. Kitagawa UTAMARO. *Woman Before a Mirror*. Last quarter of the eighteenth century. The James A. Michener Collection, the Honolulu Academy of Arts.

Plate 9. Suzuki HARUNOBU. Untitled. The James A. Michener Collection, the Honolulu Academy of Arts.

Yet although among Japanese types of female beauty Harunobu's girl is one of the most compliant and vulnerable, she is not deprived of indicators of autonomy, as a comparable Western fragile beauty would be. The autonomy of Harunobu's innocents is indicated by their position—frequently standing, and often outside, in public space—meeting lovers or, like the Sekidera Komachi in plate 4, visiting shrines.[29] (Sekidera Komachi, "Komachi Entering the Temple" is one of seven scenes from the life of poet Ono no Komachi, shown also in plate 2, which were very popular in Ukiyo-e.) In plate 5 they sit, the one on a ledge above her lover (who sits on the floor), the other alone. The aesthetic choices in their clothing and environments inform us of their tastes, education, abilities, and preferences. The gentle curves of the subtle kimono designs, each based on nature but alluding also to the season and to a wealth of literary references, suggest their temperaments. Books on the floor bespeak their literacy—which of course would include in this context famil-iarity with the classical novels, poetry, and diaries written by women and men. The calligraphy above the door in plate 5 is in seal script, an ancient Chinese script carrying references both to Confucianism and the classical Chinese past

Plate 10. Anonymous. *Shunga*. The James A. Michener Collection, the Honolulu Academy of Arts.

and revivified by the trendier Nanga school of art then flourishing in Japan, which exploited a certain conscious archaism of Chinese neo-Confucianist painting. The appointments in the room are supremely elegant, as is every nuance of the ladies' posture.[30]

Indeed it would seem that the very perfection of the outer image makes the viewer aware of the inner private self, implied and vividly felt in every image of letter writing, reading of love letters, or playing an instrument alone. In plate 6, the lady looks dreamily out onto a marshy autumn landscape, again redolent with allusions to ancient poetry. The pose vividly recalls Okumura Masanobu's print of Lady Murasaki in the process of writing *The Tale of Genji* (plate 1). The dreamy beauty is no mere passive object onto which the male ego can project his own interiority (as has been argued for the Impressionist works of similar composition and theme), but an originator of Japanese culture whose voice has been retained as central.[31] Similarly the Harunobu girl who seems so fragile in plate 4 is after all one of the great independent voices of all Japanese history, whose reputation rests as much on her resistance, her refusal to concede to others' expectations of her, as on the intensity of her poetic voice.[32]

Shunga: Erotic Art and the Intersubjective Self

Nowhere does the difference between the Western self and the Japanese self emerge more clearly than in erotic art or *shunga* (Spring Pictures). This difference is that between the Subject constructed by a relation (of dominance) to an object and the Subject constructed intersubjectively, in relation to an Other conceived and encountered as a Subject.

In explicitly erotic prints, women are *not* restricted to the role of passive object of male desire. They quite clearly appear as active desiring subjects (plates 10–14). Women are sometimes shown in positions of submission, but more often stand and sit upright (plate 12) or lie with a man who is also lying down. Either the woman (plate 11) or the man may be on top; they may be intertwined, with neither dominant (plate 13). Poses characteristic of Western erotica—the woman lying on her back with her hands behind her head, fully exposed to the viewer, or lying with her head fallen back in abandon, as if her neck were broken—are not seen in Japan until after contact with the West.[33]

These women in *shunga* are not only active, and avoiding either extreme of dominance or submission, but they are desiring. They actively reach out for the man and fondle his genitals (plate 13). They curl their toes with rapture. It is impossible to mistake their enjoyment.

The disempowerment of the nude Western sex object is missing in the Japanese examples. Nudity is important in the Western context because it signals the permission given the male viewer: deprived of social status, her nudity indicating not merely her agreement to the male gaze/fantasy/act but often a wantonness that makes her agreement beside the point, the woman is vulnerable. In Japan, on the other hand, the vulnerability of nudity is not only unnecessary but undesirable. (And nudity per se is not sexy in Japan; it was common in public bathing.) What is desirable in a woman in the Japanese pictures is a subject with whom to interact, not an object on whom to project one's own fantasy. Clothing—the choice and combination of patterns, the colors, the references—is vital to the revelation of one's Subjecthood.

The encounter with the other as full Subject is signaled by the mutual gaze into each other's eyes. All of these prints show the couple looking at each other. In *shunga,* it is not only the male who gazes at the female; the woman gazes back. Or rather, the Gaze (as it is called in representational theory) or the Look (as it is called in philosophy) is mutual—neither looks at an object, but into another Subject, with a look that creates the Other as subject rather than diminishing her or him to the status of object. While eye contact is not

Plate 11. Anonymous. *Shunga.* The James A. Michener Collection, the Honolulu Academy of Arts.

Plate 12. Suzuki HARUNOBU. Untitled. The James A. Michener Collection, the Honolulu Academy of Arts.

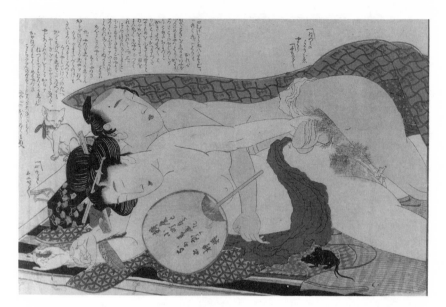

Plate 13. Katsushika HOKUSAI. *Shunga.* The James A. Michener Collection, the Honolulu Academy of Arts.

universal in these prints, it does appear in the *shunga* of major artists from the late-seventeenth century (plates 10, 11) through Harunobu in the eighteenth century (plate 12) to Hokusai in the mid-nineteenth century (plates 13, 14).

If, as Western gaze theorists maintain, one's status as subject is gained partly by the act of looking, both women and men are subjects here. As indicated by the conventions of representational practice, neither men nor women are seen as objects, and women are not denied the right to gaze.

The Female Gaze

Not only in *shunga* but generally, Japanese representations differ from Western ones in facilitating the female gaze as well as the male gaze. The Gaze is not only erotic. Ukiyo-e artists thematized perception in countless ways; they were fascinated with the instruments (mirrors, telescopes, and eyeglasses) and the phenomena of perception as a process—lantern light and fireflies and moonlight, mist and shadows and veils. They were fascinated with the act of looking.

Plate 14. Katsushika HOKUSAI. *Shunga.* The James A. Michener Collection, the Honolulu Academy of Arts.

Women looking is a major theme of Ukiyo-e. The well-known prints by Utamaro (plate 8) of women examining themselves in the mirror, paralleled by prints like Shunko's of Danjuro V (plate 3), exemplify the self as Subject taking itself as object, adopting toward itself the stance of the Other. But women assume the right to gaze in other ways as well. They are frequently voyeurs in sexual scenes (plate 12). They examine other women on the streets (plate 15), especially in the work of Kiyonaga who is famous for his complex social situations. In plate 16, three women look through a book of pictures of famous courtesans, and the housewife in black points out "That's the one" (Link, *The Feminine Image*). They look at art, as we have seen in the various Harunobu interiors. In *Gyokuwashi Emio Performing Calligraphy* (plate 7), also by Kiyonaga, the young girl is being taught calligraphy by her mother— her voice sustained, and her right to look and to judge implied by the scrolls and fans hanging on the wall. Her identity as writer, as producer of the symbolic (an identity she inherits from her mother), is clear in the writing paraphernalia, as revelatory and essential to her identity as the writing implements on the desk of a Confucian scholar.

The Japanese representations are shown to depict women with full Subjecthood and in intersubjective sexual relations with men. While Subjecthood

Plate 15. MANGETSUDŌ. *Yoshiwara Komachi Sansui (Komachi in the Yoshiwara)*. (Triptych.)
Late 1740's. The James A. Michener Collection, the Honolulu Academy of Arts.

is not exclusively male, neither is object status exclusively female. The impact
of such images must be to legitimate the female Subject and the male object.

Knowledge of Self and Other in Twentieth-Century Fiction

Twentieth-century Japanese fiction[34] has earned critical attention in the West
both for the ease with which it made its own the preoccupation with selfhood,
alienation, and personal identity (Kimball, *Crisis in Identity;* Miyoshi, *Accomplices of Silence;* Shomu and Katsumaro, *The Russian Impact on Japan;* Walker,
Japanese Novel), that were until then the province of European literature, and
for its fascination with art, aesthetics, and beauty. What has so far gone
unnoticed, however, is the interaction between these two concerns, which
amounts to an almost systematic examination of the relations between art
and the self and between art and the constitution of the Subject.[35]

When we speak of art in the West, we usually think of the works of art,
the actual objects (*hakubutsu,* or *geijutsu,* terms introduced into Japanese after
contact with the West) or the images they present. The Japanese approach to
art stresses *geidō,* the way (*dō* or *Tao*) of art, comprised of complementary

Plate 16. Torii KIYONAGA. *Discovering the Address of a Husband's Sweetheart.* c. 1790. The James A. Michener Collection, the Honolulu Academy of Arts.

processes of mastering the techniques and attitude for making works, and becoming thoroughly familiar with individual works and a genre or school from the point of view of the connoisseur, for purposes of appreciation. Both of these processes are at least as emotional and physical as they are intellectual; the approach must be appropriate, mere knowledge is insufficient. Both are assumed to be life-long processes. And they are assumed to require and justify the utmost commitment.[36] As a result, they are expected to have the deepest capacity to change the individual, to affect personal identity on the most profound level.

Because of this, art does not merely "express" a pre-given self but reveals and creates the self. And it does this not only for the artist or writer but also for its audience. But precisely in virtue of the capacity art has to create the self—that is, to change it—it requires that the self not be consistent over time (as the ideal Western self is) but be inherently interactive and fluid. Art also has the capacity to reveal the Other, to make clear to us who the Other is, better than anything else. Therefore it can also create the Other for us in some totally new way, creating possibilities of intersubjectivity that would not be possible otherwise. It plays, therefore, a role that is not merely emotional and pleasurable, but cognitive: art constructs our world, by constructing the possibilities through which we interpret our world.[37]

As a result, individuals turn to art when baffled, for help in solving problems, as in Shiga Naoya's *A Dark Night's Passing* and Yasunari Kawabata's *Sound of the Mountain*.[38] In such works, art is shown to clarify situations, particularly ethical situations, when action is called for but the appropriate action cannot be recognized. This means that art is not primarily a "leisure" activity, if by that we mean something used to take up the time when nothing more important is happening, an "escape" to take our minds off our problem. It is not "aesthetic" or "distanced" in the Kantian sense of removed from the everyday life-and-death struggle. It is integrally related to this struggle—not only metaphorically (in *A Dark Night's Passing*, encounters with art are crucial to the formation of a personal identity which will permit the hero to father a child) but literally *(The Sound of the Mountain)*. Common in such works are discussions of the arts as representations of knowledge.[39]

One example involves the temple architecture in its garden setting in Yukio Mishima's *The Temple of the Golden Pavilion*. In this story the mid-twentieth-century protagonist is sent as a child by his dying father to Kinkaku-ji, the famous fifteenth-century Golden Temple, to be educated and to prepare for the Zen priesthood. As he grows up, the beauty of the temple becomes an obsession with him, combining as it does his most vivid link with his dead father and the site of both his daily experiences and his dreams for the future—for he has been chosen to become the abbot of this temple.[40] Yet the combined forces surrounding the temple are overwhelming for him; ultimately he destroys the temple by burning it down. (This is a true story, based on transcripts of the trial.) The work of art provides the means for this act of self-transcendence and self-destruction, but it also provides the motivation—or perhaps one should say pretext.

Similarly, in Yasunari Kawabata's novel *A Thousand Cranes*, a son is dominated by his father's vision of the world, represented after his death by the vivid vision of art, in this case the tea ceremony, he has transmitted to his son. The physical evidence of his father's involvement with the art remains, in the form of tea utensils, to be constantly encountered by the son, and the tea ceremony is used in the novel to structure the two rival love affairs of the young man, his memories of his dead father, and his newly emerging understanding of his new life.[41] In both these novels, the son does not rebel against the father, nor openly resent him, but continues to seek him out, enacting the dependency relationship of *amae* (Doi, *Anatomy of Dependence*) that has been found to provide such satisfaction to Japanese males (Roland, *In Search of Self*).[42]

The novel *Masks* by Fumiko Enchi relies primarily on the masks of the Noh theater to explore the roles of art in the constitution both of knowledge and of the relations of self to other. Enchi's characters also turn to other arts, to Ukiyo-e and Buddhist painting,[43] for instance, and most consistently to the novel *The Tale of Genji*.[44]

In the Japanese novel (ideally read) one brings a broad background knowledge (with varying degrees of understanding) of the arts to which the novelist will be referring; and the acts of empathy elicited by the novel are intended to structure one's subjective knowledge of oneself and one's situation, not objective knowledge of others. Art from the viewpoint of these novelists is about knowledge, but it is about knowledge *from the other's point of view,*[45] and about ways of deliberately shattering our isolation and independence. This points up the process of coming to understand the other, while the Ukiyo-e prints reveal the full subjectivity of the figure represented.

Conclusions

The Japanese self has usually been seen as fundamentally dependent on a group for its identity (a "we-self"). More recently, the Japanese self has begun to be recognized as complex, with both interdependent and independent components (Lebra, *Japanese Culture and Behavior*).[46]

Examination of the arts—visual, literary, musical, and kinesthetic representation and presentation—often leads to quite different conclusions regarding the nature of this self than does the evidence provided by the social sciences or by studies of religious theory, history, or law. The premises upon which the Japanese have traditionally approached art differ in important ways from Western premises. As we have seen, Japanese art-forms are in many cases inherently intersubjective, both born of confidence in our ability to know the other, and justifying that confidence at the same time. Although the Japanese self may have permeable boundaries, be highly intersubjective, etc., this "we-self" coexists with (a) an intensely realized private self, and (b) (what is less commonly recognized), a fully developed Subject. This is not a we-self, not constituted through identification with a group, but independent. This typical Japanese Subject, moreover, differs from the norm established for the Western self in that it is not exclusively male, and is constituted intersubjectively as opposed to via opposition to or domination over an object.

Notes

1. The modern Western self is often imprecisely defined but is generally understood to be autonomous (or, to the extent that it is not, then immature or pathological), independent, and separated (Erickson *Childhood and Society, Identity and the Life Cycle*). In the sense in which I am using it here, it is closely related to the ego, in that it is conceived to be centered around consciousness. This model is consistent with the work of many philosophers, particularly those of the Anglo-American school, of psychologists who study "self-esteem," and of many scholars who study the self's manifestation in and dependence upon specific artistic forms such as autobiography, portraiture, etc. (Gusdorf, "Conditions and Limits," Olney, *Metaphors of Self*). It is not to be confused with the self of Jungian psychology, which was drawn up as an integrative concept which would accommodate ego, subconscious, and most importantly some transpersonal aspects of the person.

2. Roland, *Search for Self in India and Japan*. Lebra (1989) has summarized the social science findings on what she calls the "consciously socio-centric" Japanese self, which I quote for its breadth and succinctness: "If viewed through the Western lens for perceiving the self as non-contingent, autonomous, or intrinsic, the Japanese self indeed appears situationally circumscribed or *on/giri*-bound (Benedict 1946), dependency-prone (Doi 1971), rank-conscious and group-oriented (Nakane 1967), empathetic (Aida 1970), differentiated into *uchi* and *soto* or *omote* and *ura* (Bachnik 1986; Doi 1985), mindful of *sekentei* (Inoue 1977), indeterminate (Smith 1983), relativistic (Lebra 1976a), hanging "between persons" (Kimura 1972; Hamaguchi 1977), uncertain and multidimensional (Minami 1983)."

3. Dorinne Kondo's "investigation of the ways selves are constructed at the workplace, and, in particular, toward a specifically artisanal idiom of work" is an interesting companion to the present study for in spite of the fact that her work focuses on full-time employment (in a modern economy) rather than on elite amateur activity, the importance of aesthetics, the exercise of individual judgment, and the notion that the artistic work develops over a lifetime in such a way as to assist the individual in

the process of maturation *(ichininmae no ningen)* and self-realization are common to both models.

4. For a number of reasons, the notion of "Subject" may be preferable to "self" and may make the distinctively Japanese form of the "self" more perspicuous. First, it permits us to avoid the philosophical trap of searching for an essential substratum underlying accidental qualities and the changes accompanying a personal history, a search which is the product of a particular moment in the history of philosophy, namely, the Enlightenment, and the outgrowth of a particular (not universally valid) logic and linguistic formulation (namely the European languages, which, unlike Japanese, have a copula and a subject/predicate logic). Second, while the notion of the self tends to cast us into a realm of supposedly eternally valid epistemology and ontology, the notion "Subject" is an attempt to recognize the constitutive role of power relations (which always take effect in a particular formulation as set up by and within a particular historical situation) in the formation of the possibilities which are to be realized by a particular person. Third, the notion of the Subject is inherently reflexive and thus accommodates the long Japanese history of self-reflection and reflexivity (Felman *Jacques Lacan*). Finally, it takes as constitutive the act of knowing and the relation to knowledge.

5. *The Tale of Genji,* by the way, remains a vital and much-loved influence throughout Japanese history. During the Tokugawa period (1615–1868) nearly everyone but the very poorest would have had access to it and enjoyed it in some form. For the imperial court, new sets of illustrations were commissioned of the Tosa family artists and it inspired a number of architectural features in the Katsura Imperial Villa built by the Hachijo princes. How important it was in the life of the Bakufu is harder to say, but Hosokawa Yusai, to take one example, who was a retainer of Ashikaga Yoshiaki, later confidant and friend of Oda Nobunaga and Toyotomi Hideyoshi, and eventually a partisan of Tokugawa Ieyasu, was a well-known lecturer on the novel. Samurai and the new middle class, the merchants, the denizens of the pleasure quarters and all their customers would also have had access to it through the new cheaper printed editions that were being published. We may infer that they would have been familiar with the story lines, characters, and visual codes of *Genji* also from the fact that there are so many popular prints illustrating, alluding to, or parodying it. This influence continues in the twentieth century, in fiction like *The Makioka Sisters* and "As I Crossed a Bridge of Dreams" by Jun'ichiro Tanizaki, and *Masks* by Fumiko Enchi; in comic book or video versions (!), and in films. The classical poets too have remained favorites of artists and the Japanese public.

6. Link, *The Feminine Image,* p. 53.

7. Her poem reads, "O you who were new sewn, from what seed did you shoot and grow? Water weeds that float, tossed upon every wave." (Translated by Howard A. Link, ibid.)

8. It is not of course the case that no Western arts are premised upon intersubjectivity (choral singing and improvisational chamber music and jazz are) nor that they do not structure the real-world possibilities of intersubjectivity (gardens and architecture do). But in the West, such attempts must fly in the face of a much stronger tendency to base art on individual experience and expression, which are privileged in virtue of the operant theories of selfhood.

9. This makes more sense when we recall, as philosophers seem rarely to do, how spotty and unreliable our knowledge of ourselves is; it is by no means clear that we are privileged in knowing ourselves more, better, or more clearly than others know us, though we do know ourselves indifferent ways. And of course in the Japanese context in which selves are recognized to vary with context, the fluctuating nature of our knowledge of either self or Other will be less conspicuous and troublesome.

10. For discussions of arts as a medium of spiritual change see Hardacre, *Kurozumikyo* and Suzuki, *Zen and Japanese Culture*. Recent Western accommodations of relativity theory and Heisenberg's uncertainty principle, which acknowledge for the first time that the act of perception (by a Subject) changes the nature of what is perceived, while radical in terms of Western epistemology, still do not take into account that the act of observation changes the observing Subject as well.

11. This sketchy anonymity is seen also in Ukiyo-e and in Chinese painting, especially of the literati school(s), to quite similar effect. See Goldberg, this volume.

12. Murase, 66–7.

13. The difference between the relations between the host who constructs this sort of surprise for his guests and the designer/ host of the French- or Italian-style garden that surprises the unwitting guest by suddenly dousing him or her with water from a hidden spray (a Renaissance delight) is, I would suggest, the difference between the Subject constituted intersubjectively and the Subject constituted by opposition to and dominance over an Object. In such Renaissance garden practices only the owner/ host is allotted full Subjecthood; the guest is treated as an Object.

14. Thomas Kasulis's paper, "Zen and Artistry," this volume, outlines the philosophical framework within which this relationship of things with emotion becomes more understandable. Further work is needed on the implications for the understanding of art.

15. This reading is supported by the Japanese characters for "human nature" or "humanity" *(ningen)* which is written by the combination of "person" *(hito)* and "interval" or "space" *(ma)*, this latter term having the dual sense of both the space between persons, an interval (in the musical sense as a "space" or "distance" between entities) by means of which their relations are constituted, and that around them, within which they live, which comprises them in the notion of *ningen*. In this view of human nature, the "not-I" is viewed as just as important as the "I" in constituting the subject; the positive is unthinkable without the negative term. (The idea is iterated in the character for "interval" itself, which is written as a combination of gate and

moon, implying that the open space of the gate is what makes perception of the moon possible.

16. A preliminary study for this section, "Representing the Self, Representing the Other: The Gendered Subject in Japanese Art," written with Welles Hackett, was presented at a panel on gender at the Society for Cross-Cultural Research in February 1990. I would like to thank my coauthor, panel organizer Prof. Lauris McKee for her invitation to participate, and Franklin and Marshall College for its funding.

17. These themes are explored in Miller, "Canons and . . . Gender."

18. In the West selfhood has been a male preoccupation. The theory of selfhood has been written by men, usually in ways that exclude women. It tends to be based on male experience, albeit only some (elite, white) male experience, and often on types of experience unavailable to women. Although some Western women may be assigned a self and may understand themselves as Subjects, if only intermittently, the Western Subject, the active agent, is paradigmatically male. The Western model has come under criticism as applying to only a small subgroup (primarily white elite males, perhaps only extraordinary males) and to comprise an ideal (of some, not all) rather than a description.

19. Nochlin, *Women, Art and Power*, 1-2.

20. See for example the *Onna Daigaku* or "Greater Learning for Women" of Kaibara Ekken.

21. We do not have room to explicate here the connections between knowledge, control, dominance, and sight—the Look or the Gaze. It may perhaps help, however, to say that where knowledge is understood as power or control or mastery (Bacon, Hegel) and sight is taken as equivalent to knowledge (as it has been since the Enlightenment), then sight/the Look/the Gaze becomes an act of control or mastery over an object, and can never establish a relation with a Subject. See Felman for a critique of this view of knowledge vis-à-vis the need for reflexivity in the constitution of the Subject in Lacan's theory. So far, the mutual look of two Subjects at each other as a way of constituting or even acknowledging their status as subjects has received little attention.

22. This is not of course a purely artistic phenomenon but the result of a variety of sociological and economic factors, including the relative importance of the female viewer as part of the potential audience for the prints, the respect these women could command in virtue of their mastery of fashion and the arts, the fact that there was no sinfulness or shame associated with sex itself in Japan, the possibilities for economic independence or married respectability available to women who made it into the upper ranks of their profession.

23. Ladies of her time rarely showed their faces, and even their lovers would rarely have seen them in the light, but comparable male poet's faces, usually facing the viewer, are also given little individuality and would certainly not aspire to physical resemblance.

24. Ukiyo-e portraits of actual but historical personages, on the other hand, differ quite a bit in that they provide an elaborate narrative context (Pl. l, 2, 5).

25. Although Kabuki was founded by a woman, women were soon forbidden by law to perform on stage; all roles were played by men.

26. Less common but far from rare; see for example Kiyonaga's portrait *"Matsumoto Koshiro IV and Two Women,"* plate 38 in Narazaki, *The Japanese Print.*

27. In *Sukeroku,* the dominant male who enjoys all the "masculine" advantages of wealth, power, and position and could take on the role of protector to the beautiful woman, and who could become Subject if she is willing to forego her active desire and become object, is ridiculed and rejected in favor of the more effeminate and less commanding—but elegant and sensitive—love object Sukeroku (who has nothing to recommend him in terms of the warrior code).

28. Representations that objectify are those that make the person depicted into an object of sight, of desire, of imaginary or hypothetical control, for the viewer. The body is shown immobile, and passive or reactive rather than active. Body parts of particular interest to the viewer (not to the depicted object, for even indirect indication of her interest would imply her Subjecthood and undermine her status as object) may be fetishized—exaggerated or overemphasized. The body is fragmented or cropped, not treated as an organic whole. Face and head or hands may be omitted. Frequently there is mutilation, infliction of pain, killing. Her pose is usually directed toward the viewer and inviting; certainly nonthreatening. Since clothing is an important indicator of social status, it is often omitted; females are not always nude, but the nude is nearly always female. Clothing may be fetishistic or titillating (concessions to the viewer) or hindering or inadequate (denying her needs as a Subject). The objectified female usually inhabits private rather than public space. Her movements are confined. She is usually within property owned by another, not herself. Evidence within the depicted environment of her social position, rank, personality, beliefs, tastes, history, and deeds is limited or nonexistent. When the eyes of such women are not demurely cast down in silent acknowledgment of her inferior status, they issue a sexual invitation to the viewer. Other modes of engagement with the viewer rarely occur.

29. The women of the Ukiyo-e are shown inhabiting public, not just private space—even the most childlike among them travel, visit temples and shrines, and walk about on streets and in the countryside.

30. As we were going to press I discovered that the figures in this print had been identified by Roger Keyes as male, specifically as young male prostitutes (Keys, pp. 34–35). He did not give his reasons for this attribution, although he did mention in his discussion two well-known indicators of male sex that are not present in this particular print, a sword and a small shaved section at the top of the head. Several experts whom I consulted agreed that they could find nothing to indicate that the two figures were men, but Dr. Lawrence E. Marceau of the University of Delaware provided the definitive answer: according to Nakamura Shin'ichiro, et al., (p. 44),

they have to be male because of the tassles at the ends of their obi, or wide sashes. (Dr. Marceau confirmed my belief that there is nothing inherently male about either their choice of books (the *Ehon Shahou-bukuro,* published by Tachibana no Morikuni in 1720) or the inscription written under the character "Gi," or "Righteousness," in the cartouche, which he translates "In all matters humbling the self, determining the principle, lacking falsehood; this we call righteousness.")

This confusion underscores my larger point: that the attribution of Subject or Object status is independent of a person's sex. Nor is it the case that men emulated women in order to appear sexually desirable, but not the converse, for Dr. Marceau assures me that at least one other signifier of male identity, the shaved spot at the top of the head, was sometimes adopted by women who used a dash of masculinity to increase their sex appeal. Of course, if that is true, might women not on occasion adopt the obi tassles as well? Whether they have done so in this case, however, must remain unanswered here, although I think that there are three further features that suggest — without requiring — that these two figures must be, in the final analysis, male.

I am deeply grateful to Dr. Marceau both for the depth and breadth of his scholarship and for his willingness to come to my aid at top speed.

31. Historian Philip Nord has argued that this analysis of Impressionist works of women reading and in interiors ignores the force of the political implications that reading had for contemporary French Republicans, among them the Impressionists (Nord, "Republican Politics").

32. Those familiar with the full iconography of the three separate illustrative traditions that depict Komachi (the "Thirty-Six Poets" tradition dating from the Kamakura era, the Ukiyo-e "Seven Komachi's," and the Buddhist versions that make of her life a cautionary tale in six or nine episodes, culminating in her portrayal as skull and bones), will realize the full story is more complex than this. But while that story would shed interesting light on this study, there is no room for it here.

33. I have seen no depictions of overt sadism or violence toward women in Japanese art prior to contact with the West, although this does not mean they do not exist. Among the first I know of are those of Uemura Shoen, a female painter (1875–1949). See Kronhausen, *The Complete Book,* plates 350–354.

34. Throughout this paper I will use the terms "novel" and "novelist" as the equivalents of *shosetsu* and *shosetsuka* without regard to the distinctions usually made in English among novel, novella, and short story, based on the length of the work. See Miller, "Beauty and Narrative."

35. Although Masao Miyoshi (1974) has found fault with the modern Japanese novel for its inability (or refusal?) to depict "personality," this does not mean, as he concludes, that the self is unimportant in these works — only that it is understood somewhat differently.

36. This is assumed to be true of even the lowliest arts — and is the assumption

lampooned in Itami's film *Tampopo,* in which the "art" of noodle-making takes on the significance of a spiritual quest.

37. If this sounds a bit post-structuralist, it is, but I think it is not an anachronism; Japan, like China, discovered the multiplicity of interpretations about a thousand years earlier than the West, and has had more time to integrate it into mainstream culture.

38. Any number of novelists and works could illustrate these points. Not only Shiga and Kawabata, but Natsume Sōseki *(Three-Cornered World),* Nagai Kafū ("A Strange Tale from East of the River"), Ryūnosuke Akutagawa ("The Hell Screen"), Jun'ichirō Tanizaki *(Some Prefer Nettles),* and Fumiko Enchi *(Masks)* wrote novels in which characters depend upon works of art for the clarification of the world and their situation within it and for their knowledge of other characters. (The questions of the novel as an art which is particularly suitable to the construction and exploration of selfhood, though obviously related, will not be addressed here.) See Miller, "Beauty and Narrative."

39. Although such works are far from representative of twentieth-century Japanese fiction as a whole, they and their fascination with the aesthetic have received a good deal of international attention for many reasons: they have all been beautifully translated (in spite of the particular problems presented by Japanese written in this style, which tends to exploit the evocative possibilities of ambiguity and therefore to be especially difficult to render in Indo-European languages which privilege logical clarity); Tanizaki and Kawabata have written book-length essays on aesthetics; Kawabata's Nobel prize and Mishima's spectacular suicide of course drew world-wide attention; and perhaps, too, they seem to comply with condescending Western biases toward the exotic "Far East" — and, in addition to all this extranea, they are all extraordinarily powerful and important, as well as beautiful, books.

40. The powerful idea of a work of art embodying to a lonely child its dead parent has a long history in Japan. It forms the nexus of the Fox-Tadanobu subplot of the Kabuki play *Yoshitsune Senbonzakura,* in which a young fox mourning the deaths of his parents (who were sacrificed to make the skins of a magical drum) takes on the human identity of a favored courtier solely in order to be near this drum. The theme recurs in Kawabata's novel *A Thousand Cranes,* in which the dead father's continued presence, in the vessels of the tea ceremony which he has bequeathed his son, dominate the son.

41. This theme of the relation of father and son, though in many cases treated as destructive of the son (see also the Kabuki play *Terakoya*), is, I believe, in general both more positive and more common in Japanese literature and art than in the West. This may be due to the greater value placed on connectedness for Japanese men.

42. Roland's work suggests that a power hierarchy such as that recommended in Japanese Confucianism and enacted emotionally through the dependency relationships of *amae* need not be predicated on dominance of a Subject over an object as in Hegel's analysis of the master-slave relation, but can be lived out in a more inter-

subjective way, with positive trade-offs and some sense of control for both. See in particular Roland's discussion of narcissistic gratification on the part of the superior.

43. Ibuki says, "Yasuko is an ordinary woman. She's simply not on Mieko's scale. Yes, that's it, like an old painting . . . In T'ang and Sung paintings of beautiful women or in a Moronobu print of a courtesan, the main figure is always twice the size of her attendants. It's the same with Buddhist triads: the sheer size of the main image makes the smaller bodhisattvas on either side that much more approachable. Perspective has nothing to do with it, so at first the imbalance is disturbing, but then it has a way of drawing you in . . . Anyway, to me Mieko is the large-sized courtesan, and Yasuko is the little-girl attendant at her side" (Enchi, *Masks,* 13).

44. Enchi, like Tanizaki, made a modern Japanese translation of this novel.

45. On the phenomenon of taking the other's point of view and the means by which this is institutionalized and taught in Japan, see Lebra, "Migaware . . ."

46. The considerable Japanese capacity for autonomous action has been described as nonetheless dependent upon a group identification and as justifying its autonomy as being for the sake of the group (Obenchain, "Japanese and Chinese Women"). This is often the case, but one must recognize that such action still requires the individual to defy the desires/orders/expectations of the individuals who are closest and most important to the subject.

Works Cited

Aida Yuji. *Nihonjin no ishiki kozo.* Tokyo: Kodansha, 1970.

Akiyama Terukazu. *Genji E, Nihon no Bijursu* 119, 1978.

―――. "A New Attribution for a Painting Fragment to the Twelfth-Century *Tale of Genji* Scrolls," *Kokka,* no. 1011 (1978), 9-26.

―――. *Heian Jidai Sezoku-ga no Kenkyu (Secular painting in early mediaeval Japan).* Summary in French. Tokyo. 1964.

Ames, Roger T., Wimal Dissanayake and Thomas P. Kasulis, editors, *Self as Person in Asian Theory and Practice.* Albany: State University of New York Press, 1974.

Azabu Museum of Arts and Crafts. *Kabuki through the Theater Prints: Collection of the Honolulu Academy of Arts, James A. Michener Collection.* Azabu, 1990.

Bachnik, Jame M. "Time, Space and Person in Japanese Relationships." In J. Hendry and J. Webber, eds., *Interpreting Japanese Society: Anthropological Approach,* JASO Occasional Papers No. 5 Oxford: Oxford University Press.

Benedict, Ruth. *The Chrysanthemum and the Sword: Patterns of Japanese Culture.* Boston: Houghton Mifflin, 1946.

Berger, John. *Ways of Seeing.* London: British Broadcasting Corp. and Penguin Books, 1972.

Bowring, Richard trans. *Murasaki Shikibu: Her Diary and Poetic Memoirs.* Princeton: Princeton University Press, 1982.

Brower, Robert H., and Earl Miner. *Japanese Court Poetry.* Stanford: Stanford University Press, 1961.

Carrithers, Michael, Steven Collins, and Steven Lukes, eds. *The Category of the Person: Anthropology, Philosophy, History.* Cambridge: Cambridge University Press, 1985.

de Rola, Stanislas K. *Alchemy: The Secret Art.* New York: Avon Books, 1973.

Dissanayake, Wimal. "Understanding the Concept of Self: Some Western Perspectives," paper presented at the East-West Center Institute of Culture and Communication. Honolulu, 1989.

Doi Takeo. *The Anatomy of Dependence.* Tokyo: Kodansha Intl.

Elvin, Mark. "Between the Earth and Heaven: Conceptions of the Self in China." In Carrithers, *The Category.*

Enchi Fumiko. *Masks (Onna-men).* Translated by Juliet Winters Carpenter, New York: Vintage Aventura, 1983: Alfred A. Knopf, 1983, Tokyo: Kodansha Ltd., 1958.

Erickson, Erik. *Childhood and Society.* New York: Norton, 1950: revised 1964.

———. *Identity and the Life Cycle.* Psychological issues Monograph I. New York: International Universities Press, 1959.

Felman, Shoshana. *Jacques Lacan and the Adventure of Insight: Psychoanalysis in Contemporary Culture.* Cambridge, Massachusetts: Harvard University Press, 1987.

Foucault, Michel. "The Subject and Power." *Critical Inquiry* 8 (Summer 1982).

———. *Language, Counter-Memory, Practice.* Translated by Donald F. Bou-chard and Sherry Simon, Ithaca. New York: Cornell University Press, 1977.

Gilligan, Carol. 1983. *In a Different Voice: Psychological Theory and Women's Development.* Cambridge, MA: Harvard University Press, 1983.

Gusdorf, George. "Conditions and Limits of Autobiography." Translated by James Olney. *Formen der Selbstdarstellung; Analekten zu einer Geschichte des literarischen Selbstportraits,* editors Gunther Reichenkron and Erich Haase. Duncker & Humblot, 1956. Reprinted in *Autobiography: Essays Theoretical and Critical.* Princeton: Princeton University Press, 1956, 1980.

Hardacre, Helen. *Kurozumikyo and the New Religions of Japan.* Princeton: Princeton University Press, 1986.

Kasulis, T. P. *Zen Action, Zen Person.* Honolulu: The University Press of Hawaii, 1986.

Kawabata Yasyunari. *A Thousand Cranes.* Translated by Edward G. Seidensticker. New York: Knopf, 1958.

———. *The Sound of the Mountain.* Translated by Edward G. Seidensticker. New York: Knopf, 1956.

Keyes, Roger. *The Male Journey in Japanese Prints.* Berkeley: University of California Press, 1989.

Keyes, Roger S. and Keiko Mizushima. *The Theatrical World of Osaka Prints: A Collection of Eighteenth-and-Nineteenth-Century Japanese Woodblock Prints in the Philadelphia Museum of Art.* Boston: Godine, 1973.

Kimball, Arthur G. *Crisis in Identity and Contemporary Japanese Novels.* Rutland, Vermont: Charles E. Tuttle, 1973.

Kondo, Dorinne. "Multiple Selves: the aesthetics and politics of artisanal identities," in Rosenberger, Nancy R. *Sense of Self.*

Kronhausen, Phyllis, and Eberhard. *The Complete Book of Erotic Art.* New York: Bell Publishing, 1987.

Lacan, Jacques. *The Four Fundamental Concepts of Psycho-Analysis.* New York: Norton, 1978. Editions du Seuil: *Le Seminaire de Jacques Lacan, Livre XI,* 1973.

Lebra, Takie. "Migawari: The Cultural Idiom of Self-Other Exchange in Japan." In Ames, et al., 1994.

———. 1984. *Japanese Women: Constraint and Fulfillment.* Honolulu: University of Hawaii Press 1984.

———. *Japanese Patterns of Behavior.* Honolulu: University of Hawaii Press, 1976.

Lebra, Takie Sugiyama, and William P. Kebra, editors. *Japanese Culture and Behavior: Selected Readings.* Rev. ed. Honolulu: University of Hawaii Press.

Lienhardt, Godfrey. "Self: Public, Private. Some African Representations." In Carrithers, *The Category,* Cambridge, 1985.

Link, Howard A. *The Feminine Image: Women of Japan.* Honolulu: Honolulu Academy of Arts, 1985.

Miller, Mara. "Beauty and Narrative: Self, Subject and Moral Agency in Kawabata's *The Sound of the Mountain,*" in *Text and Context: the Cultural Production of Meaning.* Wimal Dissanayake, ed. University of Minnesota Press, 1997.

———. "Canons and the Challenge of Gender," *The Monist* vol. 76, no. 4 (October 1993), 477–493.

Miner, Earl. *Japanese Peotic Diaries.* Berkeley and Los Angeles: University of California Press, 1997.

Mishima Yukio. *The Temple of the Golden Pavilion.* Translated by Ivan Morris. New York: Knopf, 1959.

Miyoshi Masao. *Accomplices of Silence: The Modern Japanese Novel.* Berkeley and Los Angeles: University of California Press, 1974.

Momigliano, A. "Marcel Mauss and the Quest for the Person in Greek Biography and Autobiography," in Carrithers, et al., 1985.

Monick, Eugene. *Phallos: Sacred Image of the Masculine.* Toronto: Inner City Books, 1987.

Mulvey, Laura. "Visual Pleasure and Narrative Cinema," *Screen* 16, Number 3 (Autumn 1975).

Murase Miyeko. *Emaki: Narrative Scrolls from Japan.* New York: The Asia Society, 1983.

Nagai Kafu. 1965. "A Strange Tale from East of the River." Translated by Edward Seidensticker. In *Kafu the Scribbler.* Stanford: Stanford University Press, 1965.

Nakamura, Shin'ichro, Kobayashi Tadashi, Saeki Junko, and Hayashi Yoshikazu. *Harunobu Shinchosha: Harunobu Bijinga to Empon.* Tokyo: Shinchosha, 1992.

Nakane Chie. *Japanese Society.* Berkeley and Los Angeles: University of California Press, 1970.

Narazaki Muneshige. *Kiyonaga*. Translataed by John Bester. Tokyo, New York and San Francisco: Kodansha International Ltd., 1969.

————. *The Japanese Print: Its Evolution and Essence*. English adaptation by C. H. Mitchell. Tokyo, New York and San Francisco: Kodansha International Ltd., 1966.

Nochlin, Linda. *Women, Art and Power*. New York: Harper and Row, 1988.

Nord, Philip. "Republican Politics and the Middle-Class Interior in Mid-Nineteenth-Century France," paper read at the Center for Historical Analysis, Rutgers University, November, 1990.

Obenchain, Diane. "Japanese and Chinese Women as Emerging Selves: Some Encouraging Differences," presented at the East-West Center Institute of Culture and Communication. Honolulu, 1989.

Olney, James. *Metaphors of Self: The Meaning of Autobiography*. Princeton: Princeton University Press, 1972.

Palangyo, Peter K. *Dying in the Sun*. London, Nairobi, etc.: Heinemann Educational Books, Ltd.: African Writers Series, 1969.

Pollock, Griselda. *Vision and Difference: Femininity, Feminism and Histories of Art*. London and New York: Routledge, 1988.

Reynolds, David K. *Flowing Bridges, Quiet Waters: Japanese Psychotherapies, Morita and Naikan*. Albany: State University of New York Press, 1989.

————. *The Quiet Therapies: Japanese Pathways to Personal Growth*. Honolulu: University of Hawaii Press, 1982.

Roland, Alan. *In Search of Self in India and Japan*. Princeton: Princeton University Press, 1988.

Rosenberger, Nancy R. *Japanese Sense of Self*. Cambridge: Cambridge University Press, 1992.

Sartre, Jean-Paul. *Being and Nothingness*. Translated by Hazel E. Barnes. Philosophical Library, 1956.

Shiga Naoya. *A Dark Night's Passing*. Translated by Edwin McClellan. Tokyo: Knodansha International, 1976.

Shomu Nobori and Akamatsu Katsumaro. *The Russian Impact on Japan: Literature and Social Thought*. School of International Relations, University of Southern California, Far Eastern and Russian Research Series, number 5. Los Angeles: University of Southern California Press, 1981.

Soseki Natsume. *Three-Cornered World*. Translated by Alan Turney. Chicago: Henry Regnery Company, 1965.

Stern, Harold P. *Master Prints of Japan: Ukiyo-e Hanga*. New York: Abrams, n.d..

Suzuki, Daisetz Teitaro. *Zen and Japanese Culture*. New York: Pantheon, 1959.

Tanizaki Jun'ichiro. *Some Prefer Nettles*. New York: Knopf, 1955.

Walker, Janet A. *The Japanese Novel of the Meiji Period and the Ideal of Individualism*. Princeton: Princeton University Press, 1979.

Contributors

Roger T. Ames is a Professor of Chinese philosophy at the University of Hawaii, Director of the Center for Chinese Studies, and Editor of *Philosophy East and West*. He is a translator of Chinese classics. His major interpretive publications include *Thinking Through Confucius* (1987), *Anticipating China* (1995), and *Thinking From the Han* (1998), all with David L. Hall.

Shivani Banerjee Chakravorty is a Research Fellow at the School of Women's Studies, Jadavpur University, Calcutta, India. Her research interests include women and literature, women and media, and Third World literature. Her most recent publication is the compilation and translation into English of an anthology of Bengali Women's prose writings on the "Girl Child" in nineteenth- and twentieth-century Bengal.

Arthur C. Danto is Johnsonian Professor of Philosophy (Emeritus) at Columbia University. Among his numerous publications are *Analytical Philosophy of Action* (1973), *Narration and Knowledge* (1979), *The Transfiguration of Commonplace* (1989), and *After the End of Art: Contemporary Art and the Pale of History* (1997).

Vinay Dharwadker is Associate Professor in the Department of English at the University of Oklahoma. He is the author of *Sunday at the Lodi Gardens* (Viking, 1994), a book of poems; and the editor, with A. K. Ramanujan, of *The Oxford Anthology of Modern Indian Poetry* (1994). He has co-edited *The Collected Poems of A. K. Ramanujan* (1995), and is the general editor of *The Collected Essays of A. K. Ramanujan* (1998), both published by Oxford University Press.

He is currently completing *The Columbia Book of Indian Poetry* (Columbia University Press).

Wimal Dissanayake is an Adjunct Fellow at the East-West Center in Hawaii and Scholar-in-Residence at Hong Kong Baptist University. He is the author and editor of several books on communication, literature, and cinema, including *Melodrama and Asian Cinema* (1993) and *Colonialism and Nationalism in Asian Cinema* (1995).

Mark Elvin's two main interests are the history of the emotions and the history of the economy and environment in China. He is best known for *The Pattern of the Chinese Past* (1973), *A Cultural Atlas of China* (1983, with Caroline Blunden), *Another History* (1996), *Changing Stories in the Chinese World* (1997), and *Sediments of Time: Environment and Society in Chinese History* (1997, co-edited with Liu Tsui-jung). He is currently a Professor at the Institute of Advanced Studies in the Australian National University.

Stephen J. Goldberg is a Professor in the Department of Art at the University of Hawaii. His research interests include Chinese art and contemporary cultural theory. He has published widely on Chinese aesthetics, and is author of *The Inscriptive Subject: Tradition and the Construction of Identity in Chinese Painting and Calligraphy* (1998).

John Hay is a Professor in the Department of Art History at the University of California, Santa Cruz. He has published many articles on Chinese art history. He is the author of *Kernels of Energy, Bones of Earth: The Rock in Chinese Art* (1985) and edited *Boundaries in China* (London: Reaktion Books, 1994).

Martin W. Huang teaches in the Department of East Asian Languages and Literatures at the University of California, Irvine. His primary interests include Chinese literature and literary history. His book, *Literati and Self-Re/Presentation: Autogiographical Sensibility in the Eighteenth-Century Chinese Novel* (1995) was published by Stanford University Press.

Gayathri Rajapur Kassebaum is an ethnomusicologist, and has recently taught world music cultures and performance classes with the University of Pittsburgh's Semester at Sea (Fall 1997) and at the University of Hawaii. She is a concert performer of South Indian classical music and has done field research on the folk music of Karnataka. Her recent publications include "Improvisation in Alapana Performance: A Comparative View of Raga Shankarabharana," *Yearbook for Traditional Music* 19:45–64, New York, and two articles for the forthcoming *Garland Encyclopedia of World Music*.

Thomas P. Kasulis is Professor of Comparative Studies in the Humanities at the Ohio State University. He has been the Numata Visiting Professor in Buddhist Studies at the University of Chicago. He is the editor and co-translator of *The Body: Toward an Eastern Mind-Body Theory* and *Self as Body in Asian Theory and Practice*, and author of *Zen Self/Zen Person*.

Lucy Lower is an Associate Professor in the Department of East Asian Languages and Literatures at the University of Hawaii. She is currently engaged in research on the cultural politics of 1930s Japan and transition of modern Japanese short fiction.

Mara Miller is the author of *The Garden as an Art* and numerous articles on philosophy, comparative selfhood, aesthetics, and feminist theory. She is working on a book on the Chinese impact on English gardens, and another on gender construction in Japanese prints. She is currently a Mellon Post-Doctoral Fellow in East Asian religion and art history at Emory University.

Ashis Nandy is a leading Indian intellectual and scholar who has published widely on colonialism, self, religion, and modernity. Among his numerous publications are *Intimate Enemy: Loss and Recovery of Self* (Oxford University Press) and *The Savage Freud and Other Essays on Possible and Retrievable Selves* (Princeton University Press).

Nobuko Miyama Ochner is an Associate Professor in the Department of East Asian Languages and Literatures at the University of Hawaii. Her current academic interests center on the representation of Korea and Manchuria in Japanese literature of the early twentieth century.

Kwok-kan Tam is Professor and former Chairman of the Department of English at the Chinese University of Hong Kong. He is also Director of the Comparative Literature Programs at the Research Institute for the Humanities at the University, and editor of the *CUHK Journal of Humanities and Comparative Literature & Culture*. He has published widely in the areas of modern

Chinese literature and drama. His recent publication is a book, *New Chinese Cinema* (Oxford University Press, 1998, co-authored with Wimal Dissanayake).

Willa Jane Tanabe is Dean of the School of Hawaiian, Asian, and Pacific Studies at the University of Hawaii, and is an expert in Japanese Buddhist art. She is the author of *Paintings of the Lotus Sutra* and co-editor of *The Lotus Sutra in Japanese Culture*.

Arthur Thornhill is Associate Profesor of Japanese in the Department of East Asian Languages and Literatures at the University of Hawaii. He is the author of *Six Circles, One Dewdrop: The Religio-aesthetic World of Komparu Zenchiku* (Princeton University Press).

Terry Siu-han Yip is Head of the Department of English Language and Literature at Hong Kong Baptist University and Convenor of the Research Group in Gender Studies at David C. Lam Institute for East-West Studies at the University. She teaches English and comparative literature in her department and her research areas cover Chinese-Western literary relations, Romanticism, gender studies, and modern Chinese, Japanese, and British literature. She also serves on the editorial board of the journal *Comparative Literature & Culture*. Her articles can be found in journals and books published in Japan, Germany, Hong Kong, Slovakia, Taiwan, Mainland China, and Australia.

Index